Markku Filppula, Juhani Klemola, Anna Mauranen, Svetlana Vetchinnikova
Changing English

Topics in English Linguistics

Editors
Elizabeth Closs Traugott
Bernd Kortmann

Volume 92

Changing English

Global and Local Perspectives

Edited by
Markku Filppula
Juhani Klemola
Anna Mauranen
Svetlana Vetchinnikova

DE GRUYTER
MOUTON

ISBN 978-3-11-065333-5
e-ISBN (PDF) 978-3-11-042965-7
e-ISBN (EPUB) 978-3-11-042976-3
ISSN 1434-3452

Library of Congress Cataloging-in-Publication Data
A CIP catalog record for this book has been applied for at the Library of Congress.

Bibliographic information published by the Deutsche Nationalbibliothek
The Deutsche Nationalbibliothek lists this publication in the Deutsche Nationalbibliografie;
detailed bibliographic data are available on the Internet at http://dnb.dnb.de.

© 2019 Walter de Gruyter GmbH, Berlin/Boston
This volume is text- and page-identical with the hardback published in 2017.
Cover image: Brian Stablyk/Photographer's Choice RF/Getty Images
Typesetting: RoyalStandard, Hong Kong
Printing and binding: CPI books GmbH, Leck
♾ Printed on acid-free paper
Printed in Germany

www.degruyter.com

Table of contents

List of abbreviations —— vii

Markku Filppula, Juhani Klemola, Anna Mauranen and Svetlana Vetchinnikova
Introduction
Changing English: global and local perspectives —— xi

I Towards the study of Global English

Christian Mair
Crisis of the "Outer Circle"? – Globalisation, the weak nation state, and the need for new taxonomies in World Englishes research —— 5

Donald Winford
The Ecology of Language and the New Englishes: toward an integrative framework —— 25

II Ongoing changes in Englishes around the globe

Valentin Werner
The Present Perfect as a core feature of World Englishes —— 63

Cristina Suárez-Gómez
Innovative structures in the relative clauses of indigenized L2 Asian English varieties —— 89

Rajend Mesthrie, Sean Bowerman and Tracey Toefy
Morphosyntactic typology, contact and variation: Cape Flats English in relation to other South African Englishes in the *Mouton World Atlas of Variation in English* —— 109

Hanna Parviainen
Omission of direct objects in New Englishes —— 129

Markku Filppula and Juhani Klemola
The definite article in World Englishes —— 155

Paul Rickman
Aspects of verb complementation in New Zealand Newspaper English —— 169

Lea Meriläinen, Heli Paulasto and Paula Rautionaho
Extended uses of the progressive form in Inner, Outer and Expanding Circle Englishes —— 191

III Expanding the horizons: lingua franca, cognitive, and contact-linguistic perspectives

Anna Mauranen
A glimpse of ELF —— 223

Janus Mortensen and Spencer Hazel
Lending bureaucracy voice: negotiating English in institutional encounters —— 255

Svetlana Vetchinnikova
On the relationship between the cognitive and the communal: a complex systems perspective —— 277

Zhiming Bao
Transfer is transfer; grammaticalization is grammaticalization —— 311

Subject index —— 331
Languages and Varieties index —— 340
Author index —— 343

List of abbreviations

A	adjective (Bao)
AAVE	African American Vernacular English
ACE	*Asian Corpus of English*
ACE	*Australian Corpus of English*
ADJ	adjective (Vetchinnikova)
ADV	adverb
AmE	American English
Ao	object-related adverbial
ASAE	Afrikaner South African English
AusE	Australian English
AUX	auxiliary
B1/B2	intermediate (CEFR proficiency level)
BNC	*British National Corpus*
BrE	British English
BRICS	*acronym*: Brazil, Russia, India, China, South Africa
Brown	*Standard Corpus of Present-Day Edited American English*
Brown/LOB	*Brown University Standard Corpus of Present-Day American English/Lancaster-Oslo/Bergen Corpus* (a British English counterpart of Brown)
BSAE	Black South African English
C1/C2	advanced (CEFR proficiency level)
CAS	complex adaptive system
CCJ	*Corpus of Cyber-Jamaican*
CCN	*Corpus of Cyber-Nigerian*
CEFR	Common European Framework of Reference
CFE	Cape Flats English
CLMET	*Corpus of Late Modern English Texts*
CNZNE	*Corpus of New Zealand Newspaper English*
Co	object complement
COCA	*Corpus of Contemporary American English*
COMPL	a Completive Perfect category
CSE	Colloquial Singapore English
CSV	comma-separated (of files)
DA	definite article
DBCC	*Diachronic Blog Community Corpus*
DET	determiner
EAfrE	East African English

EFL	English as a Foreign Language
EHAB	Non-delimited (extended) habitual
EL	Ecology of Language (framework)
ELF	English as a Lingua Franca
ELFA	*Corpus of English as a Lingua Franca in Academic Settings*
ENL	English as a Native Language
ESL	English as a Second Language
ESTA	Non-delimited (extended) stative
ETE	'extraterritorial' English
EuroCAT	*European Corpus of Academic Talk*
eWAVE	*Electronic World Atlas of Varieties of English*
FjE	Fijian English
Frown/FLOB	*Freiburg – Brown Corpus of American English/Freiburg Lancaster-Oslo/Bergen Corpus of British English*
FUT	Futurate
GloWbE	*Corpus of Global Web-Based English*
HKE	Hong Kong English
ICE	*International Corpus of English* (varieties: -SIN, -GB, IND, -EA, -CAN, -HK, -PHI, -JA, -IRL, -CORE)
ICLE	*International Corpus of Learner English* (varieties: -CH (Hong Kong), -JP (Japanese), -FI (Finnish), -SW (Swedish)
IL	idiolect
IND	Indeterminate
IndE	Indian English
INF	informational (of leaves in dendrograms)
INV	involved (of leaves in dendrograms)
IrE	Irish English
ISAE	Indian South African English
JaC	Jamaican Creole
JaE	Jamaican English
Jam Eng	Jamaican English
k	thousand
KenE	Kenyan English
L1	native language
L2	second language
Ll&NW	*Corpus of Interview Data from Llandybie and North Wales*
LOC	locative
LOCNESS	*Louvain Corpus of Native English Essays*
m	million
M	model

M-coeff	M-coefficient
ME	Middle English
MEC	*Corpus of Matriculation Examination Compositions*
MICASE	*Michigan Corpus of Academic Spoken English*
ModE	Modern English
N	noun
N-CAT	Net Corpora Administration Tool
NEG	negation
NigE	Nigerian English
NORM	*acronym*: nonmobile, older, rural male
NZE	New Zealand English
Od	direct object
OE	Old English
Oi	indirect object
Op	prepositional object
OTH	other
P	pronoun
PDE	Present-Day English
PF	progressive form
PHAB	Delimited/Progressive habitual
PhiE	Philippine English
pl/PLU	plural
PoS	part of speech
PP	prepositional phrase
PRES	present tense
PRF	perfect (aspect)
pro	pronoun
PROG	progressive
PrPf	Present Perfect
PSTA	Delimited/Progressive stative
R	recipient
R.P.	Received Pronunciation
RH	Relexification Hypothesis
S	clause (Bao)
S	subject (Parviainen)
S1A	code for *Spoken Private Dialogue* (private dialogue, direct conversations and telephone calls)
SBCSAE/SBC	*Santa Barbara Corpus of Spoken American English*
SCoRE	*Singapore Corpus of Research in Education*
SED	*Survey of English Dialects*

sg	singular
SinE/SingE	Singapore English
SLA	second language acquisition
SLU	second language usage
Sp	subject-prominent (of a language)
SPst	Simple Past
StE	Standard English
SU	*Statens Uddannelsessstøtte* (Danish) literally: 'State Education Support'
SUB	Subjective
TL	target language
TOP	topic
Tp	topic-prominent (of a language)
TR	transitive
Trad EE	Traditional English English
Trad IrE	Traditional Irish English
Trad BrE	Traditional British English
TTR	type-token ratio
V	verb
VOICE	*Vienna-Oxford International Corpus of English*
VP	verb phrase
Trad WE	Traditional Welsh English
WelE	Welsh English
WR	Work-verbs
WrELFA	*Corpus of Written English as a Lingua Franca in Academic Settings*
WSAE	White South African English
WWC	*Wellington Corpus of Written New Zealand English*
X	lexical category
XP	phrase; phrasal category

Markku Filppula, Juhani Klemola, Anna Mauranen and Svetlana Vetchinnikova
Changing English: global and local perspectives

The English language has in the last couple of centuries reached a status as the world language of our day that is used as a regular means of communication by hundreds of millions of people representing very different ethnic, cultural and social backgrounds. The emergence of numerous new varieties of English and its use as a lingua franca mean that it enters into constant contact with virtually every other major language in the world. This, in turn, leads to accelerated change and variation in English itself, manifest in several domains of its grammar and lexis, as well as in its discoursal properties. In consequence, the "English language" can perhaps less than ever before be described as a unitary linguistic system or systems but rather presents an increasing range of more or less diverging or converging "Englishes". This state of affairs is recorded in large-scale surveys of varieties such as the *Mouton World Atlas of Varieties of English* (Kortmann and Lunkenheimer 2013). It is also reflected in the motley terminology used for the multiplicity of varieties: terms such as "New" vs. "Old" Englishes, "World Englishes", "post-colonial" or "extra-territorial" Englishes, "Inner, Outer, and Expanding Circle Englishes", "L1" or "native" vs. "L2" or "non-native" varieties, etc. abound in the literature (see, e.g. Crystal 2003; Schneider 2007; Mesthrie and Bhatt 2008; Jenkins 2009).

This edited collection arises from the papers read at the conference on *Changing English*, held in Helsinki, June 2013. It was organised by the GlobE Research Consortium, funded by the Finnish Academy, and led by Markku Filppula (University of Eastern Finland), Juhani Klemola (University of Tampere), and Anna Mauranen (University of Helsinki). The proposed volume examines the special nature of English both as a global and a local language, focusing on some of the ongoing changes and on the emerging new structural and discoursal characteristics of varieties of English. Although it is widely recognised that processes of language change and contact bear affinities, for example, to processes observable in second-language acquisition and lingua franca use, the research into these fields has so far not been sufficiently brought into contact with each other. The articles in this volume set out to combine all these perspectives in ways that give us a better understanding of the changing nature of English in the modern world.

The chapters in the book are divided into three parts, each of which has its own introduction describing the contents of each chapter. Part One discusses

DOI 10.1515/9783110429657-204

some general and theoretical aspects of the study of English as a global language. Christian Mair first charts out the development of "English as a World English" to "Global English" and what this means from the point of view of research into it. Abandoning the traditional classification of varieties based on the post-colonial nation-state and national standards of English, he posits a global "English Language Complex", which encompasses both standard and nonstandard varieties and presents them as a hierarchically ordered constellation of varieties. New in this hierarchy is recognition of Standard American English as the "hub" or "hyper-central variety", which subsumes under it, at the next level, several "super-central" varieties, such as British English, Australian English, Indian English, and Nigerian English. One level down, then, are "central varieties" such as Irish English, New Zealand English, and Jamaican English, while "peripheral varieties" like traditional non-standard rural dialects as well as pidgins and creoles are found at the bottom of the hierarchy.

The other chapter in the first part is authored by Donald Winford. His focus is on New Englishes, a term which for him covers both post-colonial Englishes and creoles. He argues for an integrated framework for the study of contact-induced change which would include three main components, viz. social factors and motivations, structural factors and linguistic constraints, and lastly, psycholinguistic factors involved in processes of language processing and production. According to him, this kind of approach is best equipped to explain the kind of innovative restructuring that has been found to occur in New Englishes and, unlike some alternative accounts, also provides an explanation for the actuation of contact-induced change.

The second part contains seven articles offering empirical analyses of ongoing change and contact phenomena in several varieties of English spoken in different parts of the world. The linguistic features covered in the chapters range from tense and aspect features to other "core" grammatical features such as relativisation or the uses of the definite article but also bring into discussion some less-studied phenomena such as aspects of morphosyntactic typology, verb complementation and omission of direct objects of transitive verbs. Together, they provide a good window on the diverse nature of the changes affecting varieties of present-day English.

The third part, then, comprises four articles on the use of English in the so-called "Expanding Circle", including lingua franca use. They cover non-native uses of English in numerous different kinds of settings all over the world and in various kinds of institutional encounters. Indeed, the Expanding Circle Englishes have in recent research been found to be a major source for innovative uses of English, and many of these uses can in the course of time be expected to have a modifying impact on the Outer and even Inner Circle Englishes.

Taken together, the articles in this volume cover different theoretical positions from contact-linguistic to cognitive, as well as offering empirical data-based investigations of Englishes spoken in many different kinds of setting.

We gratefully acknowledge the financial support given by the Academy of Finland, first to the research consortium *Global English: contact-linguistic, typological, and second-language acquisition* (grant no. 133119), and then its sequel, *Changing English: users and learners worldwide* (grant no. 269385). We would like to thank Professor Elizabeth Traugott, the TiEL series editor, for her expert review and incisive comments on the manuscripts of the individual chapters as well as the general structure of this volume. Dr Julie Miess, the editor in charge at de Gruyter, also deserves our thanks for her patience and professional help in various stages of the editing process. Dr Izabela Czerniak made an important contribution to this volume through her painstaking input to the copyediting of the chapters for the print production and to the compilation of the list of abbreviations. Finally, we wish to thank Ms Helen Bilton for compiling the indexes for this volume.

I Towards the study of Global English

Editors' Introduction to Part I

Part I opens the book with a discussion of some theoretical issues germane to the study of English as a global language in the changing world.

Christian Mair (*Crisis of the "Outer Circle"? – Globalisation, the weak nation state, and the need for new taxonomies in World Englishes research*) indicates the need to revise our models of varieties of English in response to changes in political and economic structures of the world. In particular, he argues that a taxonomy of World Englishes based on the idea of the nation state does no longer capture the realities of today's language use practiced in the conditions of increasing globalisation and weakening nation states. Yet, it is national varieties of English which underpin such influential models of World Englishes as Kachru's "Three Circles" of English (1992 [1985]) or Schneider's (2007) "Dynamic Model" as well as taken as the main compilation principle in many widely known corpora. He reasons that the emergence of an endonormative standard variety, which has been witnessed in some of the post-colonial nation states, is not necessarily the only possible trajectory of development and can depend on *inter alia* demographical and economical strength of the nation state in question. Building on de Swaan's World Language System (2010), he puts forward a new model, "the World System of Englishes" (Mair 2013a), which in contrast to its predecessors recognises varying importance of different national varieties on the global English rather than places them on the same level by default. For example, the model not only puts Jamaican Standard English and Jamaican Creole at two hierarchically different levels but also reverses their order implying that from a global perspective Jamaican Creole in fact enjoys more prestige than its standard counterpart. In support of the arguments, Mair compares data from Standard Nigerian English vs. Nigerian Pidgin and Standard Jamaican English vs. Jamaican Creole.

While Mair looks at the currently established hierarchical relationship between different varieties of English, Donald Winford, in the following chapter (*The Ecology of Language and the New Englishes: toward an integrative framework*), is interested in how they emerged in the first place, focusing his attention on contact varieties in particular. He argues for the importance of building a unitary framework of the evolution of New Englishes which would integrate linguistic, sociolinguistic and psycholinguistic aspects of contact-induced change rather than focus on one of them exclusively, which is a common practice due to excessive fragmentation in the discipline. Taking this view, he examines Mufwene's Ecology of Language framework in meticulous detail and finds that, though laudable in its attempt to explain language change from a sociolinguistic perspective, and especially on the basis of the macro-level social factors, it completely overlooks the psycholinguistic component. However, he argues, since post-colonial Englishes developed in settings of naturalistic second language acquisition, taking the psycholinguistic aspect of second language processing into account would seem indispensable. The omission of psycholinguistic processes involved in creation of innovations at the level of an idiolect explains, in Winford's view, why the EL framework postulates no difference between the formation of creole and non-creole varieties and between internally and externally motivated change. In other words, in Weinreich's terms, the actuation problem of change has not been sufficiently addressed in EL, Winford concludes. Yet, he continues, psycholinguistic processes of SLA, such as transfer, could readily account for innovations arising in creoles, but not in non-creoles.

The two chapters effectively set the scene for the discussion of more specific questions to follow in Part Two and Part Three of the volume, in the spirit of bringing together different perspectives and approaches to the study of English and developing a more comprehensive and informed framework of changing English in today's world.

Christian Mair
Crisis of the "Outer Circle"? – Globalisation, the weak nation state, and the need for new taxonomies in World Englishes research[1]

Abstract: The study of "varieties of English around the world", the "New Englishes" or "World Englishes" emerged at the intersection of dialectology, sociolinguistics and historical linguistics in the early 1980s and has been among the most vibrant sub-fields of English linguistics in recent years. Work in this tradition has made an important contribution to our understanding of the linguistic legacy of colonialism and the era of early post-colonial nation building. In widely accepted frameworks such as Kachru's "Three Circles" of English (1992) or Schneider's (2007) "Dynamic Model", the focus has been on the emergence and endonormative stabilisation of new national standard varieties of English. The present paper argues that this emphasis on the (post-colonial) nation state raises two problems. First, economically, politically and demographically weak nation states may fail as settings enabling full endonormative stabilisation. Secondly, recent economic, political and cultural globalisation has set in motion transnational and global linguistic flows (Alim, Ibrahim and Pennycook, eds. 2009) which have profoundly affected both standard and non-standard varieties of English. To make this point, the paper discusses data from Standard Nigerian English and Nigerian Pidgin.

Keywords: Standard Nigerian English, Nigerian Pidgin, nation state, Kachru's Three Circles model, Schneider's Dynamic Model, New Englishes, endonormativity, World Language System, English Language Complex, World System of Englishes model, Standard American English, African American Vernacular English (AAVE), Standard Jamaican English, Jamaican Creole

---

[1] The author gratefully acknowledges the financial support he has received from *Deutsche Forschungsgemeinschaft* (DFG), which funded his research on "cyber-pidgins" and "cyber-creoles" through grant MA 1652/9 ("Cyber-Creole": Jamaican Creole als Kontaktvarietät unter den Bedingungen globalisierter und computergestützter Kommunikation). In addition, I would like to thank Joseph Farquharson for his insightful comments on language use in the Jamaican webdata discussed below.

Christian Mair, University of Freiburg

DOI 10.1515/9783110429657-002

> Quite a number of people who think about language think about globalization, usually under three rubrics: the disappearance of small languages, the growing need for translation and interpretation, the spread of global English. The people who think about globalization, on the other hand, almost never think about language.
> (Mary Louise Pratt, n.d.)

1 Introduction: "national standards" as a problematical category in World Englishes?

In the modern world, national boundaries may occasionally be disputed, but in principle the world has been divided up completely, including the Antarctic, a continent without a permanent population, and various uninhabited islands scattered across the oceans. We take the nation state for granted as a basic criterion of classification in so many ways that extending the method to cover World Englishes seems natural. National varieties of English thus seem a convenient and self-evident top-level domain of classification, much like the world's population is calculated by adding up figures from individual national censuses. In Kachru's (1992) widely accepted model, nation states populate the Inner, Outer and Expanding Circles of English. The UK, the US and Australia are mentioned as important native-speaker communities of the Inner Circle (ENL). Bangladesh, India, Singapore and Zambia represent the second-language varieties of the Outer Circle (ESL), and China, Egypt and Vietnam illustrate the Expanding Circle of foreign-language use of English (EFL). In Schneider's book-length presentation of the Dynamic Model of postcolonial English, the core chapter (5, "Countries along the cycle"; 2007: 113–250) presents sixteen case studies, of which fifteen involve nation states – Fiji, Australia, New Zealand, the Philippines, Malaysia, Singapore, India, South Africa, Kenya, Tanzania, Nigeria, Cameroon, Barbados, Jamaica, Canada – and one (Hong Kong) is a special administrative region within another state.

What tends to be backgrounded in the flat hierarchy presented by such lists are issues such as whether Tanzania, South Africa and Nigeria are really on the same level when it comes to assessing the impact of a particular variety on the development of English in Africa, or on World Englishes in general.

The nation state is also the ordering principle underpinning many corpus projects in World Englishes studies. Thus, the *International Corpus of English* (ICE) does not have a regional "Caribbean component", but provides separate coverage for Jamaica, the Bahamas and Trinidad and Tobago. This is no different in the far bigger, web-derived *Corpus of Global Web-based English* (GloWbE), which covers the United States, Canada, Great Britain, Ireland, Australia, New Zealand, India, Sri Lanka, Pakistan, Bangladesh, Singapore, Malaysia, Hong

Kong, the Philippines, South Africa, Nigeria, Ghana, Kenya, Tanzania, and Jamaica. This is a significant contrast to corpora of English as a Lingua Franca (ELF), such as the *Vienna-Oxford International Corpus of English* (VOICE) or *English as a Lingua Franca in Academic Settings* (ELFA), which sample language across communicative domains rather than from regionally or nationally defined populations of speakers.

It is surprising to see a national principle at work – by default, as it were – in the classification of the New Englishes which doesn't work too well even for old and established varieties such as Standard British and Standard American English. There are spelling conventions which are followed throughout the UK, which differ from those of the US and which therefore make it possible to identify the country of origin of a written text. With regard to more central aspects of linguistic structuring, however, Peter Trudgill has long insisted that there is no national standard English for the whole of the UK and that what is usually referred to as (Standard) British English is in fact English English, i.e. the standard variety of England (e.g. Trudgill and Hannah 1982). Scotland has its own (sub-national) pronunciation, lexical and partly also grammatical norms within the UK. Received Pronunciation (R.P.), once the standard accent of a far-flung colonial empire, has little relevance beyond England as a standard norm in the UK today. In North America, Canadian orthographic practice shows that, instead of an endogenous national norm, there is competition between two different external standards within the national territory: the British, or British and Commonwealth one, and the US one.

The emergence of fully endonormative national standard varieties of English in the postcolonial world is one possible line of historical development. It is the story told about American English in Schneider's Chapter 6 ("The cycle in hindsight", 2007: 251–308), and it is a story which could be told about Australian English (cf. Schneider 2007: 118–127). We should not assume, however, that it is the *only* plausible development. Such an assumption is premature and will blind us to other possible outcomes of linguistic decolonisation.

There is no flat hierarchy among the New Englishes themselves, but clear non-reciprocal relations of influence. Developments in South African English, for example, are more likely to affect Namibian or Zambian English than the other way round.[2] A demographically and economically strong nation with a global diaspora, such as India, secures its English a global profile which is unattainable for, say, the established national standard of New Zealand or the emerging national standard of Sri Lanka. Last but not least, we should consider whether there is a minimum social and institutional threshold for a community's identification around "its own" variety of English in the post-colonial world.

---

[2] Cf. Buschfeld (2014: 194–196) for a discussion of the important, yet complex impact of South African English on English in Namibia.

Nationalist-inspired postcolonial language planning around English has succeeded in well-documented ways in Singapore (Leimgruber 2013). However, what has worked in a Southeast Asian economic powerhouse may not be applicable to the demographically more heterogeneous and institutionally less regimented environment of a Commonwealth Caribbean outpost in Central America such as Belize. Another issue is whether there is a purely demographic threshold needed to sustain the development of a fully codified endonormative standard. With a population of ca. 320,000, Iceland is a well-known case of a very small but culturally and linguistically fully autonomous nation state. The Bahamas has roughly the same number of inhabitants (ca. 360,000), but with regard to migrations, higher education and the media it is so thoroughly integrated with the United States and the rest of the Anglophone Caribbean that stable autonomy for the nation's English is unlikely. To mention an even smaller English-speaking nation state, there are no doubt locally specific ways of using English in St. Kitts and Nevis (population 50,000+), but prestige usage is very likely to be too volatile and subject to external influence for stable endonormativity.

2 The "World System of (Standard and Non-standard) Englishes"

Recognising both the persistence of global multilingualism and the privileged position occupied by English as the global *lingua franca*, de Swaan (2002) proposed a systems-theoretical analysis, which distributes the world's six to seven thousand languages into four hierarchical layers:

(a) **hyper-central language**: English
(b) **super-central languages**: Arabic, Chinese, French, German, Hindi, Japanese, Malay, Portuguese, Russian, Spanish and Swahili[3]
(c) **central languages**: e.g. Dutch, Finnish, Korean, Wolof, ...
(d) **peripheral languages**: 6,000+

As can be seen, the World Language System has a very broad base, namely thousands of peripheral languages, but little room at the top. There are no more than 100 to 150 central languages, around a dozen super-central ones, and only one hyper-central one: English, which functions as the single "hub" of the system today. In other words, while English is not the *only* language of power in the world, there is no truly global power *without* English. The BRICS states (Brazil, Russia, India, China and South Africa), emerging global players and all multilingual, are cases in point. To the extent that it contributes to the global economy, Brazil does so in Portuguese and English, as Russia does in

---

[3] In the updated 2010 version de Swaan adds Turkish to this list (2010: 57).

Russian and English. Bilingualism in Russian and Portuguese, with English excluded from the repertoire, is not as viable economically. This almost exclusive association of English with global power (albeit in multilingual constellations) is historically new. In the heyday of British Imperialism, in around 1900, the world did not have one undisputed global language yet. French was certainly a strong contender with English in politics and diplomacy, and German and French rivalled English as languages of scholarly publication. French, German and a small number of other languages are now found on the next lower level, among the "super-central" languages; they all have transnational reach, without being able to claim the global importance of English. On the level below there are the "central" languages, typically the fully standardised official languages of nation states. They are secure in their home bases, but their power, influence and attraction beyond that is limited. The "peripheral" languages are those which lack demographic weight, a written standard, media presence or other institutional support; they comprise the vast majority of the world's languages, and many in this group are threatened by extinction.

Seen as a whole, however, the World Language System constitutes "a surprisingly efficient, strongly ordered, hierarchical network, which ties together – directly or indirectly – the 6.5 billion inhabitants of the earth at the global level" (de Swaan 2010: 56). As such, and alongside the political, economic, ecological and cultural dimensions of globalisation, it represents the linguistic dimension, drawing attention to the impact of globalisation on language use and at the same time recognising the partial autonomy of the linguistic dynamics of globalisation from the other dimensions.

With regard to the *leyenda negra* of English, its alleged status as the world's number one "killer language", the World Language System shows the very partial truth of this allegation. Of course, there are numerous historical cases of English playing a role in the elimination of other languages – in the British Isles itself (Manx, Cornish), or in colonial North America or Australia. However, in the pecking order that the World Language System represents, the most immediate threat to a language is generally not from English directly, but from the neighbour from one level up. For example, Sami, a peripheral language of Finland, is under threat not from English, but from Finnish, its closest "central" neighbour. As it became established as one of the central languages of Scandinavia, Finnish, in turn, had to assert its position vis à vis Swedish and Russian, which succeeded each other as the "super-central" transnational languages in the relevant region of Northern Europe.[4]

---

4 The "English-free" Scandinavian four-language constellation was chosen to make the basic point. Of course, English is commonly present in similar constellations, especially as language of education and administration, in the postcolonial world. Here, English may well work against peripheral languages in conjunction with another language.

To gain a clearer understanding of the hierarchically structured internal variability of the "English Language Complex" (McArthur 2003; Mesthrie and Bhatt 2008) I have recently suggested applying de Swaan's systems-theoretical model to World Englishes (Mair 2013a). On this view (and paraphrasing de Swaan), the global English Language Complex presents itself as a surprisingly efficient, strongly ordered, hierarchical constellation of varieties, styles and registers which ties together – directly or indirectly – the 1-billion-plus regular users of English at the global level. Figure 1 presents the relationship obtaining among varieties:

- **the hub / hyper-central variety:** Standard American English
- **super-central varieties:**
  - **standard:** BrE, AusE, IndE, NigE, ...
  - **non-standard:** AAVE, Jam CreoleE, popular LondonE, ...
  - **further domain-specific ELF uses:** science, business, international law
- **central varieties:**
  - **standard:** IrE, NZE, JamEng, ...
  - **non-standard:** US "Southern", North-of-England, ...
- **peripheral varieties:** all traditional rurally based non-standard dialects, plus a large number of ex-colonial varieties including pidgins and creoles

Figure 1: The World System of Standard and Non-Standard Englishes (Mair 2013a)

Like de Swaan for the World Language System, I assume a single hub for the World System of Englishes, namely Standard American English. This assumption may be controversial for two reasons.

First, it could be contested by speakers of British English. However, there is clear linguistic and language-external evidence to support the global pre-eminence of American English today. For example, for several decades now there have been strong unidirectional currents of lexical borrowings from (standard and non-standard) American English to practically all other varieties, including British English, but only trickles in the reverse direction. British academic publishers sometimes follow US orthographic practice, but British orthography is not used by American publishers. American spellings tend to be favoured for borrowings from English into other languages. The whole English-speaking world is expected to be able to cope with the language of American-produced movies and books in the original, whereas globally successful British books, television series and movies are sometimes adapted to the American market by lexical adjustments or the addition of glossaries or subtitles.[5]

---

[5] A prominent example of this is provided by the books and films of the *Harry Potter* series.

Secondly, it has been argued that, especially with regard to the spoken language, Standard American English is a language-ideological myth – "a hypothetical construct" (Lippi-Green 2012: 55). This is an overstatement. I am happy to concede the point that hardly any *de facto* standardisation processes come without their fair share of language-ideological folklore and myth-making. This, however, tends to proceed from some factual base, as it does in the present case:

> American English has developed a national dialect for the usually well-educated participants in a national marketplace for goods, services, and jobs. The well-educated share a national speech pattern within their own social stratum, unlike earlier periods in the history of American English when they shared regional dialects with working-class and lower-middle-class speakers. (Kretzschmar 2004: 55)

Individual acts of subversion – such as a rap artist parodying Standard American English through "sampling" bits of it in their work – are premised on a recognition of this current sociolinguistic order. Needless to add, given the global power of the American media industry, international audiences are not totally ignorant, and in some cases even quite knowledgeable, about the contemporary sociolinguistic stratification of American English.

It is, in fact, one of the advantages of the World System of Englishes model that it systematically considers both standard and non-standard varieties of English. And sure enough, even the handful of illustrative examples given in Figure 1 supplies evidence for the weakness of the nation state and the problems of privileging the "(postcolonial) national standard variety of English" as a top-level category in classifications of World Englishes. National standard varieties of English are found on three out of four hierarchical layers in the system. Standard American English is the hub of the system, Standard British English and Standard Australian English are super-central varieties with considerable transnational reach, New Zealand English is a central variety by now securely established in its own national territory, and Jamaican Standard English is a central variety whose position within its national territory has strengthened considerably in the recent past but is not yet entirely unchallenged.

Many non-standard varieties of English are counted among the peripheral ones, as expected, but this is clearly not true for all of them. African American Vernacular English (AAVE), for example, has been shown to be at the core of some of the most powerful *global linguistic flows* (Pennycook 2008). It provides the vernacular substrate for "Hip Hop nation language", a subcultural movement which, though originating in the urban ghettoes of the US in the late 1970s and early 1980s, has since spread throughout the English-speaking world and beyond that into many other linguistic communities – a clear case of transnational impact. In the transnational and media domains AAVE has gained overt prestige which it has never had in vernacular usage in the United States itself. In this case, upgrading the prestige of a vernacular does not entirely undermine the existing sociolinguistic order. Standard American English is the national prestige variety within the US and the hub of the global English Language Complex at the same time. The national sociolinguistic orders are reversed, however, in the cases of Nigerian and Jamaican Standard English. These are prestigious varieties on the national level, where Nigerian Pidgin English and Jamaican Creole, the corresponding mass vernaculars, are stigmatised. This constellation is reversed completely in the international linguistic market, where Jamaican Creole and Nigerian Pidgin are the hotter commodities.

3 Mobility, migration, media – and the inversion of prestige

African American Vernacular English, Jamaican Creole and Nigerian Pidgin would have remained peripheral varieties of English if it had not been for their triple mobilisation – (i) in currents of physical migration, from country to city within national boundaries and subsequently also across national boundaries in the formation of diasporic communities; (ii) through association with subcultural and artistic movements (from blues through hip hop to reggae and dancehall); and (iii) through being taken up and marketed as commodities by a globally operating entertainment industry.

As has been pointed out, the mobilisation of AAVE cannot undermine the position of its corresponding standard. This is different in the cases of Jamaica and Nigeria. Standard Jamaican English and Standard Nigerian English have gained postcolonial legitimacy only within their own national territories. Unlike their corresponding pidgin or creole vernaculars they have not been mobilised beyond these limits. They play little role in the new transnational "ethnoscapes" and "mediascapes" (Appadurai 1996) opened up by migration and cultural globalisation, with the result being a loss of prestige and relevance relative to their more mobile and internationally better-known nonstandard counterparts. In the terminology proposed by Castells (2010), Standard Jamaican English and Standard Nigerian English have remained part of the traditional "space of places", whereas Jamaican Creole and Nigerian Pidgin have moved on to become part of the new "space of flows" of cultural globalisation. In these two cases it is thus the pidgin and the creole rather than the corresponding standards which need to be analysed in terms of the sociolinguistics of globalisation, which Blommaert has aptly defined as the "sociolinguistics of mobile resources and not of immobile languages" (Blommaert 2010: 180).

Empirical support for this assessment will be provided by the findings of a Freiburg-based research project (cf. also footnote 1 above), in which large web-derived corpora of texts are used to document the use of English (and other languages) by West African and Caribbean diasporic communities. One component of this database is the "Corpus of Cyber-Nigerian" (CCN), a collection of posts obtained from a web-forum (www.nairaland.com) which comprises ca. 244,048 posts produced by 11,718 members between 2005 and 2008, amounting to a total of around 17.3 million words.[6]

N-CAT (= Net Corpora Administration Tool) is the concordancing and visualisation tool which has been developed for the project. For CCN, it uses information on the country of residence of 968 key contributors to the forum to estimate the distribution of particular linguistic forms in geographical space; for 374 of these, additional information on the city of residence was obtained. Tests using frequent and geographically neutral search terms such as *the*, *good* or *house* have shown that the visualisation in the map covers a large part, usually more than two thirds, of the concordance output.

Fig. 2 below presents the map based on a search for the indefinite article *a*, which is a regionally and socially unmarked item. Because of the very high frequency of this search item,[7] the map is a good approximation of general forum activity.

Figure 2: Regional distribution of 244,048 documents containing *a* in CCN

The map shows a global diaspora with three focal areas in Nigeria itself, in the US and in the UK. The pale circles, giving the national totals, incorporate the information from the darker ones, which represent individual cities. Note that a different scale of representation is used in the production of the pale and dark

---

6 Corpus compilation has been described and some of the material has been analysed in Mair 2013a, 2013b, Mair (2016); Mair and Pfänder 2014 and Heyd and Mair 2014.
7 It actually occurs at least once in every single one of the 244,048 posts collected for the corpus.

circles, which means that the dark circles for very important cities, such as London, may turn out larger than those for their corresponding countries. This was necessary as representing entire countries with the city-scale would have led to extremely large pale circles which would have made the map impossible to read.

Out of a total of 244,048 posts, 70,620 could not be assigned to a specific location, whereas the remaining 173,428 were assigned to a country or a city and are thus visualised in the map. This means that we have a coverage of 71.1 per cent of the posts in this case. Of the documents covered and visualised, 36.8 per cent (or 63,811 posts) originate from Nigeria itself, 31.4 per cent (or 54,528 posts) from the US, and 19.3 per cent (or 33,393 posts) from the UK (with the other countries shaded in the above map accounting for the remaining 12.5 per cent or 21,696 posts).

To give an idea of the Zipfian geographical distribution observed (i.e. a small number of top countries accounting for a high proportion of the total data and a long tail of countries adding ever smaller contributions), I add the full list of countries represented, ordered by number of documents:

Canada – 4548
Spain – 2515
Germany – 1860
Malaysia – 1397
Ghana – 1360
Italy – 1206
Australia – 1112
United Arab Emirates – 960
Fiji – 747
Sierra Leone – 741
Netherlands – 618
Ireland – 476
China – 475
Belgium – 455
Norway – 440
France – 409
Japan – 347
South Africa – 275
India – 229
Liberia – 223
Benin – 213
Cameroon – 180
British Virgin Islands – 129

Cuba – 123
Brazil – 117
Finland – 84
Bulgaria – 75
Central African Republic – 48
Jamaica – 47
Papua New Guinea – 47
Egypt – 44
Switzerland – 37
United Republic of Tanzania – 36
Portugal – 28
Togo – 27
Botswana – 13
Cote d'Ivoire – 9
Namibia – 8
Romania – 8
Kenya – 7
Senegal – 6
Korea, Republic of – 4
Poland – 4
Zambia – 4
Grenada – 3
Congo – 2

If the distribution of the neutral item *a* represents the default case, any major deviation from it may be taken as *prima facie* evidence that a particular search item has regional or social indexical value. To test this, we can perform searches for known lexico-grammatical characteristics of Nigerian Standard English. They are expected to cluster in Nigeria itself, and the interesting question in the present connection concerns the extent to which these forms travel into diasporic communities. Consider, for example, the following use of the modal *will* (instead of internationally more familiar British, American or Australian English *would*) in the polite expression *would like to* (Alo and Mesthrie 2004: 815f.):

(1) **I will like to congratulate** mr seun first of all, you are an example of a champion and this project you have taken up will surely take you up and forward. (CCN [13548][8])

Figure 3 gives the relevant map, based on a concordance output of 439 documents produced by 303 members:

Figure 3: Regional distribution of 439 documents containing *will like to* in CCN

Of the 439 documents, 253 were localisable (coverage rate of 57.6 per cent). Of these, 45.8 per cent originate from Nigeria, 20.9 per cent from the US, and 18.2 per cent from the UK. As expected, much of this "local" grammatical usage

---

[8] Real user names in the Nairaland forums have been replaced by numbers in CCN in order to preserve posters' anonymity after the original posts have been removed from the forum.

clusters in Nigeria itself, and the circles in Britain and the US are smaller than in the corresponding map for *a* in Figure 2.

A common grammatical feature of noun-phrase grammar in Nigerian English is the use of plural forms for what would be considered non-count nouns in internationally more familiar English. Examples mentioned in Alo and Mesthrie (2004: 821) include *advice, aircraft, behaviour, blame, deadwood, equipment, information, personnel* and *underwear*. One such form which is frequent enough for systematic investigation in CCN is *stuffs*. Pluralisation of this word is possible in internationally familiar English in certain compounds such as *food stuffs* (*food-stuffs*, *foodstuffs*), but otherwise rare:[9]

(2)   DO SOMETHING NIGERIANS, i want to wake up and see **good stuffs about Nigeria** on t.v **Good stuffs about our leadership** and waking up to see that Governors are running around like they lost something !!!!! (CCN [6794])

Figure 4 below shows that this usage travels even less easily outside Nigeria than *will like to*:

Figure 4: Regional distribution of 451 documents containing *stuffs* in CCN

---

9 Of course, this usage is not restricted to Nigerian English, but can be found in other New Englishes, as well. In the Corpus of Global Web-based English (GloWbE, http://corpus.byu.edu/glowbe/) a search for instances of *stuffs* tagged as noun (stuffs.[n*]) shows a frequency of > 5 per million words for Nigeria, Bangladesh, Singapore and Malaysia.

The 451 documents come from a total of 233 different members. 315 documents can be located: 51.1 per cent to Nigeria, 23.5 to the US, and 13.3 to the UK.

A lexical peculiarity of Nigerian English is the use of words such as *miscreant* (for 'criminal' or 'offender'), which would be considered old-fashioned in other varieties.

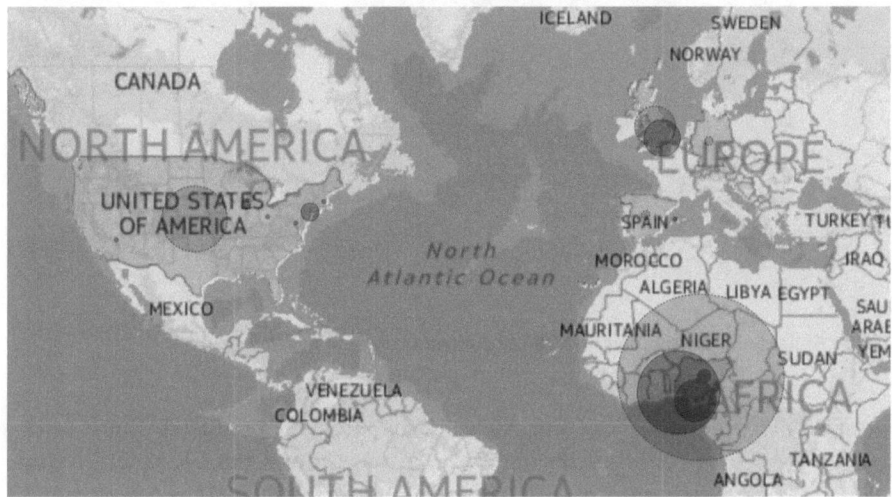

Figure 5: Regional distribution of 129 documents containing *miscreants* in CCN

Of the 169 documents, 96 are localisable, with 61.5 originating from Nigeria, 22.9 from the US, and 13.5 from the UK.[10] Again, Nigerian English usage is concentrated in Nigeria itself, with expatriate Nigerians apparently giving it up in favour of forms backed up by the Standard English norms of their new places of residence.

If one searches for common features of Nigerian Pidgin, on the other hand, no such effect is to be observed. Figure 6 presents the distribution of the highly frequent Nigerian Pidgin interrogative pronoun *wetin* ('what').

The 2,084 documents were produced by 814 members. 1449 documents were localisable, which means that the map covers 69.5 per cent of the total concordance output. Major sources of the localisable output are Nigeria (37.1 per cent, 537 documents), the US (31.3 per cent, 453), and the UK (20.8 per cent, 301). This is almost exactly the same distribution as that found for the indefinite article *a*. In other words, wherever in the world there is forum activity, there will be a

---

10 Note that similarly archaic usage is found in South Asian New Englishes. GloWbE has a frequency > 2 per million words for Nigeria, India, Pakistan and Bangladesh.

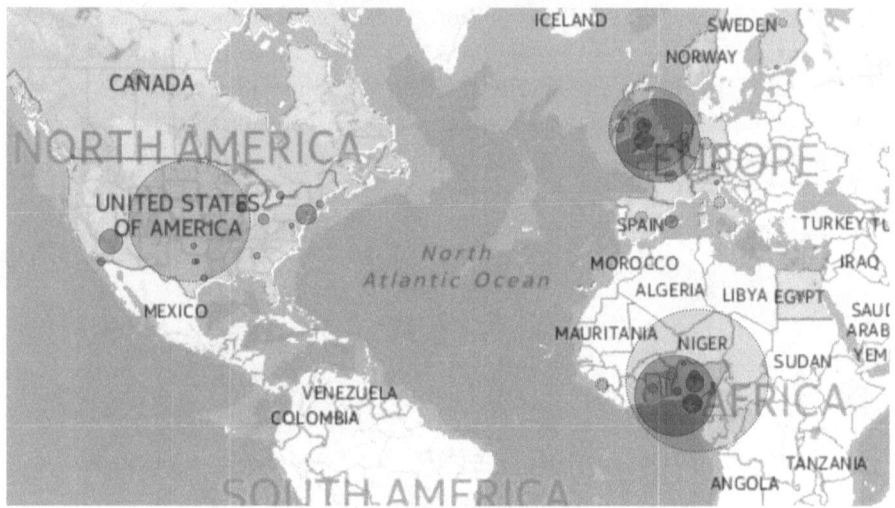

Figure 6: Regional distribution of 2,084 documents containing *wetin* in CCN

proportional amount of Nigerian Pidgin in the language produced. This is borne out by the list of countries beyond Nigeria, the US and the UK to which individual concordance entries could be attributed, which are – in the order of frequency: Canada (28), Spain (18), France and Germany (16 each), Italy and Australia (12 each), Malaysia (8), Sierra Leone (7), Fiji (6), and – at frequencies of five or less – India, China, South Africa, Ghana, Egypt, Ireland, Japan, Norway, Belgium, United Arab Emirates, Finland, Benin, and the Netherlands.

Expressions such as *wetin be* ... ('what is ...'?), *wahala* ('problem') or *na wa o* (exclamation of shock and surprise) are widely known stock phrases even among outsiders with little knowledge of Nigerian Pidgin. High frequency of *wetin* outside Nigeria thus would not necessarily imply fluency in Nigerian Pidgin, but could be evidence for symbolic use, for example, by second- and third-generation immigrants otherwise fully integrated in their new communities. This is why an additional search was undertaken for posts containing a set of three common grammatical morphemes: the focus particle *na*, the emphatic utterance-final particle *o*, and the second-person plural pronoun *una*.[11] This typically yielded material of the following type, which can be taken as evidence of fluency in Pidgin:

---

[11] The search was confined to the spellings as given here, which are the most common ones in the data. Other spellings exist.

(3) This is Rosby's first posting and you're already on fire for the lady.
Na **una** type dey carry beat women for house so. Make you take time **o**.
Me I don marry, express don leave you behind. You think say **na** play play
we come do for here. Carry ya playboy pattern go Romance section **o o**!!
(CCN, [15947])

In all, there are 382 documents meeting the search criterion, which were produced by 193 different members, with the geographical distribution represented in Figure 7:

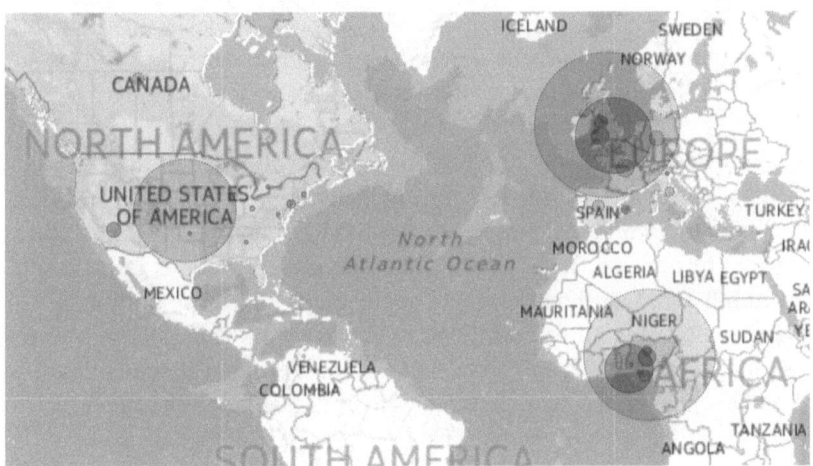

Figure 7: Regional distribution of 382 documents containing at least one instance of *na*, *una* and *o* in CCN

278 documents (72.8 per cent) could be attributed to a specific location. The biggest single contributor (34.9 per cent, 97 documents) was the UK, followed by Nigeria (31.7 per cent, 88), and the US (24.5 per cent, 68). With further passages of fluent Pidgin originating from France, Germany, Spain, Canada, Italy and Fiji, we have established further proof that Nigerian Pidgin is not confined to Nigeria itself, but continues to thrive wherever Nigerians move in the world.

As has been hinted at, a similar point can be made about the relationship between Standard Jamaican English and Jamaican Creole in the Jamaican webforum data collected for the project. The method of demonstration, however, is different. The Jamaican cyber-diaspora differs from the Nigerian one because it lacks a strong base in the historical "homeland", the island of Jamaica itself. In the absence of sufficient amounts of data from Jamaica, direct comparison with US output is not possible for most variables. Another complicating factor is that

Jamaican Creole and English are linked in an ordered continuum, which makes it more difficult to distinguish passages of Creole and English in writing than it is to distinguish English from Nigerian Pidgin.

What is striking, though, is that, when used on the web, basilectal Jamaican Creole seems to shed most of the stigma attaching to it in face-to-face interaction on the ground. Rather than denote rural origin, poverty, lack of education and general backwardness, it becomes a valuable resource which is freed up for new communicative uses in the new medium. Generally, it serves to evoke an atmosphere of *a yaad* ('at home', 'among Jamaicans'), as opposed to *inna farrin* ('in foreign' = abroad[12]). Men often use Jamaican Creole playfully to perform a tough guy persona or to engage in games of mock verbal aggression. For women, it commonly embodies the down-to-earth common-sense of the strong woman in the Caribbean tradition, as it does in the following example:

(4)   when i go visiting in Georgia and Bermuda, everyone says Hi to everyone they pass. It's so good to see it. I still say hello to strangers of my own colour here in Toronto. Sometimes they answer, sometimes they don't but that won't turn me off. Howdy and Tenky nuh bruk no square. lawx, mi did learn nuh fi eat inna di bathroom, but sometimes mi in dere putting on me makeup or combing mi hair while mi rushing to work and mi have a sangwige ..mi juss rest di egg sangwige pon a piece a tissue while me put apply di make up ..mi eat in btwn.... *sigh* life in di fast lane. (CCJ, [3316])[13]

User metadata and the deictic reference to "here in Toronto" in the text itself help localise this post reliably. Note that the first part of this brief text introduces the Caribbean as a topic. But of course there is no automatic "knee jerk" connection between mention of things Caribbean and the use of Creole. The subject of traditional norms of politeness in the Caribbean is discussed in English for quite some time, before the proverb "Howdy and Tenky nuh bruk no square" brings about the switch into Creole, probably referencing the fact that the speaker considers her politeness to be the result of her solid Caribbean upbringing. Interestingly, Creole continues when the topic moves to the stressful morning routine faced by the career woman living in the big city. Eating in the bathroom breaks

---

[12] Actually, the situation is more complex, with *farrin* referring to "outside Jamaica and the Caribbean region, and especially the US and Canada". Barbados, another Commonwealth Caribbean state, and even Spanish-speaking Cuba would not usually come under the heading of *inna farrin* (Joseph Farquharson, p.c.).

[13] CCJ stands for "Corpus of Cyber-Jamaican", which contains 16.9 million words of forum data covering the years from 2000 to 2008.

a strong traditional taboo in the Jamaican context, so that we have to read this passage as a truly heartfelt confession. The maintenance of Creole might be a way of signaling that despite her doing this un-Jamaican thing, she is still a *yaadi* deep down. We don't know whether this particular poster has frequent opportunity to use Jamaican Creole offline, but whether or not this is the case, we can be sure about one thing: Creole has accompanied this immigrant as a mobile and flexible linguistic resource in a mobile life.

4 Conclusion

The present study has raised the question whether we can go on taking the postcolonial nation state as the primary criterion for classifying standard varieties of the New Englishes. From Singapore to South Africa, several postcolonial nation-building projects have resulted in a robust sense of identification with the new state by a majority of the population and in stable institutional structures, but such success has, sadly, not been universal. The question thus arises whether there can be a strongly focussed new standard of English in an environment characterised by weak administrative and educational institutions and a lack of identification with the state. Such a situation does not invalidate the predictions of Schneider's model, but in a fragmented nation the "indigenisation"[14] of English will take place in selected sectors of the national population only. This could be described as the threat to Outer Circle endonormativity from within.

There is also a challenge to Outer Circle endonormativity from without – in all those instances in which migration and persistent external influence lead to a blurring of the national boundaries, so to speak. Referring to the results of the loosening of traditional ties between territory, community and identity in her study of Jamaica, Thomas has formulated the pointed conclusion that "Jamaica is now wherever Jamaicans are" (2004: 259). What she does *not* spell out is the linguistic result of this re-definition: the fact that Jamaican Creole, but not necessarily Standard Jamaican English, is now wherever Jamaicans are, too. It is this global presence that has caused the inversion of the traditional prestige of the standard and the creole.

When Jamaicans are in the US, in Britain or in Canada, it is usually Jamaican Creole and not Standard Jamaican English which supplies the linguistic resources

---

14 To describe the institutional and cultural indigenisation process which English undergoes in first- and second-language postcolonial settings Schneider uses the term "nativisation". I prefer *indigenisation*, to avoid a misunderstanding in which *nativisation* is taken to imply that English has become the native or first language of the population.

that speakers use to signal their identity – just as Nigerian Pidgin rather than Nigerian English serves the purpose for global Nigerian diaspora.

The "crisis of the Outer Circle" which we have described does not mean that we should reject the important insights which we owe to Kachru's or Schneider's models for the integrated description of varieties of English. What we should do, however, is to stop taking them for granted. They were developed to account for the linguistic legacy of colonialism, and for this purpose they will continue to work. But history, and the place of English in it, has moved on. Since decolonisation, essentially a period spanning the three decades between the end of World War II and the mid-1970s, much has happened in the English Language Complex which takes us into the unexplored territory between and beyond the magic Three Circles of Kachru's model.

There is, obviously, a simultaneous "crisis of the Expanding Circle" which I have not been able to cover within the scope of the present paper. The easy flow of linguistic authority and authenticity from the "norm-giving" Inner Circle through the "norm-developing" Outer Circle to the "norm-dependent" Expanding Circle is challenged when people who have been taught English as a foreign language (EFL) find themselves using it as a lingua franca (ELF) later in their lives. Such situations deserve close sociolinguistic study. The one thing I am convinced we must *not* do, however, is to take the emancipatory arguments used to defend Outer Circle endonormativity for the New Englishes and apply them to the lingua franca situation unchanged. Local communities of vernacular speakers, imagined communities (Anderson 1991[15]) rallying around codified standard languages, and communities of practice defined by shared interests and pursuits are very different forms of social organisation and will differ enormously in their language practices, attitudes and ideologies.

References

Anderson, Benedict R. 1991. *Imagined communities: reflections on the origin and spread of nationalism*. London; New York: Verso.

Appadurai, Arjun. 1996. *Modernity at large: cultural dimensions of globalisation*. Minneapolis MN: University of Minnesota Press.

Alim, H. S., A. Ibrahim, and A. Pennycook, (eds.). 2009. *Global linguistic flows: hip hop cultures, youth identities, and the politics of language*. New York: Routledge.

---

[15] The relevant quotation reads: "It is always a mistake to treat languages in the way that certain nationalist ideologues treat them – as emblems of nation-ness, like flags costumes, folk-dances, and the rest. Much the most important thing about language is its capacity for generating imagined communities, building in effect particular solidarities." (1991: 133)

Alo, Moses A., and Rajend Mesthrie. 2004. Nigerian English: morphology and syntax. In Bernd Kortmann and Edgar Schneider (with Kate Burridge, Rajend Mesthrie, Clive Upton) (eds.), *A handbook of varieties of English. Vol 2*, 813–827. Berlin: Mouton de Gruyter.

Blommaert, Jan. 2010. *The sociolinguistics of globalization*. Cambridge: Cambridge University Press.

Buschfeld, Sarah. 2014. English in Cyprus and Namibia: a critical approach to taxonomies and models of World Englishes and Second Language Acquisition research. In Sarah Buschfeld, Thomas Hoffmann, Magnus Huber, and Alexander Kautzsch, (eds.), *The evolution of Englishes: the dynamic model and beyond*, 181–202. Amsterdam: Benjamins.

Castells, Manuel. 2010. *The information age. 3 vols. I: The rise of the network society. II: The power of identity. III: End of millennium*. Oxford: Blackwell.

Coupland, Nikolas, (ed.). 2010. *The handbook of language and globalization*. Malden MA: Blackwell.

de Swaan, Abram. 2002. *Words of the world: the global language system*. Cambridge: Polity.

de Swaan, Abram. 2010. Language systems. In Nikolas Coupland (ed.), *The handbook of language and globalization*, 56–76. Malden MA: Blackwell.

Heyd, Theresa, and Christian Mair. 2014. From vernacular to digital ethnolinguistic repertoire: the case of Nigerian Pidgin. In Véronique Lacoste, Jakob Leimgruber and Thiemo Breyer, (eds.), *Indexing authenticity: sociolinguistic perspectives. FRIAS Linguae & Litterae Series*, 244–268. Berlin: de Gruyter.

Kachru, Braj, (ed.). 1992. *The other tongue: English across cultures*. 2nd ed. Urbana IL: University of Illinois Press.

Kretzschmar, William A. 2004. Regional dialects. In Edward A. Finegan and John R. Rickford, (eds.), *Language in the USA: themes for the 21st century*, 39–57. Cambridge: Cambridge University Press.

Leimgruber, Jakob. 2013. *Singapore English: structure, variation and usage*. Cambridge: Cambridge University Press.

Lippi-Green, Rosina. 2012. *English with an accent: language, ideology, and discrimination in the United States*. London and New York: Routledge.

Mair, Christian. 2013a. The World System of Englishes: accounting for the transnational importance of mobile and mediated vernaculars. *English World-Wide* 34. 253–278.

Mair, Christian. 2013b. Corpus-approaches to the vernacular web: post-colonial diasporic forums in West Africa and the Caribbean. In Katrin Röder and Ilse Wischer, (eds.), *Anglistentag 2012: Proceedings*, 397–406. Trier: WVT, 2013. [expanded reprint in *Covenant Journal of Language Studies* [Ota, Nigeria] 1. 17–31; http://journals.covenantuniversity.edu.ng/jls/published/Mair2013.pdf]

Mair, Christian, and Stefan Pfänder. 2013. Vernacular and multilingual writing in mediated spaces: web forums for post-colonial communities of practice. In Peter Auer, Martin Hilpert, Anja Stukenbrock and Benedikt Szmrecsanyi (eds.), *Space in language and linguistics: geographical, interactional, and cognitive perspectives*, 529–556. Berlin / New York: de Gruyter.

Mair, Christian. 2016. Beyond and between the Three Circles: World Englishes research in the age of globalisation. In Elena Seoane Posse and Christina Suárez-Gómez. (eds.), *World Englishes: new theoretical and methodological considerations*, 17–36. Amsterdam: Benjamins.

McArthur, Tom. 2003. World English, Euro-English, Nordic English. *English Today* 19(1). 54–58.

Mesthrie, Rajend, and Rakesh M. Bhatt. 2008. *World Englishes: the study of new varieties*. Cambridge: Cambridge University Press.

Pratt, Mary Louise. *Globalization, language, and secularization or Land of the Free, home of the phraselator*. Manuscript.

Schneider, Edgar. 2007. *Postcolonial English: varieties around the world*. Cambridge: Cambridge University Press.

Thomas, Deborah A. 2004. *Modern blackness: nationalism, globalization and the politics of culture in Jamaica*. Chapel Hill NC: Duke University Press.

Trudgill, Peter, and Jean Hannah. 1982. *International English: a guide to varieties of Standard English*. London: Arnold. [5th ed. 2008]

Donald Winford
The Ecology of Language and the New Englishes: toward an integrative framework

Abstract: Previous research has repeatedly pointed to the need for a unified framework for language contact phenomena – one that would include social factors and motivations, structural factors and linguistic constraints, and psycholinguistic factors involved in processes of language processing and production. In this paper, I argue that the New Englishes offer a promising opportunity to integrate the three components of a unified framework for the study of contact-induced change. Such a framework must address, among other things, the nature of the processes underlying contact-induced change, that is, both the actuation and implementation of change (Weinreich et al. 1968), which relate respectively to the roles played by the individual and the community in the origin and spread of change. This would be in keeping with Weinreich's observation that language contact can best be understood only "in a broad psychological and socio-cultural setting" (1953: 4). In that spirit, I assess the contribution of the Ecology of Language (EL) framework (Mufwene 2001, 2008) to our understanding of the processes by which the New Englishes emerged. In the first place, I argue that, while this framework offers valuable insight into the social ecology of contact-induced changes, it fails to provide a principled explanation for the actuation of such changes, that is, the psycholinguistic mechanisms underlying the innovations that individuals introduce into their emerging interlanguage grammars or idiolects. Secondly, contra the EL framework, I argue in favor of the traditional view that all New Englishes, including creoles, arose via natural SLA, involving processes of restructuring, not in Mufwene's sense, but in the sense intended by researchers in first and second language acquisition (Hulstijn 1990: 32). Such restructuring includes, among other things, the replication of L1 grammatical patterns in the learners' interlanguage systems (ILs), which involves the psycholinguistic mechanism of imposition, that is, applying the language production procedures of one's L1 in producing structures in an emerging L2. An approach of this kind provides principled explanations for the kinds of innovative restructuring found in the formation of the New Englishes – explanations which the EL framework has so far failed to offer. A truly comprehensive framework for the study of the New Englishes must therefore establish links between linguistic, sociolinguistic and psycholinguistic approaches to language contact and change.

Donald Winford, The Ohio State University

DOI 10.1515/9783110429657-003

Keywords: language contact, New Englishes, Ecology of Language model, creole formation, idiolect, cognitive/psycholinguistic processes, imposition, transfer, innovation, (naturalistic) second language acquisition (SLA), contact-induced change, actuation of change, implementation/propagation of change, restructuring, internally/externally motivated change, grammaticalization, simplification, creole/non-creole varieties

1 Introduction

Researchers over the last sixty years or so have repeatedly pointed to the need for us to explain language contact phenomena in terms of social factors and motivations; structural factors and linguistic constraints; and the psycholinguistic factors involved in language processing. Such an integrated framework has so far eluded scholars in Contact Linguistics more generally, and more particularly in the study of New Englishes, among which I include English-lexicon creoles. Two broad factors have contributed to this lack of unity in the field. The first has to do with degree of fragmentation in the study of New Englishes, as reflected in the division of this area of study into fairly autonomous sub-fields such as World Englishes versus Creole Linguistics, etc. The disunity is further perpetuated by the classifications of New Englishes themselves, into "indigenized varieties" versus "creoles", or "native" versus "nativized" or "L2" varieties and the like, not to mention the distinction between varieties that are due to "normal" versus "abnormal" transmission. Such fragmentation ignores the fact that all New Englishes arose under conditions of contact, generally involving natural second language acquisition, and therefore share common processes of restructuring associated with this type of language contact. The second major reason for the lack of unity has to do with fragmentation among the sub-disciplines involved in the study of New Englishes. Linguistic approaches to these varieties have devoted a great deal of attention to the structural properties of contact phenomena and their sources in the input languages, but by and large pay little attention to the role of social factors. Sociolinguistic or socio-ecological approaches focus more on social contexts at the expense of structural factors. And both types of approach generally have little to say about the role of psycholinguistic factors, hence they fall short of providing a comprehensive picture of the evolution of post-colonial Englishes. A truly integrative model of language contact must establish links between linguistic, sociolinguistic and psycholinguistic approaches to language evolution. Such a framework must address, among other things, the nature of the processes underlying contact-induced change, that is, both the actuation and the implementation of change (Weinreich et al. 1968), which relate respectively to the roles played by the individual and the community in the origin and spread of change. If, as is generally agreed, the locus of actuation (of a contact-induced innovation) is the individual bilingual, then the mechanisms or processes of change have to be explained in terms of how linguistic systems or inputs interact in the individual mind – i.e., in psycholinguistic terms. At the same time, if the locus of the propagation of change is the set of networks that link individual to individual, and each to the broader social structure, then this aspect of change must be explained in sociolinguistic terms (Backus 2009). Linguistic approaches, for their part, focus primarily on the structural aspects of language contact, and try to explain "the forms of mutual interference of languages that are in contact", as Weinreich (1953: 3) puts it.

The New Englishes offer a promising opportunity to integrate the three components of a unified framework for the study of contact-induced change. This would be in keeping with Weinreich's observation that language contact can best be understood only "in a broad psychological and socio-cultural setting" (1953: 4). In that spirit, I examine one of the frameworks that has attempted to address Weinreich's challenge, namely the "evolutionary framework" of language change, as proposed particularly in work by Mufwene (2001, 2008, etc.).[1] Mufwene's approach is built largely on his experience with creole languages, extended to all the varieties of European languages that arose in colonial settings between the 15th to 19th centuries. I will argue that, while this framework offers valuable insight into the social ecology of language change, it is less successful in explaining the (psycho)linguistic processes involved in contact-induced change, particularly the actuation of such change. In Section 2, I provide a brief overview of the EL framework. In Section 3, I discuss what this framework contributes to our understanding of the ways in which the social ecology influenced the different evolutionary paths taken by New Englishes. In Section 3, I question the adequacy of the EL model of "competition and selection" as a framework for understanding the emergence and development of the New Englishes. In particular, I argue that the EL model overlooks the heart of what is involved in the actuation question, that is, the creation of innovations that shape the character of contact languages. I further question the EL model's claim that the kinds of actuation involved in contact-induced change are essentially the same as those involved in internally-motivated change. In Section 4, I argue that the EL approach offers no principled explanation for the ways in which the grammars of the New Englishes were built up from the features provided by their source

---

1 A similar approach is offered by Croft (2000), but I do not discuss his framework here.

languages. Contra Mufwene, I argue that this process of language creation is essentially one of "restructuring" similar to that found in cases of naturalistic second language acquisition, of which creole formation is a somewhat unusual type. In Section 5, I argue that such an approach allows us to address the core of the actuation problem, that is, the psycholinguistic processes that led to the innovations which were incorporated into the grammars of the New Englishes – a dimension of explanation that is barely touched on in the EL framework. Section 6 is a brief conclusion.

2 The EL framework

The EL framework is a very ambitious attempt to explain the processes of language evolution by appealing to various "ecological" factors that motivate and regulate change. The full range of the model and the wealth of issues it addresses are quite complex, and beyond the scope of the present discussion. An extensive recent account can be found in Mufwene (2008), especially Chapter 7, and Mufwene (2014). My chief concern here is how far the EL model achieves the kind of integrative explanation that it seeks, and whether in fact it achieves its goal of accounting for all aspects of language change in a unitary framework. I examine these questions specifically in relation to the origins and evolution of the New Englishes.

As Weinreich (1953: 3) and others have pointed out, any attempt to formulate a comprehensive model of language contact must face the difficult question of how to separate the individual from the social in examining the interaction between the linguistic processes generated by language contact, on the one hand, and the sociolinguistic and psycholinguistic factors that regulate them, on the other. Among the broader issues that arise are the following:

- The question of how macro- and micro-level social factors influence the outcomes of contact.
- The question of the implementation of change, that is, their propagation through social groups, and their eventual conventionalization as part of the community language.
- The question of the actuation of change, and the locus of such actuation.
- The question of how the linguistic inputs to the contact situation affect the type and degree of change.

All of these questions are of course inter-related, and the challenge is to demonstrate how they all interact with one another in particular cases of language contact.[2] The EL model is a valuable attempt to address at least some aspects of this challenge, but it deals primarily with the first two issues above, and only partly with the last two. It does so in terms of an extended metaphor that establishes parallels, or analogies, between language evolution and biological evolution. My aim here is not to challenge or dispute the analogies drawn by the model, but rather to scrutinize how far the model itself provides a fuller understanding of the origins and evolution of contact languages such as the New Englishes.[3] I first discuss the sociolinguistic contribution of the model, or in Mufwene's terms, the "social ecology" of language change, and then go on to discuss the shortcomings in the model's treatment of the psycholinguistic aspects of language contact.

2.1 The social ecology of language evolution

In the EL framework, ecology is divided into two broad categories: the internal and external. The former consists of all those factors that are internal to the language undergoing change and evolution. The external ecology includes a wide range of both social and linguistic factors. Linguistic factors include the languages that are come into contact with the evolving language. For the moment, I am concerned only with the social ecology. Social factors operate at both the macro level (of social structure) and the micro level (of social interaction). So far, as Mufwene and Vigouroux (2013: 131) point out, the EL model has focused most of its attention on "an integrative hitherto macro-level approach that bridges sociolinguistics, the ethnography of communication and language evolution". The EL model has identified a number of macro-level social factors that influence language evolution, including the following (Mufwene and Vigouroux 2013: 111 ff):
- Differences in economic systems (which influence population structure).
- Population structures (which determine who interacts with whom).
- Demographic strengths of populations.

---

[2] A full account of how the integrated approach outlined above applies to specific cases of language contact is beyond the scope of this paper. My aim is simply to point out what I see as crucial gaps in the way the EL model addresses the above questions, and to suggest how they can be remedied.
[3] Mufwene himself points out that "the notion of language species need not be analogous to that of biological species in all respects" (2001: 2), and does a fine job of pointing out where the analogies between linguistic and biological evolution break down. See for example, Mufwene (2014: 20).

Micro-level social factors can be divided into those that reside in the individual, and those that relate to the patterns of interaction that individuals engage in. Mufwene 2014: 16) classifies the former as cases of "direct" external ecological constraints, associating them with individual speakers/signers who are "direct language ecologies". All other social factors at both the macro and micro level are treated as part of the "indirect" external ecology. The micro-level sociolinguistic component of the EL model is still in an early stage of development (Mufwene 2014; Mufwene and Vigouroux 2013). This component seems most relevant to Mufwene's views on how changes spread from individual to individual via social networks, in ways reminiscent of the work of Milroy and Milroy (1985), Eckert (2000), Labov (2001) and others. It seems to lend itself most suitably to some kind of integration with the EL model of competition and selection as the key vehicles of language change. But we are still quite far from understanding the ways in which micro-level social factors interact with others in regulating change or resolving competition among linguistic variants. This represents a promising area for future research on New Englishes, and language contact in general (See the papers in Leglise and Chamoreau (eds.) (2013) for a step in this direction). So far, the EL framework has had much more to say about the macro-level social ecologies that are relevant to the origins and development of the New Englishes, so I confine my attention to this.

2.2 Macro ecology and the New Englishes

Mufwene has argued in a number of publications that different colonization types, and the kinds of economic systems they engendered, led to differences in population structures, which directly affected the evolution of English and other European languages in their colonial settings. Thus, in general, colonies established mostly for trade purposes in places like Africa and the Pacific produced pidgins based on non-standard dialects of the lexifier language. When these and other colonies in India and South East Asia became "exploitation" colonies, standard varieties were acquired by the elite segments of the population via the scholastic medium, giving rise to "Indigenized" varieties such as Nigerian, Indian and Singapore English. By contrast, "settlement" colonies such as those in the US, Australia, New Zealand, etc, produced outcomes that were closely related to their European sources – the varieties that have been categorized as "inner circle" or "native" in some of the literature. However, as Mufwene (2013: 214) points out, "settlement colonies were not all of the same kind: variation in the ways they were settled and in the ensuing population structures bore on how English evolved." A subset of these colonies – the plantation colonies in places like the Caribbean – relied on agro-industry that required huge numbers of imported slave laborers. Such colonies produced creoles that were structurally different from the varieties that emerged in other settlement countries. The general classification proposed by Mufwene is a promising first step toward exploring the broad social contexts in which the New Englishes emerged. Indeed, it has much in common with those proposed by other scholars, such as Gupta (1997), Mintz (1971), and Schneider (2003, 2007, 2010). Such macro-level approaches provide a broad context in which to categorize the various linguistic outcomes. However, as the case of the "settlement" colonies shows, they do not by themselves account for the structural differences in outcomes within the same colony, or across colonies. For Mufwene, such differences are merely a matter of degree, and depend simply on variation in the social ecologies that produced the contact varieties, rather than differences in the processes of restructuring that produced the various outcomes. Consequently, Mufwene (2008: 149) adopts the view that "the development of creoles differs from that of other language contact phenomena (such as the "indigenization" of European languages in the Third World) more in degree than in kind."

On the face of it, this seems to reflect the very reasonable view that differences in the social ecology lead to differences in the outcomes of language contact. There is much that is attractive in Mufwene's attempt to provide a single unified account of the origins of all New Englishes – one in which the ecology "rolls the dice" to determine the various outcomes. It is a welcome attempt to revisit the relationships among members of the family of Englishes, and to explore what they share in common by way of social history and linguistic evolution. It is now well known that the boundaries between creoles, indigenized varieties, expanded pidgins etc, break down upon closer inspection of the similarities both in the social ecologies and the linguistic processes that produced them. The EL attempt to formulate a uniform model of the social ecologies that produced the New Englishes is therefore an important contribution toward the unified sociolinguistic framework we all seek.

However, Mufwene goes much further, claiming that differences in the social ecologies are all that distinguishes creoles from non-creole varieties of colonial Englishes. For Mufwene, "the differences between, for instance, American Southern English, New England English, Gullah, AAVE, Jamaican Creole and Jamaican English" can all be explained in terms of "specificities of the ecological settings of their emergence" (2008: 44). The claim that the differences between varieties as distinct as New England English and Jamaican Creole boil down to just differences in the ecological setting raises several questions. Not the least of these is whether the structural differences involved can all be accounted for by the same processes of restructuring. This in turn raises the issue of whether the

New Englishes can be seen as a distinct family of contact languages in its own right. This has of course led to bitter debate about the status and typology of creoles, which Mufwene now extends to other New Englishes.

Mufwene argues that "external history suggests that there are actually no differences in regard to the restructuring process involved" (2008: 44). Even allowing for some flexibility in the interpretation of "restructuring", this is a very strong claim indeed. It leads Mufwene to question a number of traditional assumptions about the differences between the development of creoles as opposed to non-creoles; about the differences between dialect contact and (bilingual) language contact; and indeed, the difference between internally-motivated and externally motivated change. Underlying this position is a very specific conception of how the "restructuring" processes that gave rise to the New Englishes operate. For Mufwene, they can all be accommodated within a single model of "competition and selection" – which implies that there are no differences in the actual processes that give rise to creoles as opposed to non-creoles. His adoption of this model also leads him to reject, unfortunately in my view, other models that link the processes of restructuring in New Englishes to those involved in naturalistic second language acquisition. To understand these issues better, we need first to explore the EL model of contact-induced change.

3 Selection, competition, and language evolution

Any model of language change must address a number of key problems that were identified by Weinreich et al. (1968: 183–87). These include: the constraints problem, the transition problem, the embedding problem, and the actuation problem. Perhaps the most basic of these is the actuation problem, which Weinreich et al. describe as "the very heart of the matter", and which involves questions like the following: "[w]hat factors can account for the actuation of changes? [w]hy do changes in a structural feature take place in a particular language at a given time, but not in other languages with the same feature, or in the same language at other times?" (Weinreich et al. 1968: 102). As Weinreich et al. make clear, such questions relate both to the initiation of a change in an individual's idiolect, and to its spread or implementation in a community of speakers. This reflects a long-standing view expressed as early as Paul (1880), as summarized in Weinreich et al. (1968). Paul was concerned both with the causation of change in idiolects, and the causation of change in what he called "language custom" (Weinreich et al. 1968: 107). Paul suggested that there were two mechanisms involved in change at the level of the idiolect: "spontaneous change" and "selective adoption of features from the idiolect of one's interlocutors" (op. cit, 107–108). It is particularly important for us to determine whether the locus of change is in the individual or in the community, or in other words, which aspects of change we associate with the individual versus the community.

Like Paul, the EL framework views change as involving two stages – changes in individual idiolects, and the propagation of such changes through social groups. However, this approach appears to interpret the actuation question solely in terms of the spread of innovations from idiolect to idiolect, and their gradual diffusion throughout a speech community until they become part of group or communal grammars. As a result, it has devoted little attention to the kinds of innovations in idiolects that Paul refers to as "spontaneous change", and their causation. Mufwene makes this clear when he poses the following question: "[w]hat is the relationship between the individual selections made by particular speaker/signers and the group selections that map the evolutionary trajectory of a language?" (2008: 125).

In the EL framework, one source of innovations in an idiolect is when an individual selects elements from the pool of linguistic features to which they are exposed, whether during the process of acquisition, or in the course of adjusting their speech to conform to that of their interlocutors. This reflects Paul's idea of selective adoption from other idiolects, and strictly speaking, is part of the propagation of change. The propagation of changes at group or community level similarly involves a process of selection from among competing variants – a process that is subject to its own set of "ecological" constraints, both internal (pertaining to the idiolect or dialect in question) and external (pertaining to both social and linguistic influences). This model of competition and selection at both individual and group level lends itself quite readily to an explanation of change in sociolinguistic terms. The approach is by no means new, and has been explored in numerous ways in the literature. In particular, sociolinguists have investigated the propagation of change within and across social networks (Milroy and Milroy 1985; Eckert 2000; Labov 2001); the role of "leaders" of change (Eckert 2000; Labov 2001); and the role of accommodation or divergence in promoting or inhibiting change (Giles et al. 1991). Building on these studies, the EL framework has proposed a number of social factors that operate at the micro-level of sociolinguistic structure, and contribute toward the ways in which change proceeds (see especially Mufwene and Vigouroux 2013). While this aspect of the model appears to be still undergoing development, it at least recognizes that a sociolinguistic component is an essential part of an integrated model of change. The EL framework is therefore to be commended for attempting to apply sociolinguistic models to the investigation of language change.

However, as we noted earlier, the EL model of competition and selection does not address that aspect of the actuation question that deals with innovations in an idiolect that are due to what Paul calls "spontaneous change". It therefore has little to say about how such "spontaneous" innovations arise in the first place, whether due to purely internal motivation, or external causation. The neglect of this aspect of causation seems to me to explain why the EL framework claims that there are no differences in the actual processes of restructuring that produce internally motivated changes as opposed to those due to contact with other languages. This in turn would explain why Mufwene sees no difference in kind between varieties like New England English and Jamaican Creole. In the next section, I take issue with this position, and argue for a fundamental difference between the processes of restructuring involved in the creation of contact languages like the New Englishes, as distinct from varieties like New England English.

3.1 Actuation and the difference between internally and externally motivated change

Mufwene (2001: 15) makes it quite clear that he sees no distinction between internally and externally motivated change as far as what he calls "causation" is concerned. He claims instead that the causation is the same in both cases. For him, "[t]he causation actually lies in the competition and selection that arise from the communicative system(s) available to speakers, and in both the accommodations they make to each other and the adjustments that they make to new communicative needs in their speech acts" (2001: 15). Moreover, such accommodations and adjustments "can draw materials from either the same linguistic system or separate ones" (ibid.).

Mufwene is led to this conclusion partly by his dissatisfaction with traditional historical linguistic approaches which ignore the fact that most languages that have been treated as cases of purely internally-motivated change have in fact been subject to externally-motivated change in their histories (2008: 31). He cites cases like the Romance languages, and indeed, English itself. It is now generally accepted that the contact-induced changes that affected these languages are different only in degree, but not in kind, from those found in contact varieties of English, French, etc. (Thomason 1995; Schreier and Hundt 2013). To take just one example, there is a growing scholarship which shows that "the English language has been contact-derived from its very beginnings onward" (Hundt and Schreier 2013: 1). For instance, Klemola (2013) argues that features such as the Northern Subject Rule, *self*-forms as intensifiers and reflexives, and the third person singular pronoun *en* in south-western dialects of English, all arose from contact with Celtic languages in the early history of English. Similarly, other scholars have demonstrated how contact with Old Norse, French, and Latin led to significant change in dialects of English, including even Standard English, at various points in the history of the language (Wright 2013; Thomason and Kaufman 1988: 263–331).

Mufwene is therefore right that contact with other languages has played an important role in the history of most, if not all languages, including those associated with what Thomason and Kaufman call "normal transmission". However, allowing that external contact has produced changes in languages traditionally viewed as conforming to the Stammbaum model, does not mean that the mechanisms underlying internally motivated change are identical in all respects to those involved in externally-motivated change.[4] Yet Mufwene claims that "it is in fact possible to account for language diversification around the world as generally motivated by population movements and contacts, therefore by language contact even in the cases of the so-called "internally-motivated changes" (2008: 31).

Effectively, then, for Mufwene, differences between the internally and externally-motivated change boil down to differences in the ecology of language. "Causation" is the same in both cases, and resides in the contact between individual systems, and ensuing competition and selection among the features available to speakers. This view of causation corresponds closely to Mufwene's focus on the actuation of change as primarily a matter of how changes in idiolects result from competition between (features of) other idiolects, and how they spread from individuals through social groups. It is in this light that we must view Mufwene's argument that there are no differences in the "evolutionary processes" (2001: 19) that produce creoles as opposed to their non-creole kin. Such differences, he argues, "amount to differences in outputs as determined by variation in the ecological conditions affecting *the same language restructuring equation*" [emphasis mine] (2001: 19). If this were meant simply to claim that differences in linguistic inputs and social factors lead to differences in evolutionary outcomes, one would have no problem with it. But if this is meant to imply that there is no difference between internally and externally motivated change in terms of the types and degrees of innovation that are involved, it must give us pause.

There are indeed certain similarities to be found between the two types of change, which I will illustrate briefly with an example from Suriname. The Surinamese creoles have a Completive Perfect category, expressed by *kaba* (< Portuguese *acabar* 'finish'), which appears in VP-final position, as in the following example from Sranan Tongo:

---

[4] A fair test of this claim would be to compare internally-motivated changes in a language that has little external influence, with externally-motivated changes in one that has.

(1) Sranan A   kownu doro   kaba
              DET   king   arrive COMPL
              'The king has arrived.'

Winford and Migge (2007: 84) demonstrate that the category is closely modeled on the Completive aspect category found in Gbe languages, as illustrated in the following example.

(2) Ajagbe àxɔ́su lɔ   à,   e   vá   lɔ́   vɔ̀
              King   DET TOP he come   arrive COMPL
              'As for the king, he has already arrived.'

In both the Surinamese creoles and the Gbe languages, the aspectual marker also functions as a main verb meaning 'finish'. It was this similarity that prompted the extension of the function of *kaba* to marking Completive Perfect aspect, on analogy with the similar aspectual function of verbs like *vɔ̀* in Gbe languages. This is a clear case of what Heine and Kuteva (2005) refer to as contact-induced grammaticalization. Interestingly, such cases in fact mirror processes of internally-motivated grammaticalization in non-creoles. The development of markers of Perfect (also known as Anterior) aspect from verbs meaning 'finish' follows a well-known and frequently occurring path of grammaticalization found in many languages, which Bybee (2006: 184) characterizes as follows:

"finish" > COMPLETIVE > ANTERIOR > PERFECTIVE/PAST

However, despite the evident similarities between the two types of grammaticalization, there are also significant differences between them. Traugott (1989: 50) ascribes the changes associated with internally-motivated grammaticalization to processes involved in the conventionalization of conversational implicatures. Such processes play out over successive diachronic stages, "with the constructions at each stage changing gradually, almost imperceptibly, by pragmatic inferencing, analogical extension and reanalysis" (Fischer 2011: 33). In short, internally-motivated grammaticalization tends to involve mechanisms that require a long drawn out process before the innovation becomes established in the grammar. By contrast, contact-induced grammaticalization is an instantaneous process, driven by direct transfer of the grammatical function of an element in the source language to a similar lexeme in the recipient language, based on analogy between the two.

Contact-induced grammaticalization in fact relies heavily on analogical inferencing – one of the universal cognitive abilities that come into play in many kinds of language change. I would therefore argue that analogy is the primary cognitive factor involved in contact-induced grammaticalization. But I would also suggest that the role of analogical inferencing is to trigger the actual mechanism that results in the creation of a new grammatical category. I propose that this mechanism is imposition (van Coetsem 1988; Winford 2013) and that it underlies all of these kinds of contact-induced change. It is related to more general cognitive processes that are involved in natural second language acquisition and processing, as well as in other kinds of language contact situations. Imposition is conceived of as a psycholinguistic mechanism that involves simply applying the language production and encoding procedures of a linguistically dominant language to produce a less familiar language. Other approaches have explained this process in terms of "relexification" and "reanalysis" (Lefebvre 1996), or "functional transfer" (Siegel 2003). Such explanations are quite compatible with the notion of imposition as described here, but the notion of imposition captures the psycholinguistic process involved in these types of grammaticalization more clearly by linking it more directly to the language production procedure.

A further difference between the two kinds of grammaticalization follows from this, namely that, as Fischer (2011: 42) puts it, "grammaticalization does not lead to new grammatical structures in any general sense (...) except perhaps in cases of substratum or long term contact, where new structures may enter through bilingualism or imperfect learning." It is the introduction of such "new structures" or innovations that distinguishes externally motivated change from internally motivated change. Such innovations obviously arise because of the far greater role played by input from an external language. The availability of such input to bilinguals (including incipient bilinguals or L2 learners) is a vital factor that distinguishes the evolution of contact languages (in the restricted sense of that term) from that of languages that have been subject to little or no external contact, as far as mechanisms of change are concerned.

Once an innovation is established in particular idiolects, whether through internal or external causation, it then becomes available for spread to other idiolects. At this point, then, the propagation of the innovation is subject to similar social processes and motivations. It is this similarity that Mufwene seems to have in mind when he claims that there is no difference between internally and externally motivated change as far as "causation" is concerned. Whatever our position on the relationships between the mechanisms involved in internally versus externally motivated change, we still must keep those mechanisms, which are primarily psycholinguistic, separate from the social mechanisms of competition and selection that the EL model appeals to. But surprisingly, Mufwene seems to reject this distinction as well. He argues that "[o]nce we explain, as in Mufwene

(2001) that the fundamental and only kind of contact that triggers language evolution is inter-idiolectal, then the distinction between internally and externally motivated change becomes an artificial one, mostly sociological" (2008: 31). This seems to deny any role to the mechanisms of contact-induced change involved in actuation, and the principles that govern them. The same confusion between the actuation and propagation of a change can be found in his claim that dialect contact involves the same processes of change as contact between quite distinct languages. I address this in the next section.

3.2 Dialect contact versus contact between typologically different languages

Mufwene builds on his claim that there is no difference between internally and externally motivated change by declaring: "In kind, it does not matter whether the varieties in contact are separate languages or dialects of the same language" (2008: 31). He links this claim to his EL model of change by stating that "[t]his position entails acknowledging language and/or feature competition and selection as a central part of the engine which drives language evolution" (ibid.) This is essentially what forms the basis of Mufwene's (2001: 19) argument that there are no differences in the "evolutionary processes" that produce creoles as opposed to their non-creole kin. Mufwene (2008: 44) similarly argues that "external history suggests that there are actually no differences in regard to the restructuring process involved" in the formation of New England English as opposed to Jamaican Creole

This requires us to question whether contact between dialects (as in the case of the emergence of American or Australian English) leads to the same types of contact-induced change as contact between typologically distinct languages (as in the case of creoles and indigenized Englishes). The linguistic mechanisms and constraints that operate in the latter case cannot be treated as though they were identical in all respects to those involved in cases of koineization, which involve competition among features drawn from varieties of the same language.

Indeed, what sets the New Englishes apart from transported Englishes like American or Australian English is precisely the fact that the contexts in which the former arose created the conditions for extreme processes of contact-induced change, of a type not usually associated with change due to dialect contact. A crucial difference between the two, as discussed further below, is that the emergence of creoles and indigenized Englishes involved a process of second language acquisition under conditions of restricted access to the superstrate target, leading to sometimes massive transfer of features from learners' L1s into their L2 versions of the superstrate. The extreme kinds of restructuring that resulted have been well documented for a variety of the New Englishes. For example, Mesthrie and Dunne (1990: 35–37) discuss cases of "transfer of relativization strategies from [Indic and Dravidian] substrates" in South African Indian English (SAIE). L2 speakers of English whose first language is Gujarati produce relative clauses like the following:

(3) Which-one I put in the jar, that-one is good
 "The ones [i.e. pickles] I put in the jar are the best"

Such structures are clearly modeled on Gujarati correlative constructions with a pre-nominal relative clause, as illustrated by the following example:

(4) Je   vepari   marī   sathe   avyo,   te   vepari
    CORRELAT businessman me   with   came   that   businessman
    Harilal ka   bhaī   che
    Harilal of   brother is
    "The businessman who came with me is Harilal's brother"
    [Lit: Which businessman came with me, that businessman is Harilal's brother]

Similarly, speakers whose L1 is Tamil produce L2 English structures like the following:

(5) People who got [working for them] sons, like, for them nice they can stay.
    "It is nice for people who have sons [who are] working for [the company], since they are allowed to stay on [in the barracks]."

Such structures are modeled on Tamil relative constructions such as exemplified in the following:

(6) Vaṇṇeñe   aṭicca   taccān   cenneki
    washerman.acc   beat.past.rel. part carpenter.nom   Madras.dat
    pōnān
    go.past.3sg.masc
    "The carpenter who beat the washerman went to Madras"
    [Lit. The washerman-beat(ing) carpenter went to Madras]

A wealth of similar examples of profound grammatical change can be found in the extensive literature on the New Englishes. Colloquial Singapore English

(CSE), for example, is replete with constructions modeled on its Chinese and Malay substrates. Bao and Wee (1999: 5) provide the following example of a passive construction that employs *give* in CSE:

(7) John give his boss scold
'John was scolded by his boss.'

Such passives are replicas of similar 'give' passives in Chinese substrate dialects such as Hokkien and Cantonese, as in the following Hokkien example (Matthews and Yip 2009: 383):

(8) *Ah   Hock   tapai   hor   lang   me*
    Ah   Hock   always   give   people scold
    'Ah Hock always gets scolded by people.'

Such changes due to contact with Chinese and Malay have been so deep and extensive that CSE is typologically more similar to Chinese than to English (Ritchie 1986).

All of these new structures are, of course, quite different from their counterparts in transported varieties of English such as American or Australian English. There is absolutely no evidence that similar kinds of restructuring either did, or could, occur in the situations of dialect leveling that produced these varieties. Additionally, the kinds of changes found in 'indigenized' Englishes such as South African Indian English or Colloquial Singapore English are very similar to those found in creoles (Bao 2005; Winford 2009). Mufwene's claim that all of these varieties arise as a result of similar processes of "restructuring" therefore strikes one as quite odd, particularly since it is not backed up by any discussion at all of the structures of the languages and the processes that created them. Again, Mufwene's claim seems to hinge more on differences in the social ecology than on differences in the kinds of linguistic processes involved in the emergence of New Englishes as opposed to transported Englishes. He claims, for instance, that "the distinction between the development of creole and that of non-creole varieties [is] non-structural, pointing to no particular restructuring process that can be identified as *creolization*" (2008: 44) [italics in original]. Mufwene does acknowledge that "variation in the specific language varieties involved in the contacts" is also a factor in explaining differences in the outcomes (2008: 44). For him, "the key to understanding why creoles are different from their non-creole kin that evolved from similar colonial varieties of European languages is that ... "language acquisition" is a reconstruction process, which is sensitive to the variants in competition in the pool of features available to individual learners" (2008: 85).

The process of creole formation, then, boils down to a process of competition and selection among features, similar to that involved in every kind of language reconstruction, including, presumably, L1 and L2 acquisition. The main difference is that "[i]n the case of creoles, features of the substrate languages that new appropriators of the target language had spoken before also contributed to the feature pool ... making it possible for the selection into creoles of features other than those selected into the other, non-creole varieties" (2008: 118). All of this is fine as a description of the linguistic inputs to creole formation, but it says little about the mechanisms or processes by which substrate features enter the idiolects of learners, and are made available for selection into the communal creole. This is in fact a key omission in the EL model of language change and development, since it ignores a key aspect of the actuation question, that is, how do the innovations in creole idiolects arise in the first place, or, to put it in Mufwene's terms, what regulates selections of features at the individual level "from among competing alternatives in a feature pool including both native [sic] and xenolectal [sic] features?" (2008: 125). This is, of course, a crucial question for any theory of language change. In my view, the EL approach fails to address this key aspect of change at the level of the idiolect, that is, the innovations that arise through the mechanism that Paul referred to as "spontaneous change", as it applies to cases of language contact. As a result, the EL approach fails to offer any insight into the psycholinguistic processes involved in the creation of individual grammars, whether in creole formation, or in the development of indigenized varieties. To see why this is so, we need to examine more closely what the model claims about selection and the reconstruction process in contact-induced change.

4 The restructuring process in contact languages

Recall that, in the EL framework, the process of "selection" operates at both the individual and communal levels. In cases of contact between languages, selection at the individual level involves the incorporation of both TL and "xenolectal" features into the learner's idiolect (2008: 121). Mufwene equates selection at the individual level with what he calls "[a] reconstruction process – actually the development of one's I-language or idiolect" (2008: 182). He disfavors use of the term "acquisition" (which he consistently places in shudder quotes) apparently on the grounds that learners do not actually acquire a ready-made grammar from any other speaker(s), but rather (re)build their own IL or idiolect out of the input (feature pool) they are exposed to in their social networks. Mufwene also suggests that (re)construction can also be called a restructuring process, but not in the sense of structural divergences that make creoles different from the European languages they have developed from. I would agree with this, but not with Mufwene's definition of "restructuring." I use the term in the very different sense in which researchers in both first and second language acquisition use it. With regard to first language acquisition, van Buren (1996: 190) defines it as "discarding old grammars for new ones." He adds: "As soon as new relevant data are encountered, the current grammar is restructured to accommodate the new input" (ibid.) With regard to SLA, it refers to the gradual and cumulative process of building and rebuilding the learner's developing grammar – the IL (Hulstijn 1990: 32). However, Mufwene appears to have a very different view of what "restructuring" means with regard to the formation of the New Englishes.

4.1 Restructuring in the development of New Englishes

Despite the differences in the approaches they take, most contemporary researchers of creoles and other New Englishes view the formation of these contact languages as the result of naturalistic SLA under conditions of more or less limited access to the lexifier language as a target, or of access only to second language, including pidginized, varieties of the lexifier language. Like Mufwene, scholars in the field also acknowledge that differences in the social ecology allow for differing degrees of contribution from learners' L1s, in ways that generally go beyond what is found in more "typical" cases of SLA, for instance by learners in a classroom setting, or by immigrants with continual exposure to a host community's language. However, Mufwene questions the tendency to "analogize SLA and the development of creoles in ways that suggest absolute parallelism" (2008: 156). His objection is based primarily on the fact that most research on SLA focuses on individual SLA, hence it "offers nothing that can be compared to the interidiolectal mechanisms of competition and selection that led to the emergence of communal norms in creoles" (2008: 159).[5] Once more, Mufwene's emphasis on actuation at the level of the community rather than the individual is instructive, since it ignores the important contributions that SLA research has made to our understanding of the latter. Mufwene does mention such research, but only to again reject it as irrelevant to creole formation. He claims that "[...] while research on SLA can inform us about conditions that favor transfer during L2

---

5 Scholars who work on "indigenized" varieties will find this criticism somewhat harsh, since they have not ignored the question of how communal norms arise in these cases of naturalistic SLA.

"acquisition", it cannot inform us on how substrate elements influence the development of creoles or any other languages for that matter" (2008: 158). Mufwene's view is based on his assumption that "[s]ubstrate influence is a population-level phenomenon that results from both the repeated occurrences of xenolectal elements in some idiolects and their spread within the population of speakers what other speakers simply copy them" (2008: 159). But this completely overlooks the parallels between the workings of L1 influence at the level of individual learners' ILs in both SLA and creole development.[6] These parallels are to be found in the process of restructuring referred to above. It is during this process that innovations of various types enter the individual IL systems as instances of spontaneous actuation, and are thereby made available for the processes of "selection" and propagation that yield communal systems.

In short, treating creole formation (and the development of New Englishes generally) in terms of SLA yields various insights into the development of these new systems at the level of the individual idiolect. For instance, as Plag (2008a,b, 2011) and others have argued, it provides a principled explanation of such features of creoles as the loss of bound inflectional morphology, the use of fixed word order, and other phenomena that have been attributed to "simplification." For instance, as Plag (2008a,b, 2011) and others have argued, both creoles and early Interlanguage share such features as the following:
- loss of bound inflectional morphology,
- the regularization of word order in declarative, interrogative and negative sentences, and
- other phenomena that have been attributed to "simplification," such as the preference for free forms and transparent form-to-function relationships.

Thus creoles generally lack both "inherent" inflection such as number, degree and tense-aspect (though some of this is found in certain creoles), and "contextual" inflection such as subject-verb agreement, case markers and the like. The following example illustrates:

(9) Guyanese Creole *Jan   pikni   gat   tu   buk.*
                           John child   have two   book
                           "John's child has two books."

---

6 The view that SLA processes do not provide a satisfactory account of creole origins is echoed by other adherents of the "feature pool" approach, such as Aboh and Ansaldo (2006: 50). See Plag (2011) for a refutation of this view.

These are among the features that Chambers (2004) referred to as "vernacular universals", found across the New Englishes. In addition, several aspects of creole syntax reflect those found in early interlanguage. For instance, with regard to *wh*-question formation, creoles manifest *wh*-fronting, which emerges in early IL, but they lack subject-verb inversion because this process emerges only at later stages of IL development (Pienemann 1998: 171).

(10) Guyanese Creole *Wisaid Jan bin fain di pikni–dem?*
Where John PAST find the child-PLU
"Where did John find the children?"

As far as negation is concerned, preverbal negation with a single element is practically universal in creoles, and is also typical of early IL.

(11) Sranan *Kofi no ben de na oso*
Kofi NEG PAST BE LOC house
"Kofi was not at home."

The preservation of such "unmarked" structures in creole is generally attributed to the fact that they began as pidgins or a collection of early-stage ILs which then became targets of learning for later arrivals in various (usually plantation) settings. As Plag has argued, these similarities between creoles and early ILs are due to the fact that both creole creators and early L2 learners devise similar strategies in constructing their ILs in the early stages of acquisition (See also Schumann 1978). This is because they are subject to similar processing constraints inherent in early SLA.

In addition to this, an SLA approach provides a more principled explanation of the contribution of learners' L1s to the development of individual creole grammars – a contribution that differs only in degree from that found in individual-level processes of SLA. A growing body of research has shown that transfer from learners' L1s can occur as a compensatory strategy in second language use, even in the classroom (Nemser 1991; Helms-Park 2003; Siegel 2008). For instance, Nemser (1991) shows that different types of transfer from German can be found in the L2 English of German-speaking Austrian students, depending on their level of proficiency in English. Less advanced students manifest examples of word order transfer from German in the production of *wh*-questions like the following:

(12) a. Want you yoghurt?

b. Went you home?

Similarly, Helms-Park (2003) discusses examples of transfer like the following, from the L2 English of elementary-level Vietnamese learners.

(13) a. L2 English: Suzie cooked butter melted (2003: 228)
'Suzie melted the butter'

b. Vietnamese Hoà   dun   nu'ó'c soi   (2003: 217)
               Hoa   cook(liquid)   water   boil
               'Hua boiled the water'

(14) a. L2 English Harry is shake the bell rang
                    'Harry rang the bell'

b. Vietnamese: Giáp rung   cái   chuông reo
               Giap shake CLAS   bell   ring
               'Giap rang the bell.'

As we saw earlier, the formation of the New Englishes involved similar types of restructuring of input from English and learners' L1s, producing structures modeled on the latter. Creole formation, likewise, involved replication of the grammatical structures of the substrate languages, which produced, to name a few, serial verb constructions of various types, 'say' complements, and certain tense-aspect categories that had no model in the superstrate. For instance, Migge discusses directional SVCs like the following, from Paamaka, which mirrors its counterparts in the Gbe substrate languages, as illustrated in the example from Wacigbe (Migge 2003: 96).

(15) Paamaka Den   e   hali   a   boto   e   go   a   liba
              3pl   PROG   haul   DET   boat   PROG   go   LOC   river
              'They are hauling the boat to the river.'

(16) Wacigbe ɔ   la   dɔn   saki   a   yi   afí-mé
              3pl FUT   drag   bag   DET   go   house-in
              'They'll drag the bag to the house.'

Directional SVCs like these are quite productive in the Surinamese creoles, with a wide range of directional V2s, including *kom* 'come,' *gwe* 'go away,' *komopo* 'come up,' *komoto* 'come out,' etc., all of which are modeled on substrate equivalents. We could add many other examples of the replication of West African structures in Caribbean English-lexicon creoles (see Winford 2008b for an overview). They involve the same kinds of grammatical replication that have been attested in cases of both classroom and untutored SLA. Hence the connections between the kinds of innovation found in the New Englishes and those found in cases of SLA are clear. Innovations like these require us to address the question of the actuation of change at the individual level, which is directly relevant to the (psycho)linguistic aspects of a theory of change.

5 The psycholinguistic component

It is precisely this component of a general theory of change that is most lacking in the EL framework. However, Mufwene has hinted at the need to address it in his more recent publications. For instance, he acknowledges that "the real locus of language contact is the individual speakers (Weinreich 1953: 6), the makers and hosts of a communal language qua species" (2008: 180). Similarly, Mufwene and Vigouroux point out that "the mind is ... one of the most direct ecologies of language", and that "real language contact occurs in the minds of individual speakers, where structural information is processed, and where features associated with the same or similar functions are brought into competition and can be negotiated during interactions" (2013: 113). Such observations suggest the need for an exploration of the psycholinguistic processes and principles involved in contact-induced change, but the EL framework has little to say on this. It is in precisely such exploration that the potential lies for integrating the sociolinguistic, linguistic and psycholinguistic aspects of a theory of language change. The psycholinguistic aspect addresses more directly the nature of the restructuring process involved in individual language creation. This in turn allows us to see the similarities in the processes that led to the emergence of creoles and indignenized varieties.

Researchers in contact linguistics have made various proposals about what (psycho)linguistic mechanisms and principles can best explain the innovations that individual learners create in acquiring a second language. Most of the focus here has been on the contribution of learners' L1s, so I will limit my attention to this. Some proposals have generated a great deal of sometimes acrimonious debate. Lefebvre's (1998) Relexification Hypothesis has been the target of particularly strong criticism from other scholars, including adherents of the EL framework. For instance, Mufwene maintains that "the main problem with the exclusive or primary substratist explanation is that it does not account for those creoles' features which are not exactly matched by the relevant African languages" (2008: 139). But Lefebvre and her associates have pointed out that "the RH [relexification hypothesis – DW] is NOT a claim that relexification is the one and only process involved in Creole genesis, nor is it argued that relexification can account for all the properties of Creole languages" Lumsden (1999a: 230, fn 7). Mufwene also questions whether there is any evidence from SLA that supports the RH, and cites Siegel (2006) as responding "unequivocally that there is none". However, this conclusion is based mostly on the available research on classroom SLA, most of which had found only minor evidence of L1 influence on SLA (But see Nemser 1991 for an exception.) Siegel (2006: 36) in fact acknowledges that transfer can occur as a compensatory strategy in second language use, even in the classroom (Helms-Park 2003). More recent research has provided ample evidence of the role of transfer in naturalistic SLA (Sanchez 2006), and this includes the robust literature on the role of L1 influence in the development of indigenized Englishes (Siegel 2006: 36). At the same time, SLA researchers and creolists have come to a consensus that L1 transfer plays a role in both SLA and creole formation (Lefebvre et al. 2006). Given such recognition of the links between the two kinds of second language acquisition, it is difficult to accept Mufwene's assertion that "One must look for an explanation other than imperfect learning to account for the undeniable structural differences between creole and non-creole varieties of European languages we know today" (2008: 35).

One is therefore justified in asking precisely what alternative explanation the EL framework offers for the "undeniable structural differences" between creole and non-creole varieties. Specifically, what constraints or principles lie behind the structural innovations that arise in individual learners' idiolects under L1 influence, and then spread to the communal repertoire? Mufwene describes such innovations as cases of "hybridism", which involves "the mixing of elements from different 'systems' into the same 'system'" (2008: 120). This leads to two kinds of innovation. First, there are those that arise from (partial) congruence between L1 and L2 structures, leading to a hybrid structure. An example would be the use of French word order in Haitian compound interrogatives like *ki mun* 'who' (lit. 'what person'), which is modeled partly on Gbe structures like Fongbe *me(-te)* 'who' (lit. 'person what'). A second type involves the introduction of substrate features into creoles in the absence of (partial) congruence with lexifier language structures ((2008: 143). Mufwene cites examples from Palenquero such as sentence-final negation, suffixation of the past tense marker *ba*,[7] etc., which Maurer (1987) attributes to Bantu influence. Mufwene explains such innovations as due to the "founder effect", i.e. the fact that Bantu people made up the majority of slaves brought to San Basilio. The resulting ethnolinguistic homogeneity of the slave population meant that "such xenolectal elements must have been favored by especially the sheer importance of their

---

[7] The use of suffixal *–ba* may in fact be a case of partial congruence between the substrate past suffix and the Spanish imperfective marker *–(V) ba*, as in *andaba* "was walking")

statistical frequency among the extant speakers of the colonial vernacular" (2008: 143). But Mufwene offers no account of the psycholinguistic processes that led to these kinds of "hybrid" structures.

To sum up, the EL model has proposed two factors that drive selection of substrate features in creole formation: congruence, and frequency. Mufwene adds a third factor, markedness, which he also interprets primarily in terms of frequency, transparency, salience, and presence of semantic content (2008: 131).[8] Other adherents of the EL approach have proposed other "constraints" on selection, such as the typological relationship between the languages in contact. Aboh and Ansaldo (2006) apply this feature pool approach to an explanation of the emergence of NP structure in the Surinamese creoles, appealing particularly to constraints such as those listed above to explain the absence of such features as plural and possessive inflection in Surinamese creole NPs. They argue that the process of competition and selection among features of the English and Gbe NP structures led to "a noun system [...] that has the semantic properties of noun phrases in Gbe, but the syntax of English noun phrases" Aboh and Ansaldo 2006: 49f). They specifically reject an explanation in terms of "acquisition". But, as Plag (2011) has argued, they provide no principled explanation for how the NP structures arose from "a general recombination of the linguistic features from the competing languages that made it to the F[eature] P[ool]" (ibid.). Plag also notes that the constraints they appeal to operate at the population level, as Aboh and Ansaldo themselves acknowledge (2006: 45). But Plag argues that such constraints are really at work on the individual level as well, and relate to the processing constraints that regulate SLA. He concludes that "L2 processing [...] provides a principled explanation for feature selection and feature mixing" (2011: 102). Plag concludes that "Any feature pool account would have to incorporate insights concerning the role of processing in order to explain feature selection and creation of new structure" (ibid.). In the following section, I briefly discuss how a language processing approach can shed light on the process by which L1 features enter the developing idiolects of individual learners in the emergence of New Englishes in general.

---

8 Note again that the "constraints" proposed in the EL framework appear to be constraints on selection from the available pool of features. But one finds no explanation of where the variants come from in the first place. For instance, Mufwene poses the following question as relevant to the role of markedness: "Given a choice between a PAST tense construction with an inflection on the verb (e.g. *–ed* in English) and one with a free periphrastic marker (e.g. *been*) ... which one is more likely to prevail and why?" (2008: 129). But no explanation is offered for the origin of *been* as a past marker.

5.1 Language production, imposition and the New Englishes

There is growing evidence that the innovations in New Englishes that have been attributed to mechanisms like hybridity, relexification, transfer, etc, can be better understood in terms of language processing by learners. There are two aspects of contact-induced change that can be profitably explained in terms of processing constraints. One has to do with so-called "simplification" processes such as loss of inflectional morphology, regularization of word order in declarative, interrogative and negative sentences, etc, all of which are typical of the early stages of SLA, including creole formation. As noted earlier, Plag (2008a,b) has provided an excellent account of how a processing model of SLA can explain such phenomena. The second aspect of contact-induced change that lends itself to treatment in terms of language processing (particularly production), is the way structural features are transferred from learners' L1s into a developing IL. There is general consensus that what distinguishes the development of creoles and other New Englishes from more "typical" cases of SLA is the extent and persistence of L1 influence on the former. In addition, varying degrees of L1 influence, and other factors, lead to a continuum of outcomes ranging from close approximations to the lexifier target, to radical departures from it. In the case of the New Englishes, L1 influence manifests itself primarily at later stages of IL development, and it is precisely at this point that the parallels between SLA and the emergence of vernacular New Englishes break down (Kouwenberg 2006: 206). The chief reason for this is that, unlike other cases of SLA, the emergence of vernacular New Englishes involved much less access to, and input from, the lexifier language. In fact, in many if not most cases, the major input came from pidginized or simplified L2 varieties of the lexifier. As a consequence, individual learners had to restructure their developing ILs by relying on L1 and other, universally motivated, strategies. In other words, the creators of New Englishes compensated for lack of full access to the lexifier by applying the language production processes of their L1s.

The mechanism underlying this strategy is what Siegel (2008) refers to as "functional transfer", and what van Coetsem (1988) calls imposition, which can be linked directly to language processing in bilingual speech production. It is through this mechanism that learners can transfer abstract features of their L1s to the version of the L2 that they are trying to construct. As Winford (2013, 2015) suggests, there is potential for such transfer at practically every stage of the language production process, from conceptualization to grammatical encoding, to phonological encoding. One of the most common solutions that learners adopt is to assign L1 lemmas (information about a lexical item's semantic, syntactic and related properties) to L2 lexemes whose lemmas they cannot access (Pienemann

1998: 83). By way of brief illustration, let us return to the examples of serial verb constructions in Paamaka and Wacigbe, provided earlier, repeated here for convenience.

(15) *Paamaka* Den e   hali a   boto e   go   a   liba
               3pl PROG haul DET boat PROG go   LOC river
     'They are hauling the boat to the river.'

(16) *Wacigbe* ɔ   la   dɔn   saki a   yi afi-mé
              3pl FUT drag bag   DET go house-in
     'They'll drag the bag to the house.'

As Winford (2008a: 140) argues, creole structures like these arise when the subcategorization properties of substrate motion or transfer verbs like *dɔn* are imposed on superstrate lexical items such as *hali*. Like *dɔn*, *hali* requires that its Theme be mapped onto a direct object, while its Goal must be expressed by a directional VP complement headed by a verb like *go*, which indicates the direction of the transfer. The mapping of argument structure onto syntactic form is identical in the creole and Gbe, but quite different from what we find in English. This is in fact the strategy that Lefebvre's RH treats as central to creole formation. Adherents of the Full Access/Full Transfer model of SLA also endorse this view (Sprouse 2006: 174). For imposition (or transfer of L1 encoding procedures) to take place in such cases, it is sufficient for learners merely to have access to the semantics of an L2 item, and to some extent, its syntactic category. Adherents of the RH in fact argue that congruence in meaning between a superstrate lexeme and its substrate counterpart is sufficient to trigger relexification, which they define as the "linking of the semantic and syntactic representation of [a learner's – DW] native language lexicon with new representations that are derived from the phonetic strings of a target language" (Lumsden 1999b: 130).[9]

Note that all of these models contribute to our understanding of the process that Mufwene refers to as "hybridization" in creole formation. It is therefore unfortunate that EL proponents have dismissed such contributions, even though it is true that the latter tend to over-reach in assigning too strong and exclusive a role to such mechanisms as "relexification". Despite their various shortcomings, both the RH and the Transfer models provide us with important insights into the

---

9 Myers-Scotton (2002) offers a similar explanation for the kinds of restructuring found in creole formation, arguing that they involve the mechanism of "convergence", which she defines as a "process that promotes a splitting of abstract lexical structure in one variety, and its combining with such abstract lexical structure from another variety" (2002: 99).

development of creoles and the other New Englishes. Among their important contributions is the recognition that much of contact-induced change is triggered by semantic or other kinds of congruence between L1 and L2 items. This is quite compatible with Mufwene's view that congruence of various types triggers the kinds of "hybridization" or "recombination of features" that are typical of the development of creoles and other New Englishes (Mufwene 2008: 119,122). It is this process of restructuring, driven by contact, that distinguishes the New Englishes from other varieties of colonial English in whose evolution contact with other languages played a more minor role.

6 Conclusion

An approach that takes into account the contributions from all of the models of contact-induced change proposed in the field is most likely to achieve the kind of unified theoretical framework that we are seeking. Such a framework must integrate the sociolinguistic, the linguistic, and the psycholinguistic aspects of change. First, it must account for the social processes by which change is propagated through social networks, leading to conventionalization in community grammars. The EL framework offers much that is valuable in this respect, but it can also benefit from all of the sociolinguistic research on language change. Second, the framework must account for the structural aspects of contact-induced change – the linguistic processes involved in the types of hybridization as well as internal developments found in contact situations. Here too, there is a wealth of research exploring syntactic change, grammaticalization processes and the like in contact situations. Third, an integrated model must account for the psycholinguistic processes involved in innovations at the level of individual idiolects – a fundamental aspect of the actuation question that the EL framework has so far only hinted at. Finally, we have to find a way of integrating all three of these components into the kind of inter-disciplinary model that Weinreich (1953: 4) viewed as indispensable to the field. The New Englishes, in all their variety, offer an ideal testing ground for developing such an integrated model of the origins and evolution of contact languages.

References

Aboh, Enoch O. & Umberto Ansaldo. 2006. The role of typology in language creation. In Umberto Ansaldo, Stephen Matthews & Lisa Lim (eds.), *Deconstructing creole*, 39–66. Amsterdam: John Benjamins.

Backus, Ad. 2009. Codeswitching as one piece of the puzzle of linguistic change: The case of Turkish yakmak. In Ludmila Isurin, Donald Winford & Kees de Bot (eds.), *Multidisciplinary approaches to code switching*, 307–336. Amsterdam: John Benjamins.

Bao, Zhiming. 2005. The aspectual system of Singapore English and the systemic substratist explanation. *Journal of Linguistics*, 41. 237–67.

Bybee, Joan. 2006. Language change and universals. In Ricardo Mairal and Juana Gil (eds.), *Linguistic Universals*, 179–194. Cambridge: Cambridge University Press.

Bao, Zhiming & Lionel Wee. 1999. The passive in Singapore English. *World Englishes* 18. 1–11.

Chambers, J.K. 2004. Dynamic typology and vernacular universals. In B. Kortmann (ed.), *Dialectology meets typology: Dialect grammar from a cross-linguistic perspective*, 127–145. Berlin: Mouton de Gruyter.

Croft, William. 2000. *Explaining language change: An evolutionary approach*. London: Longman.

Eckert, Penelope. 2000. *Language variation as social practice*. Oxford, Blackwell.

Fischer, Olga. 2011. Grammaticalization as analogically driven change? In Bernd Heine & Heiko Narrog (eds.), *The Oxford Handbook of Grammaticalization*, 31–42. Oxford: Oxford University Press.

Giles, Howard, Nikolas Coupland & Justine Coupland. 1991. Accommodation theory: Communication, context and consequence. In Howard Giles, Justine Coupland & Nikolas Coupland (eds.), *Contexts of Accommodation: Developments in applied sociolin*guistics, 1–68. Cambridge: Cambridge University Press.

Gupta, Anthea F. 1997. Colonisation, migration, and functions of English. In Edgar W. Schneider (ed.), *Englishes around the world: Vol. 1, General Studies, British Isles, North America*, 47–58. Amsterdam: John Benjamins.

Helms-Park, R. 2003. Transfer in SLA and creoles: The implications of causative serial verbs in the interlanguage of Vietnamese ESL learners. *Studies in Second Language Acquisition* 25. 211–244.

Heine, Bernd & Tania Kuteva. 2005. *Language contact and grammatical change*. Cambridge: Cambridge University Press.

Hulstijn, J. 1990. A comparison between information processing and the analysis/control approaches to language learning. *Applied Linguistics* 11. 30–45.

Hundt, Marianne & Daniel Schreier. 2013. Introduction: nothing but a contact language. In Daniel Schreier & Marianne Hundt (eds.), *English as a contact language*, 1–17. Cambridge: Cambridge University Press.

Jarvis, Scott & Aneta Pavlenko. 2008. *Crosslinguistic influence in language and cognition*. New York & London: Routledge.

Klemola, Juhani. 2013. English as a contact language in the British Isles. In Daniel Schreier & Marianne Hundt (eds.), *English as a contact language*, 75–87. Cambridge: Cambridge University Press.

Kouwenberg, Silvia. 2006. L1 transfer and the cut-off point for L2 acquisition processes in creole formation. In Claire Lefebvre, Lydia White and Christine Jourdan (eds.), *L2 Acquisition and Creole Genesis*, 205–219. Amsterdam: John Benjamins.

Labov, William. 2001. *Principles of linguistic change: Social Factors*. Malden, MA: Blackwell.

Lefebvre, Claire. 1998. *Creole genesis and the acquisition of grammar: The case of Haitian Creole*. Cambridge: Cambridge University Press.

Lefevbre, Claire, Lydia White and Christine Jourdan (eds.). 2006. *L2 Acquisition and Creole Genesis: Dialogues*. Amsterdam: John Benjamins.

Léglise, Isabelle & Claudine Chamoreau (eds.). 2013. *The interplay of variation and change in contact settings*. Amsterdam: John Benjamins.
Lumsden, John. 1999a. The role of relexification in creole genesis. *Journal of Pidgin and Creole Languages* 14. 225–258.
Lumsden, John. 1999b. Language acquisition and creolization. In Michel DeGraff (ed.), *Language creation and language change: Creolization, Diachrony, and Development*, 129–158. Cambridge MA/London: The MIT press.
Matthews, Stephen & Virginia Yip. 2009. Contact-induced grammaticalization: Evidence from bilingual acquisition. *Studies in Language* 33(2). 366–395.
Maurer, Philippe. 1987. La comparaison des morphèmes temporels du Papiamento et du Palenquero: Arguments contre la théorie monogénétique de la genèse des langues creoles. In Philippe Maurer & Thomas Stolz (eds.), *Varia Creolica*, 27–70. Bochum: Studienverlag Dr. N. Brockmeyer.
Meshrie, Rajend & Timothy T. Dunne. 1990. Syntactic variation in language shift: The relative clause in South African Indian English. *Language Variation and Change* 2(1). 31–56.
Migge, Bettina. 2003. *Creole formation as language contact*. Amsterdam: John Benjamins.
Milroy, James & Lesley Milroy. 1985. Linguistic, social network, and speaker innovation. *Journal of Linguistics* 21. 339–384.
Mintz, Sidney W. 1971. The socio-historical background to pidginization and creolization. In Dell Hymes (ed.), *Pidginization and creolization of languages*, 481–96. Cambridge: Cambridge University Press.
Mufwene, Salikoko. 2001. *The ecology of language evolution*. Cambridge: Cambridge University Press.
Mufwene, Salikoko. 2008. *Language evolution: Contact, competition, and change*. London: Continuum.
Mufwene, Salikoko. 2014. Language ecology, language evolution, and the actuation question. In Tor Äfari & Brit Maelhum (eds.), *The sociolinguistics of grammar*, 13–35. Amsterdam: John Benjamins.
Mufwene, Salikoko & Cécile B. Vigouroux. 2013. Individuals, populations, and timespace: Perspectives on the ecology of language. In Françoise Gadet (ed.), *Construction des connaises sociolinguistiques: Du terrain au positionnement théretique*, 111–137. Brussels: EME & intercommunications.
Myers-Scotton, Carol. 2002. *Contact Linguistics: Bilingual encounters and grammatical outcomes*. Oxford: Oxford University Press.
Nemser, W. 1991. Language contact and foreign language acquisition. In V. Ivir & D. Kalogjera (eds.), *Languages in Contact and Contrast: Essays in Contact Linguistics*, 345–64. Berlin, Mouton de Gruyter.
Odlin, Terry. 1989. *Language transfer: Crosslinguistic influence in language learning*. Cambridge: Cambridge University Press.
Paul, Herman. 1880. *Prinzipien der Sprachgeschichte*. Halle: Niemeyer.
Pienemann, M. 1998. *Language Processing and Second Language Development: Processability Theory* (Studies in Bilingualism 15). Amsterdam: John Benjamins.
Plag, Ingo. 2008a. Creoles as interlanguages: Inflectional Morphology. *Journal of Pidgin and Creole Languages* 23(1). 114–135.
Plag, Ingo. 2008b. Creoles as interlanguages: Syntactic structures. *Journal of Pidgin and Creole Languages* 23(2). 307–328.

Plag, Ingo. 2011. Creolization and admixture: Typology, feature pools, and second language acquisition. In Parth Bhatt & Tonjes Veenstra (eds.), *Creoles and Typology*. (*Journal of Pidgin and Creole Languages* 26(1). 89–110).

Ritchie, W.C. 1986. Second language acquisition and the study of non-native varieties of English: Some issues in common. *World Englishes* 5. 15–30.

Sanchez, Liliana. 2006. Bilingual grammars and creoles: Similarities between functional convergence and morphological elaboration. In C. Lefebvre, L. White & C. Jourdan (eds.), *L2 Acquisition and creole genesis*, 277–294. Amsterdam: John Benjamins.

Schneider, Edgar W. 2003. The dynamics of New Englishes: From identity construction to dialect birth. *Language* 79(2). 233–281.

Schneider, Edgar W. 2007. *Postcolonial English: Varieties Around the World*. Cambridge: Cambridge University Press.

Schneider, Edgar W. 2010. Developmental patterns of English: similar or different? In Andy Kirkpatrick (ed.), *The Routledge Handbook of World* Englishes, 372–384. London, New York: Routledge.

Schreier, Daniel & Marianne Hundt (eds.). 2013. *English as a contact language*. Cambridge: Cambridge University Press.

Schumann, John H. 1978. *The pidginization process: A model for second language acquisition*. Rowley, MA.: Newbury House.

Siegel, Jeff. 2003. Substrate influence in creoles and the role of transfer in second language acquisition. *Studies in Second Language Acquisition* 25(2). 185–209.

Siegel, Jeff. 2006. Links between SLA and Creole studies: Past and present. In Claire Lefevbre, Lydia White, & Christine Jourdan (eds.), *L2 Acquisition and Creole Genesis: Dialogues*, 15–46. Amsterdam: John Benjamins.

Siegel, Jeff. 2008. *The Emergence of Pidgin and Creole Languages*. Oxford/New York: Oxford University Press.

Sprouse, Rex A. 2006. Full transfer and relexification: Second language acquisition and creole genesis. In Claire Lefebvre, Lydia White and Christine Jourdan (eds.), *L2 Acquisition and Creole Genesis*, 169–183. Amsterdam: John Benjamins.

Thomason, Sarah Grey. 1995. Language mixture: Ordinary processes, extraordinary results. In In Carmen Silva-Corvalán (ed.), *Spanish in Four Continents: Studies in language contact and bilingualism*, 15–33. Washington DC: Georgetown University Press.

Thomason, Sarah G. & Terrence Kaufman. 1988. *Language Contact, Creolization and Genetic Linguistics*. Berkeley: University of California Press.

Traugott, Elizabeth Closs. 1989. On the rise of epistemic meanings in English: An example of subjectification in semantic change. *Language* 65(1). 31–55.

van Buren, Paul. 1996. Are there principles of universal grammar that do not apply to second language acquisition? In Peter Jordens and Josine Lalleman (eds.), *Investigating Second Language Acquisition*, 187–207. Berlin: Mouton de Gruyter.

van Coetsem, Frans. 1988. *Loan Phonology and the Two Transfer Types in Language Contact*. Dordrecht: Foris.

Weinreich, Uriel. 1953. *Languages in contact: Findings and problems*. The Hague: Mouton.

Weinreich, Uriel, William Labov & Marvin I. Herzog. 1968. Empirical foundations for a theory of change. In W.P. Lehman & Yakov Malkiel (eds.), *Directions for Historical Linguistics: A symposium*, 95–188. Austin: University of Texas Press.

Winford, Donald. 2008a. Processes of creolization and related contact-induced change. *Journal of Language Contact (JLC)*, Second Thema Issue. 124–145.

Winford, Donald. 2008b. Atlantic Creole Syntax. In Silvia Kouwenberg & John V. Singler (eds.), *The Handbook of Pidgin and Creole Studies*, 19–47. Oxford: Wiley-Blackwell.

Winford, Donald. 2009. The interplay of "universals" and contact-induced change in the emergence of New Englishes. In Markku Filppula, Juhani Klemola and Heli Paulasto (eds.), *Vernacular universals and language contacts: Evidence from varieties of English and beyond*. 206–230. London: Routledge.

Winford, Donald. 2013. On the unity of contact phenomena: the case for imposition. In Carol de Féral (ed.), *In and Out of Africa: Languages in Question. In Honour of Robert Nicolaï, Volume 1, Language contact and epistemological issues*, 43–71. Louvain-La-Neuve: Peeters.

Winford, Donald. 2015. Creole formation and second language acquisition: a language processing perspective. In Piotr P. Chruszczewski, Richard L. Lanigan and John R. Rickford (eds.), *Languages in Contact 2014*, 295–322. Wroclaw, Poland: WYDAWNICTWO WYŻSZEJ SZKOŁY FILOLOGICZNEJ WE WROCŁAWIU.

Winford, Donald & Bettina Migge. 2007. The influence of Gbe languages on the tense/aspect systems of the Surinamese creoles. In B. Migge and N. Smith (eds.), *Transatlantic Sprachbund? Special issue of the Journal of Pidgin and Creole Languages*, Vol. 22(1). 73–99.

Wright, Laura. 2013. The contact origins of Standard English. In Daniel Schreier & Marianne Hundt (eds.), *English as a contact language*, 58–74. Cambridge: Cambridge University Press.

II Ongoing changes in Englishes around the globe

Editors' Introduction to Part II

Part II of the volume, *Ongoing changes in Englishes around the globe*, presents seven case studies focusing on a range of varieties of English and linguistic phenomena. These studies offer an excellent overview of the wide compass of ongoing changes in World Englishes today.

Valentin Werner's *The Present Perfect as a core feature of World Englishes* opens the discussion in Part II. In this study, Werner presents results of his ongoing corpus-based investigation of the usage of the Present Perfect (HAVE + past participle) across World Englishes. Using material from the *International Corpus of English* family of corpora, Werner argues that the Present Perfect can be considered a core feature of World Englishes. In addition, Werner argues that comparable genres or text types are a stronger explanatory factor for associations between varieties than factors such as geographical location, variety types or mode of discourse.

The next chapter, *Innovative structures in the relative clauses of indigenized L2 Asian English varieties*, by Cristina Suárez-Gómez, is also based on data from the *International Corpus of English*. In her study, Suárez-Gómez focuses on innovative adnominal relative clause constructions in the Asian English varieties of Hong Kong, India, and Singapore. She examines the characteristics of these non-standard relative constructions taking into account the role of the superstrate variety (British English), L1 transfer, various language contact phenomena, and evolutionary factors in these norm developing varieties (based on Schneider's Dynamic Model). Suárez-Gómez argues that these constructions can best be explained as localized grammatical innovations, where the role of substrate languages is considerable.

Morphosyntactic typology as a tool for exploring the complexities of linguistic contact and variation in South Africa is the topic of the chapter on *Morphosyntactic typology, contact and variation: Cape Flats English in relation to other South African Englishes in the Mouton World Atlas of Variation in English* by Rajend Mesthrie, Sean Bowerman and Tracey Toefy. In this study, Mesthrie et al. present an overview of the morpho-syntactic features of Cape Flats English and examine the typological characteristics and relatedness of Cape Flats English and the three major varieties of South African English (L1 White SAE, L2 Black SAE, and Indian SAE) included in the *Mouton World Atlas of Variation in English* (MWAVE; Kortmann and Lunkenheimer 2013). In addition, Mesthrie et al. offer an assessment of the strengths and weaknesses of the MWAVE in the light of the complex linguistic landscape of South Africa.

DOI 10.1515/9783110429657-004

With Hanna Parviainen's chapter, *Omission of direct objects in New Englishes*, the focus shifts back to grammatical variation and change in the light of the data from the *International Corpus of English*. In her study, Parviainen examines the omission of direct object of transitive verbs in contexts where the verb cannot function intransitively, as in the following example from ICE-India: A: *Do you know Malayalam?* B: *Oh yes I speak*. The paper examines the omission of direct objects in the following nine varieties of English included in the *International Corpus of English*: Fiji, Hong Kong, India, Jamaica, Kenya, the Philippines, Singapore and British and American English. The conclusion is that the feature is most frequently found in the Asian varieties of Indian English and Singapore English. In the remaining New Englishes (FjE, KenE, PhiE, JaE and HKE), various degrees of object omission are found, while the feature is practically non-existent in the "parent varieties", British and American English.

The exploration of the *International Corpus of English* continues with Markku Filppula's and Juhani Klemola's chapter on *The definite article in World Englishes*. They examine a syntactic feature which is common in the Celtic-influenced varieties of English, but is also attested to varying degrees in other British Isles varieties and World Englishes, viz. wider use of the definite article in certain kinds of contexts. In addition to spoken data from traditional varieties of British, Irish and Welsh English, Filppula and Klemola also analyse data from 10 varieties of English world-wide, and conclude that no single explanatory factor can be found to govern the variation in the use of the definite article; language contact and substratum influence are a likely explanation in the case of Celtic Englishes, while universal or angloversal factors are more likely in the case of Asian Englishes.

In *Aspects of verb complementation in New Zealand Newspaper English*, Paul Rickman examines the complementation patterns of the verbs of prevention in a 100-million-word corpus of New Zealand English compiled by the author himself. The *Corpus of New Zealand Newspaper English* is a diachronic corpus (1995–2012) offering a representative sample of the genre of newspaper English in New Zealand. In addition to the prototypical verbs of prevention, *prevent* and *stop*, Rickman's corpus is large enough to enable the analysis of the complementation patterns of also the less frequently used verbs of prevention (*ban, bar, block, deter, discourage, dissuade, forbid, hinder, prohibit, restrain, save* and *spare*). Rickman compares the results of his analysis of NZE English with data from British English (BNC) and American English (COCA), and finds evidence of both colonial lag and other, more complex patterns of change in the NZE data.

Finally in Part II, *Extended uses of the progressive form in Inner, Outer and Expanding Circle Englishes*, by Lea Meriläinen, Heli Paulasto and Paula Rautionaho, expands the horizon by adding data from learner varieties of English in the analysis of extended uses of the progressive form (PF), especially in the stative and habitual functions. The authors conclude that the three main determining factors for the extended uses of the progressive are the type of English, the substrate language/L1 and the proficiency level of the learners. Furthermore, they argue that substrate or L1 influence is the most compelling explanatory factor, while universal strategies of SLA or angloversals do not seem to offer satisfactory explanations for the phenomena analyzed in the study.

Valentin Werner
The Present Perfect as a core feature of World Englishes[1]

Abstract: This paper presents central results from a larger corpus-based project (see Werner 2013a; 2013b; 2014) that investigates the usage of the Present Perfect (HAVE + past participle) across World Englishes. It aims at complementing other empirical studies which merely focus on differences between British and American English or which investigate the alternation of the Present Perfect with other time-reference forms.

Findings are based on material from the International Corpus of English (ICE), which has been annotated for various language-internal factors (such as semantics, preceding tense, etc.), so that the distributions and the relative importance of these factors can be analyzed. I employ explorative aggregative methods to find measures of similarity between the various varieties of English under investigation. In addition, this approach allows a systematic investigation of the influence of language-external variables (such as text types, variety types, geographical location) across all varieties. Furthermore, a case study on evidence of an allegedly extended functional range of the Present Perfect in terms of tense-like usage is presented.

The data reveal (i) that the Present Perfect can be seen as a globalized or core feature of world-wide varieties of English, and (ii) that geographical location, variety types, mode of discourse, genres and text types only have a weak effect when associations between varieties are explored; significant groupings across all varieties appear along register lines, however. The case study shows that creative usage in terms of a functional extension of the Present Perfect occurs in the ICE data, albeit largely restricted to informal speech in L1 varieties and to L2 varieties, where influence from both the substrate and through learner language is highly likely. The case study further exemplifies layering between the Present Perfect and its competitor, the Simple Past, in indefinite temporal environments.

Keywords: Present Perfect, Simple Past, involved vs. informational text type, American English (AmE), British English (BrE), International Corpus of English (ICE), L1 varieties, L2 varieties, aggregative analysis, cluster analysis, phylogenetic networks, NeighborNet

---

[1] I would like to thank Ole Schützler and an anonymous reviewer, who both commented on earlier versions of this paper.

Valentin Werner, University of Bamberg

DOI 10.1515/9783110429657-005

1 Introduction

The Present Perfect (henceforth PrPf), both in its standard version HAVE + past participle and in alternative surface constructions with a similar function usage (which will not feature in this analysis),[2] has been among the most frequently discussed issues of English grammar. While earlier research labeled it a "somewhat inconvenient case" (Bauer 1970: 189; see also Labov 1978: 13), 40 years on – and notwithstanding the bulk of literature on the subject (on which see further below and Klein 2009: 54) – the general situation does not seem to have changed, as the PrPf still "eludes a convincing analysis" (Veloudis 2003: 385). I will briefly summarize the main areas of dispute.

A first point that seems difficult is to assign the PrPf to one of the established grammatical classes. To illustrate this point, I will use the categorization approaches as developed in influential descriptive reference grammars of English (see also Werner 2013a). The two relevant approaches as contained in Quirk et al. (1985), Biber et al. (1999), and Huddleston and Pullum (2002) use different kinds of workarounds to achieve an elegant description, which, in turn, leads to inconsistencies in the overall models proposed. For instance, Huddleston and Pullum (2002) label the PrPf a "primary present" and "secondary perfect tense", but state at the same time that "past" and "perfect" form the umbrella category of "past tense" (see Figure 1).

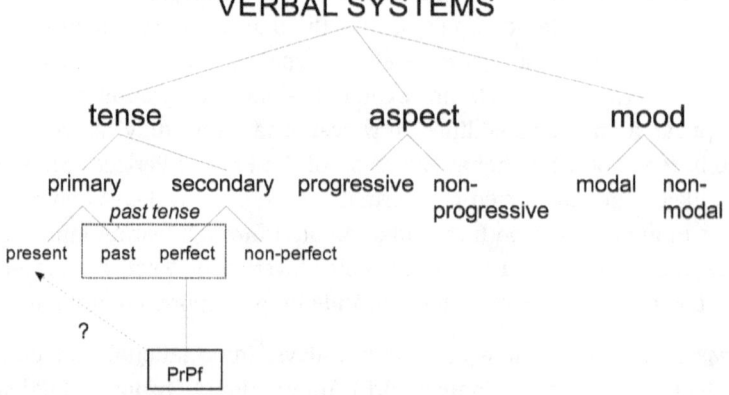

Figure 1: Grammatical categories (= verbal systems) as represented by Huddleston and Pullum (2002); adapted from Werner (2014)

---

[2] Among others, this includes occurrences with auxiliary ellipsis or without any morphological marking at all, BE-perfects, and special cases such as the *after*-perfect (as mainly found in Irish English).

Moreover, some of the grammars listed apply a purely form-based approach. The only reason why the PrPf does not qualify as tense, as is the case in the Quirkian grammar (shown in Figure 2; similarly in Biber et al. 1999), for example, is that tense is taken to be realized morphologically, while aspect is realized syntactically (hence the "morphemic boundary" between the two grammatical classes and the categorization of the PrPf as aspect in this second set of grammars; see further Section 3.2 below).

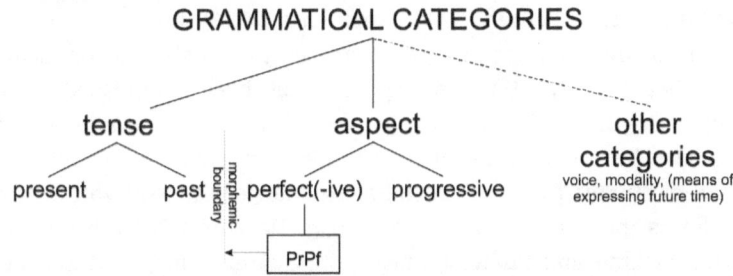

Figure 2: Grammatical categories as represented by Quirk et al. (1985)[3] and Biber et al. (1999); adapted from Werner (2014)

In addition to the analyses in descriptive grammars, a range of theoretical literature on the subject exists, largely revolving around the following topics:
- The PrPf as a grammatical category: tense vs. aspect views vs. further labels, such as "phase" or "status" (see e.g. Bauer 1970; Salkie 1989; Jaszczolt 2009);
- Semantic (and pragmatic) interpretation of the form (see e.g. McCawley 1983; Portner 2003);
- Compositionality of the form (see e.g. Klein 1992; Kortmann 1995).

While all of these works have their merits, some of their inherent weaknesses need to be exposed. First, with regard to semantic readings, depending on the individual author, between one and seven possible interpretations are given and often cross-classifications are possible. Second, another limitation that applies to both descriptive grammars and theoretical treatments of the PrPf alike is that they restrict their focus to a standard variety of British and, less often, American English. Third, many of the models presented are based on introspective analyses and constructed example sentences (but cf. Biber et al. 1999).

---

[3] Means of expressing the future are treated separately in Quirk et al. 1985 (4.41–4.48), while they are included under modals by Biber et al. 1999 (483–497), hence the notation in brackets in the figure.

Starting with Elsness's (1997) pioneering investigation, however, a few corpus-based studies (e.g. Wynne 2000; Schlüter 2002; Hundt and Smith 2009) have overcome the latter difficulty by relying on authentic language data, and have presented quantitative views of the PrPf. Still, while these works have laid the groundwork for the present and other follow-up corpus studies, I would like to argue that they leave some room for improvement. First, some of them apply the semantic models criticized for being based on mere introspection (see above); second, their conclusions partly rely on small and unbalanced corpus material, as has been noted earlier by Schlüter (2006) and Gries (2006), for instance; and third, the majority of the analyses is again restricted to British and American data. Even though the study of World Englishes has been established as a subfield of English linguistics for an extended period now, further varieties (of different types) have been considered in recent years only. Within this area, a distinction between studies focusing on the alternation of the PrPf with other time reference forms, notably the Simple Past (e.g. Davydova 2011, 2016; Yao and Collins 2012; Seoane and Suárez-Gómez 2013; Suárez-Gómez and Seoane 2013; Werner 2013b; see also the contributions in Werner, Seoane and Suárez-Gómez 2016), and within more general "inner life" analyses of the PrPf that consider contextual factors (e.g. Werner 2014) can be drawn. In the present paper, I seek to further extend the empirical perspective on the PrPf within the scope of various World Englishes. Another aspect that the present study will focus on is the systematic inclusion of text type and register – a topic that has been ignored in most analyses as yet to date.

Within the scope of this paper, I will tackle the following issues:

- Is the PrPf a core feature of World Englishes (in terms of overlap between varieties in the distributions of contextual factors) or is nativization (in terms of divergence) observable?
- Along which dimensions (e.g. geographical location, variety types) does variation occur?
- Is there evidence for effects of register, genre or text types within and across varieties?
- Do the data contain evidence of leveling between the PrPf and the Simple Past (SPst) and does this carry implications for the overall grammatical status of the PrPf?

After presenting an outline of the data and the methodology in Section 2, I will show one approach toward relating overlap and divergence of PrPf usage in different varieties in Section 3. This section has two subparts. The first one comprises a global perspective and focuses on text type effects (using aggregative methods). The second part represents a case study. It explores what corpus data from World Englishes can reveal about the grammatical status of the PrPf (see above) and its potential future development (using a predominantly qualitative approach). I will finish with a general discussion and summary in Section 4.

2 Data and methodology

2.1 The International Corpus of English

In comparison to many of today's mega-corpora of English, such as the *Corpus of Contemporary American English* (450 million words; corpus.byu.edu/coca/) or the even larger *Collins Corpus* (4.5 billion words; www.collins.co.uk/page/The+Collins+Corpus), the scope of the data used for the present study, the *International Corpus of English* (ICE; ice-corpora.net/ice/index.htm), with one million words per regional/national variety, is small. However, it has repeatedly been shown that corpora of this size are well suited for the analysis of grammatical patterns, especially for high-frequency patterns such as the PrPf (Mair 2013: 182; see further Biber 1990). Another motivation for using ICE as a synchronic corpus of different regional L1 and L2 varieties of English is that meaningful comparative analyses across these varieties are only possible with matching corpus components that all adhere to the same compilation principles and thus are as homogeneous as possible with regard to the specification of text categories (see Appendix A), the dating of the data (mostly early 1990s) and the educational background of the informants (adult speakers with at least a completed English-medium secondary school education; Greenbaum 1996: 6; for more detail see Nelson 1996: 28).[4]

For the present analysis, I used the components for Australia (ICE-AUS), Canada (ICE-CAN), Great Britain (ICE-GB), Hong Kong (ICE-HK), India (ICE-IND), Ireland (ICE-IRL), Jamaica (ICE-JA), New Zealand (ICE-NZ), the Philippines (ICE-PHI) and Singapore (ICE-SIN) as well as data from Nigeria (ICE-NIG), East Africa

---

[4] It is evident that in practice there are some differences between corpus components (e.g. as to the time period when the data was sampled or as to individual text types that are used for the individual categories), which – depending on the focus of the research – may influence results. Yet, the ICE family can be viewed as state-of-the-art for the corpus-based linguistic study of World Englishes, as recent additions such as GloWbE (Davies and Fuchs 2015), which can also be used for cross-variety analyses, are restricted to electronically-mediated communication. See the discussion presented in Hundt (2009) for a critical assessment of prospects and limitations of ICE.

(ICE-EA), and the USA (ICE-USA) for the case study.[5] As already indicated, each of the components comprises approximately one million words, while 40% of the material is written, and 60% is spoken. Each component consists of 500 texts of 2,000 words, with many of the 2,000-word text units being composite themselves (see Appendix A).

It is apparent that using this type of data facilitates (i) comparative studies with a focus on the proximity to or distance from a reference variety, most likely British English or American English, (ii) analyses of potential core features across varieties and (iii) accounts of variety-internal variation, which emerges as a growing trend in the study of World Englishes and in variational linguistics in general (Hundt and Vogel 2011: 146; Mukherjee and Schilk 2012: 194).

2.2 Extracting and coding examples

The first step toward a reliable identification of PrPf occurrences in the corpus was to create tagged versions of the corpus files, which are typically available in plain text format only (ICE-GB being one exception). To this end, part-of-speech tags were automatically applied to the corpus data through the *CLAWS* part-of-speech tagger (ucrel.lancs.ac.uk/claws/).[6]

The second step was to create a search string[7] and extract relevant tokens and their context to spreadsheets, which was done with the help of *WordSmith Tools* (Scott 2011). As I retrieved a number of false positives, such as passives, elliptical forms, combinations of modals and PrPfs, and other non-finite forms

---

[5] A note of caution applies, as only the written sections of ICE-USA were available at the time of the analysis. Therefore, additional data, deriving from Yao and Collins (2012) was used (see Section 3.2).
[6] The C5 tagset was used for the present study. For the sake of consistency, a plain text version of ICE-GB was created that was subsequently tagged again. Versions of the ICE-components that are tagged with the C7 tagset as well as with semantic tagging are available now (ice-corpora. net/ice/index.htm).
[7] The search was for instances of the PP consisting of forms of HAVE (tags *_VHB/*_VHZ) and a past participle (tags *_VBN/*_VDN/*_VHN/*_VVN) within four words to the right. The four-word range was deemed adequate as earlier studies (Schlüter 2002: 103; 2006: 136) found that more than three inserted items between auxiliary and past participle are very rare. The following tag was excluded in the automated search: got_*. The rationale behind this was to exclude the highly frequent combination HAVE *got* (+ NP), as it can virtually always be replaced by a present form HAVE + NP (Wynne 2000: 33); likewise, all instances of HAVE *got to* as a semi-modal that expresses obligation were excluded. In addition, to sharpen the focus of the analysis, progressive forms (tags *_VBG/*_VDG/*_VHG/*_VVG) were excluded due to their almost exclusive association with continuative contexts. The search procedure for the case study will be explicated below (Section 3.2).

(Bowie and Arts 2012), I had to manually exclude them from the analysis (see Werner 2014: 114–117 for a discussion of methodological issues during both the tagging and the identification stage). Still, more than 38,000 data points remained, so I opted for representative random sampling (98% confidence level, 5% margin of error), which eventually left 5,752 data points for the analysis.

The last step in the preparation of the data was to manually code each of the examples according to a number of variables suitable for establishing a kind of grammar of usage (cf. also Biber and Conrad 2009: 216) of the PrPf. The variables had been identified as influencing PrPf usage in other works, and can broadly be categorized into contextual and semantic factors (see Appendix B for underlying models, possible values and examples).

The former group comprises
- presence/absence of temporal adverbials and type of adverbial, as they are commonly viewed as important triggers of the PrPf;
- sentence type, as it is an interacting factor that may determine the presence or absence of temporal adverbials (Schlüter 2002: 242) as well as the semantic interpretation of an instance (Winford 1993: 166);
- preceding time-reference forms, as they may also act as triggers for the PrPf (Davydova 2011: 157).

The latter group consists of
- Aktionsart of the main verb, as inherent lexical aspect carries a substantial part of the meaning of the verb phrase (Schlüter 2006: 143);
- semantic reading of the sentence/clause containing a PrPf occurrence, as a universal property.

2.3 Aggregative analysis

It is one of the principal aims of this study to assess similarity and difference of various varieties on different levels (such as varieties taken as a whole, registers, genres or text types). Therefore, I opted for a multidimensional aggregative statistical approach as an exploratory method used for the identification of latent structure that would not be directly accessible with the help of manual analysis alone. The approach is particularly apt for extended sets of multidimensional data material consisting of a large number of individual data points. Two types are applied: cluster analysis (Romesburg 1984; Manning and Schütze 1999: 495–528) and phylogenetic networks (Huson and Bryant 2006), which have seen a number of applications in linguistics in recent years (e.g. Nichols and Warnow 2008; Szmrecsanyi and Wolk 2011; Kortmann and Wolk 2013; McMahon and

Maguire 2013; Fuchs and Gut 2016; Krug, Schützler and Werner 2016). The main purpose of both types is to graphically represent and reveal relationships of similarity and dissimilarity between different items (varieties, genres and text types in this study). Either unrooted tree-shaped dendrograms or network graphs emerge as the final graphical output, reducing n-dimensional spaces to two-dimensional hierarchical or non-hierarchical representations, respectively (see below).

In the present study, relative values calculated from the absolute values obtained through the coding of the individual factors serve as the input for comparison.[8] These values are entered into comma-separated files (CSV files) to make the data readable for the calculation of the similarity matrices and further processing. In these files, each column represents a register, macro-genre, or text type, and each line contains the values of the same category (e.g. all values of the same category for the factor 'type of adverbial' appear in the same line across all the text types considered).[9] See Table 1 for a snapshot view of such a file.

Table 1: Snapshot view of the top left corner of a CSV spreadsheet used as input for the calculation of the similarity matrix; column labels refer to the ICE text types (of ICE-AUS, in this case); line labels refer to the relative values of the factor 'type of adverbial', adding to 1 (rounded to second decimal place) for each factor

	AUS S1A	AUS S1B	AUS S2A	AUS S2B	AUS …
Time-position	0.20	0.32	0.26	0.25	…
Span/duration	0.14	0.32	0.42	0.38	…
Frequency	0.34	0.32	0.16	0.12	…
Sequence	0.32	0.04	0.16	0.25	…
…	…	…	…	…	…

These files are subsequently used for aggregative analysis. In the first approach, cluster analysis, items are compared pairwise within a similarity matrix and then fused into clusters that are (depending on the clustering method used)

---

8 These relative values are the ones presented in Chapter 5 of Werner (2014) for each of the varieties and the respective registers, macro-genres, and text types (unless stated otherwise). All data points had values between 0 and 1. Therefore, no standardization was needed.

9 To calculate statistical measures, *R* was used. For clustering (function *hclust*) I employed the complete linkage method (Manning and Schütze 1999: 505–507) based on the similarity of the two least similar members of a cluster. Rank-based distance matrices were created with the Spearman method. For the creation of the NeighborNet representations I used *SplitsTree* 4.12.3 ("equal angle" method). The most recent version of the program is available at www.splitstree. org (see also Huson and Bryant 2006). As input it requires a nexus file that contains a similarity matrix (see above) created in *R*.

internally maximally similar or minimally dissimilar. In any case, they are highly dissimilar to other clusters and items (Manning and Schütze 1999: 501). In the second approach, data are also clustered, but phylogenetic networks (sometimes also referred to as "phenograms") are used as an alternative (non-hierarchical) means of depicting similarities across varieties. The latter type creates network representations ("NeighborNets") that allow for a more fine-grained analysis. The added value of the NeighborNet representations is that differences, in our case between varieties, and text types, are not reductively shown in terms of absolute cluster membership and categorical (bifurcating) branching. Rather, relative distances to each of the other categories (varieties and text types) that cover the terminal nodes in the graphs are mapped. An interrelation between two nodes is indicated by boxes (splits) in the NeighborNet output. Thus, this method of graphical representation allows us to determine differences between categories that would form members of a single cluster in a hierarchical cluster analysis (see above).

3 Assessing overlap and divergence

3.1 The Present Perfect in the broader perspective

The first section will start from a bird's eye perspective on the data and illustrate the potential of the aggregative methods introduced above. Figure 3 shows a NeighborNet comparing all the data for the eleven varieties under investigation with the individual varieties as nodes or taxa. Colors indicate variety types (L1 = grey; L2 = black, GB as reference variety = underlined). The numbers that are given after each variety indicate the phase label according to Schneider's (2007) dynamic model of postcolonial Englishes. The higher the number in brackets, the further advanced the variety is in the model, so that we could also see the phase labels as some kind of sociolinguistic variety type.

First of all, it emerges that "geolinguistic signals[s]" (Szmrecsanyi 2013: 837) in the data are weak. In other words, geographical location and variety types as external factors only exert a limited influence and clear alignments between varieties of the same type (e.g. in terms of one group of L1 varieties contrasting with L2 varieties or in terms of groups according to the stage labels) do not emerge.

Instead, relationships between the varieties seem to be of a more intricate nature, and a number of further splits deserve closer inspection: As a broad trend, all the L2 (stage 3 and stage 4) varieties apart from Philippine English and Nigerian English are located toward the right hand side of Figure 3, show-

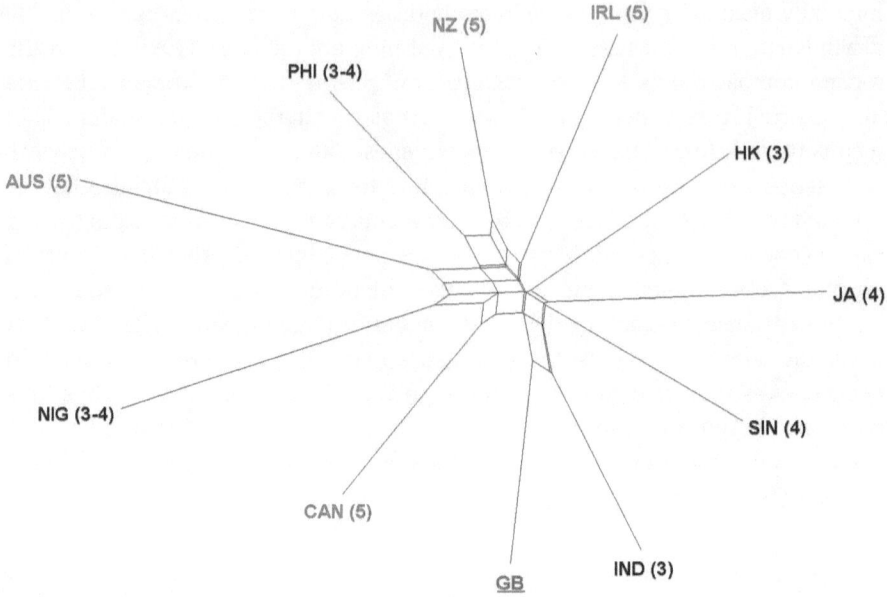

Figure 3: NeighborNet of similarity across ICE components (language-internal factors); numbers in brackets refer to variety type categorization according to Schneider (2007)

ing some association with British English. Another grouping that emerges comprises transplanted L1s (phase 5) varieties (Irish, New Zealand, and Australian English) and Philippine English. The remaining transplanted L1, Canadian English, is also close, but first shares a split with British English, to which it is also close in terms of distance. The L2 varieties align with British English, while the data show that Singapore English and Jamaican English, varieties that have developed further along the evolutionary circle (phase 4), share a split before they merge with the other L2s and British English, the colonial ancestor.

Still, no unambiguous picture emerges. For instance, Indian English as a variety of the L2 type associates closely with British English as its alleged exonormative standard. In contrast, this is not the case to the same extent for Hong Kong English, for instance. In addition, it becomes clear from Figure 3 that Nigerian English covers a special position. Similar to Philippine English, it neighbors the stage 5 varieties Canadian English and Australian English, and, compared to other L2 varieties, appears remote from British English. The latter finding is noteworthy insofar as in Nigeria British English is also still perceived as an exonormative standard to a certain extent (Awonusi 1994: 76; Gut 2012: 2–3).

However, what is most striking is the star-like shape of Figure 3, which indicates that all varieties (with the possible minor exceptions of Australian and Nigerian English) are approximately equidistant from one another. In other words, they differ by approximately the same amount, while sharing many characteristics in terms of quantitative distributions of the factors. Note further that none of the groups, that is, both L1 versus L2 and when the varieties are grouped according to Schneider's (2007) phases, emerges as statistically significant as determined by a bootstrapping test (see also Werner 2014: 305).

When we zoom in, text type effects are evident across varieties, as the cluster dendrogram shown in Figure 4 reveals. This complex dendrogram compares all twelve text type categories (see Appendix A) from the eleven varieties according to the variables described in Section 2.2 above with each other. Each leaf represents one text type, for example the one at the left margin labeled "AUS.w2f" stands for the creative writing category in Australian English.

Above all, note that variety type again does not play a role here, as clusters tend to contain texts from many different varieties. Figure 4 further demonstrates that the distribution of the variables is relatively homogeneous for some of the text types, and this applies mainly to the spoken categories. A case in point is represented by cluster B, which contains 39 out of the 44 leaves representing spoken texts. Given the findings of comparable studies of individual varieties (e.g. Werner 2014), this does not come as a major surprise, as in these analyses, spoken text types regularly emerged as more homogeneous compared to written ones (see also Biber and Conrad 2009: 261). Conversely, clusters A, C and D contain exclusively or predominantly written leaves. Some trends in terms of alignment of individual text types can be established. For instance, seven out of the eleven leaves of the popular writing (w2b) category can be found in B1, six out of eleven of persuasive writing (w2e) cluster in D1 and six out of eleven of creative writing (w2f) in D.

If we change the perspective to the broader ICE macro-genres (see Appendix A), dialogues (19/22) and, even more clearly, monologues (21/22) cluster in B, while almost half of the texts included in non-printed writing agglomerate in clusters C and D (9/22). Printed writing, which comprises a wide range of different text types, is more diverse overall but dominates in B2 (14), C1 (8), D2 (16) and A (6).

It has to be noted that a test for the statistical significance of the clusters in *R* returns only a few clusters on a lower level. No straightforward division (e.g. with a significantly different "spoken" B cluster as indicated above) can be established, which in turn suggests that – with the exception of a few outliers – the data are homogeneous even from a more fine-grained perspective, although some groupings can be observed.

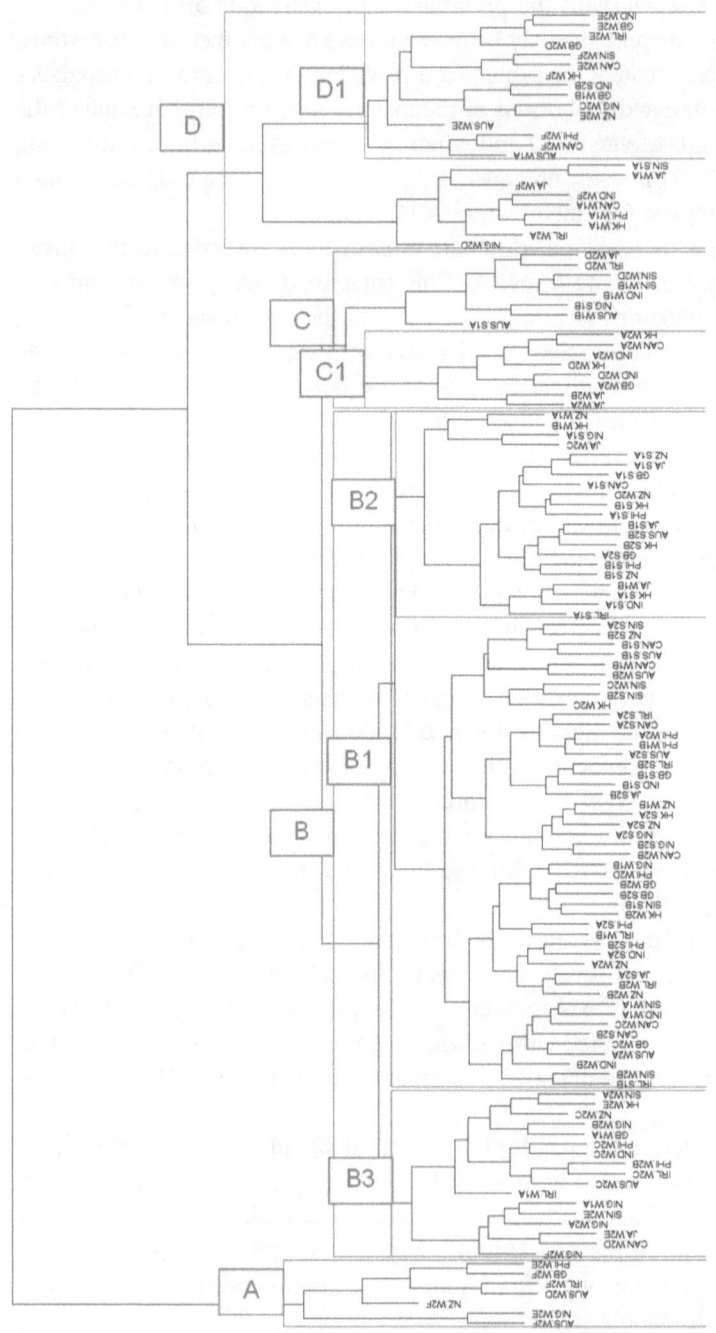

Figure 4: Cluster dendrogram of similarity across ICE text types (cophenetic correlation value = 0.88)

In contrast, significant groupings emerge when we aggregate the data and reorganize them according to the more coarse-grained categories "involved", that is spoken and non-printed, versus "informational" texts, loosely corresponding to the categorization first established in Biber (1988) as "Dimension 1" along which texts or registers may vary. The relevant dendrogram is presented as Figure 5.

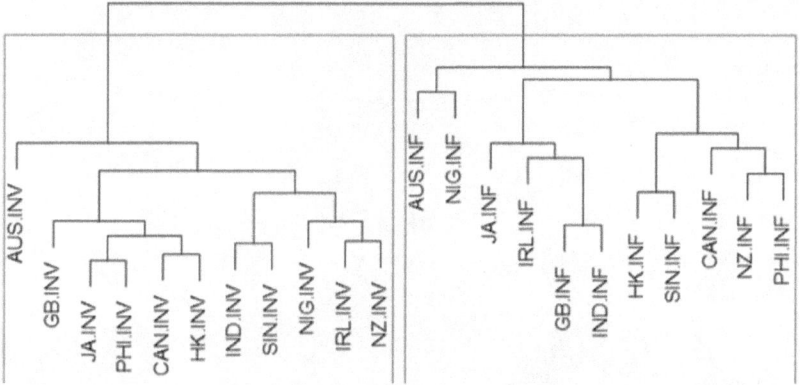

Figure 5: Cluster dendrogram across ICE components: involved (INV) vs. informational (INF) (cophenetic correlation value = 0.76)

It is evident that texts strongly associate with other texts of the same category and that a dichotomy between involved and informational language emerges. All involved leaves (INV) can be found in the left cluster, while the informational leaves (INF) all are found towards the right hand side in Figure 5. A test for statistical significance of the two highlighted clusters confirms the split.

The usefulness of the non-hierarchical perspective as an additional or even alternative means of graphical representation for this type of analysis manifests itself in Figure 6.

The contrast between the two categories involved vs. informational unambiguously appears at one glance in the non-hierarchical network representation. It is illustrated by the larger box-shaped area in the middle of the figure, which separates the two groups and intuitively indicates distance between them. It is also worth noting that, in general, distances between the individual involved nodes are shorter than between the informational nodes, which implies a greater homogeneity of the distributions of the variables in the former type.

In sum, in this aggregated view, we can robustly determine text type associations across varieties. At the same time, this implies that conceptualizations of national varieties as monolithic and clearly separable blocks may be too simplistic (see also Hundt and Vogel 2011), and in particular when individual constructions, such as the PrPf in the present case, and their usage patterns are considered (see Werner 2014: 351–356 for further discussion).

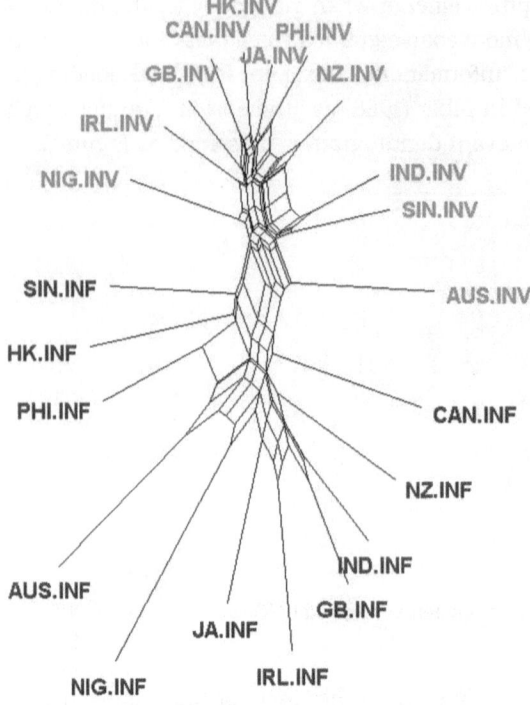

Figure 6: NeighborNet across ICE components: involved (INV) vs. informational (INF)

3.2 Present Perfect versus Simple Past

This section presents a case study that draws its motivation from the well-documented evidence for leveling between the PrPf and the SPst in some varieties of English (eWAVE feature 99; eWAVE feature 100; cf. Lunkenheimer 2012) and in particular discourse types, such as police reports (Ritz 2010) or after-match sports reportage (Walker 2011). It builds on Werner (2013b), now additionally including American English data.

We start from two initial hypotheses. First, in some varieties the PrPf may be used as a narrative tense (in the sense of Quirk et al. 1985), that is, comparable to the SPst, it can be used to create past time reference in combination with definite time adverbials. This represents a development often described in grammaticalization research and is therefore not uncommon from a synchronic typological perspective (Bybee and Dahl 1989: 68–77). Second, we also consider the counter-development, that is, use of the SPst in indefinite temporal contexts typically associated with PrPf use, which is taken as evidence for layering between the two forms (Hundt and Smith 2009: 58; Werner 2013b: 232).

To test these hypotheses, the non-trivial task of identifying contexts where PrPf and SPst are potentially interchangeable with each other without any (fundamental) change in meaning has to be solved. While a certain amount of subjectivity cannot be avoided, I opted for an approach that relies on temporal adverbials as indicators for the contexts under investigation. For the former, I searched for instances where the definite temporal adverbial constraint (as established in Klein 1992) is violated, that is, I searched for combinations of the PrPf with temporal adverbials that typically co-occur with the SPst (x + *ago*, *once*, *yesterday*, *last* + x, *in* + cardinal number).[10]

Werner (2013b: 229) has shown that in the ICE data relevant examples are scarce and, in terms of register, that they characteristically occur in spoken (and informal) data. While from a quantitative perspective the analysis has suggested a higher salience of tense-like PrPf usage in Asian varieties of English (Indian, Hong Kong, and Philippine English; see also Lunkenheimer 2012: 338–340), no statistically significant differences between the L1 and L2 variety group as a whole have emerged.

However, clear qualitative differences are traceable between variety types. In L1 varieties, occurrences of the PrPf in definite temporal contexts can be explained through pragmatic necessity or as performance errors, which ties in with Rastall (1999: 81–83). One of the types that can be identified comprises examples with iterative statements, such as (1).

(1) For example, the diagnostic and statistics manual (DSM) has been updated twice, *once in 1968, and again in 1980, with a revised version appearing in 1986* (ICE-GB w1a-007)

Here, the definite temporal adverbial constraint seems to be suspended. A second type are examples with afterthoughts or insertions, as (2) or (3).

(2) [...] but we've seen that video *months ago* (ICE-NZ s1b-009)

(3) They have also uhm I think *last year* uh given a list of of six principles (ICE-IRL s2b-001)

---

10 The view that *in the past* should not be categorized as a temporal adverbial characteristic for SPst contexts, as argued in Werner (2013b: 228), receives further support from the ICE-USA data, as the following examples show: *I think there are some areas we have underemphasized* in the past *that we ought to concentrate on.* (ICE-USA w2b-036); *Because China and the United States have constantly had conflicts* in the past [...] (ICE-USA w1a-012); *In this regard, please ensure that your critical accounting* [...] *analyzes the factors on how the company arrived at material estimates including how the estimates or assumptions have changed* in the past *and are reasonably likely to change in the future.* (ICE-USA w1b-020).

While the hesitation is explicit through *uhm* and *uh* in (3), the corpus annotation of (2) also contains a hesitation marker between *months* and *ago*. It is evident that the violation of the definite temporal adverbial constraint (without further pragmatic factors as described as a prerequisite) is common in colloquial New Zealand English, and the same applies to Australian English (eWAVE feature 100), as illustrated by (4), so these two factors may interact here.

(4) Well he's come on very quickly *last year* (ICE-AUS s2b-017)

Nevertheless, both examples above may be interpreted as instances where the speakers, although they become aware of a "performance error", accept the lack of grammatical well-formedness for pragmatic reasons. Note further that afterthought-like variants may even occur in written texts, as example (5) from the persuasive writing category illustrates.

(5) The Topaz 2 has been used in only two missions, *in 1987.* (ICE-USA w2e-004)

(6) The present tutor training system has been in effect from the inception of the tutoring center *over six years ago.* (ICE-USA w1a-003)

In a similar fashion, (6) exemplifies an instance where the definite temporal information (*six years ago*) is syntactically embedded under an indefinite construction (*from the inception...*) and therefore constitutes some kind of post-hoc specification. A similar interpretation is also conceivable for (1) above, where the focus is first on the indefinite *twice* and subsequently on definite temporality.

A third issue that seems to play a role is the subjective conception of a situation as recent and relevant by the individual speaker, which is illustrated in (7) with the apparent "recentness" interpretation of the temporal adverbial *this fall*.

(7) Meghan, who will be 4 in March, has also started school *this fall*.
(ICE-USA w1b-011)

While premodification, as in (8), is acceptable in both variety types, in L2 varieties structural subjectivity is often conveyed by a combination of definite and indefinite temporal adverbial, as in (9) (see further Werner 2014: 348–349).

(8) Oh I've had some fun *this last week* (ICE-CAN s1a-093)

(9) I would not say that women's issues have *just* started *last year* I would not even say that (ICE-EA s1a-028)

In contrast, the vast majority of the tokens from the L2 varieties exemplify innovative use. On the one hand, motivations behind these uses that clearly violate the definite adverbial constraint (see (10) and (11)) as defined above can be found in the L1 of the speakers (Davydova 2011: 172–173), where comparable structures are acceptable.

(10) You know *yesterday* I have seen some two guys speaking with you (ICE-IND s1a-049)

(11) So he admits Sir what he has stated *yesterday* was was not correct (ICE-IND s2a-063)

In addition to the impact of the substrate(s), learner effects exert some influence. This is mainly the case in terms of a larger variety of grammatical forms for one specific communicative purpose (Werner 2014: 349), which materializes in the present investigation as the occurrence of combinations of PrPfs with definite temporal adverbials, as (12) to (14) illustrate.

(12) Some of them have *once* been my best friends [...] (ICE-HK w1b-004)

(13) *Months ago* I have written Sen John Sheffield the head of the US Senate Environment Committee about the problems [...] (ICE-PHI s2b-032)

(14) We have mailed you the above DBS Card *2 weeks ago*. (ICE-SIN w1b-019)

In sum, the combination of both of these types of influence, as has previously been argued for other features (e.g. by Schneider 2012: 63–64), seems to provide a plausible motivation for the innovative, tense-like uses of the PrPf in the varieties discussed (see also Werner 2013b: 231–232). The following disclaimer applies, however: Although there is some evidence for creative usage or an extension of the functional range of the PrPf in the ICE data (in particular in the L2 varieties), relevant examples are restricted to informal speech and are rare overall. Although this would not be unlikely from a typological perspective, the data do not support a development of the PrPf into a proper variant of the SPst (or even ousting it). Thus, we can conclude that in the data, the indications for a functional extension of the PrPf are weak at present, as is also shown by converging evidence from other studies (e.g. Elsness 2014: 100). Nevertheless, on a more general note, we may speculate on the potential role substrate and learner effects plays for language change, as changes regularly start out from colloquial usage (Suárez-Gómez and Seoane 2013: 169) and later spread to more formal registers.

In addition to the foregoing qualitative analysis, a brief quantitative view seems worthwhile in order to address the second issue, leveling toward the SPst. While we may not be able to relate all varieties to each other in the same way as shown in Section 3.1 above (due to the lack of comparability of the ICE-USA and ICE-EA data),[11] we can attempt an approximation with the help of assessing the overall "openness" toward the SPst in typical PrPf contexts, again exploiting temporal adverbial contexts, now of the indefinite type. Accordingly, for the identification of examples, a search for adverbials typically associated with the PrPf (*already, yet, always, ever, never, recently, just, since*) in both PrPf and SPst contexts was conducted.

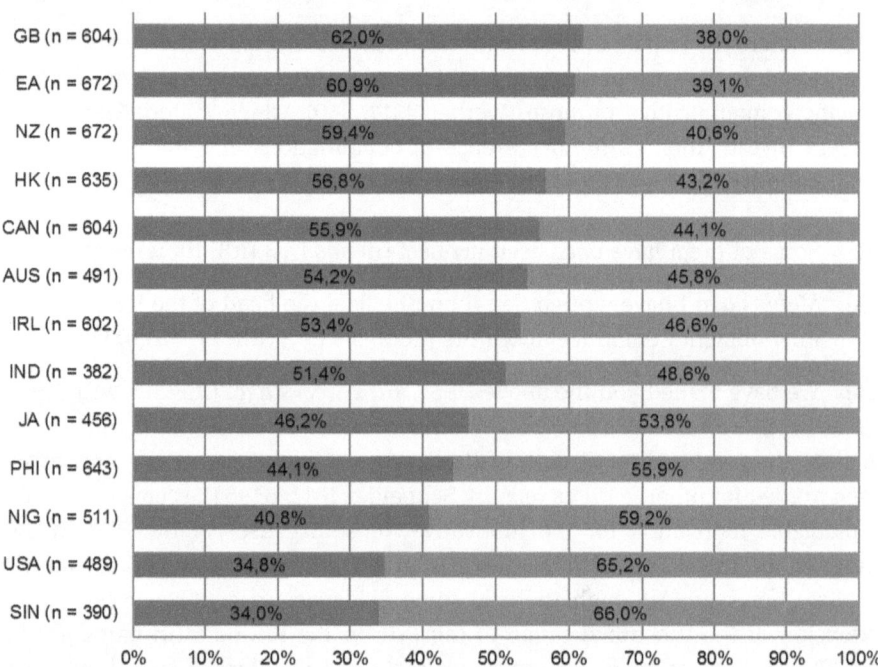

Figure 7: Ranked ratio (relative values) of PrPf (dark grey) vs. SPst (light grey) with indefinite time adverbials

While Werner (2013b) offers an analysis of distributions between SPst and PrPf co-occurring with individual adverbials, the present investigation seeks to arrive at a more global picture. Figure 7 plots the ratio of co-occurrence with either SPst or PrPf averaged across the whole set of indefinite temporal adverbials.

---

[11] As no completed version of ICE-USA is available, the values for the American data are based on the numbers provided in Yao and Collins (2012: 402), who relied on an American corpus that approximates the ICE layout and contains both spoken and written material.

Above all, it establishes that there is considerable variation in the distribution between the two forms. Figure 7 also allows establishing a hierarchy of openness toward the SPst, where Singapore and American English emerge as the most open varieties, while British and East African English appear to be most conservative. This hierarchy largely corresponds to the hierarchy of PrPf friendliness established with a different methodology in Werner (2013b: 213), and further confirms the view of American and British English as two poles on a continuum of openness toward the SPst (see Yao and Collins 2012: 399).

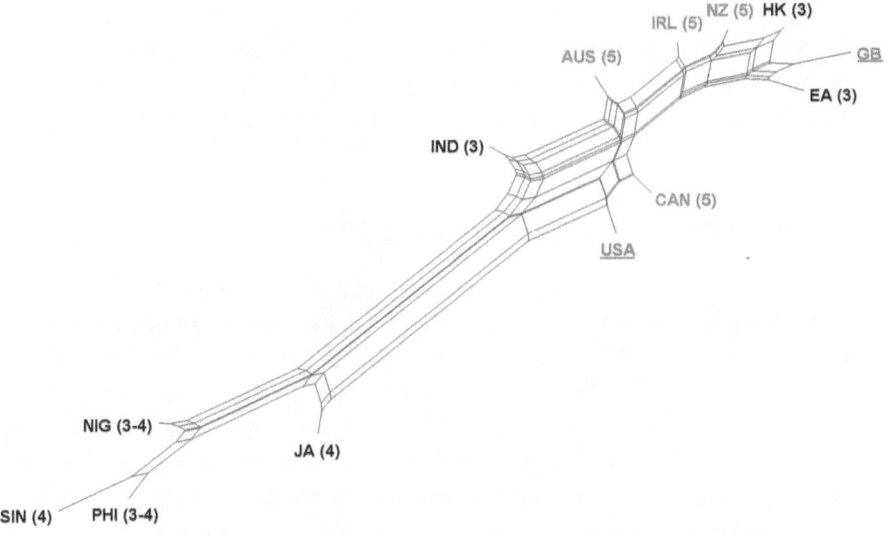

Figure 8: NeighborNet of similarity of SPst vs. PrPf across ICE components; numbers in brackets refer to variety type categorization according to Schneider (2007)

Although American English can be viewed as a variety that is open toward the SPst overall (see Figure 7), variety type plays a part when individual adverbials are considered.[12] We can identify a split along the lines of variety types that is even more clear-cut than the one found in Werner (2013b: 214–216). The NeighborNet shown in Figure 8 reveals a clear distinction between a group of varieties (Singapore, Jamaican, Philippine, and Nigerian English) that emerge as more open toward the SPst (more than 55% of the relevant contexts; see

---

12 Figure 8 is based on the relative values of the eight indefinite adverbials (see above). As *just*, *recently*, and *since* did not feature in Yao and Collins (2012), the average values across the other 12 varieties are used for American English for these items. This standard procedure applied to missing values in aggregative analyses is further explained in Krug, Schützler and Werner (2016).

above) and a group comprising the remaining varieties. The latter group includes both the reference varieties (American and British English) and the transplanted L1s (phase 5) varieties as well as the nativizing (phase 3) varieties, which arguably still show traces of exonormative orientation and therefore associate closely with the former varieties. In contrast, the group that appears removed exclusively consists of varieties that move toward or have already reached phase 4, which are viewed as being in or entering a process of endonormative stabilization. In spite of the overall distance, American English emerges as the L1 that is closest to the phase 4 varieties. These findings support the usefulness of Schneider's (2007) dynamic model as one approach for the description of World Englishes, although more features would have to be included to assess the overall applicability of this socio-historical approach for the empirical structural description of varieties of English (but see Schneider 2014: 14–15).

4 Conclusion

The results of the study highlight a number of issues. Above all, I hope to have at least partially shown what can be gained from an extension of the research focus beyond the traditional British/American paradigm. While the study of World Englishes has become an established field of English linguistics, there still lies considerable potential in structural analyses that integrate the study of varieties of all kinds. I also want to emphasize again the necessity to systematically include register-, genre- and text type-effects, which can help us to explain variation within and across varieties, as previously noted by Sand (2005: 458) and Schneider and Hundt (2012: 29–30), for example. In this regard, the largely parallel design of the ICE components could be confirmed to be a valuable asset.

The quantitative assessment of the corpus data suggest that the PrPf represents an element of the core grammar of World Englishes. In other words, there was only scarce evidence of the explicit nativization of PrPf usages. Reasons for the convergence may be that grammar represents a linguistic area where convergence is likely in general, while the homogeneous speaker group as represented in ICE and general aspects of globalization may also play a part. To be precise, differences between varieties were of a quantitative rather than a categorical nature, while fine nuances in the distributions and a restricted influence of variety types could be observed. Furthermore, the analyses showed that rather than associations within varieties or varieties of the same type, comparable genres or text types of different varieties emerged as closer to one another. This suggests a revision of the view that conceives of (regional) varieties as monolithic blocks.

The case study provided some evidence for creative language use due to substrate and learner effects, at least as regards individual aspects in the ICE data, and a similar situation applies to further case studies on semantic and pragmatic aspects of alternative surface forms appearing in PrPf contexts (Werner 2014: 322–335; see also Davydova 2011). However, the case for a change of the grammatical status of the PrPf is weak. The second part of the case study exemplified the different characteristic values of layering present in the varieties investigated. In addition, it revealed a fundamental split as to the association of indefinite temporal contexts with either PrPf or SPst along the lines of variety types. For a further assessment in terms of locating varieties in relation to British and American English, it would be desirable to have the full ICE dataset available. In addition, register effects in this domain need to be explored in more detail in the future to obtain a fuller picture.

Closely related to the previous aspect are the final notes on methodology. The present study gave an insight into the benefits of working with corpus data that share a similar layout and largely stick to the same compilation principles. In addition, it demonstrated the usefulness of combining different types of multidimensional aggregative analysis (facilitating the identification of latent structure in big datasets) with further quantitative and qualitative techniques. The extension of aggregative methods to other types of linguistic data (see Krug, Schützler and Werner 2016 for an application on questionnaire data) has the potential to reveal patterns that would otherwise remain hidden.

References

Awonusi, Victor O. 1994. The Americanization of Nigerian English. *World Englishes* 13(1). 75–82.
Bauer, Gero. 1970. The English 'Perfect' reconsidered. *Journal of Linguistics* 6. 189–198.
Biber, Douglas. 1988. *Variation across speech and writing*. Cambridge: Cambridge University Press.
Biber, Douglas. 1990. Methodological issues regarding corpus-based analyses of linguistic variation. *Literary and Linguistic Computing* 5(4). 257–269.
Biber, Douglas, Stig Johansson, Geoffrey Leech, Susan Conrad & Edward Finegan. 1999. *Longman grammar of spoken and written English*. Harlow: Longman.
Biber, Douglas & Susan Conrad. 2009. *Register, genre, and style*. Cambridge: Cambridge University Press.
Bowie, Jill & Bas Aarts. 2012. Change in the English infinitival perfect construction. In Terttu Nevalainen & Elizabeth Closs Traugott (eds.), *The Oxford handbook of the history of English*, 200–210. Oxford: Oxford University Press.
Bybee, Joan L. & Östen Dahl. 1989. The creation of tense and aspect systems in the languages of the world. *Studies in Language* 13(1). 51–103.
Comrie, Bernard. 1976. *Aspect*. Cambridge: Cambridge University Press.

Davies, Mark & Robert Fuchs. 2015. Expanding horizons in the study of World Englishes with the 1.9 billion word Global Web-based English Corpus (GloWbE). *English World-Wide* 36(1). 1–28.

Davydova, Julia. 2011. *The present perfect in non-native Englishes: A corpus-based study of variation*. Berlin: Mouton de Gruyter.

Davydova, Julia. 2016. The present perfect in New Englishes: Common patterns in situations of language contact. In Valentin Werner, Elena Seoane & Cristina Suárez-Gómez (eds.), *Re-assessing the present perfect*, 169–194. Berlin: Mouton de Gruyter.

Elsness, Johan. 1997. *The perfect and the preterite in contemporary and earlier English*. Berlin: Mouton de Gruyter.

Elsness, Johan. 2014. The present perfect and the preterite in late modern and contemporary English: A longitudinal look. In Kristin Davidse, Caroline Gentens, Lobke Ghesquière & Lieven Vandelanotte (eds.), *Corpus interrogation and grammatical patterns*, 81–103. Amsterdam: Benjamins.

Fuchs, Robert & Ulrike Gut. 2016. Register variation in intensifier usage across Asian Englishes. In Heike Pichler (ed.), *Discourse-pragmatic variation and change: Insights from English*, 183–184. Cambridge: Cambridge University Press.

Greenbaum, Sidney. 1996. Introducing ICE. In Sidney Greenbaum (ed.), *Comparing English worldwide: The International Corpus of English*, 3–12. Oxford: Clarendon Press.

Gries, Stefan Thomas. 2006. Exploring variability within and between corpora: Some methodological considerations. *Corpora* 1(2). 109–151.

Gut, Ulrike. 2012. Towards a codification of Nigerian English: The ICE Nigeria project. *Journal of the Nigeria English Studies Association* 15(1). 1–12.

Huddleston, Rodney & Geoffrey K. Pullum. 2002. *The Cambridge grammar of the English language*. Cambridge: Cambridge University Press.

Hundt, Marianne. 2009. Global English – global corpora: Report on a panel discussion at the 28th ICAME conference. In Antoinette Renouf & Andrew Kehoe (eds.), *Corpus linguistics: Refinements and reassessments*, 451–462. Amsterdam: Rodopi.

Hundt, Marianne & Nicolas Smith. 2009. The present perfect in British and American English: Has there been a change, recently? *ICAME Journal* 33. 45–63.

Hundt, Marianne & Katrin Vogel. 2011. Overuse of the progressive in ESL and learner Englishes – fact or fiction? In Joybrato Mukherjee & Marianne Hundt (eds.), *Exploring second-language varieties of English and learner Englishes: Bridging a paradigm gap*, 145–165. Amsterdam: Benjamins.

Huson, Daniel H. & David Bryant. 2006. Application of phylogenetic networks in evolutionary studies. *Molecular Biology and Evolution* 23(2). 254–267.

Jaszczolt, Kasia M. 2009. *Representing time: An essay on temporality as modality*. Oxford: Oxford University Press.

Klein, Wolfgang. 1992. The present perfect puzzle. *Language* 68(3). 525–552.

Klein, Wolfgang. 2009. How time is encoded. In Wolfgang Klein & Ping Li (eds.), *The expression of time*, 39–81. Berlin: Mouton de Gruyter.

Kortmann, Bernd. 1995. Compositionality and the perfect. In Wolfgang Riehle & Hugo Keiper (eds.), *Anglistentag 1994 Graz: Proceedings*, 183–199. Tübingen: Niemeyer.

Kortmann, Bernd & Christoph Wolk. 2013. Morphosyntactic variation in the anglophone world: A global perspective. In Bernd Kortmann & Kerstin Lunkenheimer (eds.), *The Mouton world atlas of variation in English*, 906–936. Berlin: Mouton de Gruyter.

Krug, Manfred, Ole Schützler & Valentin Werner. 2016. Integrating typological profiles and questionnaire data. In Olga Timofeeva, Anne-Christine Gardner, Alpo Honkapohja & Sarah Chevalier (eds.), *New Approaches to English Linguistics: Building Bridges*, 35–66. Amsterdam: Benjamins.

Labov, William. 1978. *The study of NonStandard English*. Urbana: National Council of Teachers of English.

Lunkenheimer, Kerstin. 2012. Tense and aspect. In Raymond Hickey (ed.), *Areal features of the Anglophone world*, 329–353. Berlin: Mouton de Gruyter.

Mair, Christian. 2013. Using 'small' corpora to document ongoing grammatical change. In Manfred Krug & Julia Schlüter (eds.), *Research methods in language variation and change*, 181–194. Cambridge: Cambridge University Press.

Manning, Christopher D. & Hinrich Schütze. 1999. *Foundations of statistical natural language processing*. London: MIT Press.

McCawley, James D. 1983. Tense and time reference in English. In Charles J. Fillmore & D. Terence Langendoen (eds.), *Studies in linguistic semantics*, 96–113. New York: Holt, Rinehart and Winston.

McMahon, April & Warren Maguire. 2013. Computing linguistic distances between varieties. In Manfred Krug & Julia Schlüter (eds.), *Research methods in language variation and change*, 421–432. Cambridge: Cambridge University Press.

Mukherjee, Joybrato & Marco Schilk. 2012. Exploring variation and change in New Englishes: Looking into the International Corpus of English (ICE) and beyond. In Terttu Nevalainen & Elizabeth Closs Traugott (eds.), *The Oxford handbook of the history of English*, 189–199. Oxford: Oxford University Press.

Nelson, Gerald. 1996. The design of the corpus. In Sidney Greenbaum (ed.), *Comparing English worldwide: The International Corpus of English*, 27–35. Oxford: Clarendon Press.

Nichols, Johanna & Tandy Warnow. 2008. Tutorial on computational linguistic phylogeny. *Language and Linguistics Compass* 2(5). 760–820.

Portner, Paul. 2003. The (temporal) semantics and (modal) pragmatics of the perfect. *Linguistics and Philosophy* 26. 459–510.

Quirk, Randolph, Sidney Greenbaum, Geoffrey N. Leech & Jan Svartvik. 1985. *A comprehensive grammar of the English language*. Harlow: Longman.

Rastall, Paul. 1999. Observations on the present perfect in English. *World Englishes* 18(1). 79–83.

Ritz, Marie-Eve A. 2010. The perfect crime? Illicit uses of the present perfect in Australian police media releases. *Journal of Pragmatics* 42. 3400–3417.

Romesburg, H. Charles. 1984. *Cluster analysis for researchers*. Belmont: Lifetime Learning.

Salkie, Raphael. 1989. Perfect and pluperfect: What is the relationship? *Journal of Linguistics* 25. 1–34.

Sand, Andrea. 2005. The effects of language contact on the morpho-syntax of English. In Lilo Moessner & Christa M. Schmidt (eds.), *Proceedings Anglistentag 2004 Aachen*, 449–460. Trier: WVT.

Schlüter, Norbert. 2002. *Present Perfect: Eine korpuslinguistische Analyse des englischen Perfekts mit Vermittlungsvorschlägen für den Sprachunterricht*. Tübingen: Narr.

Schlüter, Norbert. 2006. How reliable are the results? Comparing corpus-based studies of the present perfect. *Zeitschrift für Anglistik und Amerikanistik* 54(2). 135–148.

Schneider, Gerold & Marianne Hundt. 2012. 'Off with their heads': Profiling TAM in ICE corpora. In Marianne Hundt & Ulrike Gut (eds.), *Mapping unity and diversity world-wide: Corpus-based studies of new Englishes*, 1–34. Amsterdam: Benjamins.

Schneider, Edgar W. 2007. *Postcolonial English: Varieties around the world*. Cambridge: Cambridge University Press.

Schneider, Edgar W. 2012. Exploring the interface between World Englishes and second language acquisition – and implications for English as a lingua franca. *Journal of English as a Lingua Franca* 1(1). 57–91.

Schneider, Edgar W. 2014. New reflections on the evolutionary dynamics of world Englishes. *World Englishes* 33(1). 9–32.

Scott, Mike. 2011. *WordSmith Tools*. Liverpool: Lexical Analysis Software.

Seoane, Elena & Cristina Suárez-Gómez. 2013. The expression of the perfect in South-East Asian Englishes. *English World-Wide* 34(1). 1–25.

Suárez-Gómez, Cristina & Elena Seoane. 2013. They have published a new cultural policy that just come out: Competing forms in spoken and written New Englishes. In Kristin Bech & Gisle Andersen (eds.), *English corpus linguistics: Variation in time, space and genre*, 163–182. Amsterdam: Rodopi.

Szmrecsanyi, Benedikt. 2013. Typological profile: L1 varieties. In Bernd Kortmann & Kerstin Lunkenheimer (eds.), *The Mouton world atlas of variation in English*, 826–843. Berlin: Mouton de Gruyter.

Szmrecsanyi, Benedikt & Christoph Wolk. 2011. Holistic corpus-based dialectology. *Brazilian Journal of Applied Linguistics* 11(2). 561–592.

Veloudis, Ioannis. 2003. Possession and conversation: The case of the category perfect. In Artemis Alexiadou, Monika Rathert & Arnim von Stechow (eds.), *Perfect explorations*, 381–399. Berlin: Mouton de Gruyter.

Vendler, Zeno. 1957. Verbs and times. *The Philosophical Review* 66(2). 143–160.

Vendler, Zeno. 1967. *Linguistics in philosophy*. Ithaca: Cornell University Press.

Walker, Jim. 2011. The emergence of the narrative present perfect in British English: Reality or illusion? *Groninger Arbeiten zur germanistischen Linguistik* 53(2). 71–87.

Werner, Valentin. 2013a. The present perfect and definite temporal adverbials: Reference grammars and corpus evidence. *English Language Overseas Perspectives and Enquiries* 10(1). 9–21.

Werner, Valentin. 2013b. Temporal adverbials and the present perfect/past tense alternation. *English World-Wide* 34(2). 202–240.

Werner, Valentin. 2014. *The present perfect in World Englishes: Charting unity and diversity*. Bamberg: University of Bamberg Press.

Werner, Valentin, Elena Seoane & Cristina Suárez-Gómez, (eds.). 2016. *Re-assessing the present perfect*. Berlin: Mouton de Gruyter.

Winford, Donald. 1993. Variability in the use of perfect have in Trinidadian English: A problem of categorical and semantic mismatch. *Language Variation and Change* 5. 141–187.

Wynne, Terence. 2000. *The present perfect: A corpus-based investigation*. Stirling: University of Stirling PhD.

Yao, Xinyue & Peter Collins. 2012. The present perfect in world Englishes. *World Englishes* 31(3). 386–403.

Appendix

Appendix A. ICE text categories (respective number of 2,000-word texts indicated in brackets)

Register/mode of discourse	Macro-genre	Text type category	Text type (detailed)
Spoken (300)	Dialogues (180)	s1a Private (100)	Face-to-face conversations (90) Phone calls (10)
		s1b Public (80)	Classroom lessons (20) Broadcast discussions (20) Broadcast interviews (10) Parliamentary debates (10) Legal cross-examinations (10) Business transactions (10)
	Monologues (120)	s2a Unscripted (70)	Spontaneous commentaries (20) Unscripted speeches (30) Demonstrations (10) Legal presentations (10)
		s2b Scripted (50)	Broadcast News (20) Broadcast Talks (20) Non-broadcast Talks (10)
Written (200)	Non-printed (50)	w1a Student writing (20)	Student essays (10) Exam scripts (10)
		w1b Letters (30)	Social letters (15) Business letters (15)
	Printed (150)	w2a Academic writing (40)	Humanities (10) Social sciences (10) Natural sciences (10) Technology (10)
		w2b Popular writing (40)	Humanities (10) Social sciences (10) Natural sciences (10) Technology (10)
		w2c Reportage (20)	Press news reports (20)
		w2d Instructional writing (20)	Administrative writing (10) Skills/hobbies (10)
		w2e Persuasive writing (10)	Press editorials (10)
		w2f Creative writing (20)	Novels and short stories (20)

Appendix B. Overview of the variables coded

Presence or absence of temporal adverbial
- Type of adverbial (Quirk et al. 1985/Biber et al. 1999)
  - Adverbials of time-position (e.g. *today, yesterday, afterwards*, etc.)
  - Adverbials of span and duration (e.g. *briefly, since* X, *for* X, etc.)
  - Adverbials of frequency (e.g. *daily, twice, always, often, never*, etc.)
- Other adverbials of sequence or time relationship between two events (e.g. *already, originally*, etc.)
- Aktionsart (Vendler 1957; 1967/Comrie 1976)
  - Activity verbs (e.g. *run, eat, fly*, etc.)
  - Accomplishment verbs (e.g. *build, draw (a circle), run (a mile)*, etc.)
  - Achievement verbs (e.g. *discover, reach (the top), cross (the river)*, etc.)
  - State verbs (e.g. *love, hate, be*, etc.)
- Sentence type
  - Positive statements (e.g. *I've been in this limbo for too long*; ICE-CAN s1a-037)
  - Negative statements (e.g. *Their performance has not been good*; ICE-NZ w2c-014)
  - Questions (e.g. *Are there any other things you have left out*; ICE-JA s1b-078)
- Semantics (Schlüter 2002)
  - Indefinite past – single acts/events (e.g. *the teacher who taught us Bridge has gone*; ICE-HK s1a-042)
  - Indefinite past – multiple acts/events (e.g. *I've probably seen them a dozen times*; ICE-AUS s1a-071)
  - Continuative past – continuous acts/events (e.g. *Complaints have been known to be made when such situations have occurred, this is why the rule now rigidly applies*; ICE-IRL w2d-017)
  - Continuative past – states (e.g. *The economic team of the present administration during its first year has been superior in cohesiveness effectiveness and clarity in purpose*; ICE-PHI s2b-026)
- Preceding time reference

Cristina Suárez-Gómez
Innovative structures in the relative clauses of indigenized L2 Asian English varieties[1]

Abstract: This paper examines morphosyntactic variation in World Englishes, looking specifically at processes of relativization. Drawing on data from *the International Corpus of English*, it analyzes adnominal relative clauses in the spoken language of a selection of international varieties of English, namely those of Hong-Kong, India and Singapore. The study presents a qualitative analysis of relative structures and explores specific constructions which are found in these World Englishes but not – or only very exceptionally – in standard English. The existence of these constructions is examined in light of the following factors:
(i) influence of the target language or geographical variety of English that acted as the colonizer language (British English)
(ii) L1 transfer, which determines the preference of certain relative markers over others (e.g. preference for *wh-* forms in Indian English)
(iii) language contact phenomena, which accounts for the occurrence of certain innovative structures as globalized features of world-wide varieties of English, following *The Electronic World Atlas of Varieties of English* (Kortmann and Lunkenheimer 2013)
(iv) evolutionary factors in these norm-developing varieties taking into account the different degree of development of the corresponding localized variety of English, following Schneider's Dynamic Model (2007).

A clear picture should thus emerge of the role and strength of superstrate and substrate influences on grammatical variation in World Englishes, taking relative clauses as a case in point.

Keywords: morphosyntax, relative clauses, L1 transfer, innovation, adnominal relative clause, correlative structures, relativization, morphosyntactic variation, International Corpus of English (ICE), Hong Kong English, Indian English, Singapore English, Electronic World Atlas of Varieties of English (eWAVE), L2 varieties, language contact

---

[1] I gratefully acknowledge the support of the Spanish Ministry of Science and Competitiveness (Grant No. FFI2014-53930-P). Thanks also go to the anonymous reviewers of this article and to Elena Seoane for helpful comments and suggestions.

Cristina Suárez-Gómez, Universitat de les Illes Balears

DOI 10.1515/9783110429657-006

1 Introduction

Research on relative clauses and relativization processes has generated a substantial amount of work over the years, especially with regard to the distribution of relative words within the relative clause and the factors that condition this, both in Standard English (Quirk 1957; Aarts 1993; Guy and Bayley 1995; Ball 1996; Tottie 1997) and in regional varieties of the most traditional Englishes, namely British (Romaine 1982; Tagliamonte 2002; Herrman 2003; Tagliamonte et al 2005; Cheshire, Adger and Fox 2013) and American English (Tottie and Harvie 2000). More recently, the analysis of relative words has become extended to postcolonial varieties of English (Gut and Coronel 2012; Huber 2012; Suárez-Gómez 2014, 2015), especially from a quantitative point of view. It has been observed here that relative markers in varieties of English around the world show differences with respect to their distribution in standard English, although differences from the norm are minimal, and the divergence found is usually related to a different use of the same features, either in terms of frequency of use or stylistic preferences, and these differences do not generally affect grammaticality conditions (see Huber 2012: 240). Such divergent structures in L2 varieties of English have often been ignored on the grounds that they are performance or planning errors or are considered exceptional structures, and hence have most often been omitted from quantitative analyses. This view will be challenged in the present paper, because although quantitative analyses tend to confirm the fact that they occur less frequently than other, more canonical constructions, they are not isolated cases. On the contrary, they are found in many different varieties and may represent either features of contact varieties or local features which, though used tentatively, may become consolidated as innovative features over time. For this purpose, following Hundt (2016), I adopt Hung's (2009: 229) definition of 'innovative feature' as "a non-standard form which is not limited to learners of English alone but can commonly be found among speakers of all levels of proficiency." Hung applied this definition to phonological features, considering that in phonology an innovative feature "is found in neither the speaker's L1 nor the target language (though it may indirectly show the influence of either of both), but is apparently a new and/or unique feature of the L2" (Hung 2009: 228). Given the stability of grammar, we can consider that an innovative feature in grammar does not necessarily have to be absent in the target language, but might simply have a different use and distribution.

The aim of this paper is to analyze the local developments of global features in the realm of relativization which appear to represent 'innovative features' in the sense that they are not necessarily attributable to the relevant L1s or the standard variety of the target language, but might be influenced by either one or both of these, or the result of the development of the contact varieties themselves. In other words, the aim here is to determine whether the relative clauses object of study represent global features in the different varieties of English (both native and non-native) or, rather, are local norms specific to some varieties which are ephemeral or become innovative features, and thus to see whether they may constitute instances of incipient change. Within relative constructions, only adnominal structures, that is, those referring back to a nominal antecedent, will be taken into account. The analysis will be carried out in three postcolonial varieties of English. These three varieties feature in a larger project on morphosyntactic variation in Asian varieties of English, which in part determines their choice here.

The varieties under study here are indigenized L2 varieties from the Outer Circle in a norm-developing process. In fact, from an evolutionary perspective, Schneider (2007) has shown that these postcolonial varieties develop local linguistic norms, which are the result of constant relationships and communication needs between the colonizers and the local population. He classified the development according to different phases. In the first two phases ('foundation' and 'exonormative stabilization') the languages in contact remain distinct; from the third phase onwards ('nativization'), the local population is conscious of a new identity and of a new local linguistic system, shown in the "formation of new linguistic habits, and an increasing frequency of usage of certain forms and patterns in a given region" (Schneider 2007: 28). This becomes consolidated in the phase of 'endonormative stabilization' and is affected by general phenomena of language variation and change in the phase of 'differentiation', the fifth and last phase of development acknowledged in Schneider's model. Indian English and Hong Kong English illustrate the phase of 'nativization', and Singapore English is slightly more advanced in that it corresponds to the 'endonormative stabilization' phase.[2]

2 Relative clauses in postcolonial varieties

Research on relative clauses and relativization processes has generated a considerable number of studies over the years (see Section 1 for references). However, research on relative clauses in postcolonial varieties of English is less common, and only very recently have any quantitative studies been seen.

---

[2] For reasons of consistency I will adopt Schneider's classification for the three varieties, although I am aware that in the case of Indian English Mukherkjee (2007) argued that it is already in phase 4.

Taking a quantitative approach, Gut and Coronel (2012) studied relative clauses in four new Englishes (Singapore, the Philippines, Nigeria and Jamaica) and showed that the distribution does not differ substantially from British and American English. In fact, as already mentioned, divergence between L2 varieties and the "norm" at the level of grammar (both morphology and, especially, syntax) tends to be minimal (Hundt 2009: 287), and this also affects relative clauses, as noted by Huber (2012: 240) for relative clauses in Ghanaian English: "by and large, GhE relative clauses, taken individually, are not ungrammatical in BrE, which is still the professed target as far as the morphology and syntax of English in Ghana are concerned". However, Gut and Coronel (2012: 231) observe that there is one type of construction recurrently used in the four varieties, and absent in standard varieties of English, namely relative clauses with prepositional and phrasal verbs with missing prepositions, and that this occurs in both spoken and written language. Other important differences, not associated with grammaticality conditions, are the distributional frequencies of relativizers; Gut and Coronel note the frequent use of *whose* with non-human antecedents in PhilE (2012: 228) and the dominance of *that* in every context in NigE (2012: 224), the latter also corroborated by Huber (2012: 223) with respect to Ghanaian English, in what seems to be a geographical tendency in West-Africa.

A comparison of relativizers in IndE, HKE and SingE shows that IndE prefers *wh-* pronominal relativizers, irrespective of the context, as opposed to HKE and to a lesser extent SingE, where invariable *that* dominates (Suárez-Gómez 2014; 2015). The preference in IndE for *wh-* relativizers and the preference in HKE for invariable *that* has been put down to L1 influence. Additionally, a closer look at different linguistic parameters shows that both the syntactic function of the relativizer and the animacy of the antecedent are very influential, and there is a clear preference for *who* with human antecedents functioning as subject in the three varieties, something also found by Cheshire, Adger and Fox (2013) in the variety of English spoken in a multicultural area of London; as a consequence, the use of *that* in this context decreases, as opposed to non-human antecedents, which show a preference for *that* in HKE and SingE, and *which* in IndE.

Hung (2001) also mentions a specific structure of HKE in which a zero relativizer functions as subject, which he attributes to L1 transfer; regarding SingE, Alsagoff and Ho (1998) report the use of the *one* construction, again seen as an instance of L1 transfer. Gisborne (2000) identifies aspects of HKE which "are apparently unique to the system of Hong Kong English" (369), among which he mentions in passing the use of *where* relatives with a directional as well as a locative meaning. Other relevant structures listed by Gisborne, and also reported by Newbrook for L2 varieties (1998), are the use of zero subject relativizers (also Hung 2001), the presence of resumptive pronouns in lower positions of the accessibility hierarchy, the omission of the preposition in cases where the relativizer functions as complement of a preposition (see Gut and Coronel, above), and the blurring between restrictive and non-restrictive relative structures.

The scant literature on relativization in postcolonial varieties of English shows distributional similarities in the use of relative words between these varieties and L1 varieties, such as British English and American English. From a more qualitative point of view, however, some studies mention a number of low frequency structures found in different varieties, although these are not analyzed further. Therefore, my own study concentrates on a selection of low frequency relative structures which have not thus far received much attention in the literature in the varieties under analysis: Indian English, Hong Kong English and Singapore English.

3 Data and methodology

The data here are drawn from the ICE corpora (*International Corpus of English*, http://ice-corpora.net/ice/index.htm), and represent an acrolectal variety of the English spoken in each of the countries concerned. They include the speech of adult males and females (over 18 years), all born and raised in the country, who received formal education in English. Samples were taken from the Spoken Private Dialogue section (coded as S1A, private dialogue, direct conversations and telephone calls) of the relevant ICE corpora, that is, ICE-HKE, ICE-IND and ICE-SIN, which together amount to c. 600,000 words (200,000 per variety). Spoken language was used since this is generally acknowledged to show a greater degree of variation than written language and is also generally considered to be the most vernacular (Kortmann 2006: 615).

The data retrieval comprised two steps. The first was automatic; with the help of the concordance program *AntConc* 3.2.4 all examples introduced by explicit relativizers introducing adnominal relative clauses were retrieved (*who*, *which*, *whose*, *whom*, *that*, *where*, *when* and *why*). This search returned over 28,000 examples for the three varieties. The second – and more important – step entailed a manual analysis. All examples had to be considered individually in order to exclude non-relevant examples, such as cases of *wh-* words introducing interrogative constructions (1), or the use of *that* as a demonstrative (2) or as a complementizer introducing complement clauses (3):

(1) *Who* won the election?

(2) *That* person arrived late.

(3) I know *that* you arrived late.

An additional manual analysis which entailed the reading of the whole corpus (S1A files) followed, in order to collect further unintroduced cases, those introduced by relativizer zero, since automatic retrieval of these was not possible, in that all the corpora were not tagged. The total number of adnominal relative clauses in the S1A files of the three Asian varieties was 1,926.

Bearing in mind that the study deals with adnominal relative clauses, several subtypes of related constructions had to be excluded. This was the case with sentential relative clauses (4) and nominal relative clauses (5):

(4) The streets were wet, *which* was expected because it had been raining.

(5) *What* you have mentioned is important.

The retrieval of examples shows that the majority of them are congruent with standard varieties of English (see Suárez-Gómez 2014 for a detailed analysis); however, there are some examples representing constructions which are not considered in current grammars of contemporary English, and some are indeed absent nowadays in standard varieties of English. The analysis of these data will show that although these occur less frequently than other more canonical constructions, they are not isolated cases, and most of the times are found in different varieties. The following section includes the description and analysis of these examples.

4 Analysis

The peculiarity of the constructions in our database is that they have often been ignored in analyses of relativization, catalogued as grammatical mistakes in standard English or as performance errors. Such a view will be challenged in this paper, because although the quantitative analyses have shown that they are less frequently used than other more canonical constructions, they are not exceptional cases and occasionally also occur in written texts. Moreover, they are also reported in descriptions of varieties of English from around the world, such as *The Electronic World Atlas of Varieties of English* (hereafter eWave) (Kortmann and Lunkenheimer 2013), which underlines their relevance. EWave records morphosyntactic variation in spontaneous spoken English in around 70 varieties, not only traditional dialects but also high-contact L1 varieties, indigenized L2 varieties, plus English-based pidgins and creoles world-wide. Therefore, rather than mistakes or errors, some examples of these constructions might well prove to be emergent features in relativization processes. The aim of this section is to provide a description of these and determine their origin.

4.1 Lack of human/non-human coreferentiality of *which-who*

One of the most significant parameters for the selection of a specific relativizer in adnominal relative clauses of the English language is the human/non-human feature of the antecedent. Within the *wh-* paradigm of relativizers in English *which* is used with non-human antecedents and *who(m)* with human ones, meanwhile *whose, that* and zero may combine with both human and non-human antecedents. This distribution of *wh-* relativizers has been present in the English language for almost 300 years, having been established during the course of the 18th century (Rissanen 1999: 294). Nevertheless, there are some examples which do not comply with this distribution and do not fulfil the animacy coreferentiality between the *wh-* relativizer and the antecedent. This has been recorded in regional British dialects (Herrmann 2003), also reported in eWave (Kortmann and Lunkenheimer 2013: feature 186), as well as by Gut and Coronel (2012: 231) in a selection of postcolonial varieties. Such examples are also recorded in my database, as illustrated by example (6).

(6) Most of the government school is is worse because they have to accept those student *which is not accepted by other* [...] *school*
 <ICE-HK:S1A-034#202:1:B>

Their frequency is included in Table 1.

Table 1: Lack of animacy coreferentiality between antecedent and relativizer[3]

	HKE	IndE	SingE
Human antecedent + *which*	6/83[4] (6%)	4/190 (2.1%)	–
Non-human antecedent + *who*	1/224 (0.4%)	1/228 (0.4%)	2/170 (1.2%)

A qualitative analysis of the examples in which a human antecedent combines with *which* shows that the antecedent *student(s)* occurs three times, more frequently than any other antecedent. Another relevant finding is that human antecedents of *which* are antecedents with generic meaning (e.g. *people, friend, woman, kids*), with the exception of example (7) with the antecedent *terrorist*.

---

[3] Since the objects of study are low-frequency phenomena, no statistical tests of significance can be carried out and only frequency of occurrence will be reported.
[4] The figures in the tables represent the number of occurrences of the phenomenon under study (in this case 6 instances of *which* with human antecedents in HKE) within the total number of *whichs* in HKE (83 in this case) and the frequency of *whichs* combining with human antecedents within all the *whichs* that occur in the corpus of HKE (6%).

(7) Only if you return that uh terrorist *which you've uh arrested*
    <ICE-IND:S1A-054#47:1:A>

The combination of the generic noun *people* with the relativizer *which* is also recorded in the *Corpus of Global Web-based English* (hereafter GloWbE) (Davies and Fuchs 2015), providing evidence from a written source.

(8) As indicated in the Active Senior Project, there is still a group of old people *which is not able* to benefit from ICT even if it is developed amongst a network of seniors (example from GloWbE).

In addition to the mismatch motivated by human antecedents and *which*, Table 1 also includes sporadic examples of non-human antecedents resumed by the relativizer *who*. This is a less frequent combination, found in only four cases. Examples (9) and (10) clearly illustrate this mismatch:

(9) Saw this book Myths and Legends in of Singapore published by VJ Times *who got things like got chapters like Pulau Hantu* <ICE-SIN:S1A-030#269:1:B>

(10) And there's sort of contract car *who drive me to whatever the starting point is* <ICE-HK:S1A-100>

In some other cases, the combination between a non-human antecedent and *who* may easily be explained as the result of referential extensions, as in example (11), in which the antecedent *department stores* is used in combination with the relativizer *who*, but the interpretation making reference to 'the people who work there' being very clear:

(11) But anyway anyway I think of all the local stores ah I mean the department stores they are the one of the ones *who are doing better lah*
    <ICE-SIN:S1A-082#58:1:A>

In addition, there are a few examples in which the pronoun *who* combines with *animals*, and although these are not in themselves human antecedents, the criterion of animacy can be used to justify the use of *who* in that animals, especially pets, may combine with *who*, as in example (12):

(12) The animals *who live in your house* are just just so lucky
    <ICE-SIN:S1A-100#125:1:A>

It is difficult, initially, to say whether these examples of lack of animacy agreement between antecedent and relativizer constitute planning mistakes or emergent features in the varieties under examination. Although they are not very frequent, there are several arguments in favor of their consideration as relevant linguistic features. The laxity in the agreement rules can be interpreted as an instance of simplification. Such simplification strategies are often associated with L2 varieties (Schneider 2007: 82, 89). Additionally, this phenomenon has been reported in a selection of postcolonial varieties of English analyzed by Gut and Coronel (2012: 231), which are further represented with the results provided by Table 1.

4.2 Relativizer *that* in NRRCs

Relative clauses are traditionally classified into restrictive or non-restrictive, depending on the information the relative clause provides about the antecedent and the degree of specificity of the antecedent. Apart from semantic cues, this distinction is supported grammatically, orthographically, prosodically and pragmatically. Restrictives are distinguished from non-restrictives essentially in terms of the type of noun used to license the relative clause and the type of relativizer used to introduce the relative clause, although this view has often been challenged, in that the dichotomy restrictive vs non-restrictive can be considered a continuum, rather than a binary category (Bache and Jacobsen 1980; Jacobsson 1994; see also Hundt and Denison 2013).

Whereas on a theoretical level restrictive and non-restrictive relative clauses are clearly distinguishable, when trying to classify real examples, the blurring of any such distinction becomes most evident. In order to classify the examples of my database, I followed the traditional semantic criterion of degree of specification of the antecedent. This analysis shows that the prescriptive use of *wh*-relativizers in non-restrictive relative clauses no longer holds, and *that* is usually found introducing non-restrictive relative clauses, as in example (13):

(13) It's very natural that focus is on Panduranga when it's a temple of Mahalaxmi <,> uhm <,> you find Mahalaxmi only there <,> not her husband *that is in Tirupati* <ICE-IND:S1A-004#59:1:B>

This variation of the relativizer introducing non-restrictive relative clauses has itself been noted in the literature (Newbrook 1998; Gut and Coronel 2012: 231) and is also listed in eWave (Kortmann and Lunkenheimer 2013: feature 185). According to eWave, this feature is absent in both IndE and HKE, contra my own data, as shown by Table 2:

Table 2: Frequency of *that* in non-restrictive relative clauses

	HKE	IndE	SingE
Non-restrictive *that*	14/99 (14.1%)	11/118 (9.3%)	–

The results from Table 2 are of special relevance in that they show the existence of a construction in Indian English which has not previously been reported, and further reinforces the existence of such a construction in Hong Kong English.

The frequent use of *that* in the context of non-restrictive clauses (around 10%) argues against considering this feature an error, and indicates that instead it should be an innovation in the system of relativizers. Several arguments can be used to justify this use of the relativizer *that*. Using *that* restores a levelling in the paradigm of relativizers, so that the same elements (*wh-* words and *that*) are available irrespective of the type of relative clause. This ties in nicely with the lack of clear boundaries between restrictive and non-restrictive relative clauses, more markedly so in spoken conversation. Although in grammars of English the possibility of *that* in non-restrictive relative clauses in PDE is only mentioned in passing (Quirk et al. 1985: 1250, Biber et al. 1999: 611, Huddleston and Pullum 2002: 1056), the fuzziness between restrictive and non-restrictive relative clauses has a long tradition in the literature of relativization.

4.3 *Where* referring to meanings other than 'place'

The favoured context of *where* in the realm of relativization is in nominal relative clauses (*Where I usually go is*...), in which the antecedent and the relativizer are fused. *Where* also occurs in standard English in adnominal relative clauses whose antecedent refers to a locative meaning, as in *the place where*, in combination with antecedents meaning 'place'. In some cases such combinations, in particular with generic antecedents such as *place*, have been considered fossilized expressions or collocations (Biber et al. 1999: 624).

It has been found, however, that the relativizer *where* may occur in combination with antecedents that do not express 'place', in early African American English (Kautzsch 2008: 543) and also in eWave (Kormann and Lunkenheimer 2013: feature 189), this being especially pervasive in English-based pidgins and creoles, and in L1 varieties such as Irish English.

Table 3 shows the occurrence of *where* expressing meanings other than place in my corpus:

Table 3: Frequency of *where* in non-locative contexts

	HKE	IndE	SingE
Non-locative *where*	–	–	4/41 (9.7%)

In these four examples *where* combines with antecedents expressing 'time' (e.g. *day, time(s), period*), as example (14) shows:

(14) Because they were the reporter was quite curious because Sunday is
the day *where* most of the stores make their money you see
<ICE-SIN:S1A-082#19:1:A>

A deeper analysis of the relativizer *where* in its default use indicating 'place' reveals a very high incidence in terms of absolute frequencies in both IndE and SingE. Its high frequency in IndE can be linked to the prevalence of *wh-* words in relative clauses over invariable relativizers, which has been explained in terms of a strong educational policy underlying the learning of English in India (Suárez-Gómez 2015). More surprising is the use of *where* in SingE, if we take into account that in this variety invariable *that* is the most frequent relativizer (Suárez-Gómez 2014: 9), as a result of L1 transfer from Chinese (Alsagoff and Lick 1998: 129), which resorts to invariable relativizers to introduce relative clauses. The hypothesis to account for the frequent use of *where* in SingE is that *where* may be becoming an invariable relativizer for Singaporeans (see Suárez-Gómez 2015), and this is supported mainly by the use of *where* in non-locative contexts, as well as by the high-frequency of use of *where* in only one context, considering that the favourite relativizers in adnominal relative clauses in this context are *that/zero*. Further analyses of SingE will confirm whether this hypothesis holds, and hence whether we can talk about a local use of the relativizer *where*.

4.4 *What* as an adnominal relativizer

In traditional grammars, the catalogue of *wh-* relativizers used to introduce adnominal relative clauses is restricted to *who/whom/whose* and *which*. Regional varieties of British English also include *what* in the repertoire of these relativizers. *What* as an adnominal relativizer has been present throughout the history of the English language, but it is no longer recognized as such in standard English. Rather, it tends to be employed to represent uneducated or dialectal speech (Poussa 1988: 443). On the oral level, dialectal studies acknowledge the use of *what* as an adnominal relativizer (see Wolfram and Christian (1976: 121) in Appalachian English, Schneider (1989: 214) in AAVE and Tagliamonte (2002) and Herrman (2003) in BrE). This phenomenon has also been reported by Kortmann and Lunkenheimer in eWave (2013: feature 190), occurring in many English-based Caribbean creoles, but also pervasive in traditional L1s such as East Anglian English. However, it is not found in HKE or IndE. This contrasts with the data from my corpus of Asian Englishes, in which this phenomenon is indeed attested, as Table 4 shows and example (15) illustrates:

Table 4: Frequency of what in adnominal relative clauses

	HKE	IndE	SingE
Adnominal *what*	–	8/644 (1.2%)	1/503 (0.2%)

(15) But one difference *what I find* is that in this generation maybe it is the influence of the TV <ICE-IND:S1A-072#43:1:B>

The fact that eight out of nine examples in my data are from the variety of English spoken in India reflects previous findings on the distribution of relativizers in this variety, in which it was found that *wh-* words in adnominal relative clauses are particularly frequent in Indian English over varieties such as HKE and SingE (Suárez-Gómez 2014: 9; 2015). This preference for *wh-* words in IndE is seen to be reinforced by the use of a minor relativizer, *what* as an adnominal relativizer.

A careful analysis of these examples reveals that the most frequent antecedent used in this context is represented by generic antecedents such as *thing* on its own or as part of a compound (e.g. indefinite pronoun *everything*) (see example (16)) in what seems to function as a sort of fossilized combination.

(16) Well is it the dowry are we going to be, are we going to, get everything *what you want* <ICE-IND:S1A-074#57:1:A>

This combination is also commonly found in GloWbE (Davies and Fuchs 2015), based on data from written sources, as examples (17)–(19) illustrate:

(17) Only *thing what we have to do* is to establish within ourselves our Spirit. (Australian English)

(18) *The thing what strikes me* is that lately the "gatekeeper" bashing has subsided. (Irish English)

(19) Big bloggers are making lots of money online and I'd say *the same thing what they told us.* (Bangladesh English)

As was the case with *that* in non-restrictive contexts, it seems clear that the use of *what* as an adnominal relativizer should also be taken into consideration as an option in relative clauses: it is frequently used in different varieties of English, and is favoured in contexts in which it resumes a generic antecedent, acting as a sort of collocation. In addition, its use in written contexts allows us to conclude that this feature is more established, especially in Indian English.

4.5 Double relativizers

Another feature reported in eWave is the "relativizer doubling" phenomenon (Kortmann and Lunkenheimer 2013: feature 191), that is, the presence of two relative markers to introduce a relative clause, as in example (20) from AAVE. Even though it may be found in L1s, L2s, pidgins and creoles, this feature is very rare.

(20) But these, these little fellahs *that which had stayed befo' God prayin'...* (Schneider 2008: 770, EAAVE)

My database also contains cases of double relativizers, as shown in Table 5.

Table 5: Frequency of double relativizers

	HKE	IndE	SingE
Double relativizers	8/779 (1%)	–	8/503 (1.6%)

My first interpretation was that these were simply performance errors, either planning errors, slips of the tongue or false starts, bearing in mind that in spoken language it is very difficult to know if such cases are intentional ("relativizer doubling") or are merely instances of repetition associated with false starts in spoken discourse. The latter interpretation also makes sense if we take into account that all the examples which contain a doubled relativizer in my corpus use the same form, either *that* (21) or a *wh-* word (22):

(21) The only thing *that that give me sub to it* is the pay <ICE-SIN:S1A-088#258:1:A>

(22) Cecilia said she has a friend *who who knows some shops that will bring her around* so she'll call me along <ICE-SIN:S1A-001#13:1:B>

In fact, the error interpretation seems the most feasible interpretation in examples such as (23), in which there is not only repetition of the relativizer, but also several other repeated words (example (24)):

(23) Because it's difficult it's difficult to find a partner *who is who who's* on the same level as you <ICE-SIN:S1A-063#73:1:A>

(24) I think you better discuss some *which country you want to visit which countries which which which you want to visit* in Europe <ICE-SIN:S1A-038#140:1:A>

Surprisingly, a search of the combinations *that that, which which* and *who who* in GloWbe (Davies and Fuchs 2015) shows that *that that* is entirely absent from the corpus, as opposed to *which which* and *who who* which do occur in the varieties of interest here. As noted above, the results from GloWbE are from written sources, which means that they are used as a conscious device and therefore they are less likely to be interpreted as planning errors and false starts.

Although the lack of any discernable pattern in the distribution of these combinations prevents us from reaching any definite conclusion as to whether they can be considered a sporadic indigenized feature or errors, their presence in sources based on written data – as well as in catalogues of language variation in different varieties of English – reinforces their interpretation as potential relevant features.

4.6 Correlative structures

A recurrent element in my corpus, and which also entails repetition, is the 'correlative structure'. Such structures are typically cases of left-dislocated constructions in that a constituent is preposed (placed at the left periphery) and then repeated by means of a pronoun in the main clause, as in examples (25), in which the subject is dislocated, and (26), with object dislocation:

(25) You know most of the people *who who go to north for medical studies* <,> *they* are really scared <ICE-IND:S1A-090#97:1:B>

(26) The problem *that you work on* <,> you have to present *that* also <ICE-IND:S1A-013#151:1:B>

In these constructions, a constituent is fronted and then resumed by a pronominal item, illustrating left-dislocation, a common syntactic device in discourse to give salience to the topic in conversation (Givón 1993: 210). Left-dislocated structures are also simplifying devices (Prince 1997: 124) in that they facilitate discourse processing.

They are considered ungrammatical in present-day Standard English. Nevertheless, they are listed in Kortmann and Lunkenheimer's catalogue (2013: feature 196) with special incidence in Malaysian English. These constructions are also reported by Lange with respect to Indian English (2012: 161) and one of the reasons she gives to account for them is the substrate influence (2012: 163, 194) from Dravidian languages, where clausal relative clauses are avoided and instead topic-comment structures are favoured (see also Sridhar 1992: 144). Thus, the structural constraints on relative clause formation shared by Dravidian languages, achieved by participialization, are retained (Sridhar 1992: 144).

In my database, correlative structures are also recorded, and they are very much a recurrent feature of Indian English, as illustrated in Table 6:

Table 6: Frequency of correlative structures

	HKE	IndE	SingE
Correlative structures	–	27/644 (4.2%)	–

Table 6 shows that these constructions are confined to IndE (27/644 examples, 4.2%), being absent in both Hong Kong and Singapore English.

In addition to Dravidian languages, L1 transfer from Hindi can also be proposed as an influencing factor. Relative clauses in Hindi resort to the so-called "non-reduction relativization strategy" (Maxwell 1979: 358; McCawley 2004). In example (27) relativization is achieved by means of the pronominal element *jo* which is then repeated (*vo*) in the main clause (Srivastav 1991:642):

(27) [RC ***jo*** laRkii kjaRii hai] ***vo*** lambii hai
　　　　who girl standing is DEM tall is
　　'The girl who is standing is tall'

In conclusion, the use of correlative structures in Indian English seems to represent an indigenized grammatical feature motivated by the combination of the superstratal way of forming relative clauses influenced by substratal features, leading thus to a construction which exists neither in the L1 nor in the target language, but which becomes an innovative structure in the emergent variety.

4.7 Preposition chopping

Relativizers functioning as complements of a preposition usually show two different structures: a structure in which the preposition remains stranded, and this may occur with any type of relativizer, either *that* and zero and, less frequently but possible, a *wh-* word and a structure in which the preposition is pied-piped to the front with the relativizer it licenses. This latter structure is only possible with *wh-* relativizers. A look at eWave reveals that there is a third possibility, which Kortmann and Lunkenheimer call "preposition chopping" (2013: feature 198), and which refers to the phenomenon whereby a stranded preposition is deleted, but where the meaning can be construed from the context, as in example (28):

(28) … like a big yard *that you do gardening an'all* [in deleted]
(African English, Mesthrie 2008c: 629)

This feature is pervasive in IndE and Malaysian English, as reported in eWave, but it also occurs in L1 varieties (Australian English and Irish English), L2 varieties (Cameroon English and Indian South African English) and English-based pidgins (Butler English) and creoles (Jamaican Creole). In eWave it is not recorded in HKE, as opposed to the information provided by Newbrook (1998: 48–49) and Gisborne (2000: 366) who observe this feature in contexts of verbs which have a particle, either prepositional or phrasal verbs. According to Newbrook, this frequency in Asian varieties which emerged as a result of contact between English and Chinese, is explained through L1 transfer.

My corpus contains examples illustrating this phenomenon from the three varieties (see examples (29)–(31)), as summarized in Table 7:

Table 7: Frequency of preposition chopping

	HKE	IndE	SingE
Preposition chopping	4/57 (7%)	1/40 (2.5%)	1/31 (3.2%)

(29) They've reached a real good status to over the men in each and every field *that they have participated* <CE-IND:S1A-011#45:1:F>

(30) Uh the one *that I am very interested* is the one at do you pronounce as Bifort or what <ICE-SIN:S1A-043#162:1:B>

(31) It's kind of vaguely related to this piece *that I was been talking*
<ICE-HK:S1A-019#268:1:A>

One example from each variety is clearly not representative enough to reach any definite conclusions, but there are four examples in HKE, the same number as pied-piped constructions in this variety. In that it arises through the influence of the substrate, as observed by Newbrook (1998), it is surprising that it does not have the same incidence in SingE, a variety of English in which Chinese also plays a role. An additional argument to justify this structure is related to a simplification strategy associated with L2 varieties whereby non-functional elements are avoided in search of a more isomorphic structure. In these constructions the preposition is not necessary in that the meaning can be easily inferred from the context.

5 Summary and conclusions

This study has presented an analysis of innovative features related to relativization in three Asian varieties of English, those of Hong Kong, India and Singapore. Such features are innovative in that they cannot be found in standard English, and thus their existence in the different Englishes cannot be attributed to the target language, in this case British English, the superstrate of the three varieties. Likewise, these features are also global, since they occur in different varieties of English with no geographic relation and therefore their presence in these Englishes cannot be explained wholly in terms of the target language. These innovative structures in L2 varieties of English have often been considered performance or planning errors, and thus omitted from statistical analyses. The present paper challenges this view and demonstrates that, although they occur less frequently than other more canonical constructions, and are generally regarded as low-frequency phenomena, they are not isolated cases and deserve deeper examination. They occur in different varieties and represent local features of contact varieties which may be emerging tentatively and which over time may consolidate and become innovative features. Such an interpretation is reinforced by the fact that the varieties are norm-developing, and have already reached phase 3, a phase in which new linguistic features are displayed.

These features include the use of relativizer *that* in non-restrictive relative clauses, *what* as an adnominal relativizer and the coreferentiality mismatch between human antecedents and the relativizer *which*. They occur in all the varieties analyzed, and are also reported in other varieties of English, both L2 varieties and traditional L1 varieties. These three features have a long tradition in the history of the English language and, although they are not accepted in prescriptive grammars, their extended use throughout the Anglophone world, both in Inner and Outer varieties, demonstrates their relevance in analyses of relative clauses. In the case of *what* as an adnominal relativizer, the presence in written sources illustrated by GloWbE (Davies and Fuchs 2015) reinforces such conclusion.

There are other features which are much more exotic in the sense that they occur in one variety, yet occur only very sporadically, or are even absent, in other varieties. In this case, rather than a global change, we are dealing with a localized grammatical innovation occurring in varieties from the Outer Circle. Among this group of features we find the use of non-locative *where* in SingE, which seems to have become an invariable relativizer in this variety of English. Other local features are the use of double relativizers in HKE and SingE. The fact that they are present in written sources, and also documented in GloWbE (Davies and Fuchs 2015), shows that they are established features. Finally, two additional features of a local nature have been attributed to substratal effects. One is the occurrence of preposition chopping in HKE, from Chinese transfer, and the other is illustrated by 'correlative constructions', a recurring feature of Indian English, influenced by substrate languages, both the Dravidian and the Hindi dominant L1s.

References

Aarts, Flor. 1993. *Who, whom, that* and Ø in two corpora of spoken English. *English Today* 35. 19–22.
Alsagoff, Lubna & Ho Chee Lick. 1998. The relative clause in colloquial Singapore English. *World Englishes* 17(2). 127–138.
Bache, Carl & Leif Kvistgaard Jakobsen. 1980. On the distinction between restrictive and non-restrictive relative clauses in modern English. *Lingua* 52. 243–267.
Ball, Catherine. 1996. A diachronic study of relative markers in spoken and written English, *Language Variation and Change* 8(2). 227–258.
Biber, Douglas, Stig Johansson, Geoffrey Leech, Susan Conrad & Edward Finegan. 1999. *Longman grammar of spoken and written English*. Harlow: Longman.
Cheshire, Jenny, David Adger & Sue Fox. 2013. Relative *who* and the actuation problem. *Lingua* 126. 51–77.
Davies, Mark & Robert Fuchs. 2015. Expanding horizons in the study of World Englishes with the 1.9 billion word Global Web-based English Corpus (GloWbE). *English World-Wide* 36. 1–28.
Erdmann, Peter. 1980. On the history of subject contact-clauses in English. *Folia Linguistica Historica* I: 139–170.
Gisborne, Nikolas. 2000. Relative clauses in Hong Kong English. *World Englishes* 19. 357–371.
Givón, Talmy. 1993. *English Grammar. A Function-based Introduction*. Amsterdam & Philadelphia: Benjamins.

Gut, Ulrike & Lilian Coronel. 2012. Relatives worldwide. In Marianne Hundt & Ulrike Gut (eds.), *Mapping unity and diversity worldwide: Corpus-based studies of New Englishes*, 215–242. Amsterdam: Benjamins.
Guy, Gregory R. & Robert Bayley. 1995. On the choice of relative pronouns in English. *American Speech* 70(2). 148–172.
Herrmann, Tanja. 2003. *Relative clauses in dialects of English: A typological approach*. Freiburg, Germany: University of Freiburg dissertation.
Huber, Magnus. 2012. Syntactic and variational complexity in British and Ghanaian English. Relative clause formation in the written parts of the International Corpus of English. In Bernd Kortmann & Benedikt Szmrecyani (eds.), *Linguistic complexity: Second language acquisition, indigenization, contact*, 218–242. Berlin: Walter de Gruyter.
Huddleston, Rodney & Geoffrey K. Pullum. 2002. *The Cambridge grammar of the English language*. Cambridge: Cambridge University Press.
Hundt, Marianne. 2009. Global feature – local norms? A case study on the progressive passive. In Lucia Siebers & Thomas Hoffmann (eds.), *World Englishes – Problems, Properties and Prospects*. Amsterdam & Philadelphia: Benjamins, 287–308.
Hundt, Marianne. 2016. *Error, feature, (incipient) change – or something else altogether?* On the role of low-frequency deviant patterns for the description of Englishes. In E. Seoane and C. Suárez-Goméz (eds.), *Worlds Englishes: New Theoretical and Methodological Considerations*, 37–60. Amsterdam: Benjamins.
Hundt, Marianne & David Denison. 2013. Defining relatives. *Journal of English Linguistics* 41(2). 135–167.
Hund, Tony T.N. 2001. Interlanguage analysis as an input to grammar teaching, *PASAA* 19. 337–356.
Hung, Tony T.N. 2009. Innovation in second language phonology. In Lucia Siebers & Thomas Hoffmann (eds.), *World Englishes – Problems, Properties and Prospects*, 227–38. Amsterdam: Benjamins.
Jacobsson, Bengt. 1994. Nonrestrictive relative that-clauses revisited. *Studia Neophilologica* 66. 181–195.
Kautzsch, Alexander. 2008. Earlier African American English: morphology and syntax. In Edgar W. Schneider (ed.), *Varieties of English. Vol 2. The Americas and the Caribbean*, 534–550. Berlin & New York: Mouton de Gruyter.
Keenan, Edward & Bernd Comrie. 1977. Noun phrase accessibility and universal grammar. *Linguistic Inquiry* 8(1). 63–99.
Kortmann, Bernd & Kerstin Lunkenheimer (eds.). 2013. *The electronic world atlas of varieties of English* [eWAVE]. Leipzig: Max Planck Institute for Evolutionary Anthropology. http://www.ewave-atlas.org/ (28 January 2014).
Lange, Claudia. 2012. *The syntax of spoken Indian English*. Amsterdam: Benjamins.
Maxwell, Dan. 1979. Strategies of relativization and NP accessibility. *Language* 55. 352–371.
McCawley, James D. 2004. Remarks on adsentential, adnominal and extraposed relative clauses in Hindi. In Dayal Veneeta & Anoop Mahajan (eds.), *Clause structure in South Asian languages*. Dordrecht: Kluwer, 291–311.
Mukherjee, Joybrato. 2007. Steady states in the evolution of New Englishes: present-day Indian English as an equilibrium. *Journal of English Linguistics* 35. 157–187.
Newbrook, Mark. 1998. Which way? That way? Variation and ongoing changes in the English relative clause. *World Englishes* 17(1). 43–59.

Poussa, Patricia. 1988. The relative WHAT: two kinds of evidence. In Jacek Fisiak (ed.), *Historical and Dialectology. Regional and Social*, 443–474. Berlin: Mouton de Gruyter.
Prince, Ellen F. 1997. On the functions of left-dislocation in English discourse. In Akio Kamio (ed.), *Directions in Functional Linguistics*, 117–143. Amsterdam: Benjamins.
Quirk, Randolph. 1957. Relative clauses in educated spoken English. *English Studies* 38. 97–109.
Quirk, Randolph, Sidney Greenbaum, Geoffrey Leech & Jan Svartvik. 1985. *A comprehensive grammar of the English language*. London: Longman.
Rissanen, Matti. 1999. Syntax. In Roger Lass (ed.), *The Cambridge History of the English Language, vol. III, 1476–1776*, 187–331. Cambridge: Cambridge University Press.
Romaine, Suzanne. 1982. *Socio-historical Linguistics. Its Status and Methodology*. Cambridge: Cambridge University Press.
Schneider, Edgar. 1989. *American earlier Black English*. Tuscaloosa: University of Alabama Press.
Schneider, Edgar. 2007. *Postcolonial English. Varieties around the world*. Cambridge: Cambridge University Press.
Schneider, Edgar W. (ed.). 2008. *Varieties of English. Vol 2. The Americas and the Caribbean*. Berlin and New York: Mouton de Gruyter.
Sridhar, Shikaripur N. 1992. The ecology of bilingual competence: Language interaction in the syntax of indigenized varieties of English. *World Englishes* 11(2–3). 141–150.
Srivastav, Venneta. 1991. The syntax and semantics of correlatives. *Natural Language and Linguistic Theory* 9(4). 637–686.
Suárez-Gómez, Cristina. 2014. Relative clauses in Southeast Asian Englishes, *Journal of English Linguistics* 42. 245–268.
Suárez-Gómez, Cristina. 2015. *The places where English is spoken*: adverbial relative clauses in World Englishes. *World Englishes* 34(4). 620–635.
Tagliamonte, Sali. 2002. Variation and change in the British relative marker system. In Patricia Poussa (ed.), *Dialect contact on the North Sea Littoral*, 147–165. Munich: Lincom Europa.
Tagliamonte, Sali, Jennifer Smith & Helen Lawrence. 2005. No taming the vernacular! Insights from the relatives in northern Britain. *Language Variation and Change* 17(1). 75–112.
Tottie, Gunnel. 1997. Relatively speaking. Relative marker usage in the British National Corpus. In Terttu Nevalainen & Leena Kahlas-Tarkka (eds.), *To explain the present: Studies in the changing English language in honour of Matti Rissanen*, 465–481. Helsinki: Société Néophilologique.
Tottie, Gunnel & Dawn Harvie. 2000. It's all relative: Relativization strategies in early African American English. In Shana Poplack (ed.), *The English history of African American English*, 198–230. Oxford: Blackwell.
Wolfram, Walt & Donna Christian. 1976. *Appalachian Speech*. Arlington, VA: Center for Applied Linguistics.

Databases

International corpus of English – homepage http://ice-corpora.net/ice/importantnote.htm

Rajend Mesthrie, Sean Bowerman and Tracey Toefy
Morphosyntactic typology, contact and variation: Cape Flats English in relation to other South African Englishes in the *Mouton World Atlas of Variation in English*[1]

Abstract: In this paper we present an overview of the morphosyntactic features of Cape Flats English, a variety that evolved among people formerly classified "coloured" in South Africa, as distinct from black and white groupings. We do so within the framework provided by Kortmann and Lunkenheimer (2012) in their comprehensive comparison of 235 morphosyntactic features in 74 varieties of English. Three major varieties of South African English featured in the survey (Black, White and Indian South African Englishes). This paper fills the gap in respect of Cape Flats English, which is demographically the major variety of English in the city of Cape Town and environs. The 235 features were rated according to their absence or presence in the dialect, and with due regard to frequency. These judgements were based on descriptions in the literature, heavily supplemented by our own observations and experience of the dialect. We conclude that, statistically, Cape Flats English coheres with all three varieties of South African English in the original survey; but more especially with White South African English. This similarity is in large part due to the influence of Afrikaans in Cape Flats English and White South African English, which has less influence on Black and Indian South African Englishes. In terms of theoretical focus, the paper provides an assessment of the methodology and generalisations of Kortmann and Lunkenheimer (2012). We argue that their typological-cum-geographical approach is a robust one. However, their general conclusion that variety type (pidgin/creole, L2, L1) is more important globally than geographical proximity does not apply in the case of South Africa, where areal and social convergence operates across the L1 vs L2 dichotomy. That the South African varieties should show overall morphosyntactic similarities in global terms, despite the degree of social segregation in the country's past, is a new insight.

---

[1] Funding for this research comes from the National Research Foundation's SARCHI chair grant of Rajend Mesthrie (number 64805) for Migration, Language and Social Change, as well as the University of Cape Town, via the Research Committee. We are grateful to Bernd Kortmann and his FRIAS colleagues at Freiburg who generated important graphs used in the paper, and Bertus Van Rooy of North West University for his insights from other South African corpora.

Rajend Mesthrie, Sean Bowerman and Tracey Toefy, University of Cape Town

DOI 10.1515/9783110429657-007

Keywords: Mouton World Atlas of Variation in English (MWAVE), South African English, Cape Flats English, White South African English (WSAE), Black South African English (BSAE), Indian South African English (ISAE), Afrikaner South African English (ASAE), Afrikaans, Coloured community, L1 varieties, L2 varieties, bilingualism, NeighborNet

1 Introduction

This chapter serves two purposes. It gives an overview of the morphosyntactic features of Cape Flats English, a major variety spoken in Cape Town and surrounding areas (henceforth CFE). This overview is presented in terms of the layout of the *Mouton World Atlas of Variation in English* (or MWAVE Kortmann and Lunkenheimer 2012, henceforth MWAVE). Three major varieties of South African English are treated in MWAVE, but CFE is not one of them. After presenting the salient features of the variety we offer a comparison between the four varieties from South Africa in terms of a NeighborNet diagram (Bryant and Moulton 2004) that gives a graphic placement of the four varieties in terms of each other, as well as their overall place in the atlas. The second purpose of this chapter is to offer an appraisal of MWAVE, its mechanisms and the plausibility of its placement of varieties.

2 Sociohistorical background

English in South Africa exists in a highly multilingual context. Even the variety most directly traceable to (southern) British descent (from 1820 onwards) has been influenced by co-existence with other languages, viz. Afrikaans and African languages like Zulu, Xhosa and Sotho. For the most part this influence is lexical, though there is some syntactic and phonetic influence from Afrikaans, especially (see e.g. Branford 1996; Jeffery and Van Rooy 2004; and Bekker 2009 respectively). This statement is less true of varieties of English that developed as second languages. Here the impact of the first languages of various communities, as well as conditions of separation long characteristic of South Africa have resulted in influences at all levels of linguistic structure, not just the lexicon. A selection of references backing up this claim includes Bowerman (2004), Watermeyer (1996), Buthelezi (1995) and Mesthrie (2004a and b) for syntax and Lanham and Macdonald (1979), Van Rooy (2004) and Mesthrie (2004c) for phonology of the different varieties. These references cover four of the five major varieties of English in South Africa: White South African English (WSAE), Black South African English (BSAE), Indian South African English (ISAE) and Afrikaner South African English (ASAE). The ethnic/colour labels are unfortunate, but remain a tangible reminder of a hierarchical and segregated past, whose main sociolinguistic effects remain (see e.g. de Klerk 1996; Coetzee-Van Rooy and Van Rooy 2005). However, much new scholarship has documented trends amongst the young middle-classes that go against the old labelling, largely due to new social networks being forged via multiracial schooling (e.g. Mesthrie 2010; Toefy 2014; Wilmot 2014). These studies are largely of a sociophonetic nature and will accordingly not be touched on here. The above categorisation should not serve to exclude the speech of new migrants, especially from other parts of Africa, whose influences in the post-apartheid era await detailed study. Varieties spoken by "Coloured" communities are treated in detail below.

The South African sense of the term 'Coloured' needs explication, referring to a group or groups that are considered not 'White', 'Black' or 'Indian'. The term is not an innocent one: it is highly contested in South Africa, because the labelling was partly imposed from outside, by people in power who have used the categorisation largely to exclude people from civil privileges. As Zimitri Erasmus (2001:15) puts it: "blackness and whiteness are [not] themselves given, coherent and homogeneous identities". The exploitative and traumatic consequences for people put into the "Coloured" category are discussed inter alia by Erasmus (2001). Opposition to the term largely comes from academics and the politically aware. The historian Adhikari (2009: x) cautions that states and ruling groups do not create identities among their subjects and "while they may reinforce, constrain or manipulate such identities with varying degrees of success, bearers in the first instance create and negotiate their own social identities". On the ground, historical and social forces – including enforced segregation – have shaped a community consciousness that accepts terms like *bruin* (Afrikaans for 'brown') or *Coloured*.

It was partly for reasons of political sensitivity that in advising Malan (1996) Mesthrie coined the term "Cape Flats English" in about 1994, to avoid the then highly charged label "Cape Coloured English". The term CFE is not, however, totally accurate, as there are other varieties spoken on the vast Cape Flats, a mostly sandy and wind-swept region between the urban centres of Cape Town and Stellenbosch, set aside in apartheid times for "non-white" occupation. Black South African English is also spoken here as a second language by mainly Xhosa speakers. And there are enclaves of Indian suburbs within the Cape Flats. However, Coloured people form a demographic majority on the flats and in greater Cape Town, a statistic that has not changed in the post-apartheid era, despite in-migration from other parts of South Africa and the continent. More importantly, the English of Coloured people exerts some influence on the speech of Black and Indian children in some schools and youthful peer groups (see Mesthrie and McCormick 1994; Meierkord 2012). It might be argued that the time for opposition to apartheid labelling is over and that the term "Cape Coloured English" be deemed more appropriate. However, the term "Coloured English" to describe a single entity in South Africa is probably not warranted, since region and ethnicity interact in complex ways – see Mesthrie (2013) for /t/ and /d/ amongst Indian and Coloured groups and Mesthrie, Chevalier and Dunne (2015) for the BATH vowel. For the time being we will stick to the CFE label.

Historically, the making of communities that were later to be labelled "Coloured" is a complex one, with different regional nuances. Several major groupings and encounters contributed to this history: the indigenous Khoi and San strands, a European strand of Dutch and allied settlers and sailors from the 17th C, a Xhosa strand, and a large contingent of slaves from the East Indies (of what are today Indonesia and India), Madagascar, and parts of Africa like Angola and Mozambique. A loose association of people treated largely as an underclass, nevertheless formed some coherence around the use of a particular version of Cape Dutch. This variety was an important feeder into what gelled into Afrikaans, and the term 'Kaaps' is in vogue for a modern urban development, showing much code-switching with English (see McCormick 1995, 2003; Roberge 2002). Afrikaans and its Kaaps instantiation are important background influences over CFE, and several of the features itemised in the appendix owe their existence to similarities with this substrate.

Although speakers of CFE do not have a name for the variety, this is in fact true of all the varieties of South African English. It is the linguists who have proffered labels on the grounds of mainly linguistic characteristics; no one really claims to speak "Black", "White" or "Coloured" varieties (see Coetzee-Van Rooy and Van Rooy 2005 on issues of labelling). In the case of CFE, although residing in the same city, there are vocabulary items that are salient within the community that are unused and even unknown to most White speakers in the city. These include *crown birthday* 'a special birthday in which one's age coincides with the day of the month one was born'; the adjective *never-minded* 'careless, not caring about doing one's work properly' and *quickly* 'for a little while' (as in *hold on quickly*). Perhaps the most identifiable feature of the dialect is its intonation and other rhythmical patterns, which have yet to be studied in the linguistic detail they deserve. The literature on CFE is relatively small, but pithy. Full length studies are McCormick (1989, 2003) on sociolinguistic dynamics and patterns of code switching with Afrikaans; Wood (1987) on phonetics and social differentiation; Finn (2002) on phonetics and convergences with Afrikaans; and Toefy (2014) on post-apartheid sociophonetic differentiation among younger speakers. Good chapter length overviews are McCormick (1995, 2004), Malan (1996) and Finn (2004).

The *Mouton World Atlas of Variation in English* (Kortmann and Lunkenheimer 2012) is a comprehensive comparative survey of the use of 235 morphosyntactic features in 74 varieties of English. These varieties are drawn from across the spectrum of Inner Circle Englishes, Outer Circle L2 Englishes, as well as English-based Pidgins and Creoles, but not the EFL of the Expanding Circle. The project utilised the NeighbourNet statistical technique to produce clusters of varieties according to their morphosyntactic characteristics. Of particular interest to World Englishes studies is the fact that L2 varieties from Africa and Asia (plus Malta and Fiji) form one branch distinct from the other MWAVE varieties. This paper will examine the results for South African English – viz. L1 White SAE, historically the main and most influential variety; L2 Black SAE, now growing in importance as a major L2 of the country and majority dialect of parliament; and Indian SAE, a "language shift variety" that arose as an L2 that then stabilised with limited contact with White SAE.

The present study uses the template of Kortmann and Lunkenheimer (2012), who produced a checklist of 235 mainly morphosyntactic features that showed some degree of variation in varieties of present-day English. Their survey of 74 varieties included 18 ESL varieties, 30 regional varieties of L1 English and 26 English-based pidgins and Creoles. The categories used by the editors were slightly different, but do not affect the present analysis: low-contact traditional L1 dialects; high-contact L1 varieties; L2 varieties; Pidgins; Creoles. CFE does not fit readily into either categorisation, since it encompasses a range from L2 speakers of English, through fluent ambilinguals having roughly equal proficiency in English and Afrikaans, to L1 speakers (with secondary competence in Afrikaans). In this sense it might be analysable in terms of Schenider's (2007) framework for the evolution of Englishes (see further Coetzee-Van Rooy (2014) and Van Rooy (2014) on the possible application of this model to South Africa). The 235 features of the MWAVE survey were divided into 13 sections as follows: I *Pronouns*; II *Noun phrase*; III *Tense and aspect*; IV *Modal verbs* ; V *Verb morphology* ; VI *Voice* VII *Negation*; VIII *Agreement*; IX *Relativization*; X *Complementation*; XI *Adverbial subordination*; XII *Adverbs and prepositions*; XIII *Discourse organization and word order*. The features analysed are the most common ones reported in the 'World Englishes' and English dialectology literature that differ from the grammar of standard English. The rating responses per individual item devised by Kortmann and Lunkenheimer are as follows: *obligatory or pervasive (A)*; *neither pervasive nor extremely rare (B)*; *extremely rare (C)*; *absent (D)*; *not applicable (X)*; *no information available (?)*. In the appendix we itemise the features of CFE that fall under the first three categories as A, B and C respectively, with examples. These features and the ratings are based on our experience of the variety, notes taken over an extended period, as well as interviews with speakers reported on in Mesthrie (2013) and Toefy (2014).

3 Notable aspects of the MWAVE profile of CFE

The most characteristic features of CFE result from being part of a bilingual repertoire (with Afrikaans) for a majority of its speakers. The intimate bilingualism involves extensive switching and mixing in informal contexts, though in the most formal contexts and in communicating with outsiders there is a large degree of "unmixing". Two paradoxical statements by interviewees in Kay McCormick's (1989) extensive research in parts of District Six, Cape Town in the 1980s capture the intimacy of this bilingualism. One speaker remarked "When I speak Afrikaans I use mainly English words", while another responded to the question "Which languages do you speak" with "*Ek kan net Engels praat*". The latter speaker stated, without apparent irony, that he could only speak English, but did so entirely in Afrikaans. McCormick convincingly demonstrates that a consequence of this community bilingualism is a large degree of convergence between English and Afrikaans, not necessarily found among monolingual or standard speakers outside the community. Where vocabulary is concerned, there is a give and take between the two languages. An Afrikaans word like *sturvy* 'stiff, stuck up' (of persons) or *deurmekaar* ('mixed up, confused') might be retained when a person is using English, for their expressive informal qualities. As McCormick shows, lexical switching in the other direction is more common in formal discourse, e.g. at a community meeting words like *meeting, functions, minutes* and *chairman* predominate to the exclusion of the standard Afrikaans equivalents. Convergence is also notable in the syntax of the two codes. Like Dutch and German, Afrikaans is a "V2 language", which means that the tensed constituent (auxiliary or verb) appears in the second position of the declarative main clause (Ponelis 1991: 495f). Verbs only hold tense when they occur without an auxiliary, so the lexical verb only appears in the second clausal position if it is unaccompanied by an auxiliary. Where the verb occurs together with the auxiliary, it is the auxiliary that occupies the second clausal position, and the verb appears in the final position in the clause, i.e. after the object. For example:

No auxiliary, verb tensed and in second position:
(1) Die   kinders   skop   die   bal.
    the   children   kick   the   ball
    'The children kick the ball'

Simple past: auxiliary 'het' tensed, and in second position; Verb final
(2) Die   kinders   het   die   bal   ge-skop
    the   children   PAST   the   ball   PAST-kick
    'The children kicked the ball.'

In subordinate clauses, the tensed element occurs in clause-final position. If the verb is tensed (i.e. unaccompanied by an auxiliary), then it appears in the final position; if accompanied by an auxiliary, then the auxiliary appears in the final slot, and the verb takes up the penultimate position:

(3) ... dat   die   kinders   die   bal   skop
        that   the   children   the   ball   kick
    '... that the children kick the ball'

(4) ... dat   die   kinders   die   bal   geskop   het
        that   the   children   the   ball   PAST.kick   PAST
    '... that the children kicked the ball'

McCormick (1995: 205) finds that these rules are sometimes violated in District Six bilingual speech, with sentences like *Ons moet study altwee* ('We must study both') being a common alternative to the standard Afrikaans equivalent *Ons moet altwee bestudeer*. For the purposes of this chapter, the examples that go the other way round are the more relevant. A frequent rule in CFE is to place time adverbials before place adverbials if they occur in a sequence. Thus *I'm going now home* instead of *I'm going home now* shows a word-order preference of Afrikaans. Likewise adjacency violations which permit a time adverbial to intervene between a verb and its subcategorized direct object NP may occur under Afrikaans influence: *My daddy bring me tonight chips*. This sentence shows another convergent feature: the use of the present for the near future [feature 117]. (The lack of the –s concord on the verb is discussed in the next paragraph). Another tense feature that McCormick argues to be based on Afrikaans is the use of unstressed *do* [feature 103], as a convergence towards the usual way of expressing the past tense in Afrikaans by *het* + *ge-* + unmarked verb. Here *het* is historically the perfect auxiliary 'have' and *ge-* the perfect prefix. In present day Afrikaans, this perfect 'auxiliary + past participle' construction is the norm for past tense constructions, the simple past and present perfect no longer being distinguished. An alternate explanation for the impetus for unstressed *do* by Mesthrie (1999) is offered below. Another example of calquing or near-calquing involving past verbs comes from idioms like *(X) did scold him out* '(X) scolded him; gave him a thorough scolding'. The Afrikaans template is given in (5) below:

(5) *(X) het   hom   uit-ge-skel*
     PAST   him   out-PAST-scold
     '(X) gave him a good scolding'.

Similar idioms like *to throw her wet* 'to splash her' and *to throw someone with a stone* 'to throw a stone at someone' show calquing involving Afrikaans syntax and lexis. One of our favourite sentences involving the latter construction is *He threw me over the hedge with a stone* 'He threw a stone over the hedge at me'. Since this example given in Pettman (1913) is from an Afrikaans-English bilingual speaker from outside the CFE community, it is an example of the overlaps between CFE and Afrikaner English, or even between CFE and broader varieties of SAE characteristic of Afrikaans-English bilinguals. The example shows the different semantics of the Afrikaans verb *gooi* 'to throw' which can also mean 'to hit, hurt by throwing'.

Convergence can also be detected in the lack of verb concord marking in the present sg. in CFE (or actually variable marking of *–s* for 3rd person sg.; feature 170), since Afrikaans verbs do not conjugate for number. As McCormick (2003: 227) concedes, sentences like *Then he pick them up* could be a second language acquisition feature (showing the selective production of redundant markers) or be based on the Afrikaans system. Finally, some prominent discourse markers complete the picture of convergence via code-switching turned borrowing. The invariant tag *nê* 'not so, isn't it' is particularly salient in the CFE community in Afrikaans as well as English. This also applies to the particle *mos* 'indeed, anyhow', whose exact meaning can be hard to pin down ('You are *mos* going to the shop, so you may as well get milk for me') – see Jantjies and Van Dulm (2012).

Mesthrie (1999) suggests that in two important features CFE may well show little or no Afrikaans influence, despite claims to the contrary. These features are more likely retentions of historical features of English that were lost in Standard and/or in White SAE. The first construction is the dative of advantage in *I'm going to buy me a car*, which is frequently misanalysed by teachers as a non-standard reflexive. But as feature 9 of the MWAVE survey shows, this is a feature of *inter alia* Irish English, Chicano English and Bahamas English (rated B in all three varieties), and was once standard (Mesthrie 1999). Since a corpus of settler letters of 19th C South Africa shows the dative of advantage to be a regular feature (*I dug me a well*), it would appear to have passed on to second language speakers and survives in CFE, but not in mainstream White SAE. Mesthrie proposes that this analysis also holds in part for the use of unstressed *do* in CFE (*Who did throw that?*, *I did eat that*). He queries whether this is an Afrikaans-based feature based on a form like (dialectal) Afrikaans in (6) below:

(6) *Ek het daai ge-ëet*
    I   PAST that PAST-eat'.
    'I ate that'

Firstly, the equivalent verb form in Afrikaans cited as a calque for unstressed *do* is not *doen* 'do', but *het* 'have'. Secondly, there is no equivalent in the English form to the prefix *ge-*, the historically perfect prefix in Afrikaans. (Such a form would be something like archaic English *y(e)-* as a prefix). Mesthrie notes that on pragmatic grounds the analogy does not work very well either. The Afrikaans forms in *het* + *ge-* + verb stem are all unmarked, whereas English unstressed *do* serves a highlighting function with new information. More crucially, he provides ample evidence of unstressed *do* in the King James Bible as well as in missionary letters of 19th C Cape Colony, South Africa. Since Christianity was an important strand in the making of the Coloured community in the 19th C, it is likely that these were the main historical sources for unstressed *do*, which must therefore be taken as a retention, rather than innovation based on Afrikaans. However, as with the dative of advantage a degree of reinforcement from Afrikaans cannot be ruled out.

A final noteworthy aspect of the profile of CFE is its use of the second person plural *yous* (sometimes spelt *youse*), a form associated with Irish immigration and influence in places as far apart as Liverpool, New York and Sydney. In CFE the form has final devoicing (yet another convergent rule with Afrikaans), hence [ju:s]. It is not clear whether this is an example of Irish influence in the dialect or a coincidental innovation. Other possibly coincidental similarities with Irish English include (a) occasional examples of *do be*, but more so among children, (b) different scope of negation with *hope* and *doubt* (e.g. *I don't hope he'll come today* = 'I hope he won't come today'), and (c) the dative of advantage.

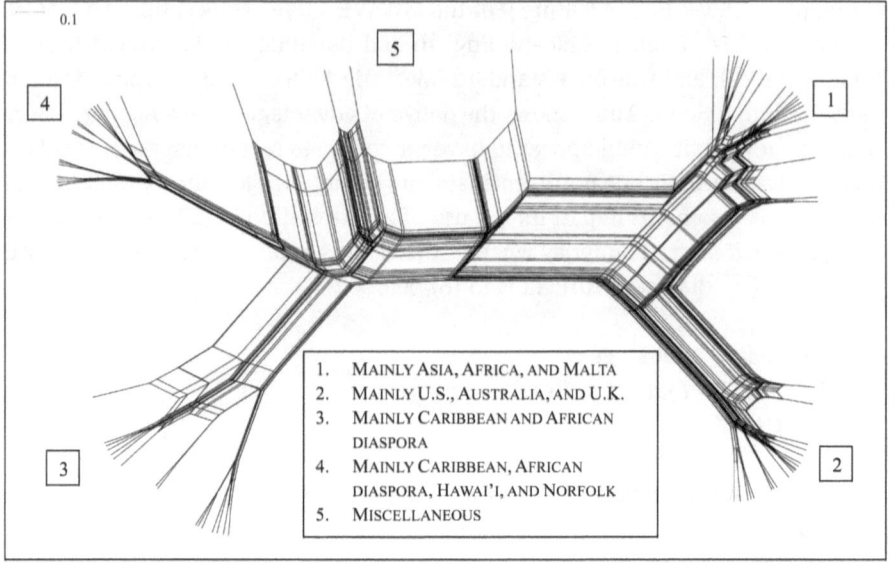

Figure 1: A Neighbornet comparison of 75 varieties of "World Englishes", showing similarities in a set of 134 linguistic features (courtesy Kortmann and Lunkenheimer)

4 The Neighbornet comparisons

Figure 1 is an update of a "Neighbornet" diagram compiled by Kortmann and Lunkenheimer (2012: 930), taking into account all 135 features of the 74 varieties originally studied in the project. Neighbornet is a powerful statistical tool that arises out of bioinformatics and genetic modelling (Bryant and Moulton 2004) and is used in linguistic typological characterisations (Cysouw 2007). In Figure 1 the different branches (or clusters) of the "fallen tree" represent distinct subsets within the data arrived at on the basis of similarities in linguistic features. The main branches do show a large degree of geographical cohesion. However, Kortmann and Lunkenheimer stress that variety type (L1, L2, Pidgin, or Creole) is an even stronger correlate than geography. Figure 1 is a revision of the original map in Kortmann and Lunkenheimer (2012: 930; larger version as insert, inside-back cover) that now includes CFE as a 75th variety to be slotted in.[2] As far

---

[2] We thank Bernd Kortmann and Kerstin Lunkenheimer for incorporating our completed questionnaire for CFE into their database in April 2013, and providing us with the revised diagrams produced here as figures 1 and 2.

as CFE is concerned, cluster 4, comprising South Asia, Africa and Malta, is of especial relevance.

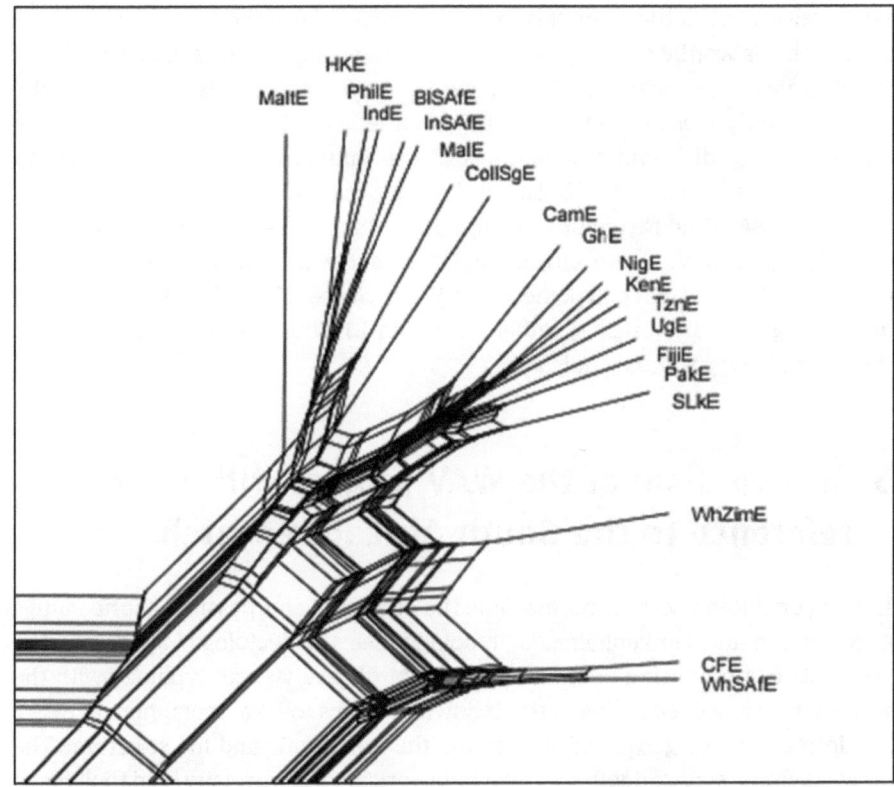

Figure 2: *A close-up of the bottom-left corner of figure 1, showing the placement of CFE within cluster1* (courtesy Kortmann and Lunkenheimer)

Figure 2 provides a close-up of cluster 1, which is made up of varieties from several areas: chiefly Africa and South Asia (Sri Lanka, Pakistan, India), and some varieties from the South Pacific (Fiji), Southeast Asia (Philippines, Malaysia, Singapore) and Europe (Malta). Africa presents the largest numbers of varieties in cluster 1: traditional L2 varieties of East Africa (Tanzania, Uganda, Kenya), West Africa (Ghana, Nigeria); Central Africa (Cameroon), the L1 varieties of Whites in Zimbabwe and South Africa, and the remaining varieties of South Africa. Figure 2 thus shows that purely on the basis of the 235 features of the survey, CFE slots in with other varieties of English in Africa, both L1 and L2, as well as with L2 varieties of South and Southeast Asia and a small miscellaneous group made up of Malta and Fiji. The similarities with Asia rest largely on similarities in processes of second language acquisition. Similarities with other African countries are suggestive of growing areal tendencies and the give-and-take between L1 Settler varieties and L2 varieties developed in colonial classrooms. This is worthy of further investigation. The comparison with South African varieties is what concerns us here. Figure 2 shows that CFE is closest to White SAE, and fairly close to Black and Indian varieties of SAE. This time the prime reason for the differential similarities is the influence of Afrikaans upon L1 White SAE, as well as on CFE. This influence occurs to a lesser extent in Black and Indian SAE. The Neighbornet comparisons thus make an important syntactic discrimination within South African Englishes that, while plausible, is not initially obvious. (We could have hypothesised CFE to cluster closely with varieties that are, or began as L2 varieties, rather than with L1 White SAE). For South Africa the methodology is thus vindicated.

5 An appraisal of the WAV project with main reference to the South African research

In this concluding section we examine the strengths and possible shortcomings of Kortmann and Lunkenheimer's "typology meets dialectology" approach. The synthesis is a promising one, marrying the bird's eye view of typology with the worm's eye view of sociolinguistics (allowing worms to have metaphorical eyes). The former favours geographical breadth, the synchronic and the structural. The latter favours social depth, the socio-historical and diversity/variation/local identity. That these might not be entirely compatible can be seen from our insistence in section 2 about the importance of the bilingual context for CFE and of switching and mixing. Two other caveats should be noted. The first pertains to the 'C' category in MWAVE ("the feature exists but is extremely rare"). For the present survey this pertains to a fairly large set of 17 features (see 1, 3, 16, 28, 43 etc. in the appendix). The question can be raised whether such extremely rare features should be deleted. Deleting the rare items for South African varieties leads to a slight realignment of the MWAVE profile presented in Figure 2: according to Kortmann (p.c. 2013), who ran the alternate analysis for us, CFE would remain in cluster 1 (as we might expect), but move closer to the other South African varieties, especially to Indian SAE. This slight swing within cluster 1 based on inclusion or exclusion of 'C' is a difficult problem to solve, and perhaps one best served by detailed corpus studies of individual features in years to come. We note further that in MWAVE, two varieties might have the same rating for a feature described structurally (e.g. special 2nd person pl. form), but the difference in surface form might be sociolinguistically salient within a territory. Thus CFE and Indian SAE may both have such a pronoun, but the difference between *yous* of CFE and *y'all* of the latter is socially significant.

We now turn to Kortmann and Lunkenheimer's conclusion that in connection with MWAVE, variety type is a stronger indicator of similarities than area: geography – they propose – matters only if we compare the morphosyntax of dialects belonging to the same variety type. For South Africa it would appear that the areal factor is perhaps stronger. The four varieties surveyed are respectively: an L1 par excellence (White SAE), a variety implicated in stable bilingualism and switching but which veers between L1 and L2 for different speakers (CFE), a variety that is solidly L2 (traditional Black SAE), and a language-shift variety (Indian SAE). That these should cohere fairly close together (and with other African L2 varieties) seems a strong indication of areal effects counteracting variety type in this particular branch of MWAVE. That the South African varieties should evince overall morphosyntactic similarities in global terms, despite the degree of social segregation in the country's past stressed earlier in this chapter is a new insight. Where South African analysts have stressed morphosyntactic differences (for an exception see Van Rooy 2017), MWAVE affords a broader comparison, including a "similarity of absences". In MWAVE terms, although the South African varieties show internal differences, they are ultimately united in *not* sharing traditional features and/or innovations characteristic of (especially) creoles and other L1 varieties in the survey. In this way morphosyntax may well be the common bond (see Sahgal and Agnihotri 1985), or at least more of a bond than might be apparent to users of ethnolects (and their analysts).

Some caution in interpreting MWAVE in absolute terms, rather than relative to the 235 features selected for analysis is warranted. Kortmann and Lunkenheimer (2012: 4) confirm that their selection was based on the most commonly reported features in the literature of English world-wide: "the vast majority of features ... are not unique to any one variety, and are widely discussed in the literature on morphosyntactic variation in English". The results might have looked different if other criteria were chosen. In particular how "deeply" one reaches into creoles, language shift and bilingual mixed varieties for the MWAVE feature pool could skew results differently. Currently, the least non-standard variety in MWAVE, judged by the number of non-standard features, is Tok Pisin (Kortmann and Lunkenheimer 2012: 917). Yet no one would want to argue that being the least non-standard makes Tok Pisin the most standard of the MWAVE varieties. We assume that Tok Pisin has the fewest of the *selected* non-standard features, but would also rank low in having standard features of English (had those been counted in MWAVE).

To conclude, the MWAVE results for CFE in relation to the rest of SAE are interesting and plausible. Overall, the MWAVE morphosyntactic comparisons speak very well to the complexities of contact and variation in South Africa.

References

Adhikari, Mohamed. 2009. From Narratives of miscegenation to post-modernist re-imagining: Towards a historiography of Coloured identity in South Africa. In Mohamed Adhikari (ed.), *Burdened by Race: Coloured Identities in Southern Africa*, 1–24. Cape Town: UCT Press.

Bekker, Ian. 2009. The vowels of South African English. North West University (South Africa) unpublished PhD dissertation.

Bowerman, Sean. 2004. White South African English: Phonology. In Edgar W. Schneider, Kate Burridge, Bernd Kortmann, Rajend Mesthrie & Clive Upton (eds.), *A Handbook of Varieties of English: Volume I*. 931–944. Berlin: Mouton de Gruyter.

Branford, William. 1996. English in South African Society: A Preliminary Overview. *Focus on South Africa* 15. 35–52.

Bryant, David, and Vincent Moulton. 2004. Neighbor-net: an agglomerative method for the construction of phylogenetic networks. *Molecular Biology and Evolution*. 21(2). 255–265.

Buthelezi, Qedusizi. 1995. South African Black English: lexical and syntactic characteristics. In Rajend Mesthrie (ed.), *Language and social history: Studies in South African* sociolinguistics, 242–50. Cape Town: David Philip.

Coetzee-van Rooy, Susan. 2014. The Identity Issue in Bi- and Multiracial Repertoires in South Africa: Implications for Schneider's Dynamic Model. In Sarah Buschfeld, Thomas Hoffmann, Magnus Huber & Alexander Kautzsch (eds.), *The Evolution of Englishes: The Dynamic Model and Beyond*, 39–57. Amsterdam: Benjamins.

Coetzee-van Rooy, Susan & Bertus van Rooy. 2005. South African English: Labels, Comprehensibility and Status. *World Englishes* 24(1). 1–19.

Cysouw, Michael. 2007. New approaches to cluster analysis of typological indices. In Reinhard Köhler, and Peter Grzbek (eds.), *Exact Methods in the Study of Language and Text*, 61–76. Berlin: Mouton de Gruyter.

De Klerk, Vivian. 1996. Introduction. In Vivian De Klerk (ed.), *Focus on South Africa*, 7–18. Amsterdam: Benjamins.

Erasmus, Zimitri. 2001. Introduction: Re-imagining Coloured identities in post-apartheid South Africa. In Zimitri Erasmus (ed.), *Coloured by History, Shaped by Place*, 13–28. Cape Town: Kwela.

Finn, Peter Alexander. 2002. Interlanguage, language shift and phonological change in the development of Cape Flats English. University of York unpublished PhD thesis.

Finn, Peter. 2004. Cape Flats English: Phonology. In Edgar W. Schneider, Kate Burridge, Bernd Kortmann, Rajend Mesthrie & Clive Upton (eds.), *A Handbook of Varieties of English: Volume 1*, 965–984. Berlin: Mouton de Gruyter.

Jantjies, Wesley & Ondene van Dulm. *Mos* as a discourse marker in rural Cape Afrikaans. *Language Matters* 43(1). 3–20.

Jeffery, Chris & Bertus van Rooy. 2004. Emphasizer *now* in colloquial South African English. *World Englishes* 23(2). 269–280.

Kortmann, Bernd, and Kerstin Lunkenheimer. (eds.). 2012. *The Mouton World Atlas of Variation in English*. Berlin: De Gruyter – Mouton.

Lanham, Leonard W. & Carol Ann Macdonald. 1979. *The Standard in South African English and its Social History*. Heidelberg: Julius Groos.

Malan, Karen. 1996. Cape Flats English. In Vivian de Klerk (ed.), *Focus on South Africa*. 125–148. Amsterdam: John Benjamins.

McCormick, Kay. 1989. English and Afrikaans in District Six: a sociolinguistic study. Cape Town: University of Cape Town Unpublished PhD thesis.

McCormick, Kay. 1995. Code-Switching, code-mixing and convergence in Cape Town. In Rajend Mesthrie (ed.), *Language and Social History: Studies in South African Sociolinguistics*, 193–208. Cape Town: David Phillip.

McCormick, Kay. 2003. *Language in Cape Town's District Six*. Oxford: Oxford University Press.

McCormick, Kay. 2004. Cape Flats English: Morphology and syntax. In Edgar W. Schneider, Kate Burridge, Bernd Kortmann, Rajend Mesthrie & Clive Upton (eds.), *A Handbook of Varieties of English: Volume II*, 993–1006. Berlin: Mouton de Gruyter.

Meierkord, Christiane. 2012. *Interactions across Englishes: Linguistic Choices in Local and International Contact Situations*. Cambridge University Press.

Mesthrie, Rajend. 1999. Fifty ways to say 'I do': Tracing the origins of unstressed *do* in Cape Flats English, South Africa. *South African Journal of Linguistics* 17(1). 58–71.

Mesthrie, Rajend. 2004a. Black South African English: morphology and syntax. In Bernd Kortmann, Kate Burridge, Rajend Mesthrie, Edgar W. Schneider & Clive Upton (eds.), *A Handbook of Varieties of English: Volume II*, 962–973. Berlin: Mouton de Gruyter.

Mesthrie, Rajend. 2004b. Indian South African English: morphology and syntax. In Bernd Kortmann, Kate Burridge, Rajend Mesthrie, Edgar W. Schneider & Clive Upton (eds.) *A Handbook of Varieties of English: Volume* II, 974–992. Berlin: Mouton de Gruyter.

Mesthrie, Rajend. 2004c. Indian South African English: phonology. In Edgar W. Schneider, Kate Burridge, Bernd Kortmann, Rajend Mesthrie & Clive Upton (eds.), *A Handbook of Varieties of English: Volume* 1, 953–963. Berlin: Mouton de Gruyter.

Mesthrie, Rajend. 2010. Sociophonetics and social change: Deracialisation of the GOOSE vowel in South African English. *Journal of Sociolinguistics* 14(1). 3–33.

Mesthrie, Rajend. 2012. Ethnicity, substrate and place: the dynamics of Coloured and Indian English in five South African cities in relation to the variable (t). *Language Variation and Change* 24(3). 371–396.

Mesthrie, Rajend, Alida Chevalier & Timothy Dunne. 2015. A Regional and Social Dialectology of the BATH Vowel in South African English. *Language Variation and Change* 27(1): 1–30.

Mesthrie, Rajend & Kay McCormick. 1994. Standardisation and Variation in South African English. *SPIL Plus* 26. 181–201.

Pettman, Charles. 1913. *Africanderisms: a glossary of South African colloquial words and phrases*. London: Longmans, Green & Co.

Ponelis, F.A. 1991. *Afrikaanse Sintaksis*. Pretoria: J. L. van Schaik.

Roberge, Paul T. 2002. Afrikaans: considering origins. In Rajend Mesthrie (ed.), *Language in South Africa*. Cambridge: Cambridge University Press. 79–103.

Sahgal, Anju, and Rama Kant Agnihotri. 1985. Syntax – The common bond: Acceptability of syntactic deviances in Indian English. *English World-Wide* 6(1). 117–129.

Schneider, Edgar W. 2007. *Postcolonial English: Varieties around the World*. Cambridge University Press.
Toefy, Tracey. 2014. Sociophonetics and Class Differentiation: A study of working- and middle-class English in Cape Town's Coloured Community. University of Cape Town unpublished PhD thesis.
Van Rooy, Bertus. 2004. Black South African English: Phonology. In Edgar W. Schneider, Kate Burridge, Bernd Kortmann, Rajend Mesthrie & Clive Upton (eds.), *A Handbook of Varieties of English: Volume 1*, 943–954. Berlin: Mouton de Gruyter.
Van Rooy, Bertus. 2014. Convergence and Endonormativity at Phase 4 of the Dynamic Model. In Sarah Buschfeld, Thomas Hoffmann, Magnus Huber & Alexander Kautzsch (eds.), *The Evolution of Englishes: The Dynamic Model and Beyond*, 21–38. Amsterdam: John Benjamins.
Van Rooy, Bertus. 2017. English in South Africa. In Markku Filppula, Juhani Klemola & Devyani Sharma (eds.), *The Oxford Handbook of World Englishes*, 508–530. Oxford: Oxford University Press.
Wasserman, Ronel & Bertus van Rooy. 2014. The development of modals of obligation and necessity in White South African English through contact with Afrikaans. *Journal of English Linguistics* 42. 31–50.
Watermeyer, Susan. 1996. Afrikaans English. In Vivian de Klerk (ed.), *English around the World: Focus on South Africa*, 99–124. Amsterdam/Philadelphia: Benjamins.
Wilmot, Kirsten. 2014. "Coconuts" and the middle-class: Identity change and the emergence of a new prestigious English variety in South Africa. *English Word-Wide* 35(3). 306–337.
Wood, Tahir M. 1987. Perceptions of, and Attitudes towards Varieties of English in the Cape Peninsula, with particular reference to the 'Coloured Community'. Rhodes University MA dissertation.

Appendix

Overview of attested features in Cape Flats English

#	Feature	CFE example	rating
	I. Pronouns, pronoun exchange, nominal gender		
1	she / her used for inanimate referents	She's a beaut. (said of a car, mainly)	C
3	alternative forms / phrases for referential (non-dummy) it	I can't get the thing out of the bag.	C
7	me instead of I in co-ordinate subjects	Now me and Elizabeth speaks English	A
8	myself / meself instead of I in co-ordinate subjects	She invited myself and my one friend.	B
9	benefactive / personal dative construction (using the object form of the pronoun)	I'm gonna buy me one of those.	A
14	no number distinction in reflexives (i.e. plural forms ending in –self)	We did it ourself.	B
16	emphatic reflexives with own	He did it his ownself.	C
28	use of us + NP in subject function	Us did eat.	C
34	forms or phrases for the 2nd person plural pronoun other than you	Are yous going to the show? You people, you all just sit there.	A
41	singular it for plural they in anaphoric use (with non-human elements)	You can only get it at Woolworths (referring to shoes)	B
42	object pronoun drop	A: I thought I lost my ticket. B: Did you find?	B
43	subject pronoun drop: referential pronouns	A: Did you buy the shoes? B: No – sold out!	C
	II. Noun Phrase		
52	associative plural marked by postposed and them / them all / dem	Marlene-them's car was stolen.	A
54	group plurals (i.e. plural marker attached to the end of an entire phrase)	How many brother-in-laws do you really have?	B
62	use of zero article where StE has definite article	When I went to Belgravia so I started taking Ø bus to school.	B
63	use of zero article where StE has indefinite article	I was Ø altar boy then.	B
71	no number distinction in demonstratives	He is just one of that people that doesn't do anything.	A
78	double comparatives and superlatives	more happier; more superior	B

	III. Verb Phrase: tense and aspect		
88	wider range of uses of progressive *be* + V-*ing* than in StE: extension to stative verbs	*She's not staying by us.*	C
93	other non-standard habitual markers: analytic	*I do be sick in winter.*	C
96	*there* plus past participle in resultative contexts	*There's cables been stolen at Retreat.*	C
99	levelling of the difference between present perfect and simple past: simple past for StE present perfect	*I ate already* (= 'I've eaten').	A
101	simple present for continuative or experiential perfect	*We five months here already and we did nothing.*	A
103	*do* as unstressed tense marker (without habitual or other aspect meanings)	*Who did throw that?*	A
109	perfective marker *already*	*Were you there already?*	A
113	loosening of sequence of tenses rule	*He said he came here last week* (= '…he had come last week')	B
117	present tense forms for neutral future reference	*I take it later.*	B
	IV. Verb Phrase: modal verbs		
123	present tense forms of modals used where StE has past tense forms	*I can [= 'could'] smack him for doing that.*	B
127	non-standard use of modals for politeness reasons	*Must I buy you some food?*	C
	V. Verb Phrase: verb morphology		
131	levelling of past tense/past participle verb forms: past participle replacing the past tense form	*I seen him yesterday.*	C
147	*was* for conditional *were*	*If I was young again….*	B
	VII. Negation		
154	multiple negation / negative concord	*Nobody can do nothing about it.*	B
158	invariant *don't* for all persons in the present tense	*That child don't have a daddy.*	B
159	*never* as preverbal past tense negator	*I never saw the goose again* [= didn't see]	B
165	invariant non-concord tags (including *eh?*)	*You first go to the left, né.*	A

VIII. Agreement

170	invariant present tense forms due to zero marking for the third person singular	And she say she donno what's wrong with him [for sg. forms].	B
171	invariant present tense forms due to generalization of 3rd person –s to all persons	The books gets dirty. [for pl. forms].	B
172	existential / presentational *there's / there is / there was* with plural subjects	There was prawns that I still think about today.	A
173	variant forms of dummy subject *there* in existential clauses, e.g. *they, it* or zero	It must have been two or three families sharing a room.	B
180	*was / were* generalization	We was very forceful.	B

IX. Relativization

190	relativizer *what* or a form derived from *what*	...all that stuff what she took...	C

X. Complementation

204	*as what / than what* in comparative clauses	It's more than what I expected.	C

XI. Adverbial subordination

214	conjunction doubling: clause + conj. + conj. + clause	Because-why I think her mother was also doing drugs at the time she was diabetic.	B
215	conjunction doubling: correlative conjunctions	So I took the ball after the ref indicted where the mark is, so I tapped the ball.	C

XII. Adverbs and prepositions

216	omission of StE prepositions	Zelda died the Friday.	B
220	degree modifier adverbs have the same form as adjectives	It's real good.	C
221	other adverbs have the same form as adjectives	People look at him strange.	B

XIII. Discourse organization and word order

227	inverted word order in indirect questions	I was wondering what am I gonna do.	B
228	no inversion / no auxiliaries in wh-questions	Where you going now?	C
229	no inversion / no auxiliaries in main clause *yes / no* questions	You coming tomorrow?	C
234	*like* as a focusing device	I've lived there for like about ten years.	C
235	*like* as a quotative particle	(Global middle class English, not really a traditional feature of CFE.)	B

Hanna Parviainen
Omission of direct objects in New Englishes

Abstract: This chapter examines the omission of direct objects of transitive verbs as in A: *Do you know Malayalam?* B: *Oh yes I speak.* (ICE-IND) in contexts where the verb does not function intransitively. The English varieties examined for this study come from Fiji, Hong Kong, India, Jamaica, Kenya, the Philippines and Singapore and the superstrate varieties from Britain and America were also included in the data. The study analyses the frequency of the phenomenon in sentences where the verbs *bring, buy, enjoy, find, give, love, make, offer* and *show* are used transitively. The focus of this quantitative study is on spoken language while possible substrate influences on the varieties are also discussed. The data for Fiji, Hong Kong, Indian, Jamaican, Kenyan, Philippine, Singaporean and British English were obtained from the spoken sections of the *International Corpus of English* (ICE), whereas American English was studied by using the *Santa Barbara Corpus of Spoken American English* (SBCSAE). The results of the study indicate that the tendency to omit direct objects is strongest in IndE and SinE, while the feature was rarest in BrE, JaE and AmE.

Keywords: transitivity, structural vs semantic, transitive verb, monotransitive vs ditransitive, direct object, omission of direct object, substrate vs superstrate language, Founder Principle, indigenous language, agreement system, topic-comment, topic-prominence, universal, acquisitional, diffusion, areal convergence

1 Introduction

The tendency to omit objects is a common feature in many languages spoken around the world, but widespread use of the feature has not been attested in traditional inner circle varieties such as British (BrE) and American English (AmE). In contrast, Platt et al. (1984: 117) have noted that "there is a tendency [in New Englishes], particularly in colloquial speech, to imply the subject or the object pronoun of a sentence rather than state it explicitly." More detailed descriptions of the spread of the feature include the English varieties of Hong Kong (HKE) (Platt 1982: 410), India (IndE) (Subbārāo 2012: 28), Malaysia (Baskaran

---

Hanna Parviainen, University of Tampere

DOI 10.1515/9783110429657-008

2004: 1080), Sri Lanka (Platt et al. 1984: 117), Singapore (SinE) and the Philippines (PhiE) (Platt et al., cited in Bhatt 2004: 1026). In addition, Platt et al. (1984: 117) have stated that the feature is also used in "African Englishes", though they do not elaborate on this issue further.

According to Kortmann and Lunkenheimer's (2013, http://www.ewave-atlas.org/parameters/42) *Electronic World Atlas of Varieties of English*[1] (eWAVE), the omission of object pronouns is "pervasive or obligatory" in Maltese English, Kenyan English (KenE), IndE, HKE, "Colloquial Singapore English", Malaysian English, Rope River Creole, "pure Fiji English"[2] and Tok Pisin. In addition, Englishes where the feature is argued to be "neither pervasive nor extremely rare" include such varieties as PhiE, Butler English and Sri Lankan English (ibid.). Interestingly, despite these estimations of the frequency of the feature, no quantitative studies based on comparative data have yet been conducted which would examine the exact spread and frequency of this feature in New Englishes.

This chapter presents a quantitative study of the frequency with which direct objects are omitted in Fijian English (FjE), HKE, IndE, Jamaican English (JaE), KenE, PhiE, and SinE. In addition, British (BrE) and American (AmE) Englishes have been included as the 'source' varieties of the other Englishes examined here. The main focus of the analysis is on the quantitative analysis of the data, although some qualitative aspects will also be addressed when considered relevant.

2 Transitivity in English

Kittilä (2010: 346) defines linguistic transitivity as "the formal and semantic features associated with [...] the linguistic coding of basic events [...] in which a volitionally acting, typically human agent targets its action at a thoroughly affected patient". According to Kittilä (2002: 78–9), the marking of transitive clauses in English is primarily motivated by "the number of core participants", which he defines as "participants that inhere in the semantics of events". In intransitive clauses such as (1), there is only one core participant, the subject (S) (*he*), whereas in transitive clauses (examples [2] and [3]) the number of core

---

[1] eWAVE is an online database which presents estimates of the frequencies of different morphosyntactic features in different varieties of English. The data comes from a questionnaire filled by 80 informants who are all experts in their field.
[2] This refers to the basilectal form of FjE (Kortmann and Lunkenheimer (http://ewave-atlas.org/parameters/42#2/7.0/7.6).

participants is two, as both the S (*the dog, she*) and the direct object (Od) (*the ball, a book*) are present.

(1) He read. (SV)

(2) The dog ate *the ball*. (SVOd)

(3) She was reading *a book* in the park. (SVOdA)

Although both verbs and clauses can be categorised as transitive, Huddleston and Pullum (2002: 216) note that it is ultimately the verb which determines the transitivity of both; for example, the verb *read* permits both the omission (1) and the presence (3) of the object and thus also determines the transitivity of the clause.

Huddleston and Pullum (2002: 218) divide the category of transitive verbs further to monotransitives, which can be either ordinary (2) or complex (examples [4] and [5]), and ditransitives, which can have only ordinary (6) structures:

(4) She considered *him* quite handsome. (SVOdCo)

(5) The neighbours kept *the dog* inside the house. (SVOdAo)

(6) She sent him *a letter*. (SVOiOd)

As (2) shows, ordinary monotransitive verbs are followed by only one core argument, the Od, which according to Carter and McCarthy (2006: 498) is invariably a noun phrase or its equivalent such as a nominal clause. The second subclass of this category consists of complex transitive verbs, which, as Quirk et al. (1985: 55–6) note, are followed by an Od and an object complement (Co) as in (4), or an object-related adverbial (Ao) as in (5). Ditransitives, in contrast, have an additional core participant, the indirect object (Oi), which according to Carter and McCarthy (2006: 499) cannot occur without the Od. Kittilä (2006: 1) argues that "canonical three-participant events involve an animate agent, an inanimate theme (i.e. the thing transferred) and an animate recipient", which in (6) are *she* (S), *a letter* (Od) and *him* (Oi). Furthermore, Dixon (2000: 41) suggests that in the English language, the syntactic functions of constituents are indicated by their order in the clause and therefore, the indirect object usually precedes the direct object, as Quirk et al. (1985: 54) note. In addition, indirect objects can frequently be placed after the Od, which turns them into prepositional objects (Op) (Quirk et al. 1985: 1208), as (7) shows.

(7) She sent *a letter* to him. (SVOdOp)

Many researchers (see, for example, Kittilä 2010; Hopper and Thompson 1980) focusing on semantic transitivity have argued against the intransitive-transitive dichotomy of structural definitions presented above; in contrast, they prefer to view transitivity as a continuum, which takes into consideration the various nuances such as kinesis, agency, affectedness, volitionality, and the number of participants that contribute to the transitivity of a clause.[3] For example, although both (2) and (3) are transitive, the object (*the ball*) in (2) is more affected by the action than the object (*the book*) in (3) and therefore, the former is placed higher in the transitivity continuum than the latter. However, as Kittilä notes (2002: 79), transitivity in the English language is fundamentally determined by the number of core participants, which justifies the structural approach used here.

3 Data and Methods

3.1 Data

With the exception of AmE, data for all varieties included in the study come from the *International Corpus of English* (ICE), a family of corpora where each corpus consists of 600,000 words of spoken and 400,000 words of written English. Since the focus of this study is on a feature that is most prominent in colloquial language, only the most informal category, 'Private conversations', will be examined here. 'Private conversations' consists of approximately 200,000 words in all Asian corpora, ICE-JA and ICE-GB, whereas only smaller amounts of data are available in ICE-EA (60,000) and ICE-FJ[4] (55,000). As the spoken component of ICE-US has not been published yet, the data representing spoken AmE come from the *Santa Barbara Corpus of Spoken American English* (SBCSAE). The use of the SBCSAE is a justified choice, since data from this corpus will also form a part of the unpublished ICE-US.[5]

3.2 Methods

The nine verbs selected for the study are *bring, buy, enjoy, find, give, love, make, offer* and *show*[6], which also represent different levels of transitivity: for example,

---

[3] For a detailed list of high and low transitivity features, see Hopper and Thompson (1980: 252).
[4] At the time of writing, ICE-FJ has not yet been published. I would like to thank Prof. Marianne Hundt for the opportunity to assist in the compilation of the corpora and granting me access to the unpublished data.
[5] For more information, see http://www.linguistics.ucsb.edu/research/santa-barbara-corpus.
[6] This selection of verbs that favour transitive uses is also supported by Mukherjee and Gries (2009: 40) to some extent.

the objects of verbs such as *make* and *give* tend to be more thoroughly affected by the action than the objects of *love* and *show,* and therefore, the former verbs are usually placed higher in the transitivity continuum than the latter. The searches were conducted using WordSmith Tools 6.0, which enables the search for not only individual words from the data, but also provides a link to the original file where the search hit is located.[7]

In the first phase of the analysis, all instances of verbs were collected from the data and analysed manually: all sentences where the verbs were used transitively but were not accompanied by an overt direct object were separated from the canonical transitive sentences, whereas instances of repetition, false starts and other unclear cases were discarded. The sentences where no Od was present were then subjected to a detailed analysis where several clues in the transcription were examined in order to ensure that the direct objects had indeed been omitted. For example, if the omitted pronoun was followed by a pause, as in (8), it was analysed as an example where the speaker did not intend to add an Od after the verb.

(8)　A: Well do you *enjoy* <,>

　　　B: Yeah <,> I like that work <w> I'll </w> *enjoy* more <,>

(ICE-IND:S1A-043#55-6)

Unfortunately, some files in the corpora did not contain any pause markings, as (9) shows; in such cases, that particular section of the dialogue was examined in greater detail.

(9)　B: How 'bout the <.> ing </.> ano the others <.> whe </.> when will we *buy*

　　　B: When will we go out and *buy*

　　　A: Friday　　　　　　　　　　　　　　　　(ICE-PHI:S1A-014#36-8)

In (9), speaker B repeats his/her question, but both times does not add the Od after *buy,* and hence, the omission of the object in speaker B's repeated question

---

[7] The search parameters were set to exclude all instances of the corpora marked as 'extra-corpus material' (<X>*</X>), 'editorial comments' (<&>*</&>), 'untranscribed text' (<O>*</O>) and transcriber's corrections (<+>*</+>).The exclusion of the first three tags were based on the recommendations given in the ICE homepage (http://ice-corpora.net/ice/importantnote.htm). The decision to exclude also 'Transcriber's corrections' was based on the personal observation that many corpora (especially ICE-IND), contained many words and sentences which were corrected by the transcribers.

was considered to be deliberate. Also, no sections of speaker A and B's turns have been marked as overlapping and therefore, object omissions in sentences such as these were not considered to be caused by interruptions. In addition, instances where the speaker continued with their turn although the Od of the transitive verb had been left out were considered to be indications of deliberate object omission; an example of this is provided in (10).

(10) A: I don't want a chocolate eclair but you cannot *give* to Ai Hui because she <O> coughs </O> (ICE-SIN:S1A-021#100:1:)

After this detailed analysis, all instances of transitive verbs that were not followed by direct objects were included in the data.

In order to determine the frequency of the feature in New Englishes, the number of omitted objects was compared with the overall number of canonical transitive constructions in the data using the X-coefficient, which is an adaptation of the V-coefficient (Smitterberg 2005: 44).[8] The X-coefficient relates the number of transitive verbs with omitted objects to the total number of transitive verbs, as shown below

$X = N_{ZERO}\ Od\ /\ N_{TRANS} \times 10,000.$

Since all nine verbs examined for this chapter can be used as intransitives and transitives (though they favour the latter), the use of the X-coefficient enables a variationist approach to the data, where the canonical transitive constructions and the transitive constructions with omitted direct objects form the two variants of the transitive clause.

4 Results

As was mentioned in the introduction, the tendency to omit object pronouns has been argued to be a common feature in many New Englishes. Figure 1 and Table 1 below present the results on the nine varieties of English from the highest to the lowest.

---

8 The V-coefficient (the *V* stands for 'verb') is used to relate the number of progressives to the number of verb phrases in a text (Smitterberg 2005: 44–5).

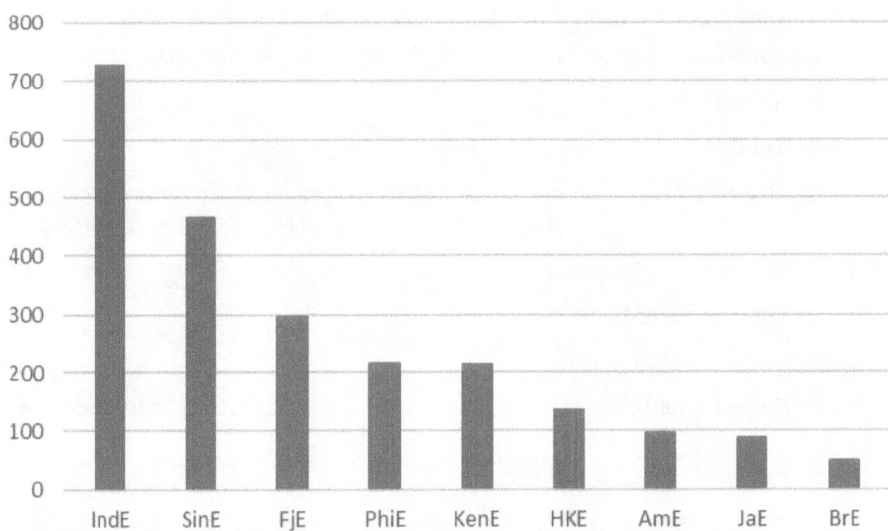

Figure 1: Frequency of direct object omission in nine varieties of English, X-coefficient

Table 1: Frequency of omitted direct objects, X-coefficient

	Canonical transitives	Transitives with zero Od	X-coefficient
IndE	981	77	728
SinE	1023	50	466
FjE	262	8	296
PhiE	1085	24	216
KenE	318	7	215
HKE	1011	14	137
AmE	818	8	97
JaE	1004	9	89
BrE	829	4	48

The results in Table 1 show that the tendency to omit direct objects is most frequent in IndE, followed by SinE, FjE, PhiE, KenE, HKE, AmE, JaE and BrE, in descending order. The overall distribution between the varieties is statistically significant ($p < 0.001$), while the only statistically significant difference between individual varieties can be found between IndE and SinE ($p < 0.05$) (for detailed figures, see Appendix 1). Examples from each variety are provided in (11) to (19):

(11) A: Who doesn't loves <,> <indig> sarees </indig> <,> <{> <[>yeah <,> Kanchipuram <indig> sarees </indig> and <O> one word </O>

B: <[> Yeah </[> </{>

B: You don't *love*?

C: Oh <w> I'm </w> not much interested in <,> <{> <[> dressing up </[>

(ICE-IND:S1A-029#166-169)

(12) A: Did your brother *make*

A: I'm sure he did

B: He no he didn't *make*

B: He just bought it   (ICE-SIN:S1A-066#93-6)

(13) A: rum yeah rum I can drink

B: hot stuff eh?

A: yeah hot stuff it's good <,,>

A: basically the imported ones <,,>

B: what the imported ones?

A: yeah imported <,> just like Red Label and all those <,> from abroad not the Fiji rum <,> <{><[>very strong</[> <,,> <O>laugh</O> I can *buy* <,,>

(ICE-FJ-S1A-090)

(14) B: ... I got so much interested that in her assignment in the <-_>in the<-/> story

I would miss doing anything else but not that not to get good marks but I *enjoyed* and I would read that book over and over again...

(ICE-EA-convers2-K)

(15) B: I am keeping my doors open but then I know I cannot *find*

A: Uh uhm okay I understand I know   (ICE-PHI:S1A-018#113-4)

(16) B: So I uhm<,,> ask the parents to bring in the vouchers

A: Yes

B: Other parents who did not *bring* in uhm explained that <}> <->

(ICE-JA:S1A-098#23-25)

(17) A: Yeah they they had take some photographs uh and <,> they *showed* to me and I I think uh it's very beautiful yeah (ICE-HK:S1A-042#508:1:A)

(18) B: Oh we were going through the uh <,> I was *showing* Mike and uh Dinah on Thursday

B: and we were going through the C V <,> (ICE-GB:S1A-016 #176-178)

(19) NANCY: And so he needed change. Like two fives for a ten or something. So she *gave* him.

(H) And then, he kept it?

He didn't give her like the ten you know? (SBCSAE0050)

The structural and semantic transitivity of a clause can sometimes disagree and, as Kittilä (2002: 37) notes, the number of arguments in a clause in such cases is usually lower than the number of participants involved. This holds true also in (11) to (19), as they all lack a core argument which is implied in the surrounding context. For example, although the surface structure of *So she gave him* in (19) could be interpreted as an ordinary monotransitive, the surrounding context reveals that it is in fact a ditransitive where the direct object is omitted: the woman in question gave the man *change* (Od), although only *she* (S) and *him* (Oi) are mentioned in the clause.

Although direct object omission occurs in all the varieties, there are also great differences between them; the frequencies of BrE and AmE are among the lowest, which supports the argument that the feature was not transmitted to the other English varieties from the two superstrates. Thus, the origins of the tendency to omit direct objects must be located elsewhere. IndE has the highest frequencies of object omission and it is followed by SinE and FjE; interestingly, both Singapore and Fiji have ethnic Indian minorities which still speak Indian languages as their L1, and it is therefore possible that the heightened frequencies in SinE and FjE are caused by the presence of the ethnic Indian minorities in the data. However, considering that the ethnic Indians comprise only approximately nine per cent of the Singaporean population (Population trends 2013, Department of Statistics), whereas the frequency of direct object omission in the SinE data is over 60 per cent of the corresponding frequency of IndE, it is highly unlikely that the proportion of ethnic Indians in the SinE data is large enough to solely explain the high frequencies of SinE[9].

---

9 Unfortunately, the speaker information of ICE-SIN is not available and therefore, it is not possible to present estimations on the distribution or the strength of the feature among the different ethnic groups of Singapore.

In the case of FjE, the possibility of an ethnic Indian minority could indeed explain the results, as Indo-Fijians form almost 40 per cent of the Fijian population (2007 Population Census, Fiji Bureau of Statistics), and they form approximately 50 per cent of the informants in the ICE-FJ data used for this study. In fact, in six out of the eight instances where the direct object had been omitted, the speaker was of Indo-Fijian ethnicity. However, since the remaining two hits came from a Rotuman and a Fijian, it is clear that Indo-Fijians do not form the sole ethnic group using this feature.

Heightened frequencies of object omission can also be found in PhiE and KenE, where the tendency to use the feature is equally strong. Interestingly, HKE uses direct object omission the least when compared with the other Asian Englishes included in the study, and it is thus closest to its source variety, BrE. This supports the observations made by Mukherjee and Gries (2009), whose collostructional analysis on the patterns of transitive and intransitive verbs indicates that HKE aligns itself closer to BrE than the two other Asian varieties (SinE and IndE) included in their study. The closeness of HKE to BrE has also been observed by Rautionaho (2014). The results on JaE are also interesting, as the variety is aptly positioned between its past and present superstrates, BrE and AmE.

5 Omission of direct objects in substrate languages

As mentioned above, the frequency at which speakers of New Englishes omit direct objects could be linked to local language influence, and therefore, the existence of a similar linguistic feature in the substrates of these varieties must be examined in greater detail. Since the total number of languages spoken in India, Singapore, Fiji, the Philippines, Kenya, Hong Kong and Jamaica exceeds the scope of this study, only the major languages from each country were selected for closer examination. This restriction is a justified choice, as the languages with the largest numbers of speakers are also more prominently represented in the "feature pool" of each variety. The term is an integral part of Mufwene's (2001: 3–6) "Founder principle", which suggests that, in contact situations, the different languages (and varieties) spoken by the population form a pool from which different features emerge through competition and selection and become manifested in the new language (or variety). Thus, if the tendency to omit direct objects is common in the larger local languages, substrate influence could provide a plausible explanation for the increased use of the feature in New Englishes.[10] However, before proceeding with the analysis, a more detailed account of the languages and the motivation for their inclusion should be presented.

Hindi is the only indigenous language of India with official status[11], and since it is also the largest substrate language of IndE with 41 per cent of the population speaking it as their L1 (Graddol 2010: 51), the selection of Indian languages examined here is restricted to only Hindi. The official local languages of Singapore are Mandarin Chinese, Malay and Tamil, but only the first of these is of greater relevance to this study, since, as Lim (2007: 453, 456) argues, the forms of Malay and Tamil used by the Malay and Indian communities of Singapore are not significant in the contact dynamics of the area. In contrast, Bazaar Malay and Hokkien should be examined closer, as they both functioned as lingua francas in the Singaporean area (Gupta 1992: 327).[12] In addition, Cantonese and Teochew have been noted to be important substrates for SinE (Ansaldo 2004: 132), but only the former will be examined here, since Teochew differs from Hokkien only in its phonology.[13] Cantonese is also the only major substrate for HKE, as it is the L1 of approximately 90 per cent of the population (Thematic Household Survey Report No. 51, Census and Statistics Department 2013). The majority of Fijians speak either Fijian or Fiji Hindi as their L1 (2007 Population Census, Fiji Bureau of Statistics), and thus both languages are included in the analysis. The language situation in Kenya is more complex, as the official languages, English and Swahili, are mostly used as lingua francas in the country where multiple local languages are spoken as L1. Therefore, in addition to Swahili, two locally spoken languages, Kikuyu and Luo, are included here, as they are the biggest languages of the two major language branches (Bantu and Nilo-Saharan) spoken in the country (Population and Housing Census 2009, Kenya National Bureau of Statistics). The two official languages of the Philippines are English and the Tagalog-based Filipino, and the latter also has the largest number of speakers in the country, approximately 28 per cent of the population

---

10 This approach is not new, as the founder principle has also been applied in studies on, for example, language evolution and ecology in Asia (Ansaldo 2009) and new dialect formation processes in London (Cheshire et al. 2011).
11 There are also 22 other associate languages which are recognised in the Indian constitution, but none of the speaker populations of these languages represent even 10 per cent of India's total population (Graddol 2010: 51). Therefore, it can be argued that Hindi has the strongest representation in the feature pool of IndE.
12 According to Lim (2007: 453–4), Bazaar Malay was used by the whole of the Singaporean population whereas Hokkien was used among the Chinese speaking population – both were replaced by English during the 1970s and 80s (Lim 2007: 453–4).
13 Bao Zhiming, personal communication, 14.3.2013.

(2011 Philippines in Figures, National Statistics Office). Despite the relatively low proportion of native speakers of Tagalog in the Philippines, restricting the selection to this language is a justified choice since, as Schachter (1976: 493) notes, "the languages of the Philippines are sufficiently similar that examples from any one language can safely be taken as paradigmatic". Jamaican Creole (JaC) is the most important substrate of JaE (Patrick 2004: 408), and thus the local creole should also be examined here.

5.1 Rich agreement

For some languages, the tendency to omit objects can be explained with the language's rich agreement system, which makes stating the object explicitly redundant. This rationale can be applied to some of the languages listed above, as the morphologies of Hindi (20), Fijian (21), Swahili (22), Kikuyu (23) and Luo (24) are complex enough to explain to some degree the tendency to omit object pronouns in IndE, FjE and KenE.[14]

(20) mẽne   kahi:.
     1SG-erg said-fs
     'I said (it) to him/her.'   (Koul 2008: 214)

(21) [e   ronqo-ta] tiko   na   marama.
     3SG   hold-TR   CNT   DET   woman.
     'The woman is holding him.'   (Aranovich 2013: 467)

(22) ni-na-ku-ona
     1SG-PRES-2SG.OBJ-see
     'I see you.'   (Myachina 1981: 64)

(23) nĩ-a-ra-mũ-rĩ-ĩr-a   waru
     fp-3SG.SUB-PRES-3SG.OBJ-eat-A-fv   10potato
     'She/he is eating food for her/him.'   (Mugane 1997: 159)

---

14 The question of Fiji Hindi morphology remains open, as no examples were found where the direct object was omitted due to rich morphology. Siegel (1988: 121) has argued that Fiji Hindi is a morphologically simplified form of Hindi, which is "derived from several different Indian Hindi dialects". Therefore, it is possible that the process of simplification has resulted in the weakening of the tendency in the language. Nevertheless, since Fiji Hindi has been mentioned to allow pro drop (see, for example, Gounder 2011), the scarceness of data on Fiji Hindi could also explain why no examples of this tendency were found for this paper.

(24) o-tedo-n(i)-a-gi
      3SG-cook-for/to-1SG.OBJ-them
      'He cooks them for me' (Stafford 1967: 17)

In (20), the object of the Hindi sentence can be omitted because "the verb [...] *kahna*: is inflected for an implied generic feminine object" (Koul 2008: 214). (21), in turn, is an example from Fijian, where the pronoun *him* is omitted; according to Kittilä (2002: 91), transitivity in (Boumaa) Fijian is signalled by verbal affixes, which is why, as Aranovich (2013: 467) points out, the omission of objects is allowed in some contexts. The omission of objects is also possible in Swahili, where "the independent arguments are very often eliminated and participants are referred to by agreement affixes only", as Kittilä (2002: 98) notes. Interestingly, this tendency can be observed in both of the Bantu languages examined here, as the subject and object are signalled in the verbs of not only (22) from Swahili but also (23) from Kikuyu. The same can also be seen in (24) from Luo where, according to Stafford (1967: 17), object pronouns can be reduced to verbal affixes. As the examples above indicate, a rich morphology in the substrate languages can indeed explain why object omission is common in some New Englishes, although there are also some restrictions as to the applicability of this explanation in some languages.[15]

5.2 Topic-prominence

Although rich morphology in the substrates of IndE, FjE and KenE can indeed explain why objects are omitted in these three varieties, this cannot explain why the same feature is also found in other Asian Englishes such as SinE, where the substratum consists mostly of isolating languages with a poor morphology. As an answer to this question, Sato (2011: 362) suggests the following:

> there is more than one grammatical source for the liberal omission of grammatical elements in the syntax. Classical pro-drop languages like Spanish [...] allow agreement-based drop because their inflectional morphology is rich enough to recover the missing element from agreement. Agreementless, topic-prominent languages allow [radical pro drop] because of the distinct topic structure underlain by topic prominence.

---

[15] Mugane (1997: 159) notes that in Kikuyu, the number of object prefixes attached to the verb is restricted to one and thus, the language allows the omission of only one object in a sentence. In addition, Aranovich (2013: 496) argues that objects belonging to the first of three categories in Fijian are "licensed by an -*a* suffix on the verb", which he considers to be "an agreement marker [that identifies] an empty *pro* in the position of complement of V". Therefore, object omission is possible also in Fijian, although the use of the feature is more constrained.

This view is supported by Li and Thompson (1976: 409), who note that "many structural phenomena of a language can be explained on the basis of whether the basic structure of its sentence is analysed as subject-predicate or topic-comment"; since many Asian languages are topic-prominent (see, for example, Sato 2011; Junghare 1988), this could explain some of the results presented in this paper.

According to Li and Thompson (1976: 484), the notion of topic is universal, but it is manifested differently in subject-prominent (Sp) and topic-prominent (Tp) languages; the differences between these two types are demonstrated in (25) and (26).

(25) John   hit Mary
     Subject Predicate   (Li and Thompson 1976: 459)

(26) *Nei-xie shumu   shù-shēn   dà*
     those   trees   tree-trunk big
       Topic   Comment
     "Those trees, the trunks are big."
                                         (Adapted from Li and Thompson 1976: 462)

(27) As for education,   John prefers Bertrand Russell's ideas
        Topic   Comment   (Li and Thompson 1976: 459)

(25) shows the structure of a basic, unmarked sentence in English, which is an Sp language where the main components are the subject and the predicate. In contrast, (26) from Mandarin Chinese shows the unmarked structure of a sentence in a Tp language where 'those trees' functions as the topic and thus signals what the sentence is about, whereas the comment ('the trunks are big') provides further information about that topic. Li and Thompson (1976: 484) note that "subjects are essentially grammaticalized topics", and therefore they are also assigned some of the properties of the topic. Here it should be noted that defining a language as Sp does not necessarily mean that it cannot have topic-comment structures or vice versa; as (27) shows, the topic-comment structure is also possible in English, where it is used as a special construction. Furthermore, the subject (*John*) and topic (*as for education*) are located in different arguments, which shows that the topic and subject do not always coincide although they are closely connected.

In their analysis of aspects that distinguish Tp languages from Sp languages, Li and Thompson (1976: 466–71) provide a list of eight features that are summarised in Table 2.

Table 2: Characteristics of Tp languages (based on Li and Thompson 1976)

Feature	Description
a) Surface coding	The topic is coded (e.g. always in initial position) in Tp languages whereas coding of the subject might not be necessary
b) The passive construction	Passivization does not exist, it is rare, or it has special meaning
c) "Dummy" subjects	Not used
d) "Double subject"	Occur in all Tp languages
e) Controlling co-reference	The topic (and not the subject) controls the omission of the co-referent constituent in Tp languages
f) V-final languages	Tp languages are frequently verb-final
g) Constraints on topic constituent	Anything can function as the topic
h) Basicness of topic-comment sentences	Topic-comment sentence types are considered to be "basic"

Importantly, Li and Thompson (1976: 483) note that "[a]s with all typological distinctions, [...] it is clear that we are speaking of a continuum". Therefore, the stronger these features are in a language, the more Tp it is. One specific feature, 'Controlling co-reference' is of special interest for the topic of the present paper, as it explains why certain languages allow the omission of objects despite their poor morphology. According to this principle, objects and other constituents can be freely omitted when their referent is the topic and thus recoverable from the context; (28) from Mandarin Chinese is an example of this.

(28) *Nèike shù yèzi dà, suǒyi wǒ bu xǐhuan ___.*
     that tree leaves big so 1SG not like
     'That tree (topic), the leaves are big, so I don't like (it)'
                                         (Li and Thompson 1967: 469)

In (28), the object of dislike is *that tree*, which is also the topic and therefore, there is no need for the speaker to provide the coreferential object pronoun *it* in the comment.

Many Chinese dialects, together with Bazaar Malay, have been argued to be Tp (Li and Thompson 1976; Yip and Matthews 2007: 135; Khin Khin Aye 2005: 153). Examples of object omission controlled by the topic are provided in (29) to (30) from Cantonese and (31) from Bazaar Malay.

(29) [TOPIC *ni1 gin6 saam1*]$_i$ *ngo5 hou2 zung1ji3* e$_i$.
         this CL   dress   1SG   very like   this
'This dress, I like [it] a lot.'   (Yip and Matthews 2007: 135)

(30) [TOPIC Ø]$_i$ *ngo5 hou2 zung1ji3* e$_i$.
                    1SG very like
'I like [it] a lot.'   (Yip and Matthews 2007: 135)

(31) *Nanti saya kawan tahu.*
     wait   1SG   friend know
'Wait (for a while), my friends know (Malay, that is, how to speak Malay).'
                                                    (Khin Khin Aye 2005: 160)

Yip and Matthews (2007: 134–5) argue that "just as a missing object can refer back to an overt sentence topic" as in (29), "so it can refer to a topic which is implied but not stated" as in (30). As could be expected, Yip and Matthews (2007: 135) link this tendency to the "'topic-prominent' characteristics of Chinese as a whole". The same tendency can be seen in (31) in Bazaar Malay where, as Khin Khin Aye (2005: 149–50) notes, "the object NP can [...] be omitted as long as it can be inferred either from the context or from knowledge shared between the interlocutors".

The classification of Hindi is slightly more problematic, since some scholars, such as Kidwai (2004: 255), claim that Hindi is an Sp language[16], whereas others (see, for example Junghare 1988: 316; Sato 2011: 362) argue that the language is in fact more Tp.[17] According to Junghare (1988: 322), "the zero pronouns occur more in conversational varieties of [Hindi]"; an example of object omission licensed by topic-prominence is provided in (32).

(32) *jonko khat   milā leki usne   Ø Ø dikhāyā nahī*
     John   letter got   but   3SG.M   showed   not
'John received the letter but he didn't show (it) (to me).'
                                                    (Junghare 1988: 325)

---

[16] Also Li and Thompson (1976) argue that Indo-European languages are Sp.
[17] Interestingly, Li and Thompson (1976) also distinguish a third category, languages that are both Tp and Sp, where "there are two equally important distinct sentence constructions, the subject-predicate construction and the topic-comment construction". However, defining the exact location of Hindi on the Tp-Sp continuum according to the eight categories mentioned above would exceed the scope of this paper.

(33) ke   surū   kar-is   rahā
      who   start do–PF   AUX
      'Who started (it)?'   (Siegel 1988: 128)

The same phenomena can also be seen in (33) from Fiji Hindi, where the omission of the direct object is licensed by the anaphoric reference of the omitted pronoun to the topic, which is clear from the context.

Li and Thompson (1976: 459) suggest that there are some languages where "the subject and the topic have merged and are no longer distinguishable in all sentence types" and thus, they are neither Tp nor Sp. Interestingly, many Philippine languages, including Tagalog, belong to this category (see, for example, Li and Thompson 1976; Schachter 1976; Shibatani 1991). Despite this, Himmelmann (1999: 232) argues that "[z]ero-options exist for both actors and undergoers in all kinds of semantically transitive constructions in Tagalog" as (34) shows.

(34) Huhugasan   ko   and=mga=pinggan, at   pupunasan   mo
      FUT-wash-DV1.   SG.GEN   NOM=PL=dish   and FUT-dry-DV   2.SG.GEN
      'I will wash the dishes, and you will dry (them).'   (Kroeger 1993: 34)

According to Kroeger (1993: 33), "Tagalog allows [zero anaphora] to apply quite freely", though it "requires that the antecedent actually precede the null pronoun, whether in the same sentence or in discourse context", which is illustrated well in (34).

Interestingly, Li and Thompson (1976: 460) argue that languages of the Niger-Congo language family, which includes such Bantu languages as Swahili and Kikuyu, are Sp. Furthermore, the eight characteristics of Li and Thompson (1976) cannot be found in Swahili to the same extent as in prominently Tp languages[18], and it is therefore unlikely that the Bantu substrates are as strongly Tp as, for example, Chinese dialects. JaC has also been noted to be Sp (Sato 2011: 362) which, according to Neeleman and Szendrői (2007: 690; also Kortmann and Lunkenheimer 2013), does not allow (radical) pro drop. However, Loftman Bailey (1966: 80) contradicts this view by stating that "if there is anything in the context which makes it clear what the direct object is, then that object is deletable" as in (35).

---

18 See Augustin's (2007) discussion on Swahili topic structures.

(35) *huu sel yu di tebl*
'Who sold you the table?'

Jak sel me
'Jack sold (it to) me.' (Loftman Bailey 1966: 80)

Again, the key issue seems to be the relatedness of the omitted object to the topic of the conversation. This issue will be discussed further below.

Kittilä (2002: 77) suggests that in a large number of languages "everything that can be inferred from the context is either omitted or is not marked explicitly", and the discussion above supports this view. In fact, many of the sources cited above note that object omission occurs in the context of conversations, and since "the topic [...] is primarily a discourse notion", as Junghare (1988: 322) points out, it is not surprising that examples of object omission licensed by the topic can be found in the spoken genres of virtually all substrates. Furthermore, since the data examined for this study represents informal spoken English, finding some instances of omitted objects in all colloquial varieties of English is something to be expected. What is important to note here is that, firstly, there are clear differences between the English varieties as to how frequently objects are omitted, and secondly, these differences seem to be linked to the topic prominence of the substrates. In Sp languages, the subject has many of the properties of the topic, and thus, sentences where the object can be omitted because it refers to the topic are rare. In contrast, there are fewer restrictions as to what can function as the topic in Tp languages and, as a consequence, omitted objects referring to the topic also occur more frequently.

Topic prominence does not, however, fully explain the results, since objects are omitted in IndE more frequently than in SinE, although Tp is more prominent in the substrates of the latter. In addition to Hindi, rich agreement and object omission are known to be common in many other South Asian languages (see, for example, Subbārāo 2012: 28; Butt 2001: 2). Therefore, a possible explanation for the difference between the results on IndE and SinE is that the high frequency of object omission in IndE is caused by the interplay of Tp and rich morphology in the substrates. Another interesting observation is the difference between the frequencies of SinE and HKE, since Cantonese is a major substrate of both varieties. A possible explanation for this is that ICE-HK contains more acrolectal English when compared with the other ICE-corpora[19], though it is difficult to estimate whether this detail alone is enough to explain the differences between the varieties. In contrast, the results on FjE can indeed be explained by substrate

---

[19] Lisa Lim, personal communication, 19.4.2013.

influence, as most of the ICE-FJ informants whose speech contained omitted objects were Indo-Fijians, and thus, their L1 is Fijian Hindi.[20] Interestingly, not all of the substrates of PhiE, KenE and JaE examined here were as prominently Tp as those of IndE, SinE, and FjE. Of these three varieties, KenE is the only one where the substrates have morphologies rich enough to explain some level of object omission in the local variety of English, and it is thus interesting that the tendency to omit objects in the variety is not higher than in PhiE.

6 Discussion

Whenever a feature is noted to be common in New Englishes, the explanations offered may vary from linguistic universals to substrate influence and second language acquisition, and often more than one of these alternatives can be regarded as a plausible explanation. Since object omission occurs more frequently in the New Englishes included in the present study than in BrE and AmE, the possibility of other explaining factors should also be addressed here. Sharma (2012) presents a useful theoretical framework, which provides the order in which these competing explanations should be considered. According to Sharma (2012), the explanations can be divided into four main types: 'Properties shared with the superstrate' (A), 'Properties shared with the substrate' (B), 'Acquisitional universals' (C) and 'General universals' (D). Furthermore, Sharma (2012: 221) argues that "[i]t is logical to *first* examine the languages in contact (Types A and B) for proximate causes of shared features before appealing to more general motivations [of Types C and D]". This order will also be followed in this section. Importantly, Sharma (2012: 219) notes that these alternatives should be explored only after "genuine similarity [in the use of the feature] has been established" in the varieties. As was noted in the introduction of this chapter, broad remarks have been presented on the tendency in New Englishes to drop (object) pronouns. However, as the results of the present study indicate, a joint tendency in New Englishes can at least be observed in the case of direct object omission. Therefore, Sharma's (2012: 219) requirement of genuine similarity is met.

According to Sharma (2012: 222), Type A explanations include 'Founder effects', 'Exogenous prestige-driven mimicry' and 'Diffusion from one variety to another'. Since the tendency to omit object pronouns is weaker in the superstrate varieties, which are also the old (BrE) and new (AmE) prestige varieties,

---

[20] Despite the likelihood of this explanation, it should also be acknowledged that the results may be partially skewed by the smaller amount of data available on FjE.

'Founder effects' and 'Exogenous prestige-driven mimicry' do not provide plausible explanations for the prominent use of objet omission in New Englishes. In contrast, the possibility of 'Diffusion from one new variety to another' should be explored further, as the frequencies of IndE, followed by SinE stand out from the results on the other New Englishes. Interestingly, some of the results of recent studies (Hundt et al. 2012: 163; Bernaisch and Gries 2015) suggest that IndE could indeed function as a linguistic epicentre in South Asia (see also Mair 2013: 263–4). Furthermore, although there is no diachronic data available on the majority of Asian Englishes, Parviainen and Fuchs (submitted) have used the apparent-time method to show that some innovative features are more established in IndE than in Southeast Asian Englishes, which supports the idea of IndE having some level of influence on Southeast Asian varieties. The differences between the results on SinE and HKE could further support the idea of diffusion from IndE to SinE: even if the low frequencies of HKE were caused by the differences in the ICE-SIN and ICE-HK data, it seems questionable whether this could solely explain the difference between SinE and HKE results. Therefore, the influence of IndE could have strengthened the tendency to omit object pronouns in SinE, although the possibility of independent development in the latter variety cannot be completely ruled out either.

Sharma (2012: 223) lists 'Accidental resemblance' and 'Areal convergence' under 'Properties shared with the substrate' (Type B) explanations. As the discussion in the previous section shows, substrate influence provides a plausible explanation for many of the results presented here. South and Southeast Asia have functioned as 'melting pots' of various cultures and languages for centuries, which has resulted in linguistic convergence of many languages spoken in the region.[21] Therefore, 'Areal convergence' should be considered the more likely explanation of the two. Furthermore, the levels of Tp in the substrates of the remaining Englishes fall somewhere between the strong Tp of SinE substrates and the strong Sp of English, and the frequencies of object omission in these varieties are also located somewhere between the two. Therefore, substrate influence is the most likely explanation for the differences in the tendency of omitting direct objects in the majority of New Englishes.

Gundel (noted in Junghare 1988: 322) suggests that it is ultimately the topic that controls the zero NP-anaphora in all languages, which would explain why

---

[21] Junghare (1988: 326) suggests that the reason why the Indo-Aryan language branch is more Tp than Sp, despite the fact that Sanskrit (together with other Indo-European languages) had become Sp already by the classical period, is because the other languages spoken in South Asia area are more Tp. Thus, their influence could have caused the Indo-Aryan languages such as Hindi to become more Tp in the course of time.

some examples of object omission were also found in spoken BrE and AmE. Despite this, generic explanations based on language universals should be considered with greater caution. Sharma (2012: 223) argues that "[t]rue emergence of universals would only be certain if the substrates do *not* have a particular feature, and yet the feature arises in offspring varieties of English". Because the concept of topic is predominantly a discourse notion (see Junghare 1988: 322, above), the fact that the data examined comes from private conversations can explain why some instances of object omission are found in all varieties included in the present study. However, because there are also great differences between the English varieties, and because these differences can be explained with substrate influence, it is ultimately the substrate that explains the distribution of the feature among English varieties. Furthermore, as Sharma (2012: 224) notes, "[i]n the absence of either Type A or B explanations it is reasonable to *next* consider the possibility of SLA effects (Type C) before assuming the wider operation of genuine universals (Type D)". Therefore, since Type B (and possibly Type A in the case of SinE) can explain the results presented here, there is no need to look further for explaining factors for object omission in New Englishes. As was mentioned in the introduction, according to Kortmann and Lunkenheimer's (2013) eWAVE database, the omission of object pronouns is "pervasive or obligatory" in IndE, SinE[22], FjE[23], KenE and HKE, whereas "the feature is neither pervasive nor extremely rare" in PhiE. Furthermore, "attested absence of the feature" can be found in JaE (and JaC), AmE and BrE (Kortmann and Lunkeheimer 2013). The results of the present study support the majority of these arguments, although some conflicting observations can also be made. IndE, SinE, FjE and KenE indeed all favour the use of the feature more than the other varieties included in the study, thus supporting some of the arguments presented by Kortmann and Lunkenheimer (2013), but the differences between these four varieties are greater than one would expect based on the eWAVE classification.[24] The other interesting observation is that HKE, which according to Kortmann and Lunkenheimer (2013) favours object pronoun omission strongly, is actually located

---

[22] Kortmann and Lunkenheimer (2013) actually note that the feature is common in "Colloquial Singapore English (Singlish)". Since the data used for this study comes from the category 'Private conversations' and represents informal language use in Singapore, it could be argued that the data examined for this paper is close to Singlish.

[23] According to eWAVE, basilectal FjE does favour the omission of object pronouns, whereas acrolectal FjE does not. Although ICE-FJ contains acrolectal FjE, the data used for this study comes from the section 'Private conversations' and thus represents a more colloquial form of the local variety. This could explain the results obtained from ICE-FJ to some extent.

[24] ICE-IND has been argued to contain more basi/mesolectal English, but considering that only the most informal register of all the corpora were examined in this paper, it is unlikely that this detail would solely explain the high frequencies of IndE.

between KenE and AmE. Another observation worth noting is that the PhiE variety favours the feature as much as KenE, although Kortmann and Lunkenheimer (2013) suggest that the feature is more pervasive in the latter variety. In contrast, the low frequencies of JaE were consistent with the eWAVE data.

7 Conclusion

This paper has examined the frequency of direct object omission in nine varieties of English. The focus has been on spoken informal language and the results indicate that there are clear differences between even those varieties which the previous literature suggest to be convergent. The results support the conclusion that the omission of direct objects is motivated by substrate influence and, in the case of SinE, possible IndE influence. There are many features in New Englishes that descriptive studies have noted to be "common", but as the results of the present study indicate, more comparative data-driven research is still needed, as they can provide interesting insights for the study of Englishes.

References

Ansaldo, Umberto. 2004. The evolution of Singapore English: Finding the matrix. In Lisa Lim (ed.), *Singapore English: A grammatical description*, 127–149. Amsterdam/Philadelphia: John Benjamins.

Ansaldo, Umberto. 2009. *Contact Languages: ecology and evolution in Asia*. Cambridge: Cambridge University Press.

Aranovich, Raúl. 2013. Transitivity and Polysynthesis in Fijian. *Language* 89. 465–500.

Augustin, Maryanne. 2007. Topic and Focus in Swahili. *Graduate Institute of Applied Linguistics (GIAL) Electronic Notes Series* 1. 1–12.

Baskaran, Loga. 2004. Malaysian English: morphology and syntax. In Bernd Kortmann, Kate Burridge, Rajend Mesthrie, Edgar W. Schneider and Clive Upton (eds.), *A Handbook of Varieties of English, Vol. 2: Morphology and Syntax*, 1073–1085. Berlin: Mouton de Gruyter.

Bhatt. Rakesh M. 2004. Indian English: syntax. In Bernd Kortmann, Kate Burridge, Rajend Mesthrie, Edgar W. Schneider and Clive Upton (eds.), *A Handbook of Varieties of English, Vol 2: Morphology and Syntax*, 1017–1030. Berlin: Mouton de Gruyter.

Bernaisch, Tobias and Stefan Th. Gries. 2015, May. Identifying linguistic epicentres empirically: The case of South Asian Englishes. Unpublished conference paper presented at ICAME36, Trier, Germany.

Carter, Ronald and Michael McCarthy. 2006. *Cambridge Grammar of English*. Cambridge: Cambridge University Press.

Cheshire, Jenny, Paul Kerswill, Sue Fox and Eivind Torgersen. 2011. Contact, the feature pool and the speech community: the emergence of Multicultural London English. *Journal of Sociolinguistics* 15. 151–196.

Dixon, R. M.W. 2000. A typology of causatives. In R. M. W. Dixon and Alexandra Y. Aikhenvald (eds.), *Changing valency: case studies in transitivity*, 30–83. Cambridge: Cambridge University Press.
Gounder, Farzana. 2011. *Indentured identities: resistance and accommodation in plantation era Fiji*. Philadelphia: John Benjamins Publishing Company.
Graddol, David. 2010. *English Next India*. London: British Council.
Gupta, Anthea Fraser. 1992. Contact features of Singapore Colloquial English. In Kingsley Bolton and Helen Kwok (eds.), *Sociolinguistics Today: international perspectives*, 323–345. London: Routledge.
Himmelmann, Nicolaus P. 1999. The lack of zero anaphora and incipient personal marking in Tagalog. *Oceanic Linguistics* 38. 231–269.
Huddleston, Rodney and Geoffrey K. Pullum. 2002. *The Cambridge Grammar of the English Language*. Cambridge: Cambridge University Press.
Hundt, Marianne, Hoffmann, Sebastian and Mukherjee, Joybrato. 2012. The Hypothetical Subjunctive in South Asian Englishes – Local Developments in the Use of a Global Construction. *English World-Wide* 33. 147–164.
Hopper, P. J. and S.A. Thompson. 1980. Transitivity in Grammar and Discourse. *Language* 56. 251–99.
Junghare, Indira Y. 1988. Topic-prominence and zero NP-anaphora in Marathi and Hindi. In Mohammad Ali Jazayery and Werner Winter (eds.), *Languages and Cultures*, 309–328. Berlin: Mouton de Gruyter.
Khin Khin Aye. 2005. *Bazaar Malay: history, grammar and contact*. Unpublished PhD thesis, University of Singapore.
Kidwai, Ayesha. 2004. The topic interpretation in universal grammar: evidence from Kashmiri (and German). In Veneeta Dayal and Anoop Mahajan (eds.), *Clause Structure in South Asian Languages*, 253–289. Boston: Kluwer Academic Publishing.
Kittilä, Seppo. 2002. *Transitivity: towards a comprehensive typology*. Turku: University of Turku.
Kittilä, Seppo. 2006. Object-, animacy- and role-based strategies: a typology of object marking. *Studies in Language* 30. 1–32.
Kittilä, Seppo. 2010. Transitivity typology. In Jae Jung Song (ed.), *The Oxford Handbook of Linguistic Typology*, 346–367. Oxford: Oxford University Press.
Koul, Omkar N. 2008. *Modern Hindi Grammar*. Hyattsville: Dunwoody Press.
Kroeger, Paul. 1993. *Phrase Structure and Grammatical Relations in Tagalog*. Stanford: CSLI Publications.
Li, Charles N. and Sandra A. Thompson. 1976. Subject and Topic: A New Typology of Language. In Charles N. Li (ed.), *Subject and Topic*, 458–489. New York: Academic Press.
Lim, Lisa. 2007. Mergers and acquisitions: on the ages and origins of Singapore English particles. *World Englishes* 26. 446–473.
Loftman Bailey, Beryl. 1966. *Jamaican Creole Syntax: A Transformational Approach*. New York: Cambridge University Press.
Mair, Christian. 2013. The world system of Englishes: Accounting for the transnational importance of mobile and mediated vernaculars. *English World-Wide* 34. 253–278.
Mufwene, Salikoko S. 2001. *Ecology of Language Evolution*. Cambridge: Cambridge University Press.
Mugane, John M. 1997. *A Paradigmatic Grammar of Gĩkũyũ*. Stanford: CSLI Publications.
Mukherjee, Joybrato and Stefan Th. Gries. 2009. Collostructional nativisation in New Englishes. *English World-Wide* 30. 27–51.

Myachina, E.N. 1981. *The Swahili language: a descriptive grammar*. Trans. G. L. Cambell. London: Routledge & Kegan Paul.

Neeleman, A., Szendrői, K. 2007. Radical pro drop and the morphology of pronouns. *Linguistic Inquiry* 38. 671–714.

Parviainen, Hanna and Robert Fuchs. (submitted). An apparent-time investigation into clause-final focus particles in Asian Englishes.

Patrick, Peter L. 2004. Jamaican Creole: morphology and syntax. In Bernd Kortmann, Kate Burridge, Rajend Mesthrie, Edgar W. Schneider and Clive Upton (eds.), *A Handbook of Varieties of English. Volume 2. Morphology and Syntax*, 407–438. Berlin/New York: Mouton de Gruyter.

Platt, John T. 1982. English in Singapore, Malaysia and Hong Kong. In Richard V. Bailey and Manfred Görlach (eds.), *English as a World Language*, 384–414. Cambridge: Cambridge University Press.

Platt, John, Heidi Weber and Ho Mian Lian. 1984. *The New Englishes*. London: Routledge and Kegan Paul.

Quirk, Randolph, Sidney Greenbaum, Geoffrey Leech and Jan Svartvik. 1985. *A Comprehensive Grammar of the English Language*. London: Longman.

Rautionaho, Paula. 2014. *Variation in the Progressive: a Corpus-based Study into World Englishes*. PhD dissertation, University of Tampere.

Sato, Yosuke. 2011. Radical pro drop and fusional pronominal morphology in Colloquial Singapore English: Reply to Neeleman and Szendroi. *Linguistic Inquiry* 42. 356–365.

Schachter, Paul. 1976. The subject in Philippine languages. In Charles N. Li (ed.), *Subject and Topic*, 491–518. New York: Academic Press.

Sharma, Devyani. 2012. Shared features in New Englishes. In Raymond Hickey (ed.), *Areal Features of the Anglophone World*, 211–232. Berlin: De Gruyter Mouton.

Shibatani, Masayoshi. 1991. Grammaticization of topic into subject. In Elizabeth Closs Traugott and Bernd Heine (eds.), *Approaches to Grammaticalization, Vol 2: Focus on types of grammatical markers*, 93–133. Amsterdam: John Benjamins.

Siegel, Jeff. 1988. The development of Fiji Hindustani. In Richard K. Barz and Jeff Siegel (eds.), *Language Transplanted: the development of overseas Hindi*, 121–149. Wiesbaden: Harrassowitz.

Smitterberg, Erik. 2005. *The Progressive in 19th-century English: A Process of Integration*. Amsterdam: Rodopi.

Stafford, Roy Lawrence. 1967. *An Elementary Luo Grammar: with vocabularies*. Nairobi: Oxford University Press.

Subbārāo, Kārumūri V. 2012. *South Asian Languages: A Syntactic Typology*. Cambridge: Cambridge University Press.

Yip, Virginia and Steven Matthews. 2007. *The Bilingual Child: early development and language contact*. Cambridge: Cambridge University Press.

Electronic sources

Butt, Miriam. 2001. *Case, Agreement, Pronoun Incorporation and Pro-Drop in South Asian Languages*. (Handout, talk held at the Workshop on The Role of Agreement in Argument Structure, Utrecht) http://ling.uni-konstanz.de/pages/home/butt/ (Accessed 13.2.2014)

Census and Statistics Department, Hong Kong Special Administrative Region. *Thematic Household Survey Report* No. 51. http://www.statistics.gov.hk/pub/B11302512013XXXXB0100.pdf (Accessed 9.10.2013)

Department of Statistics, Singapore, *Population trends 2013* http://www.singstat.gov.sg/publications/publications_and_papers/population_and_population_structure/population2013.pdf (Accessed 7.11.2013)

Fiji Bureau of Statistics, *2007 Population Census* http://www.spc.int/prism/fjtest/Census2007/census07_index2.htm (Accessed 6.6.2014)

International corpus of English –homepage http://ice-corpora.net/ice/importantnote.htm (Accessed 27.11.2011)

National Statistics Office, Republic of the Philippines, *2011 Philippines in Figures*. http://www.census.gov.ph/sites/default/files/2013%20PIF.pdf (Accessed 16.2.2014)

Santa Barbara Corpus of Spoken American English -homepage http://www.linguistics.ucsb.edu/research/santa-barbara-corpus (Accessed 1.9.2014)

Kenya National Bureau of Statistics. *Population and Housing Census 2009, Volume 2- Population and Household Distribution by Socio-Economic Characteristics*. http://www.knbs.or.ke/index.php?option=com_phocadownload&view=category&id=109:population-and-housing-census-2009&Itemid=599 (Accessed 26.6.2014)

Kortmann, Bernd and Kerstin Lunkenheimer, (eds.). 2013. *The Electronic World Atlas of Varieties of English*. Leipzig: Max Planck Institute for Evolutionary Anthropology. http://ewave-atlas.org (Accessed 25.11. 2013)

Appendix

Appendix 1: Chi-square values of the figures presented in Table 1

Overall distribution	X-squared = 148.034, df = 8, p-value < 2.2e-16***
IndE-SinE	X-squared = 6.0564, df = 1, p-value = 0.01386*
SinE-FjE	X-squared = 1.1206, df = 1, p-value = 0.2898
FjE-PhiE	X-squared = 0.3097, df = 1, p-value = 0.5779
PhiE-KenE	X-squared = 0, df = 1, p-value = 1
KenE-HKE	X-squared = 0.5521, df = 1, p-value = 0.4574
HKE-AmE	X-squared = 0.3231, df = 1, p-value = 0.5698
AmE-JaE	X-squared = 0, df = 1, p-value = 1
JaE-BrE	X-squared = 0.5839, df = 1, p-value = 0.4448

Markku Filppula and Juhani Klemola
The definite article in World Englishes[1]

Abstract: Article usage is an area of syntax where a great deal of variation exists in different varieties of English. This study focuses on the uses of the definite article in two specific types of context: with names of social institutions and with the quantifying expressions *both of, half of, most of,* when followed by a postmodifying *of*-phrase. Differences in usage are known to exist between British and American English but in this study the scope is extended to selected varieties spoken in different parts of the world. The social distinction between standard and non-standard language is also examined with respect to British Isles varieties. Language contacts leading to substratal influence on article usage, universal semantic or pragmatic constraints, and possible "angloversal" features emerge as the main factors that can provide plausible explanations for a large part of the variability in definite article usage.

Keywords: definite article, names of social institutions, quantifying expressions, variation, language contact, dialect contact, substratum influence, universal, angloversal, standard vs. non-standard, Animacy Hierarchy, Inner and Outer Circle Englishes

1 Introduction

Article usage is a particularly complex area of grammar as it lies in the crossroads of syntax, semantics and pragmatics. It is therefore not surprising to find a great deal of both diachronic and synchronic variation in article usage between different varieties of English. What makes the study of this variation even more interesting is that it can also occur within a variety, including Standard English itself. For example, in British English names of illnesses or ailments can occur either without an article or with the definite article (DA), thus *(the) measles, (the) whooping cough, (the) headache,* etc. (see, e.g. Quirk et al. 1985: 270–272).

---

[1] This research and the writing of this article were supported by the Academy of Finland funding for the research consortium entitled *Changing English: users and learners worldwide* (grants no. 269114 and 269385), which we gratefully acknowledge.

Markku Filppula, University of Eastern Finland
Juhani Klemola, University of Tampere

DOI 10.1515/9783110429657-009

Similar examples can be cited from most other varieties, and variation is especially common in those that have emerged from contacts with some other language or languages, which may have a different system of article usage or no articles at all. Obvious examples of such varieties are not hard to come by amongst postcolonial Englishes (see, e.g. Sand 2004; Mesthrie and Bhatt 2008: 47–52; Siemund 2013: 90–91, 97–100, and Kortmann and Lunkenheimer 2013, feature items 60–65).

Because of the complex nature of article usage, we have in this paper narrowed down our focus to some non-standard aspects of the use of the definite article. In the context of the British Isles and Ireland, such uses have been noted to be one of the characteristic features of the most Celtic-influenced varieties of English, such as Irish English (see, e.g. Harris 1993; Filppula 1999; Hickey 2007), but they are also attested to varying degrees in other British Isles varieties and World Englishes. Thus, in their survey of varieties of English around the world, Kortmann and Szmrecsanyi (2004) found that irregular use of articles (including also other than the definite article) was among the Worldwide Top 12 features of non-standard varieties of English, attested in 33 of the 46 varieties in the *World Atlas of Varieties of English* (WAVE) survey[2]. It turned out to be a top feature in the British Isles, the Caribbean, Australia, Africa and Asia, but not in America and the Pacific. Variation in article usage is also treated in some detail in Mesthrie and Bhatt (2008: 47–52), who provide plenty of examples from different varieties across the globe and from several Asian varieties, in particular. Siemund (2013: 100–105), in turn, discusses the same phenomena and especially the marking of definiteness from a cross-linguistic, cross-dialectal and typological point of view.

2 Object and aims of this study

The features examined in this paper are, first, the use and non-use of the definite article with names of *social institutions* and, secondly, certain types of *quantifying expressions*. The social institutions selected for closer examination are: *church, college, hospital, school,* and *university,* when used in the institutional sense and not referring to the any specific church, college, school, etc., thus, *be in/at (the) school, go to (the) church/college/hospital* etc. The quantifying expressions to be

---

[2] In the enlarged survey published in electronic form, eWAVE – *The Electronic World Atlas of Varieties of English* (see http://www.ewave-atlas.org/; Kortmann and Lunkenheimer 2013), the number of investigated varieties was increased to 76, including 26 pidgin and creole Englishes.

studied are: *both of, half of, most of,* when followed by a postmodifying *of*-phrase, as in *(the) both/half/most of them.*

As our starting-point we will use the descriptions of article usage in British Standard English given in Quirk et al. (1985: 277–279) and Biber et al. (1999: 261–263). According to both sources, the definite article is typically left out in British StE with the following types of nouns in the following kinds of context:
- non-specific or generic plural NPs;
- names of social institutions such as *school, church,* or *hospital* when used with non-specific reference;
- quantifying expressions such as *most, both, half* when followed by a postmodifying *of*-phrase;
- names of languages, festive days or seasons;
- means of transport or communication.

Our aim is to investigate to what extent the definite article is either left out or used with the names of social institutions and with the mentioned kinds of quantifying expressions in different varieties of English, both traditional and standard, spoken in different kinds of sociohistorical settings world-wide. We also want to examine the factors determining the use of the definite article, and more specifically, the possible role of the following factors:
(i) distinction between standard and non-standard varieties;
(ii) influence of language and/or dialect contacts;
(iii) influence of universal or "angloversal" features of language or (in the case of the latter) of English.

3 Databases

Our first set of set of data represents non-standard traditional varieties of spoken in the British Isles and Ireland. These include:
- **Traditional English English** (Trad EE): *Survey of English Dialects* (SED) *tape-recordings*; interviews with NORM-type[3] informants dating mainly back to the 1950s and early 1960s;
- **Traditional Irish English** (Trad IrE): corpus collected and compiled by Markku Filppula and others in the late 1970s and the early 1980s; informal interviews with elderly speakers with minimum education from four different

---
3 The acronym NORM stands for 'nonmobile, older, rural male' (see Chambers and Trudgill 1980).

regions in the south of Ireland: Counties Clare, Kerry, and Wicklow, and the city of Dublin; most of the informants from the (south)-west of Ireland had some Irish and some lived close to Irish-speaking areas.
- **Traditional Welsh English** (Trad WE):): corpora collected and compiled by Heli Paulasto in Llandybie, Carmarthenshire, south-west Wales, between 1995 and 2000; nearly all the informants were first-language Welsh speakers and had minimum education.

The evidence obtainable from these corpora will be used in this study to examine the effect of the non-standard – standard distinction on definite article usage, the latter being represented by the second set described below. Furthermore, the conservative nature of especially the Traditional British English data opens up a window into nineteenth-century regional English(es) and thus allows some diachronic comparisons to be made.

The second set of data is drawn from a selection of Englishes from the *spoken and unscripted parts* of the *International Corpus of English* corpora, which have been designed to represent the national standard English variety in each of the countries included (for discussion of the data-collection principles and composition of the corpora, visit http://ice-corpora.net/ice/). For American English we have used the Santa Barbara Corpus of Spoken American English (SBCSAE), a widely used surrogate for the as of yet unpublished ICE-USA.

The following varieties were selected for this study:
- **American English** (SBCSAE);
- **British English** (ICE-GB);
- **Canadian English** (ICE-CAN);
- **East African English** (ICE-East Africa);
- **Hong Kong English** (ICE-Hong Kong);
- **Indian English** (ICE-India);
- **Irish English** (ICE-Ireland);
- **Jamaican English** (ICE-Jamaica);
- **Philippines English** (ICE-Philippines);
- **Singapore English** (ICE-Singapore).

The ICE databases consist of transcripts of speech obtained from various types of spoken situations involving educated speakers: dialogue and monologue, face-to-face conversations and radio interviews, lectures, and sportscasts. Stylistically, they range from the informal and colloquial to more formal situations. The size of the individual corpora varies from 500,000 to 600,000 words.[4]

---

[4] The SBCSAE sample we have used is somewhat smaller (ca. 250,000 words) than the spoken parts of ICE-corpora included in the study.

The Asian and African corpora and varieties depicted in these corpora share the following general characteristics:
- they represent (mostly) non-native, yet to a certain extent institutionalised varieties of English, having developed through the educational system(s) of each country;
- they are generally spoken as an L2 in their respective countries;
- they display a wide range of functional and sociolinguistic uses; and
- they may reflect substratal or other influences from the other language(s) involved in the contact setting.

In our comparative set-up, the postcolonial varieties serve an important role in making it possible to assess the extent to which a given feature of article usage is due to influence from a substratal language or, if that can be excluded, whether it could be considered a universal feature of one type or another.

4 Results

We will start off with some examples from the databases to illustrate the types of use of the DA examined. This will be followed by a survey of the distribution of DA and zero article, first, in the nonstandard traditional varieties of British, Welsh, and Irish Englishes and second, in the data from the standard ICE varieties. In the discussion part, then, an attempt is made to assess the role of the possible explanatory factors (non-standard – standard distinction, language/dialect contacts, universal/angloversal features).

The following examples from the corpora we have analysed illustrate uses of the definite article which deviate from the usages described in standard textbooks on English grammar and can in this sense be considered non-standard:

(1) So he say- he came back and he says I'm going to send you to *the hospital*. I think you've had a heart attack. (WE, Llandybie: MT)

(2) B: Apparently there are less people traveling now because of the weather

A: Uh I heard in the news that uh this morning the elementary and high school uh students uh are are excused to go to *the school* right now <,> but in certain areas I think only (ICE-PHI: S1A-050)

(3) so he told me <-/>he told me<-/> that you see in Canada people don't care about going to *the church* (ICE East Africa: S1A-016)

(4) A man who thinks about this <?> filling </?> things etcetera <,> he has missed his way in *the college* (ICE-IND: S2A-035)

(5) B: So Kareen Chow asked me to go. Would you go?
A: Depending on what is going on between *the both* of them (ICE-SIN: S1A-061)

(6) AC: I'd three brothers and two sisters, and they're all gone bar [/] bar [\] me.
MB: Hmm.
AC: Yes. But *the most* of them, well only one that did worse than eighty. (SED: Man2: AC)

Definite article usage – or indeed, article usage in general – is an area of grammar that is not governed by categorical rules. Furthermore, definite article usage is to some extent variable in any variety of English, including so-called Standard English, and depends on a variety of pragmatic and other factors (cf. Sand 2003: 416, 425). In the case of *university* and *hospital*, for example, it can be difficult to draw the line between non-specific references to these institutions (as in *go to university/be in hospital*), as opposed to references to actual buildings or places. It is well known that British and American English differ in this respect: in British English, there is a strong tendency not to use the definite article with *university* and *hospital* when the reference is to the institution rather than the actual building, whereas in American English, the definite article is required in these contexts (see Quirk et al 1985: 277; Tottie 2001: 148).

4.1 Non-standard uses of the definite article in vernacular British Isles varieties

The results of our analysis of the use of the definite article in the contexts examined are shown in Figure 1 and Table 1.

In Traditional English English, the percentage of non-standard uses of the definite article in the contexts examined is very low at 3.4%. There is little evidence for definite article use with any of the investigated items, with more than one instance of the definite article being found only with *school* (3), *hospital* (2) and *most of/on* (3). In the traditional Welsh English corpus, the percentage of the non-standard use of the definite article is somewhat higher level than in Trad EE, at 6.8%. In Welsh English, the highest numbers of instances occur with *hospital* (4), *both of* (3) and *school* (2).[5] The highest percentage of use of

---

5 In addition, the definite article is frequently used in our corpus of Welsh English with names of languages. This is not unexpected, since the construction has a Welsh parallel. We counted 8 instances of *the Welsh* ('Welsh language') and 4 instances of *the English*.

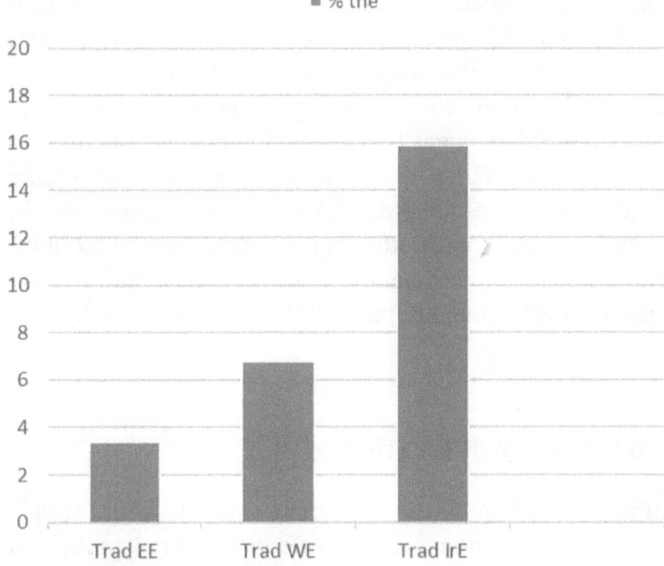

Figure 1: Percentage of non-standard uses of the definite article in Traditional dialects of English, Welsh and Irish English

Table 1: Definite article usage in Traditional dialects of English, Welsh and Irish English, frequencies normalised per 100,000 words (absolute figures in parentheses)

Corpus	The	Ø	Total	% the
Trad EE (515,000)	2.1 (11)	60.0 (309)	62.1 (320)	3.4
Trad WE (61,400)	14.7 (9)	202.0 (124)	216.6 (133)	6.8
Trad IrE (158,000)	13.3 (21)	70.3 (111)	83.5 (132)	15.9

the definite article in the contexts examined, however, is clearly in the traditional Irish English corpus. More than one instance of the definite article is found with *school* (3), *most of* (13), and *half of* (2). Moreover, definite article is the preferred choice in our IrE corpus with *most of* (13 out of 20); the other quantifying expressions show considerably lower frequencies, (1 of 1 for *both of*, 2 of 4 for *half of*).[6]

---

[6] Like WE, IrE often has the definite article with names of languages and especially with that of the indigenous language, Irish (12 instances of *the Irish*, 3 of *the English* in our corpus).

The wider use of the definite article in Welsh English and Irish English is to be expected on the basis of parallel usages in the respective Celtic languages. Thus, in Welsh, names of social institutions are used with the definite article, and the definite article is also used with quantifying expressions (as in e.g. *y ddau* 'the both') and names of languages (*y Saesneg* 'the English (language)') (Thorne 1993: 97–100). In the case of Irish, the parallels to the use of the definite article with names of social institutions are even closer than in the case of Welsh, and these parallels extend, in fact, to most other non-standard uses found in IrE such as names of certain illnesses, place-names, seasons, feasts, and abstract nouns (see Christian Brothers 1976: 6–8; Filppula 1999, section 5.2 for a detailed discussion).

4.2 Definite article usage in ICE varieties

Next, we turn to definite article usage in the ICE varieties investigated. Figure 2 and Table 2 show the percentage of non-standard uses of the definite article in the ten ICE varieties included in our analysis.

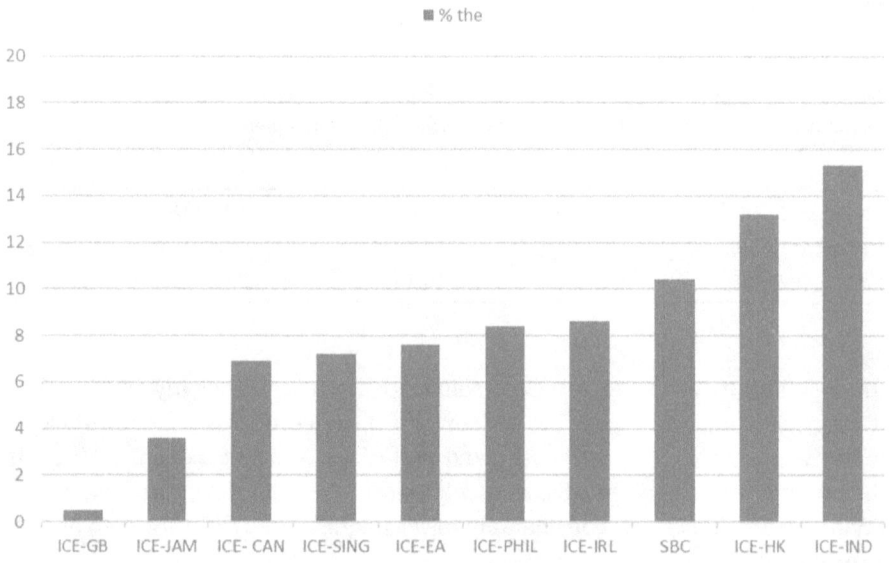

Figure 2: Percentage of non-standard uses of the definite article in ICE varieties of English

Table 2: Definite article usage in ICE varieties of English, frequencies normalised per 100,000 words (absolute figures in parentheses)

Corpus	The	Ø	Total	% the
ICE-GB (528,500)	0.2 (1)	40.1 (212)	40.3 (213)	0.5
SBCSAE (277,500)	4.3 (12)	37.1 (103)	41.4 (115)	10.4
ICE-CAN (535,400)	4.5 (24)	65.4 (350)	69.9 (374)	6.9
ICE-EAfr (261,600)	6.7 (18)	81.5 (220)	88.2 (238)	7.6
ICE-HK (598,400)	14.9 (89)	97.9 (586)	112.8 (675)	13.2
ICE-IND (553,400)	8.1 (46)	44.9 (255)	53.0 (301)	15.3
ICE-IRL (525,500)	4.0 (21)	42.6 (224)	46.6 (245)	8.6
ICE-JA (525,000)	3.4 (18)	93.2 (489)	96.6 (507)	3.6
ICE-PHIL (555,700)	3.9 (22)	42.3 (241)	46.2 (263)	8.4
ICE-SING (496,200)	3.7 (20)	47.0 (257)	50.7 (277)	7.2

As our results show, British English shows by far the lowest frequency of non-standard usages of the definite article at 0.5%. The opposite end of the continuum is represented by the Asian varieties, Hong Kong English (13.2%)[7] and Indian English (15.3%), where the frequency of non-standard uses of the definite article is comparable to that of traditional Irish English. Between these extremes, a number of geographically dispersed varieties form a relatively homogenous group in terms of the frequency of non-standard usages of the definite article (ICE-CAN 6.9%, ICEN-SING 7.2%, ICE-EA 7.6%, ICE-PHIL 8.4%, ICE-IRL 8.6%, SBCSAE 10.4%[8]). Jamaican English, on the other hand, is clearly an outlier, falling between the extremely low frequency of non-standard uses of the definite article in British English and the large group of postcolonial varieties of English.

5 Discussion

The *standard – non-standard* distinction emerges from our results as one significant factor explaining the differences between the varieties examined. Thus,

---

[7] In principle, all the ICE corpora should represent a comparable range of text types. However, as Rautionaho (2014: 159–161) has shown, the spontaneous conversations (S1A) in ICE-HK appear to be rather different compared to the other ICE corpora. This can be seen, for example, in the list of the most frequent verbs in ICE-HK, where ICE-HK clearly differs from all the other ICE corpora.
[8] It must be pointed out, however, that the relatively high frequency of non-standard usages of the definite article in the SBCSAE, representing American English, is to a large extent due to the categorical use of the definite article with *hospital* in the SBCSAE.

TradIrE and ICE-IRL, on one hand, and TradBrE and ICE-GB (though slightly less so), on the other, diverge from each other in their rates of use of the definite article in the kinds of context investigated. This is hardly the full story, though. The clear difference between the educated varieties of IrE (represented by ICE-IRL) and BrE (ICE-GB) suggests influence from some other sources, too. *Language (and dialect) contacts* could be one such factor. This is supported by the language-contact background of the Irish varieties, which is also evident from the higher figures for TradIrE as compared with educated IrE, not to mention several empirical studies of article usage in IrE dialects from early on (e.g. Joyce 1910; Henry 1957; Filppula 1999; Hickey 2007). It is plausible to assume that the influence from the corresponding Irish usages has seeped through into even the present-day educated varieties of IrE. Its likelihood is increased by the fact that Irish substratal influence shows itself in many other grammatical features of educated IrE (see, e.g. Kirk and Kallen 2007; Hickey 2007). This line of reasoning is also backed up by Trudgill's (2011) distinction between "high" and "low" contact varieties. In our database Standard BrE represents the former, while TradEngE represents the latter. All others (including AmE but with the exception of JamE) also belong to the high-contact varieties. As for JamE, there may well be a difference between the standard variety (as in the ICE corpus) and Jamaican creole but that comparison cannot be made on the basis of the current database.

That said, substratal influence cannot be considered the common denominator for all "postcolonial" or "contact" varieties. These include AmE, which displays a relatively high rate of use of non-standard definite articles on the basis of the SBC data. The same also holds for some of the African and Asian varieties. As Sand (2003), among others, points out, many of the relevant regional substratum languages (e.g. Hindi and Chinese) do not possess a definite article. It is also noteworthy that at least in SingE and EAfrE the general tendency is towards omission of articles and other determiners rather than "overuse" of the definite article (Wee 2004; Schmied 2004). In fact, Platt, Weber and Ho (1984: 52–59) have noted a shift in what they call the "New Englishes" from the definite/indefinite distinction to a specific/non-specific distinction, affecting the way articles are used. Documenting this would, however, require a comprehensive study of not only all instances of the definite, indefinite and zero articles in the databases but also other means of indicating specificity/non-specificity of noun phrases such as the use of demonstrative pronouns, and this was not possible within the bounds of the present study.

In the absence of clear substratal parallels and of the kind of sociolinguistic circumstances that would favour substratal influences, a third possible explanation could be *universal* or *angloversal* linguistic features which would then help explain the observed similarities between most of the postcolonial varieties.

Following up this lead, Sand (2003) proposes that definiteness is linked to the well-known Animacy Hierarchy. This hierarchy is universal in nature and has the categories "human" and "proper noun" on top of the list of identifiability of referring expressions. For instance, social and domestic institutions relate to human activities and are thus uniquely identifiable to the hearer; quantifiers, in turn, "logically" adopt the definite article and are universal in that sense. According to Sand, at least some uses of the definite article shared across varieties are therefore not the result of substratal influences but can be explained by universal or angloversal factors such as the Animacy Hierarchy or other general semantic considerations. In another context (see Sand 2004) she expands on this link between definiteness and humanness. She refers to Whaley (1997: 172–73) who has claimed that the Animacy Hierarchy is sociocentrically orientated in that "speakers and writers tend to place most importance on themselves and those listening to them". According to Whaley, this centrality of human referents in discourse then explains why they tend to be definite (and thus occur with the definite article) more often than nonhuman noun phrases (Whaley 1997: 173; quoted here from Sand 2004: 295).

Sharma (2005), also writing on the possible influence of universal pragmatic and discoursal factors, discusses the use of the definite article in Indian English. She finds evidence for both commonly cited L1 effects but also for new, possibly universal, pragmatic functions. Her general conclusion is that, rather than acting as opposing forces, language transfer and universals may work together to produce a mixture of standard and non-standard uses of the definite article (Sharma 2005: 563).

Siemund (2013: 522) is an even more recent study that looks at over-use and under-use of articles and discusses the various factors behind the observed variability in article usage across varieties of English. One of the generalisations emerging from his study is that in non-standard Englishes variability in article usage occurs mostly in those contexts where the standard usage also shows some amount of variation, e.g. in names of diseases, social institutions, seasons, and "cultural uses" (Siemund 2013: 98, 101). Siemund's findings are supported by the results of our study, which revealed considerable variation in the frequencies of non-standard uses in virtually all varieties except Standard BrE.

Another observation in Siemund's study deserves to be noted, too: over-use and under-use of articles often occur concurrently especially in second-language varieties, which of course greatly adds to the variability in article usage (Siemund 2013: 99). A great deal seems to depend on whether the first language of speakers acquiring English has definite or indefinite articles in its grammatical system. According to Siemund, a contact situation easily leads learners to impose or reinterpret the article system of their own language upon that of English. This in turn may result in overuse or underuse of the definite article or the other means of marking definiteness (or indefiniteness) in English (Siemund 2013: 101). Relying on Dryer's (2011) comparative survey of the article systems in the world's languages, Siemund further notes that about one third of the world's languages do not possess either definite or indefinite articles but use some other means of marking them (ibid.). It is obvious that quite a number of these languages are in close contact with English and thus add their own flavour to the general picture of article usage across varieties of English worldwide.

Finally, our results may be compared with those of Wahid (2013), who assesses, amongst other factors, the effects of variety type (i.e., the classification of Englishes into Inner and Outer Circle Englishes) vs. usage type or register on definite article usage. Somewhat surprisingly, Wahid's results show that register is more influential in definite article usage than the division into Inner and Outer Circle Englishes. However, Wahid notes some "marked uses" of the definite article among the Outer Circle varieties but even these are according to Wahid structural (such as presence of a postmodifying phrase) or situational in nature (Wahid 2013: 39). The discussion of our findings above makes it clear that they are in some contrast to those of Wahid: variety type is a factor differentiating especially between the Inner Circle varieties spoken in Britain and most of the Inner or Outer Circle varieties spoken in colonial and postcolonial contexts. It should also be noted that Wahid's study does not consider differences based on lexical categories at all, which is where clear differences exist on the basis of our results.

6 Conclusion

As has become evident, no single factor can be said to explain the observed variability of definite article usage in the Englishes investigated in this study. Instead, one has to assume a complex interplay of factors including linguistic and sociohistorical factors. Among the latter, the relevance of the standard – non-standard distinction was shown by comparisons between the British and Irish varieties, for which both types of data were available. As for the other varieties examined here, the relevance of this distinction awaits further study and appropriate data.

Substratum influence and, more generally, the effects of language contacts are best in evidence in the Celtic varieties of English, but are there, too, possibly reinforced by universal factors. For the Asian and African Englishes, it is harder to identify plausible substratal sources in the absence of the definite article in many of the relevant substrate languages. In these cases, universal or "angloversal" tendencies appear to provide better explanations.

References

Biber, Douglas, Edward Finegan, Stig Johansson, Susan Conrad and Geoffrey Leech. 1999. *Longman Grammar of Spoken and Written English*. London: Longman.
Chambers, J. K. and Peter Trudgill. 1980. *Dialectology*. Cambridge: Cambridge University Press.
Christian Brothers. 1976. *New Irish Grammar*. Dublin: Fallons.
Dryer, Matthew. 2011. Definite Articles. In Dryer, Matthew S. & Haspelmath, Martin (eds.), *The World Atlas of Language Structures Online*. Leipzig: Max Planck Institute for Evolutionary Anthropology. (Available online at http://wals.info/chapter/37)
Filppula, Markku. 1999. *The Grammar of Irish English: Language in Hibernian Style*. London: Routledge.
Harris, John. 1993. The grammar of Irish English. In Milroy, James and Lesley Milroy (eds.), *Real English. The Grammar of English Dialects in the British Isles*, 139–186. London: Longman.
Hickey, Raymond 2007. *Irish English: History and Present-day Forms*. Cambridge: Cambridge University Press.
Kirk, John M. and Jeffrey L. Kallen. 2007. Assessing Celticity in a corpus of Irish Standard English. In Hildegard L. C. Tristram (ed.), *The Celtic languages in contact: Papers from the workshop within the framework of the XIII International Congress of Celtic Studies, Bonn, 26–27 July 2007*, 270–298. Potsdam: Universitätsverlag Potsdam.
Klemola, Juhani and Mark Jones. 1999. The Leeds Corpus of English Dialects–project. In Upton, Clive and Katie Wales (eds.), *Dialectal Variation in English: Proceedings of the Harold Orton Centenary Conference 1998*, 17–30. Leeds: Leeds Studies in English.
Kortmann, Bernd, Burridge, Kate, Mesthrie, Rajend, Schneider, Edgar and Upton, Clive. 2004. *A Handbook of Varieties of English, Vol. 2: Morphology and Syntax*. Berlin & New York: Mouton de Gruyter.
Kortmann, Bernd and Szmrecsanyi, Benedikt. 2004. Global synopsis: morphological and syntactic variation in English. In Bernd Kortmann, Burridge, Kate, Mesthrie, Rajend, Schneider, Edgar and Upton, Clive (eds.), *A Handbook of Varieties of English, Vol. 2: Morphology and Syntax*, 1142–1202. Berlin & New York: Mouton de Gruyter.
Kortmann, Bernd and Lunkenheimer, Kerstin (eds.). 2013. *The Electronic World Atlas of Varieties of English*. Leipzig: Max Planck Institute for Evolutionary Anthropology. (Available online at http://ewave-atlas.org, Accessed on 2016-06-22.).
Lim, Lisa. (ed.). 2004. *Singapore English: A Grammatical Description*. Amsterdam / Philadelphia: John Benjamins.
Mesthrie, Rajend and Rakesh M. Bhatt. 2008. *World Englishes: The Study of New Linguistic Varieties*. Cambridge: Cambridge University Press.
Platt, John, Weber, Heidi and Ho, Mian Lian. 1984. *The New Englishes*. London, Boston, Melbourne and Henley: Routledge and Kegan Paul.
Quirk, Randolph, Sidney Greenbaum, Geoffrey Leech and Jan Svartvik. 1985. *A Comprehensive Grammar of the English Language*. London: Longman.
Rautionaho, Paula. 2014. *Variation in the Progressive: A Corpus-based Study into World Englishes*. (Acta Universitatis Tamperensis 1997). Tampere. Tampere University Press.
Sand, Andrea. 2003. The Definite Article in Irish English and Other Contact Varieties of English. In Hildegard L.C. Tristram (ed.), *The Celtic Englishes III*, 413–430. Heidelberg: Winter.
Sand, Andrea. 2004. Shared morpho-syntactic features in contact varieties of English: article use. *World Englishes* 23 (2). 281–298.

Schmied, Josef. 2004. East African English (Kenya, Uganda, Tanzania): morphology and syntax. In Bernd Kortmann, Kate Burridge, Rajend Mesthrie, Edgar Schneider, Clive Upton (eds.), *A Handbook of Varieties of English, Vol.2: Morphology and Syntax*, 929–947. Berlin and New York: Mouton de Gruyter.

Sharma, Devyani. 2005. Language transfer and discourse universals in Indian English article use. *Studies in Second Language Acquisition* 27(4). 535–566.

Siemund, Peter. 2013. *Varieties of English: A Typological Approach*. Cambridge: Cambridge University Press.

Thorne, David A. 1993. *A Comprehensive Welsh Grammar*. Oxford: Blackwell.

Tottie, Gunnel. 2001. *An Introduction to American English*. Oxford: Blackwell.

Trudgill, Peter. 2011. *Sociolinguistic Typology: Social Determinants of Linguistic Complexity*. Oxford: Oxford University Press.

Wahid, Ridwan. 2013. Definite article usage across varieties of English. *World Englishes* 32(1). 23–41.

Wee, Lionel. 2004. Singapore English: morphology and syntax. In Bernd Kortmann, Burridge, Kate, Mesthrie, Rajend, Schneider, Edgar and Upton, Clive (eds.), *A Handbook of Varieties of English, Vol. 2: Morphology and Syntax*, 1058–1072. Berlin & New York: Mouton de Gruyter.

Whaley, Lindsay J. 1997. *An Introduction to Typology: The Unity and Diversity of Language*. Thousand Oaks: Sage.

Paul Rickman
Aspects of Verb Complementation in New Zealand Newspaper English[1]

Abstract: The present paper describes a new diachronic corpus of New Zealand newspaper English compiled at the University of Tampere. Using material from the Fairfax archives, the corpus covers selected periods from the last two decades, and comprises approximately 100 million words. Using data from the corpus in addition to pre-existing data on British and American English, the paper then explores aspects of the complementation patterns of the verbs of prevention. The study aims to highlight selected aspects of NZE usage in comparison to BrE usage, with the older postcolonial variety AmE used as a point of reference. The study goes on to discuss the direction of change discernible in the development of NZE, with reference to the concept of 'colonial lag'. It is argued that while certain changes may be classified as developmental lags, examples of other types of diachronic change, including innovation, are also evident.

Keywords: New Zealand English (NZE), British English (BrE), American English (AmE), complementation, verbs of prevention, colonial lag, diachronic change, newspaper language, Corpus of New Zealand Newspaper English (CNZNE), British National Corpus (BNC), Corpus of Contemporary American English (COCA), Corpus of Late Modern English Texts (CLMET3.0)

1 Introduction

The main Southern Hemisphere Englishes – New Zealand, Australian and South African – have provided fertile ground for linguistic analysis, and what is emerging is a picture of young nations that are comfortable with their identities – a large part of that identity being the language that they take pride in calling their own. In each of these three varieties, English has taken on its own unique

---

[1] This research was made possible by funding from the Academy of Finland, under the GlobE consortium. The author would like to thank all members of the consortium, the audience at ChangE Helsinki 2013 and an anonymous reviewer for helpful comments on the paper.

Paul Rickman, University of Tampere

DOI 10.1515/9783110429657-010

flavour, having absorbed features of the pre-existing native language(s), and, in the case of NZE at least, the old and the new now exist side by side. In New Zealand, both English and Māori have official status, and the lexical presence and influence of the latter in New Zealand today is clear and undeniable, evident in place names, terms for flora and fauna, and, perhaps to a lesser extent, more general vocabulary items (see e.g. Davies and Maclagan 2006; Macalister 2006).

The view that New Zealand English (NZE) is a separate and unique variety of English is not new, with commentary and studies on its various phonological and lexical features dating back many years (for a summary see Gordon and Abell 1990). However, the view that NZE contains unique grammatical features was only established in more recent decades. Regarding genuine syntactic New Zealandisms, it was recently noted that "there are actually relatively few syntactic features that are wholly unique to New Zealand" (Hay et al. 2008: 47), and some 20 years prior to that, it was noted that any differences that exist are not radical, but are manifest in "matters of degree rather than in categorical distinctions" (Bauer 1989b: 82). In the closing years of the twentieth century, Hundt (1998) presented a convincing argument supporting the view that several aspects of NZE grammar do serve to set it apart from the other main varieties, and it has been argued that "even if, in terms of grammar, usage in New Zealand is found to agree closely with the standards of the United States and Britain, that does not mean that it makes no sense to speak of New Zealand English morphosyntax" (Hundt et al. 2008: 305).

The present paper aims to contribute to the literature on NZE by using new NZE data alongside BrE and AmE data to address the question of "colonial lag" and other manifestations of postcolonial linguistic development and differentiation. The paper is structured as follows: Section 2 describes a new corpus compiled at the University of Tampere in order to support further studies on NZE; Sections 3 presents a study of the sentential complements of the *prevent*-type verbs, with evidence from NZE, BrE, and AmE corpora. A diachronic approach is taken, allowing categorisation of the apparent changes underway in NZE within the framework of the six-way typology of diachronic change proposed in Hundt (2009). Section 4 summarises the colonial lag question, introduces the typological framework, and provides a discussion of results. Here I provide evidence in support of the idea that the linguistic "lag" scenario is only a small part of a more complex system of changes taking place in NZE. Section 5 provides concluding remarks.

2 The New Zealand Newspaper Corpus[2]

Basing research on corpora consisting entirely of newspaper material requires little justification these days; a look at some recent work (Macalister 2001; Rohdenburg 2002; Mukherjee and Hoffmann 2006; Davies and Maclagan 2006; Calude and James 2011) shows that a carefully compiled corpus of media language can provide a solid foundation for linguistic analysis, provided the usual restrictions regarding generalisability of results are kept in mind.

The currently available set of NZE corpora are well compiled and useful for a wide range of research goals, but they are nevertheless small by today's standards, and therefore unsuitable for certain uses. In a recent study on constructions in four varieties of English, Mair found aspects of his investigation restricted by the small size of the corpora used, commenting at one point that his results are "bedeviled by the very low figures in some cells" (Mair 2009: 271). The corpora were the Brown/LOB quartet for written AmE and BrE, the Wellington Corpus of Written New Zealand English (WWC) and the Australian Corpus of English (ACE) for written NZE and AusE. The latter two are based on the Brown/LOB template, with 1980s/90s material, allowing comparison to Frown/FLOB. For spoken English, Mair used the 600,000 word spoken sections of the ICE corpora, which, as noted above, were not large enough to give a full picture of the patterns associated with some predicates. In an earlier study Hundt et al. comment that "the data on *dare* from the one-million-word corpora are too meagre to verify any hypotheses on diachronic change or regional variation" (Hundt et al. 2008: 319), and some years prior to that Bauer noted the sparse data available for *farewell*, *screen*, and *appeal* in the same group of corpora (Bauer 2001).

With size thus being one of the main prerequisites, I set about compiling a corpus of NZE newspaper text (The Corpus of New Zealand Newspaper English – CNZNE) using material from the archives of Fairfax Media.[3] Fairfax is one of the main media groups in Australasia, controlling publications that span the length of New Zealand and include major metropolitan newspapers from three of the four main centres – Auckland, Wellington, and Christchurch – as well as several provincial papers. Care was taken to ensure that papers from as many different regions of the country as possible were included, since, while it is generally

---

[2] Prof. Dr. Sebastian Hoffmann gave valuable and much needed assistance in the compilation of the corpus in connection with the data retrieval and processing, for which I am extremely grateful. All Perl scripts used in the process were written by him.
[3] Fairfax Media New Zealand kindly granted permission for their material to be republished in my work.

acknowledged that NZE is more homogeneous than BrE and AmE, there is still known to be some, albeit minor, regional variation (Turner 1966: 163 ff.; Bauer and Bauer 2000; Hay et al. 2008: 95 ff.; Calude and James 2011).

The aim was to compile a diachronic corpus, the earlier sub-section of which would parallel the British National Corpus (BNC)[4] newspaper sub-section. The composition of the BNC sub-corpus, according to the numbers retrieved from the BNCweb (CQP-Edition) interface, is given in Table 1.

Table 1: BNC newspaper sub-section word counts

Arts	593,014
Commerce	850,071
Editorial	102,718
Miscellaneous	1,040,943
Report	3,403,683
Science	121,199
Social	1,234,095
Sports	1,333,385
Tabloid	733,066
Total	9,412,174

While BNC news material covers the period 1985–93, the Fairfax archives contain electronic material going back only as far as 1995, which was deemed close enough to the BNC time frame to allow valid comparison.[5] From the period 1995–98, one-year samples (which included all available material) were taken from a selection of 10 broadsheet newspapers (nine daily and one weekly), and two-year samples were taken from two weekly tabloid newspapers. Two-year tabloid samples were taken in order to try and increase the amount of this type of material, which still remains somewhat lower in comparison to broadsheet material than the ratio found in the BNC.

One- and two-year samples (which, again, included all available material) of the same papers, where possible, were taken from the 2010–12 period, forming the second section to the corpus. The 2010–12 sub-section contains material from only 10 papers, due to the fact that in 2002 two of the newspapers merged, and in 2006 one of the tabloids ceased its contribution to the archives. Table 2 provides the details of both sub-sections of the NZE corpus.

---

[4] A genre-balanced corpus comprising 100 million words of British English (90% written, 10% spoken) covering the years 1960–1993.

[5] Details of the BNC newspaper material show that the majority of the data, which is mainly taken from the larger metropolitan papers *The Independent*, *The Guardian*, and *The Daily Telegraph*, is from the period Oct 1989–Apr 1992.

Table 2: Newspapers, periods sampled, and word counts in the CNZNE

Newspaper	Period Sampled	Word Tokens
Section 1: 1995–98		
Daily News*	Aug 1996–Jul 1997	2,676,265
Dominion**	Jan 1995–Dec 1995	7,725,459
Evening Post**	Jan 1996–Dec 1996	6,874,558
Evening Standard*	Jun 1996–May 1997	2,158,689
Nelson Mail	Jul 1997–Jun 1998	2,221,658
Press	Jan 1997–Dec 1997	3,710,614
Southland Times	Mar 1997–Feb 1998	4,223,612
Sunday News (tabloid)	Dec 1995–Nov 1997	3,626,271
Sunday Star Times	Dec 1995–Nov 1996	4,096,501
Timaru Herald	Jul 1996–Jun 1997	1,422,032
Truth (tabloid)***	Dec 1995–Nov 1997	808,631
Waikato Times	May 1996–Apr 1997	3,049,242
Total		42,593,532
Section 2: 2010–12		
Dominion Post	Jan 2011–Dec 2011	10,142,874
Manawatu Standard	Jan 2011–Dec 2011	5,022,767
Nelson Mail	Jan 2010–Dec 2010	4,668,709
Press	Jan 2012–Dec 2012	10,980,886
Southland Times	Jan 2012–Dec 2012	5,940,329
Sunday News (tabloid)	Jan 2010–Dec 2011	3,435,614
Sunday Star Times	Jan 2012–Dec 2012	3,583,489
Taranaki Daily News	Jan 2010–Dec 2010	4,809,591
Timaru Herald	Jan 2011–Dec 2011	4,134,794
Waikato Times	Jan 2010–Dec 2010	5,775,395
Total		58,494,448

* name of paper changed – *Daily News* Section 1 = *Taranaki Daily News* Section 2; *Evening Standard* Section 1 = *Manawatu Standard* Section 2
** merged to become *Dominion Post* in Section 2
*** not found in the archive after 2006

The sample periods of the 2010–12 sub-section are noticeably more uniform than those of the earlier sub-section. This is due to most of the newspapers having begun electronic archiving at different times in the mid-1990s – not always at the beginning of the calendar year – and the date from which each paper first appears in the electronic archive was taken as the starting point for each paper's sample period. When compiling the 2010–12 sub-section on the other hand, the priority was to maximise the gap between the two sub-sections, while spreading the sample years out over a three-year period in an attempt to minimise or avoid the duplicate problem (discussed below).

The Fairfax archives provide relatively clean material consisting of the full text of each article, title, name of author if available, and a set of tags denoting section, sub-section, topic and sub-topic. As well as texts from all the usual newspaper sub-genres, the archives naturally also include all normal newspaper service information. Macalister (2001: 37) mentions this type of text, defining it as "lists – sports results, tv programmes, share prices, weather forecasts, and so on". He chose to exclude it from his work, and I have done the same, on the grounds that it does not contribute much towards a clear picture of the aspects of NZE under investigation. (1) below is an example of service information text, and (2) is an abridged article from the sports sub-genre.

(1) BOX OFFICE
1 (new) Transformers: Dark of the Moon 2 (1) Cars 2 3 (2) Bridesmaids 4 (4) Bad Teacher 5 (3) Green Lantern 6 (8) My Afternoons with Margueritte 7 (5) X-Men: First Class 8 (6) The Hangover Part II ... (Dominion Post, 2011)

(2) The Canterbury Crusaders will name their team tomorrow.... The players from outside the region are: Mark Weedon (North Harbour), Norman Maxwell (Northland), Pat Lam (North Harbour), Andy Miller (Bay of Plenty) and Graham Dempster (South Canterbury) ... (Sunday News, 1995)

In order to deal with service information text as efficiently and objectively as possible, a Perl script was used to identify and remove articles whose content exceeds predefined thresholds for the number of words consisting of numerical characters, or beginning with a capital letter (*word* defined here as any character or series of characters separated on either side by a white space). The thresholds were set, based on consideration of the material, at 15 per cent for numericals and 45 per cent for capitals. The full text of example (1) exceeds both numerical and capital thresholds, at 19.66 per cent and 56.84 per cent respectively; while (2) exceeds only the capital threshold, at 49.06 per cent (articles exceeding either or both thresholds were removed). Service information-type text accounted for approximately seven million words in the original set of texts in the 1995–98 section, and around 10 million in the 2010–12 section.[6]

---

[6] Another issue, concerning the presence of duplicate articles in the material, surfaced when test concordances were being carried out with an early version of the corpus. It seems that sometime between the mid-1990s and 2012, publications within the Fairfax group began sharing articles to a much greater extent than they had done previously, i.e. the same article is published in more than one Fairfax newspaper, often with slight paraphrasing, or sometimes with none. This results in excessive numbers of duplicate, triplicate and even quadruplicate tokens showing up in the search results. Indeed, duplicates are found in other, more high-profile corpora to a

The corpus has been tagged for part-of-speech, using the CLAWS4 tagger (Garside and Smith 1997) – the same software that was used to tag the BNC. At this stage it is not possible to carry out genre-specific searches of the corpus.

To summarise, the CNZNE was designed and compiled for the purpose of researching grammatical patterns in NZE that have thus far been beyond the reach of existing corpora. Comparison with BNC – and indeed COCA (1995–99) – newspaper data is possible. The CNZNE period covers the greater part of the last two decades; a period in which enormous advances in information technology and global communications have taken place, and for this reason alone investigations into change and variation in postcolonial Englishes over this period are justified, and can be expected to produce worthwhile results.

3 Verbs of prevention: background and preliminary results

3.1 Background

In this part of the paper CNZNE data is used alongside BrE and AmE data to investigate the variable use of the complementiser/preposition[7] *from* with verbs of prevention in NZE, BrE, and AmE. The pattern in question is V + NP + (*from*) + *-ing*, as illustrated in examples (3–7) below with the two prototypical verbs of this class, *prevent* and *stop*.

(3)   ... to drag their careless owners out of range of exploding barbecues or *prevent their foolish children from gulping* down bottles of bleach. (CNZNE, Evening Post, 1996)

(4)   Now only bad luck or selectorial whims look capable of *preventing the pair representing* New Zealand at next year's Games in Dublin. (CNZNE, Sunday Star Times, 1997)

---

certain extent, but I wanted to eliminate them from the CNZNE as much as possible. The chosen solution was to run all 2010–12 data sharing the same sample year through the plagiarism detection software Wcopyfind, which resulted in the detection of around 13,000 articles that were more or less copies of other articles. These were removed, reducing the word count of the 2010–12 section to 58,494,448. The 1995–98 section did not require this step, as the duplicate issue here is minimal.

7 *From* in *prevent*-type patterns has been analysed as a complementiser (see e.g. Rosenbaum 1967: 89ff; Aarts 1990), and the label *complementiser/preposition* is used in Mair's work. In the present study however, while recognising the implication of these earlier works, for the sake of simplicity I adopt a permissive attitude towards terminology and use the label *preposition*.

(5) Antony was struck with polio as a young boy. This *prevented his pursuing the musical career he almost certainly would have chosen.* (CNZNE, Sunday Star Times, 1997)[8]

(6) ... appears to have lost the house he mortgaged to fund a case aimed at *stopping the creationists from "peddling* their poppycock to schoolchildren". (CNZNE, Daily News, 1997)

(7) His response was neither clever nor funny but that didn't *stop him flying* to Ohio to deliver his line and make himself look a total jerk. (CNZNE, Southland Times, 1997)

Variable preposition use with these verbs in some varieties of English is an area that is well covered in the literature, the earlier work documenting both quantitative and qualitative aspects of the variation. The present study takes a quantitative approach, using new data to assess the recent trends in NZE. The new NZE data will also shed light on the less frequently used verbs *ban, bar, block, deter, discourage, dissuade, forbid, hinder, prohibit, restrain, save* and *spare*,[9] the details of which have been difficult to assess with the smaller corpora.

Earlier work, based on the Brown/LOB quartet and the WWC (Mair 2009), has found that regarding *prevent*, NZE resembles BrE in making use of both the *from* and *from*-less patterns in varying degrees, while AmE speakers, on the other hand, favour the former, more explicit version almost exclusively. The general situation with *stop* was found to be similar to that of *prevent*, though use of the *from*-less variant with *stop* was somewhat more advanced than *prevent* in BrE. There has been a pronounced shift in BrE speaker preference over the past century in the case of both of these verbs, and it has been noted

---

8 (5) represents the pattern that is commonly referred to in the literature as *poss -ing*: a possessive/genitive NP preceding the gerund. The *poss -ing* pattern in this context is no longer as common as it once was, nowadays being mainly restricted to formal registers, and structures with pronominal NPs or NPs with personal reference (Quirk et al. 1985: §16.42), and its presence in the corpora used for this study was indeed found to be minimal. It has also been pointed out that *prevent* and *stop* differ in respect to their compatibility with the *poss -ing* pattern, with *stop* being less likely to license it (Huddleston and Pullum 2002: 1238; Heyvaert et al. 2005: 83–84). More to the point, *poss -ing* does not accommodate *from* with *prevent*, nor any other verbs in this group (Rudanko 1989: 118). All tokens of this type are therefore excluded from the analysis section below.

9 This group of 12 of the lesser-used verbs of prevention/discouragement was selected from the larger group as being those which may promise at least some degree of variation with *from*. While some small benefits might have arisen from the inclusion of more verbs, the analysis of every verb from e.g. Huddleston and Pullum's (2002: 657) list was seen as casting the net unnecessarily wide.

that "changes in the complementation of *prevent* represent one of the rare instances in which the grammars of the British and American standard have definitely moved apart in the course of the twentieth century" (Mair 2006: 130). Mair confirms that over the course of approximately one century the *from*-less pattern with *prevent*, having been at one time also a possibility in AmE, was all but eradicated from that variety, and gained ground with some speed in BrE.

It has also been noted that "a similar trend seems to be affecting the entire semantic class of what could be called verbs of prevention" (Mair 2006: 132). This observation both justifies research into the wider group of verbs, and provides grounds for some of the assumptions that it will be necessary to make in the present research. These assumptions are necessary due to the unfortunate fact that this study does not have access to BrE newspaper data from the 2010–12 period to match the recent CNZNE material, and it will therefore not be possible to provide evidence of BrE movement over the past two decades. Mair's view lends weight to the assumption that the BrE shift in favour of the *from*-less variant is widespread – affecting the whole semantic class – and ongoing.

Much of the earlier discussion in the literature surrounding this class of verbs is of a qualitative nature, and the question of factors motivating the variable preposition usage has been approached from several angles (Poutsma 1904: 649; Jespersen 1940: 148; Rohdenburg 2002; Rudanko 2002; Herbst et al. 2004; Dixon 2005; Mair 2009; Sellgren 2010). The subject of much of this earlier discussion lies outside the scope of the present study, but one previously noted structural factor bears mentioning here: Rohdenburg's (1996: 151) Complexity Principle states that "in the case of more or less explicit grammatical options the more explicit one(s) will tend to be favored in cognitively more complex environments". The principle suggests that in the present context, sentences hosting one or more features that contribute to increased cognitive complexity (passives and other types of structural discontinuity, complex NPs etc.) would tend to include the preposition, in order to ease the processing burden. This is indeed the case when the matrix clause is in the passive voice, where, with the majority of verbs in this group, there is little option but to include it in Present-day English[10] (Huddleston and Pullum 2002: 1238). The following tokens, from NZE and BrE illustrate *prevent*, *stop*, and *ban* in the passive.

(8)   Every day deaf New Zealanders are *prevented from* doing something that hearing New Zealanders take for granted. (CNZNE, Southland Times, 2012)

---

[10] Huddleston and Pullum (*ibid.*) note that the *from*-less passive is possible "very marginally with *prevent* and *stop* (?*She was prevented/stopped writing to us*)".

(9) The accident report also said the company should be *stopped from* operating out of Porirua Harbour ... (CNZNE, Evening Post, 1996)

(10) Kim Basinger is refusing to open an Argentinian disco named after her unless blondes are *banned from* standing near her in a photo session. (BNC, CEK 2986)

Due to this lack of variation, passive tokens are omitted from the results in the data analysis section below. One verb, however, in an interesting departure from the behaviour of the rest of the class, does allow *from* omission with the passive in all three varieties:

(11) Wellington supporters were *spared* having to watch the clinical dissection of their team as it happened. (CNZNE, Dominion, 1995)

(12) Since it's breakfast, you are mercifully *spared* ordering salad, because salad comes with a metronomically-recited choice of dressing ... (BNC, AL3 1518)

(13) With the machine I was *spared* having to relay dissertations. (COCA, NEWS, 1998)

From-less *spare* passives are indeed found in the corpus data, but in very low numbers.[11] For the sake of consistency therefore, they will be omitted along with the rest of the passives.

3.2 Data and methodology

The data used for this section are taken from both sub-sections of the CNZNE (42.6 m. + 58.5 m. words), the BNC newspaper sub-section (9.4 m. words), and the Corpus of Contemporary American English (COCA)[12] (1995–1999) news sub-section (20.4 m. words). As is well known, AmE shows little variation in the use of *from* with *prevent* and *stop* (Mair 2009), and so AmE data is used in this study only as a point of reference. With this in mind, the large numbers of COCA tokens for some verbs were thinned down to more manageable random samples

---

[11] CNZNE 1995–98: two tokens; CNZNE 2010–12: two tokens; BNC: two tokens; COCA: one token.
[12] A genre-balanced corpus comprising 450 million words of American English, covering the period 1990–2012, compiled by Mark Davies at Brigham Young University.

for analysis.[13] With the main focus being NZE and BrE, all available data for these varieties has been used.

In addition, it will be helpful at times to look beyond the boundaries of the corpora mentioned above, and therefore brief reference is made to evidence from the entire BNC and COCA, as well as the latest version of the Corpus of Late Modern English Texts (CLMET3.0).[14] This extra material, while not matching the genre of the main data set under investigation here, is employed only to provide clues as to the behaviour of certain verbs – in the case of CLMET3.0 – in years past.

The CNZNE and CLMET3.0 were processed with AntConc 3.2.4w concordancing software. The BNC and COCA were accessed through the BNCweb (CQP-Edition) interface and the BYU interface respectively. With corpus word counts being unbalanced, normalised frequencies are given alongside raw numbers in all tables and charts below.

3.3 Results

At this point I introduce the synchronic (1990s) data from the three varieties, with Table 3 below containing both the normalised frequencies and the raw frequencies for all predicates in the CNZNE 1995–98, the BNC and COCA. The table lists the two prototypical members of the group, prevent and stop, first, then the remaining 12 in alphabetical order.

As mentioned earlier, all examples of the *poss -ing* pattern and matrix clause passives are excluded from these figures, as there is no possibility of prepositional variation. These omissions, coupled with the genre bias introduced by the use of newspaper corpora, mean that the results given here are not directly comparable with results of earlier work. Despite this, on a general level the profile for NZE that emerges here appears to agree with that suggested in earlier work; NZE exhibits a broadly BrE profile. The avoidance of the *from*-less pattern with all verbs of the group in AmE is also clear.

---

13 A search for the lemma [prevent] returns 1608 hits. From these, 500 were selected at random and analysed, which resulted in the raw numbers given in Table 3. Normalised frequencies were calculated according to the reduced size of the total available data set (31.09% of all hits). The same procedure was followed for [stop].[v*] (500 from a total of 4968) and [save].[v*] (500 from a total of 3103). All other verbs produced more manageable numbers of hits.

14 CLMET3.0 contains around 34.4 m. words of genre-balanced BrE text from the period 1710–1920, arranged in three sub-sections (1710–1780, 1780–1850, 1850–1920). Compiled by Hendrik De Smet, Hans-Jürgen Diller and Jukka Tyrkkö (https://perswww.kuleuven.be/~u0044428/).

Table 3: Prevention verbs in NZE, BrE and AmE

	CNZNE 1995–98	BNC	COCA
prevent + NP + *-ing*	21.2 (904)	29.5 (278)	0.3 (2)
prevent + NP + *from* + *-ing*	19.5 (832)	23.5 (221)	30.5 (194)
stop + NP + *-ing*	31.1 (1325)	39.9 (376)	0.5 (1)
stop + NP + *from* + *-ing*	13.5 (575)	8.0 (75)	13.6 (28)
ban + NP + *-ing*	0.3 (13)	0.1 (1)	–
ban + NP + *from* + *-ing*	2.6 (110)	5.1 (44)	1.5 (30)
bar + NP + *-ing*	0.1 (6)	–	0.0 (1)
bar + NP + *from* + *-ing*	1.2 (51)	2.3 (22)	5.4 (110)
block + NP + *-ing*	0.2 (10)	0.2 (2)	–
block + NP + *from* + *-ing*	0.3 (14)	0.1 (1)	1.3 (26)
deter + NP + *-ing*	0.3 (11)	0.1 (1)	–
deter + NP + *from* + *-ing*	2.5 (107)	2.4 (23)	0.8 (17)
discourage + NP + *-ing*	0.4 (18)	0.1 (1)	0.0 (1)
discourage + NP + *from* + *-ing*	2.1 (90)	2.1 (20)	4.6 (94)
dissuade + NP + *-ing*	–	–	–
dissuade + NP + *from* + *-ing*	0.8 (36)	0.6 (6)	0.7 (15)
forbid + NP + *-ing*	0.2 (8)	–	0.0 (1)
forbid + NP + *from* + *-ing*	0.5 (21)	1.1 (10)	1.9 (38)
hinder + NP + *-ing*	0.1 (3)	0.2 (2)	–
hinder + NP + *from* + *-ing*	0.0 (1)	0.1 (1)	0.2 (5)
prohibit + NP + *-ing*	0.4 (19)	–	–
prohibit + NP + *from* + *-ing*	0.9 (39)	0.7 (7)	7.9 (161)
restrain + NP + *-ing*	–	–	–
restrain + NP + *from* + *-ing*	0.4 (16)	0.6 (6)	0.3 (6)
save + NP + *-ing*	0.9 (37)	1.1 (10)	–
save + NP + *from* + *-ing*	2.2 (92)	3.4 (32)	3.0 (10)
spare + NP + *-ing*	0.0 (1)	–	–
spare + NP + *from* + *-ing*	0.1 (4)	0.2 (2)	0.2 (4)

Numbers outside brackets represent normalised frequencies per one million words; bracketed numbers represent raw figures.
COCA normalised frequencies for *prevent*, *stop* and *save* were calculated based on adjusted corpus numbers. See footnote 13 for further details.

No tokens of the *from*-less complement were found with *dissuade* and *restrain* in the corpora, despite speculation that with all but one (*keep*) of the verbs in Huddleston and Pullum's (2002, 657) list, "*from*-less variants are possible in theory, and – on the strength of the *prevent* model – expected in British English." (Mair 2006: 132). An extended search covering the entire BNC also failed to turn up any relevant tokens. *Dissuade* and *restrain* will therefore receive no further attention in the analysis section below.

Section 4 below provides the main analysis of the results, where the more recent NZE data is placed alongside the synchronic data. The issue of colonial lag is also raised in Section 4, since the discussion here aims to classify all instances of change according to this framework.

4 Discussion

This section opens with a discussion of colonial lag, the conceptual background against which the subsequent data analysis will be conducted. In the analysis section, the verbs, rather than being treated separately, are treated in groups according to similarity of changes apparent.

4.1 Colonial lag

A number of recent studies on variation among varieties of English make reference to the concept of 'colonial lag'. The term itself was coined in the mid-twentieth century (Marckwardt 1958: 80) to label a phenomenon that had been the subject of comment since the late nineteenth century, and is typically used to refer to older, now archaic features of the original mother country language which are still used in the language of a colony. The term 'colonial innovation' similarly refers to cases of linguistic innovation in the language of the colony. The concept and terminology have been critically discussed and further refined in recent years (see e.g. Görlach 1987; Trudgill 1999 and 2004; Bauer 2002; Dollinger 2006; Hundt 2009). The discussion I focus on here is that of Hundt (2009: 14), who notes that "the dichotomy of 'colonial lag' and 'colonial innovation' – especially when it is applied to features of post-colonial English [...] – implies a far too simplistic view of the much more complex patterns and processes of language change". Hundt goes on to restrict colonial lag to one of a wider set of six possible scenarios in the development of grammatical features of postcolonial Englishes. The term 'colonial' English is replaced with 'extraterritorial' English (ETE) (following Lass 1990, cited in Hundt 2009: 15), and 'lag' is superseded by 'conservatism' to avoid any negative and misleading connotations. The six scenarios outlined by Hundt are:

(a) Extraterritorial conservatism: older forms of home country usage are retained in the ETE
(b) Extraterritorial innovation
(c) Truly divergent patterns develop in both varieties
(d) Parallel developments in both varieties

(e) The revival of an older form in either variety
(f) Kick-down developments: what starts out as conservatism gathers momentum to overtake home country usage, and becomes innovation

Hundt's case study concerns BrE and AmE, and indeed she is able to categorise all divergent features she addresses according to the above typology. In the case of the two main varieties of English, there appears to be little need to allow for an additional scenario, one which might prove relevant when dealing with less dominant varieties. In this regard I suggest a seventh possibility – scenario (g): change under the influence of another main variety. This would be a case in which a variety (e.g. NZE) that has traditionally been seen as being grammatically closer to one main variety (BrE) than the other (AmE), begins to exhibit grammatical tendencies more associated with AmE.[15] With the addition of this extra scenario, the seven-way typology can be applied to the data, and will be referenced throughout the discussion below.

On a final note, it is important, particularly in the context of NZE, to consider Trudgill's view, that a degree of lag is likely to be present, at least for a short time, in the language of a certain type of founder society.[16] All in all there appears to have been a complex blend of forces at work on the emerging NZE dialect during the lifetimes of the first generations of New Zealanders, and straightforward explanations of variation and change are not always going to be possible.

4.2 *Prevent* and *stop*

Table 4 presents the data on the two main verbs from the 1995–98 and 2010–12 sections of the CNZNE.

---

15 It must be pointed out that in the absence of the comparable 2010-12 BrE data, any potential scenario (g) classifications – or indeed any classifications that require knowledge of current BrE trends – can only really be speculative at this point, since there is no way of knowing whether it is in fact AmE that is providing the model for NZE.

16 In Trudgill's view, a lag can occur when "there is no common peer-group dialect for children to acquire in first-generation colonial situations involving dialect mixture" (Trudgill 2004: 34). The children therefore reach adulthood speaking more like their parents than is normally the case, and the language of the colony is thus prevented from following the natural paths of development by the space of around one generation. The early New Zealand settlers were just this type of mixed-dialect founder group; a good proportion originated from various parts of the British Isles and spoke a wide variety of dialects, and there was very little or no pre-established English-speaking population in most of the areas in which they settled. Figures denoting the origins of the early settlers, according to census data from the year 1881, are: England 49%; Scotland 22%; Ireland 20%; Australia 7%; Wales 1%; North America 1%. (from McKinnon 1997, cited in Trudgill et al. 2000).

Table 4: *Prevent* and *stop* in NZE (1995–98 and 2010–12)

	CNZNE 1995–98	CNZNE 2010–12
prevent + NP + *-ing*	21.2 (904)	15.8 (925)
prevent + NP + *from* + *-ing*	19.5 (832)	20.3 (1190)
stop + NP + *-ing*	31.1 (1325)	27.1 (1585)
stop + NP + *from* + *-ing*	13.5 (575)	16.2 (948)

Numbers outside brackets represent normalised frequencies per one million words; bracketed numbers represent raw figures.

The situation in NZE with the two main verbs of this group is somewhat surprising, with the data suggesting change in NZE over the CNZNE period in favour of the more explicit pattern with both verbs – a reversal of the same type of shift that has taken place in BrE over the twentieth century. Note that due to the absence of sufficient diachronic data no such movement has actually been documented in NZE, but it is reasonable to assume that a shift very similar to that which BrE has experienced has taken place.

Concerning NZE developments from the perspective of colonial lag, the twentieth-century restructuring of the patterns of sentential complements for *prevent* and *stop* could, up until the late 1900s, have been classed as a lag, since it could be seen as though NZE was following and trailing behind the BrE lead. It now appears that NZE is in the process of reverting to the more explicit pattern, which could arguably be seen as a result of AmE influence. Keeping in mind the important fact that comparable 2010–12 BrE data is unavailable, and thus going on the assumption that the BrE change continues in favour of the *from*-less option, I suggest scenario (g): change under the influence of another main variety, as a classification for *prevent* and *stop*, pending the availability of BrE data.

4.3 *Forbid, hinder, prohibit,* and *save*

Table 5 gives the data on these verbs from the 2010–12 section of the CNZNE, alongside the earlier data of Table 3 for comparison.

These four verbs are grouped together by virtue of their being the only four – outside of the two main verbs – that are found in CLMET3.0 (in low numbers) with the *from*-less complement. The following tokens illustrate this earlier BrE usage.

Table 5: *Forbid, hinder, prohibit* and *save* in NZE (1995–98 and 2010–12)

	CNZNE 1995–98	CNZNE 2010–12
forbid + NP + *-ing*	0.2 (8)	0.0 (2)
forbid + NP + *from* + *-ing*	0.5 (21)	0.4 (22)
hinder + NP + *-ing*	0.1 (3)	0.1 (3)
hinder + NP + *from* + *-ing*	0.0 (1)	0.1 (4)
prohibit + NP + *-ing*	0.4 (19)	0.2 (10)
prohibit + NP + *from* + *-ing*	0.9 (39)	1.2 (70)
save + NP + *-ing*	0.8 (37)	0.7 (39)
save + NP + *from* + *-ing*	1.9 (92)	2.5 (146)

Numbers outside brackets represent normalised frequencies per one million words; bracketed numbers represent raw figures.

(14) … but should inimical circumstances *forbid* me closing with your kind offer … (CLMET 2)

(15) We went to bed rather fatigued, but not so much so as to *hinder* us getting up this morning to mount Skiddaw. (CLMET 2)

(16) Paul *prohibits* all Christians, in every age, celebrating it at all. (CLMET 3)

(17) It'll *save* you having to walk from the Maypole, there and back again. (CLMET 3)

Two of these – *forbid* and *prohibit* – are not found governing *from*-less complements in the BNC data; an absence which may indicate a rise and subsequent fall of that pattern in BrE, and present a counterargument to the assumption that the BrE move toward the *from*-less complement is taking place among all verbs of this class. *Forbid* and *prohibit* are found with *from*-less complements in the CNZNE however, with numbers declining across the period of the last two decades. The fortunes of the *from*-less complement in NZE could thus be seen as tracing the same course as BrE, but lagging behind by at least one generation. Scenario (a): ETE conservatism (colonial lag) therefore seems an appropriate classification of the progress of *forbid* and *prohibit*.

In the case of *save*, diachronic NZE shows only a slight drop in the *from*-less complement between sub-corpora. The drop being so slight, it could easily be a case of random fluctuation, and thus relatively unremarkable. *Save* does, however, stand out from the rest of the group, in recording the highest use of the *from*-less complement behind the two main verbs *prevent* and *stop* in both NZE and BrE, as well as having been noticed (Mair 2006) to be acting like the prototypical prevention verbs in BrE, showing a clear predilection for the *from*-less pattern. Furthermore, the NZE rise in the more explicit pattern is something to be noted; it may also be instructive to take account of the raw frequencies in comparison to the normalised data in this regard. For the above reasons I would suggest that *save* is likely to be following the same path as *prevent* and *stop* in NZE, that is, an apparent return to the more explicit complement pattern, possibly under AmE influence: scenario (g). As with *prevent* and *stop* in the previous section, this classification is speculative, pending the missing BrE data.

Hinder maintains similar numbers in both halves of the CNZNE, and aside from not being attested in the *from*-less form in AmE, it shows no major discrepancy in numbers across varieties. As noted above, it is attested in CLMET3.0 – where the more explicit complement far outweighs the less explicit – and is still evident, with a total of only three tokens, in the BNC, where the more explicit complement happens to be in the minority. It could be assumed to be following the course of *prevent* and *stop* in BrE, but with numbers overall being too low to reveal much, *hinder* will not be categorised here.

4.4 *Bar* and *spare*

Bar and *spare* are both found with the *from*-less complement in the CNZNE data but not the BNC data. In total, NZE yields six *from*-less tokens of *bar*, and one of *spare*, all of which are in the 1995–98 sub-section. Table 6 presents the relevant data.

Table 6: *Bar* and *spare* in NZE (1995–98 and 2010–12)

	CNZNE 1995–98	CNZNE 2010–12
bar + NP + *-ing*	0.1 (6)	–
bar + NP + *from* + *-ing*	1.2 (51)	1.0 (59)
spare + NP + *-ing*	0.0 (1)	–
spare + NP + *from* + *-ing*	0.1 (4)	0.0 (2)

Numbers outside brackets represent normalised frequencies per one million words; bracketed numbers represent raw figures.

Expanding the search to take in the entire BNC and COCA reveals that the *spare* + NP + *-ing* pattern is in fact also to be found in both BrE and AmE, as attested by the following tokens.

(18) I have fetched in enough buckets of coal this afternoon to *spare* you having to carry them in tomorrow. (BNC, fiction, HGE 1179)

(19) His slouch hat *spared* him being cut by the mirror shards raining down around him. (COCA, FIC, 2008)

With AmE generally not conducive to the *from*-less complement, the fact that there are several other examples of this type in COCA – as well as the issue of *from*-less passivisation in NZE, BrE, and AmE (§3.1) – separates *spare* from the other verbs here, and makes it a worthwhile topic for further research. In the meantime, it will not be classified here, due to low numbers and incomplete data.

Bar + NP + *-ing*, also the subject of an expanded search of the BNC and COCA, is found only in NZE – with a fairly convincing six tokens – and in AmE. One token, from NZE, is given below.

(20) Wellington lawyer Tony Ford said the law *barred* relatives claiming exemplary damages after a death. (Evening Post 1996)

The *bar* + NP + *-ing* pattern could be a candidate for scenario (b): ETE innovation. A complication, however, is presented by the fact that *bar* + NP + *-ing* is found only in the 1995–98 section, and not the later section of the CNZNE. Future research will have to determine whether the case for innovation can be upheld.

4.5 *Ban, block, deter* and *discourage*

The remaining four verbs are all found with the *from*-less complement in the modern data. Table 7 below provides the relevant numbers.

Table 7: *Ban, block, deter* and *discourage* in NZE (1995–98 and 2010–12)

	CNZNE 1995–98	CNZNE 2010–12
ban + NP + *-ing*	0.3 (13)	0.2 (10)
ban + NP + *from* + *-ing*	2.4 (110)	2.8 (162)
block + NP + *-ing*	0.2 (10)	0.1 (5)
block + NP + *from* + *-ing*	0.3 (14)	0.7 (43)
deter + NP + *-ing*	0.3 (11)	0.2 (14)
deter + NP + *from* + *-ing*	2.5 (107)	2.1 (124)
discourage + NP + *-ing*	0.3 (18)	0.1 (8)
discourage + NP + *from* + *-ing*	2.1 (90)	2.1 (124)

Numbers outside brackets represent normalised frequencies per one million words; bracketed numbers represent raw figures.

Absence of the *from*-less complement from CLMET3.0 would indicate that the use of this complement with these verbs is a twentieth-century addition to both BrE and NZE. The *from*-less pattern with *ban, block, deter*, and *discourage* in NZE, while being equal to or – in most cases – higher than that of BrE in the 1990s, shows a decline (at least with *ban, block*, and *discourage*) over the period between the NZE sub-corpora. This appears to be a situation where a pattern has emerged at roughly the same time in both varieties – although admittedly it is not possible to discern the progression timeline in each variety from the current data – and is now beginning to drop out of use in at least one of those varieties (comment cannot be made on recent BrE developments). Classification under Hundt's type (d) change: parallel developments in both varieties, would seem appropriate.

5 Conclusion

Bigger is not always better, but when focus is on the lesser-used predicates in a language, corpus size becomes all-important. Various earlier studies mention target predicates, then, due to the lack of suitably large corpora, fail to provide conclusive results. To address this, a diachronic newspaper corpus was compiled and put to the test in a case study on the complementation of 14 *prevent*-type verbs. The results show that the creation of the corpus was justified (though admittedly two of the chosen verbs were still not well represented), and the literature on NZE will benefit from it.

Certain aspects of the results of the case study go some small way towards strengthening the justification for spending more time on investigating New Zealand grammar, as it sits in relation to the main varieties of English. The diachronic overview of the last two decades of NZE newspaper language given here allows qualification of the comment that, in regard to this area of the grammar, "no rapid recent "Americanization" of usage can be observed" (Mair 2009: 263): it does appear that, in the case of *prevent* and *stop* – and at least one of the minor verbs from the group – NZE usage is beginning to drift away from the BrE model, possibly under the influence of AmE, though it would be rash to apply the term "Americanization" at this stage. This was not found to be the case for all verbs of this semantic group; in fact one important finding of this study was that while some – *prevent, stop* etc. – appear to be drifting in one direction, many are still apparently on the same path as their BrE counterparts. Thus the assumption that all verbs of prevention are following the same trend – movement in the BrE direction – cannot be upheld. It is important to reiterate the caveat that, until these results are cross-checked against the relevant BrE data, they must remain speculative at this point. The present study, therefore, opens up possibilities for future research, and provides justification for the creation of a comparable corpus of BrE newspaper data.

The present study supports the view, expressed in much of the literature on extraterritorial Englishes, that while there often is a type of lag evident in one area of the grammar of an extraterritorial variety, belated development is only a small part in the more complex system of change taking place in the different varieties of English worldwide. Hundt suggests six possible scenarios for extraterritorial English change, I have added one more to that list, and four of these scenarios were applied to 10 of the verbs analysed here.

References

Primary sources

BNC – The British National Corpus (http://www.natcorp.ox.ac.uk/)
COCA – The Corpus of Contemporary American English (http://corpus.byu.edu/coca/)
CLMET3.0 – The Corpus of Late Modern English Texts, version 3.0 (https://perswww.kuleuven.be/~u0044428/clmet3_0.htm)
CNZNE – The Corpus of New Zealand Newspaper English

Secondary sources

Aarts, Bas. 1990. Prevent-type verbs in a GB-framework. UCL *Working Papers in Linguistics* 2. 147–164.
Bauer, Laurie. 1989b. The verb have in New Zealand English. *English World-Wide* 10(1). 69–83.
Bauer, Laurie. 2001. Some verb complements in New Zealand English. *New Zealand English Journal* 15. 29–34.
Bauer, Laurie. 2002. *An Introduction to International Varieties of English*. Edinburgh: Edinburgh University Press.
Bauer, Laurie & Winifred Bauer. 2000. Nova Zelandia est omnis divisa in partes tres. *New Zealand English Journal* 14. 7–17.
Calude, Andreea & Paul James. 2011. A diachronic corpus of New Zealand newspapers. *New Zealand English Journal* 25. 35–52.
Davies, Carolyn & Margaret Maclagan. 2006. Maori words – read all about it: testing the presence of 13 Maori words in four New Zealand newspapers from 1997 to 2004. *Te Reo* 49. 73–99.
Dixon, R. M. W. 2005. *A Semantic Approach to English Grammar*. Oxford: Oxford University Press.
Dollinger, Stefan. 2006. The modal auxiliaries have to and must in the Corpus of Early Ontario English: Gradient change and colonial lag. *Canadian Journal of Linguistics* 51(2). 287–308.

Garside, R., and Smith, N. 1997. A hybrid grammatical tagger: CLAWS4. In Garside, R., Leech, G., and McEnery, A. (eds.), *Corpus Annotation: Linguistic Information from Computer Text Corpora*, 102–121. Longman, London.
Gordon, Elizabeth & Marcia Abell. 1990. 'This objectionable colonial dialect': Historical and contemporary attitudes to New Zealand speech. In Bell, Allan & Janet Holmes (eds.), *New Zealand Ways of Speaking English*, 21–48. Clevedon: Multilingual Matters Ltd.
Görlach, Manfred. 1987. Colonial lag? The alleged conservative character of American English and other 'colonial' varieties. *English World-Wide* 8. 41–60.
Hay, Jennifer, Margaret Maclagan, & Elizabeth Gordon. 2008. *New Zealand English*. Cambridge: Cambridge University Press.
Herbst, T., D. Heath, I. Roe & D. Götz. 2004. *A Valency Dictionary of English*. Berlin: Mouton de Gruyter.
Heyvaert Lisbet, Hella Rogiers & Nadine Vermeylen. 2005. Pronominal Determiners in Gerundive Nominalization: A "Case" Study. *English Studies* 86(1). 71–88.
Huddleston, Rodney & Geoffrey Pullum. 2002. *The Cambridge Grammar of the English Language*. Cambridge: Cambridge University Press.
Hundt, Marianne. 1998. *New Zealand English Grammar – Fact or Fiction?* Amsterdam: John Benjamins.
Hundt, Marianne, Jennifer Hay & Elizabeth Gordon. 2008. New Zealand English: morphosyntax. In Burridge, K. & Bernard Kortmann (eds.), *Varieties of English: The Pacific and Australasia*, 305–340. Berlin: Mouton de Gruyter.
Hundt, Marianne. 2009. Colonial lag, colonial innovation or simply language change? In Rohdenburg, Günter & Julia Schlüter (eds.), *One Language, Two Grammars?*, 13–37. Cambridge: Cambridge University Press.
Jespersen, Otto. 1940. *A Modern English Grammar on Historic Principles. 7 vols.* Copenhagen: Munksgaard.
King, Michael. 2003. *The Penguin History of New Zealand*. Auckland and London: Penguin Books.
Macalister, John. 2001. Introducing a New Zealand newspaper corpus. *New Zealand English Journal* 15. 35–41.
Macalister, John. 2006. The Māori presence in the New Zealand English lexicon, 1850–2000. *English World-Wide* 27. 1–24.
Mair, Christian. 2006. *Twentieth Century English*. Cambridge: Cambridge University Press.
Mair, Christian. 2009. Infinitival and gerundial complements. In Peters, P., P. Collins and A. M. Smith (eds.), *Comparative Studies in Australian and New Zealand English*, 263–276. Amsterdam: John Benjamins.
Marckwardt, Albert. 1958. *American English*. New York: Oxford University Press.
Mukherjee, Joybrato & Sebastian Hoffmann. 2006. Describing verb-complementational profiles of New Englishes: A pilot study of Indian English. *English World-Wide* 27(2). 147–173.
Poutsma, Hendrik. 1904. *A Grammar of Late Modern English: Part 1 – The Sentence*. Groningen: P. Noordhoff.
Quirk, Randolph, Sidney Greenbaum, Geoffrey Leech & Jan Svartvik. 1985. *A Comprehensive Grammar of the English Language*. London: Longman.
Rohdenburg, Günter. 1996. Cognitive complexity and increased grammatical explicitness in English. *Cognitive Linguistics* 7(2). 149–182.
Rohdenburg, Günter. 2002. Processing complexity and the variable use of prepositions in English. In Cuyckens, H. & Radden, G. (eds), *Perspectives on Prepositions*, 79–100. Max Niemeyer: Tübingen.

Rosenbaum, Peter. 1967. *The Grammar of English Predicate Complement Constructions*. Cambridge: MIT Press.
Rudanko, Juhani. 1989. *Complementation and Case Grammar: A Syntactic and Semantic Study of Selected Patterns of Complementation in Present-day English*. Albany, New York: State University of New York Press.
Rudanko, Juhani. 2002. *Complements and Constructions: Corpus-based Studies on Sentential Complements in English in Recent Centuries*. Lanham MD: University Press of America.
Sellgren, Elina. 2010. Prevent and the battle of the –ing clauses. In Lenker, U., J. Huber & R. Mailhammer (eds.), *English Historical Linguistics 2008: Volume 1: The history of English verbal and nominal constructions*, 45–62. Amsterdam: John Benjamins.
Trudgill, Peter. 1999. A window on the past: "Colonial lag" and New Zealand evidence for the phonology of nineteenth-century English. *American Speech* 74(3). 227–239.
Trudgill, Peter. 2004. *New Dialect Formation*. Edinburgh: Edinburgh University Press.
Trudgill, Peter, Elizabeth Gordon, Gillian Lewis & Margaret MacLagan. 2000. Determinism in new-dialect formation and the genesis of New Zealand English. *Journal of Linguistics* 36(2). 299–318.
Turner, G. W. 1966. *The English Language in Australia and New Zealand*. London: Longman.

Lea Meriläinen, Heli Paulasto and Paula Rautionaho
Extended uses of the progressive form in Inner, Outer and Expanding Circle Englishes

Abstract: This article examines extended uses of the progressive form (PF), especially the stative and habitual functions, across Inner, Outer and Expanding Circle Englishes. Extended use of PF has been observed in numerous L1 and L2 varieties, and it is often characterized as an angloversal (i.e, a shared non-standard feature) found in Englishes worldwide. Although this feature is sometimes explained with factors relating to second language acquisition (SLA) and teaching in the context of L2 varieties, it has been less examined in English used by foreign language learners. Some recent studies have compared non-standard uses of PF across a range of English as a native language (ENL), English as a second language (ESL) and English as a foreign language (EFL) varieties, but there is, thus far, no systematic description of the semantically extended (esp. habitual and stative) uses of PF in a large sample of Englishes. In the present study, the functional variation of PF is examined in a large number of Englishes representing ENL, ESL and EFL, taking into consideration the fact that the functional variation is linked to the ongoing general increase of the construction over the past few centuries. The results reveal considerable variation in terms of the frequency and functions of PF between the corpora. The factors which primarily account for extended use of PF are the type of English (ENL, ESL, EFL), the substrate language or the learners' L1, and in the case of EFL data, the learners' proficiency level. The present results do not lend support for the angloversality of extended PF use as a general learner language feature.

Keywords: progressive form (PF), stative use, habitual use, angloversal, Kachru's Three Circles model, Inner Circle, Outer Circle, Expanding Circle, English as a foreign language (EFL), English as a second language (ESL), learner English, World Englishes, substrate language, transfer

1 Introduction

Non-standard use of the progressive form (PF) has been widely discussed in earlier literature on World Englishes (e.g., Platt et al. 1984; Mesthrie and Bhatt

---

Lea Meriläinen and Heli Paulasto, University of Eastern Finland
Paula Rautionaho, University of Tampere

2008). It is a feature that may be regarded as an *angloversal*, i.e., a shared non-standard feature across geographically distant varieties of English (for a review of the notion, see, e.g. Meriläinen and Paulasto 2017). Angloversals (a term introduced by Mair 2003) have drawn considerable interest over the past decade in connection with the mapping of morphosyntactic variation in Englishes world-wide (e.g. Kortmann and Szmrecsanyi 2004; Kortmann and Lunkenheimer 2013). Earlier research suggests various sources for these shared features: endogenous development, contact influence, or universals of vernacular English, cognitive processing or second language acquisition (see, e.g. Filppula et al. 2009a; Meriläinen and Paulasto 2017).

The focus of this article is on extended uses of PF, especially to stative and habitual functions, which are reported to be globally widespread (see Kortmann and Lunkenheimer 2013). Although this feature has been examined in numerous earlier studies (e.g., Gachelin 1997; van Rooy 2006, 2014; Paulasto 2006, 2014; Collins 2008; Sharma 2009; Filppula et al. 2009b; Rautionaho 2014), systematic comparisons of non-standard semantic functions across different types of Englishes are still in short supply. The present study undertakes such a comparison in a wide variety of corpora representing Inner Circle, Outer Circle and Expanding Circle Englishes, which are generally associated with English as a native language (ENL), English as a second language (ESL) and English as a foreign language (EFL), respectively (Kachru 1985)[1]. Through such a comparison, this study aims at promoting research into these different types of Englishes under a joint framework (see Mukherjee and Hundt 2011), and shedding new light on the possible roles of transfer and/or universals of second language acquisition (SLA) in the development of angloversals. The variation in the semantic functions of PF also connects to the general increase in its use over the past centuries and to the new or more prominent functions that PF has adopted in several varieties and registers (e.g. Smitterberg 2005; Leech et al. 2009; Kranich 2010). The present study examines the variation in the functions of PF also in the light of these ongoing changes.

The following sections discuss the typical functions of PF and its recent developments, and briefly introduce earlier studies on PF across ENL, ESL and EFL. Sections 4 and 5 outline the empirical part of this paper. The results are then presented in terms of frequencies of use and semantic categories of PF in

---

[1] We are aware of the possible mismatch between Inner Circle and ENL, Outer Circle and ESL, and Expanding Circle and EFL (e.g., Hundt and Vogel 2011; Edwards 2014) as well as the critical points of view towards these categories. However, we consider them useful for methodological purposes and will be using these labels interchangeably throughout this article, as customarily done in World Englishes research. In line with Szmrecsanyi and Kortmann (2011: 169), we approach the distinctions between ENL, ESL and EFL as an empirical question rather than as an 'a-priori issue'.

the three types of Englishes, with a focus on the imperfective and, in particular, the extended stative and habitual functions. Finally, the results are discussed in relation to the commonalities and differences that emerge between the corpora and the variables which are found to be the most influential in constraining or enabling extended uses of PF across the investigated varieties and learner Englishes.

2 The progressive form: recent developments

The construction called progressive form (i.e., BE + V–*ing*) has attracted considerable attention in recent years because it is a structure that is currently undergoing a change in English; not only has the use of PF increased in frequency over the past few centuries, but it has also expanded in its scope and developed new functions in several varieties, genres and registers (e.g. Smitterberg 2005; Leech et al. 2009; Kranich 2010). Historically, PF has grammaticalized from a stylistic device in OE and ME into a full-fledged aspectual marker in ModE (see, e.g. Leech et al. 2009: 121–122; Kranich 2010). As a sub-category of the imperfective aspect[2], the basic function of PF is the progressive one, i.e. indicating that an activity is in progress, incomplete, and has limited duration (Quirk et al. 1985: 197–198). Besides its aspectual function, PF has 'special functions', denoting events which are actualized in the future, or which are habitual or nondurative (e.g. Leech et al. 2009: 119). In the latter cases, PF may convey a subjective (negative) speaker attitude or interpretation of a given situation or event (Kranich 2010: 61–76).

There are various reasons for the growing use of PF in PDE. In their corpus-based diachronic study of British English (BrE) and American English (AmE), Leech et al. (2009: 122–143) explain the increased frequency of PF with colloquialization, as the highest frequencies are attested in press, fiction and speech-like registers (e.g., face-to-face conversations, broadcast discussions or private letters). Functionally speaking, the primary factor in the increased overall use of PF in BrE appears to be the subjective (interpretative) function, as shown in Kranich (2010: 228).[3] Similarly, Smitterberg (2005: 174) ascribes the change to the increased use of 'not-solely-aspectual' progressives as well as that of stative verbs.

---

[2] Non-progressive imperfective situations are typically stative or generic-habitual ones. These are conveyed either through the simple present and past verb phrases or a specific habitual construction, such as *used to* + V (see, e.g. Comrie 1976: 24–40).
[3] Rautionaho (2014: 193) examines four subcategories within the general subjective function and shows that there is in fact a great deal of variation across Englishes, most varieties indicating a preference for narrative PF use.

The English PF is unusually wide in its scope in comparison to other languages with a progressive category. The above non-aspectual uses are partly the reason for this, but PF also has a tendency to extend to the imperfective non-progressive domains of stativity and habituality. This characteristic is of special interest in this article, because stative and habitual extension are prime examples of the non-traditional uses that PF has acquired in varieties of English. The previous, above-mentioned studies in World Englishes therefore set a point of comparison for examining similar uses across a broader range of corpora, including English by foreign language learners.

Stative use of PF is constrained in standard BrE and AmE, as it continues to be unacceptable with verbs indicating prototypical states (e.g., *we're owning a house in the country*; Quirk et al. 1985: 198–199; see also Leech et al. 2009: 292). However, specific conditions, such as temporal delimitation or subjectivity, permit the use of most stative verbs in PF, including verbs of perception and sensation (e.g. *you're imagining things*), cognition, emotion and attitude (e.g. *that will be much sooner than you're thinking*), having and being (e.g. *the British Government is being deliberately slow*) and stance (e.g. *we are living in a crucial time*; examples from Leech et al. 2009: 129–130). PF thus softens the distinction between the lexical situation types of stative and dynamic verbs (see Kranich 2010: 49–54). Similarly, the combination of PF with habitual activities is described as being possible in certain contexts only: when the activity in question has a limited duration (cf. *the professor types his own letters* vs. *the professor is typing his own letters while his secretary ill*), when it combines with progressivity (e.g. *whenever I see her, she's always working in the garden*; examples from Quirk et al. 1985: 199) or when PF is modified by a time adverbial such as *always*, expressing the speaker's subjective attitude (e.g. *I imagine you're always battling in school*; Leech et al. 2009: 134, see also Smitterberg 2005: 210–217). In our categorization of the functions of PF in Section 5, we set the aspectual functions apart from the subjective ones.

In spite of the above restrictions, several contact-induced varieties of English display stative and habitual uses that remain extremely rare in standard BrE or AmE. These extended uses are discussed further in the following sections.

3 The progressive form in World Englishes and learner English

According to the *electronic World Atlas of Varieties of English* (eWAVE; Kortmann and Lunkenheimer 2013), extension of PF to stative verbs (e.g. *I'm liking this*) is pervasive or common in 38/76 varieties, and extension to habitual contexts (e.g.

I am often playing computer games on Saturday and Sunday) in 20/76 varieties. The majority of the varieties where these extended uses are found are high-contact L1 and L2 varieties. In earlier studies, extension of PF to stative contexts is considered a feature of many indigenized L2 varieties, which has been explained with, for instance, an overemphasis on PF in English teaching or the fluidity of the distinction between stative and dynamic verbs in StE, thus giving rise to overgeneralization by ESL speakers (Platt et al. 1984: 72–74; Mesthrie and Bhatt 2008: 67). Extended habitual functions of PF have been examined less, but they are also reported in several contact-induced varieties, including Welsh English, Black South African English and Indian English (e.g., Paulasto 2006, 2014; van Rooy 2006, 2014; Sharma 2009; Rautionaho 2014). Gachelin (1997) explains the widespread extended uses of PF in varieties of English with the aspect-prominence of numerous substrate languages in Africa and Asia as well as in the Celtic countries (see also Sharma 2009; Filppula et al. 2009b; Paulasto 2014).

Although language contact and second language acquisition (SLA) appear to factor behind this feature in several studies, non-standard uses of PF are examined relatively little in English used by foreign language learners. Evidence from EFL learners would be highly relevant for the study of this feature as well as of other angloversals, for it may open new perspectives on the SLA-related explanations behind these shared features. Some studies report quantitative 'overuse' of PF in Swedish-speaking and German-speaking EFL learners' written English, but semantically their PF usage is mainly standard-like (e.g. Virtanen 1997; Axelsson and Hahn 2001; Römer 2005). Ranta (2013) examines English as a lingua franca interaction by speakers from various L1 backgrounds, and finds no evidence for overuse of PF by non-native speakers in comparison to native speakers. Both speaker groups also manifest qualitatively similar, albeit relatively few, extended uses, which Ranta (2013: 104) interprets as a feature of spoken English grammar in general.

The scarcity of studies examining this feature in EFL is partly due to the fact that World Englishes and learner English have long been studied within different paradigms (see Mukherjee and Hundt 2011), and thus the study of angloversals has not yet been systematically extended to learner English (but see Meriläinen and Paulasto 2017). Studies involving comparisons of PF in ENL, ESL and EFL include van Rooy (2006), Hundt and Vogel (2011), Davydova (2012), and Edwards (2014). Van Rooy (2006) compares Black South African English (ESL) and English by German learners (EFL), and finds substrate-induced extension of PF in ESL, while EFL appears to model itself on Inner Circle norms. Hundt and Vogel (2011) examine the frequencies and non-standard (esp. stative) uses of PF across a number of ESL and EFL varieties, and conclude that unlike ESL varieties, learner English tends to rely on prototypical uses of PF and does not tolerate the combination of PF with stative verbs. Davydova (2012) examines PF, among a number of other features, in Indian English and in English spoken in Russia, and finds hardly any overgeneralization in Russian learner English in contrast to Indian English. Edwards (2014) observes that PF use in Dutch English (traditionally regarded as EFL) has characteristics of both EFL and ESL varieties, demonstrating norm orientation in terms of the overall frequency but more frequent use of extended functions than in Singapore English (yet less than in Indian English). It is noteworthy, however, that these studies have primarily looked at EFL learners or users whose L1 does not mark lexical aspect (German, Dutch, Swedish, Finnish), and who are at advanced levels of English proficiency and therefore likely to be highly aware of the norms of standard English. Further studies on EFL learners and comparisons of ESL and EFL are needed in order to ascertain whether these two types of non-native Englishes exhibit similar types of extended uses of PF. As Hundt and Vogel (2011: 146) emphasize, it is important to take a number of Inner, Outer and Expanding Circle Englishes on board such comparisons in order to account for variation within these groups before drawing conclusions as to the characteristics of ENL, ESL or EFL as a whole. Several studies point to ENL, ESL and EFL varieties forming a cline rather than neat categories (see Mukherjee and Hundt 2011), which warrants further empirical investigations involving a wide variety of corpora representing these different types of Englishes.

4 Aims and research questions

This study aims at obtaining mutually comparable results on extended uses of PF across Inner, Outer and Expanding Circle Englishes, and advancing systematic research into ENL, ESL and EFL within a unified framework, as encouraged by Mukherjee and Hundt (2011). Although PF has been the focus of numerous earlier studies, many of these studies have examined a limited range of varieties or variety types, have applied differing criteria for the classification of extended uses of PF, or have adopted a so-called "bird's-eye view" in order to chart apparent similarities or universals across varieties (e.g. Kortmann and Szmrecsanyi 2004). Moreover, most of these earlier studies have focused on stative uses of PF, while habitual uses, despite being widespread (e.g. Kortmann and Lunkenheimer 2013), have received less attention. These earlier studies have undoubtedly established extended uses of PF as a potential angloversal, but it is still unclear as to whether the examined features really are similar in terms of their types, frequencies or distribution in different Englishes. As pointed out by Sharma (2009: 171), in order to ascertain the genuine universality of a given feature, the semantic and grammatical conditioning of this feature must be placed under close scrutiny in order to eliminate substrate or transfer effects.

More specifically, this study addresses the following research questions:
1. How frequent is the progressive form across different types of Englishes?
2. How commonly is the progressive form extended in stative and habitual contexts in the examined varieties?
3. Which factors account for extended use and variation across different Englishes? The variables we examine are the type of English (ENL, ESL, EFL), L1/substrate language, and in the case of EFL data, the proficiency level of the learners.

This study is a contribution to the discussion on the roles of universal vs. contact-induced sources of extended uses of PF through the application of similar criteria for the identification and classification of this feature across Inner, Outer and Expanding Circle Englishes, and by including data from EFL corpora, where the learners' L1 is unambiguously identified. The most commonly used database in World Englishes research, the *International Corpus of English*, lacks metadata on the speakers' L1s. EFL corpora, such as the *International Corpus of Learner English* (Granger et al. 2009), enable controlling for this variable, which has the potential to shed new light on the possible roles of transfer and/or universals of SLA behind angloversals.

5 Data and methods

Our data include several corpora of Inner, Outer and Expanding Circle Englishes, which are listed in Table 1. The Inner Circle data covers spoken BrE (ICE-GB), AmE (SBCSAE) and, as a contact-induced variety, Welsh English (WelE), represented by a corpus of interview data (Ll&NW) from Llandybie (south-west of Wales) and North Wales (see Paulasto 2006). Present-day BrE is complemented with diachronic data from the SED tape recordings (see Klemola and Jones 1999), which consist of non-structured interviews with non-mobile older rural male (NORM) informants. In addition to these spoken English corpora, we also include written English data from the LOCNESS, the reference corpus for the ICLE, in order to account for the comparability of written learner English data and Inner Circle corpora.

Outer Circle Englishes are represented by Indian (IndE), Singapore (SingE), Kenyan (KenE) and Hong Kong English (HKE) from the International Corpus of English (ICE) private conversations sections. The varieties arise from different geographic locations and substrate backgrounds, and they can be considered to represent different phases of Schneider's Dynamic Model (2003, 2007), SingE being the most and HKE the least advanced of the varieties.

Expanding Circle Englishes include written essays by L1 Finnish, Swedish, Japanese and Chinese learners from the ICLE and a corpus of Matriculation Examination Compositions (MEC) by speakers of Finnish and Swedish (Meriläinen 2010). These four learner groups were chosen in order to compare learners with aspect-marking (Japanese, Chinese) vs. non-aspect-marking (Finnish, Swedish) L1s. The MEC allows for examining written data by Finnish-speaking and Swedish-speaking students of a lower proficiency level. The ICLE subcorpora are known to vary as to the proficiency level of the learner groups; while the Finnish and Swedish learners in the ICLE generally fall into levels C1 and C2 (advanced level) of the Common European Framework of Reference (CEFR), the Japanese and Chinese learners only reach level B2 or lower (intermediate level; Granger et al. 2009: 12). The MEC represents L1 Finnish and Swedish learners of an intermediate level (CEFR B1-B2; Meriläinen 2010: 45). This enables examining the effects of L2 proficiency, which has been shown to affect the degree of L1 influence (Jarvis and Pavlenko 2008: 201–203). Furthermore, the L1 Chinese subcorpus of the ICLE provides an interesting point of comparison to ICE-HK. For the purposes of this study, the data from ICLE-CH was compiled so that it only contains data from Hong Kong, thus representing a borderline case between ESL and EFL. We are aware of the challenges of comparing written and spoken data, as PF has been shown to be more frequent in spoken English than in written English (see, e.g. Collins 2008; Leech et al. 2009; Hilbert and Krug 2012). Comparable spoken English data from EFL learners was not available at the time of conducting this study, but conclusions as to the types and frequencies of PF across Englishes are drawn with care, taking into consideration the possible effects of the mode of communication.

Table 1: The data

Inner Circle	Trad EngE	Survey of English Dialects (SED)
	BrE	ICE-GB
	AmE	Santa Barbara Corpus (SBCSAE)
		Louvain Corpus of Native English Essays (LOCNESS)
	WelE	Llandybie and North Wales (Ll&NW)
Outer Circle	IndE	ICE-IND
	SingE	ICE-SIN
	KenE	ICE-EA
	HKE	ICE-HK
Expanding Circle	L1 Finnish	ICLE-FI
		Corpus of Matriculation Examination Compositions (MEC)
	L1 Swedish	ICLE-SW
		Corpus of Matriculation Examination Compositions (MEC)
	L1 Japanese	ICLE-JP
	L1 Chinese	ICLE-CH (Hong Kong)

For this study, we selected c. 100,000 words from each corpus.[4] PF constructions were searched with different forms of the auxiliary verb BE (including contracted forms) followed by the form *ing (with a maximum of three words in between). Irrelevant instances were weeded out manually. These include *be going to* with future reference, appositively used participles, gerunds and predicative adjectives (following Smitterberg 2005; Leech et al. 2009: 122). Perfect progressive instances (HAVE + BE + V-*ing*) were considered semantically so distinctive (and rare; Biber et al. 1999: 461) that they were also omitted from the study. From each corpus, we randomly selected 200 instances for detailed semantic analysis.

The semantic classification is based on the functions of PF in StE (Quirk et al. 1985; Römer 2005; Smitterberg 2005; Leech et al. 2009; Kranich 2010; Levin 2013; Smith and Leech 2013) and certain contact-induced varieties (Paulasto 2006, Sharma 2009). The primary functions of PF are imperfective ones, which are further divided into the progressive (ex. 1–2), delimited/progressive stative (3–4) and delimited/progressive habitual (5–6) functions, as described in Section 2. The extended stative and habitual uses, which we are primarily concerned with, are situations which do not conform to the descriptions of these functions in the above StE-based studies. The main distinguishing factors are that they are temporally non-delimited and non-subjective. Extended stative uses (ex. 7–8) describe fully stable situations and can involve prototypical states, where PF is rare, e.g. *exist*, *know*, *love*, *understand*. Extended habitual situations (9–10) can also be generic ones, but they do not describe the habitual situation as progressive or vice versa.

Non-aspectual functions include the futurate, where PF may or may not combine with the auxiliary *will* (ex. 11–12), and the subjective function (the term used by Kranich 2010), which involves speaker attitude, emotivity, or stylistic use of PF. The subjective category consists of three sub-types: subjective use with *always* or similar adverbials (usually expressing negative speaker attitude; ex. 13), subjective use without *always* (here including tentative, intensifying, experiential, emotive and narrative uses; ex. 14) and interpretive use (ex. 15; see, e.g. Leech et al. 2009: 134–36; Kranich 2010: 62–68).[5] In addition, we found it

---

[4] The exceptions are the Kenyan subcorpus of ICE-EA where the private dialogue section is only c. 54,000 words (Hudson-Ettle and Schmied 1999: 53) and the L1 Swedish subcorpus of the MEC, which only contains c. 30,000 words due to limited availability of the data (see Meriläinen 2010 for a more detailed description of corpus compilation). The differing sizes of the corpora are taken into account in the analysis of the results.

[5] Despite its versatility, the subjective function is not central for the present study. For closer descriptions of the types of usages included in this category, we thus refer you to the above-mentioned sources and to Huddleston and Pullum (2002: 165–67), Smitterberg (2005: 207–41), and Couper-Kuhlen (1995).

necessary to form a separate category of so-called work-verbs (*work, teach, study, farm*) for two reasons: situations describing a person's employment are semantically ambiguous, having the potential to be considered either habitual or stative (see Brinton 1987: 199), and as the topics of conversation in the ICE corpora often concern work and studies, these verbs can be so frequent in the data that including them in, e.g. one or the other habitual category would distort the results. The category of 'other' includes passive (ex. 18) and perfective (19) instances as well as some lexically nonstandard learner usages (20). The indeterminate category was resorted to when the context was unclear or when it was impossible to assign a specific occurrence to any single category with reasonable certainty.

Progressive (PROG)
(1) I'*m reading* the Treasure Island at the moment (ICE-GB)
(2) ... when you *were talking* to him you was like pretty drunk (ICE-HK)

Delimited/Progressive stative (PSTA)
(3) ... if we don't say that uhm you have a responsibility to do it then it's like we *are being* lax you see (ICE-SIN)
(4) You know what I *was thinking* of doing? (SBCSAE)

Delimited/Progressive habitual (PHAB)
(5) They *are practicing* it everyday and night (ICLE-JP)
(6) ... he'*d be running* around, d- in the street with his diapers on. (SBCSAE)

Non-delimited (extended) stative (ESTA)
(7) English *is being* a universal language (ICLE-JP)
(8) ... almost everybody *is having* a car (ICE-EA Kenya)

Non-delimited (extended) habitual (EHAB)
(9) Like my family all the people they *are taking* non-veg (ICE-IND)
(10) ... two or three of us *were riding* up to Llandeilo, every day (Ll&NW)

Futurate (FUT)
(11) ... these people *aren't going* home alone tonight (SBCSAE)
(12) There I'*ll be spending* my time in house only (ICE-IND)

Subjective (SUB)

(13) ... he *was always being oppressed* by [...] women (ICE-SIN)

(14) I'*m thinking*, God, these guys don't waste any time. (SBCSAE)

(15) If you speak English you *are showing* off (ICE-IND)

Work-verbs (WR)

(16) I mean we *are working* in the accounts department (ICE-EA Kenya)

(17) ... he and his sister *was farming* (Ll&NW)

Other (e.g. passive, perfective; OTH)

(18) ... recycling of waste *is carrying* out in our dairly life (ICLE-CH)

(19) I *was hurting* my back (SED)

(20) Since that time animals freedom *is losing* little by little ('is disappearing'; MEC-FI)

Indeterminate (IND)

It must be acknowledged that semantic categorizations such as this are necessarily somewhat subjective. The advantage of research collaboration is that we scrutinized each other's analyses and therefore had to justify our choices. We are therefore fairly confident of the consistency of the categories.

6 The results: The progressive form across Englishes

6.1 Total frequencies

Figure 1 presents the M-coefficients (i.e. instances per 100,000 words) of PF use in all investigated corpora. There is a clear difference in frequencies between the ICE corpora on the one hand, the private spoken sections yielding high frequencies, and the written learner corpora and LOCNESS, on the other. This difference is in accordance with the observations in Biber et al. (1999: 462) and Leech et al. (2009: 124–27) that the progressive form is used in conversation more frequently than in the written genres, academic writing in particular. Note that the ICLE subcorpora are indeed found at the left-side edge of the figure, while the MEC results are closer to the ICE corpora in frequencies.

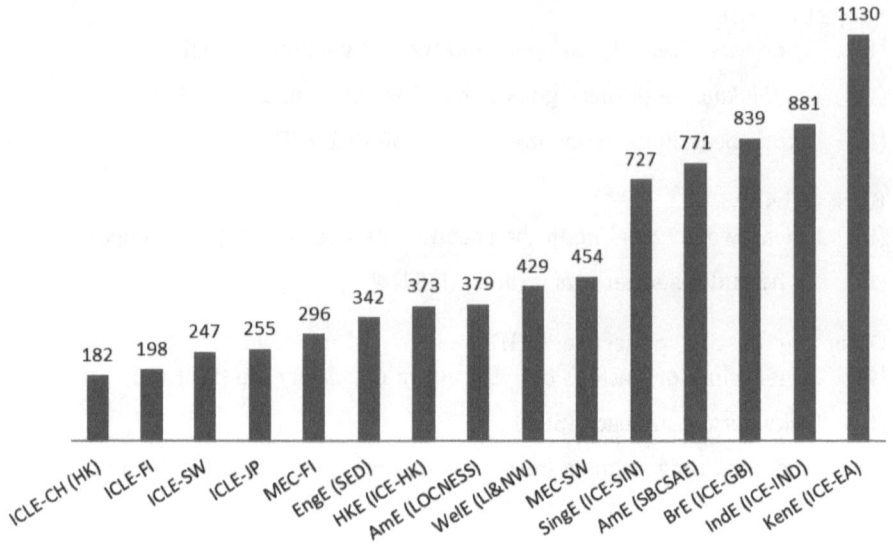

Figure 1: M-coefficients of PF use in all corpora

However, clustering near the written corpora are also the traditional EngE corpus and the WelE corpus. In this case, the comparatively low figures may be partly explained by the different method of data collection, as these corpora consist of interview data rather than casual private conversations.[6] Variation is quite notable among the private spoken sections of the ICE corpora, too. ICE-HK displays very low frequencies in comparison to other similar corpora, and the result is mirrored by the written ICLE-CH Hong Kong, which has the lowest PF use of all. The ICE corpora do not cluster according to variety type: there are no clear differences between L1 and L2/contact varieties but rather a cline from lower frequency contact varieties, HKE and SingE, through AmE and BrE to the high frequency contact varieties, IndE and, in particular, KenE. There appears to be a correlation between the analyticity/syntheticity of the primary substrate languages (Cantonese and Mandarin in HKE and the Chinese languages plus Malay and Tamil in SingE versus Hindi and Tamil in IndE and the Bantu languages in KenE) and the frequencies of PF: The substrate influence causes either under or overuse of PF in comparison to BrE and AmE. Let us see how the frequencies relate to the semantic functions of PF in the various corpora, however.

---

[6] The interviewer's speech has been omitted from the word count.

6.2 Semantic distribution in all corpora

Figure 2 gives the semantic functions of the investigated instances in the corpora, ordered from British and American L1 varieties to contact-induced and L2 varieties and on to the learner corpora. Some corpora have fewer than 200 instances in total.[7] At first glance the figure looks rather messy: There are no clear patterns which would align with this order of the corpora. One can see, however, that the academic written corpora are characterized by majority use of the central PROG function of PF, with close to or over 120 instances, i.e. 59–74%.[8]

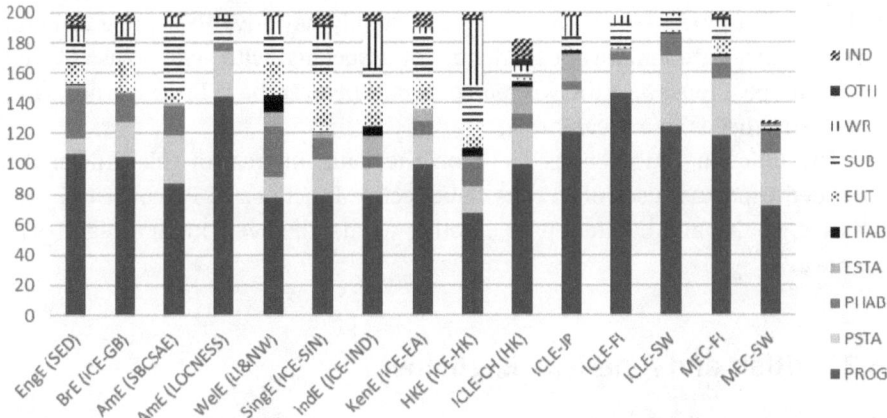

Figure 2: Semantic distribution of all or 200 random instances of PF per corpus (absolute numbers)

A second observation is that there are great distributional differences between the corpora as regards the categories of FUT, SUB and WR. In the final case, this is indicative of the topics discussed in the corpora, as *working*, *teaching* and *studying* are in a major role in the private conversations of ICE-IND and ICE-HK. As regards future tense and subjective use of PF, the variation probably reflects actual variety-specific differences in the usability of the construction in these functions (see also Rautionaho 2014: 208–210). FUT is particularly frequent in SingE and IndE. It may be reinforced by substrate influence in IndE, as the Hindi progressive marker *rahna* is also used for the future tense (Sharma 2009:

---

[7] The purpose of Figure 2 is to give a comprehensive idea of the semantic distribution observed in the data. As it also includes the non-aspectual categories, we do not test the distribution for statistical significance but leave this to the forthcoming subsections.
[8] In MEC-SW PROG instances amount to 56% and in ICLE-CH (HK) to 54%.

185). In contrast, there are no FUT instances at all in AmE LOCNESS and very few in the written learner corpora, either, apart from the intermediate MEC-FI. In Finnish, futurate is not marked grammatically but indicated using the present tense, which may explain the use of the present progressive for this purpose. Generally speaking, however, the preference for futurate PF in spoken rather than written corpora is in accordance with Leech et al. (2009: 132).

The subjective function types are found in all corpora. They are most characteristic of spoken AmE, KenE, HKE and SingE (11–23% of all instances) and least common in learner corpora (2–8%). The main exception to this trend is ICE-IND with only 9 (4.5%) SUB instances. Different corpora favour different SUB function types: spoken AmE employs mainly narrative PFs, while in KenE most instances are tentative, experiential or associated with stylistic use of *say/tell* in the past tense.[9] In the written corpora, however, be it L1 or learner data, interpretive use is in a greater role.

The following subsections focus on the main interest of this article: the extended aspectual uses of PF. The imperfective functions of PF consist of progressive, stative and habitual uses, in other words, the five bottom categories in Figure 2.

6.3 British and American Englishes

When grouping the Inner Circle corpora together in Figure 3, with the imperfective categories only, we can see that extended habitual and stative uses are generally very infrequent (combined M-coefficient under 7.8 in all but WelE).[10] In ICE-GB and the American corpora this is to be expected, as they represent standard L1 varieties. There is also no historical basis for expecting a high percentage of extended use from the traditional vernacular SED corpus, as observed in Section 2; it is in fact noteworthy that standard, delimited/progressive use of PF with stative verbs (PSTA) is considerably more frequent in the present-day BrE and AmE corpora than in the older SED. The use of PF in this context has increased from the 18th to the 20th century, as shown by Smitterberg (2005: 174) and Kranich (2010: 228), and the present results confirm their observations.

The WelE data diverge from the pattern, producing a statistically highly significant difference ($p < 0.001$)[11] in extended vs. standard use among the corpora

---

9 See Rautionaho (2014: 191–197) for more detailed results on the subjective function in World Englishes.
10 See Table 2 in the appendix for the raw figures.
11 Because of the low number of instances in some cells, we used Pearson's Chi-squared test with a simulated p-value (based on 2000 replicates; Monte Carlo simulation, Hope 1968).

(combined M-coefficient at 45.05). Although interview-based, the corpus is fairly vernacular in style, including also rural, elderly informants. The difference from the SED with its NORM informants is therefore quite striking. The extended uses in WelE result from Welsh substrate influence (e.g. Fife 1990: 368–70; Paulasto 2014: 266–267), the Welsh imperfective periphrasis being used for habitual as well as progressive situations and with the majority of stative verbs. It is noteworthy, though, that 7 of the 10 ESTA instances in WelE involve *living*, a stance verb which nevertheless is used in nondelimited contexts here. Extended stative use of PF in WelE is therefore lexically quite constrained (see also Paulasto 2014: 263).

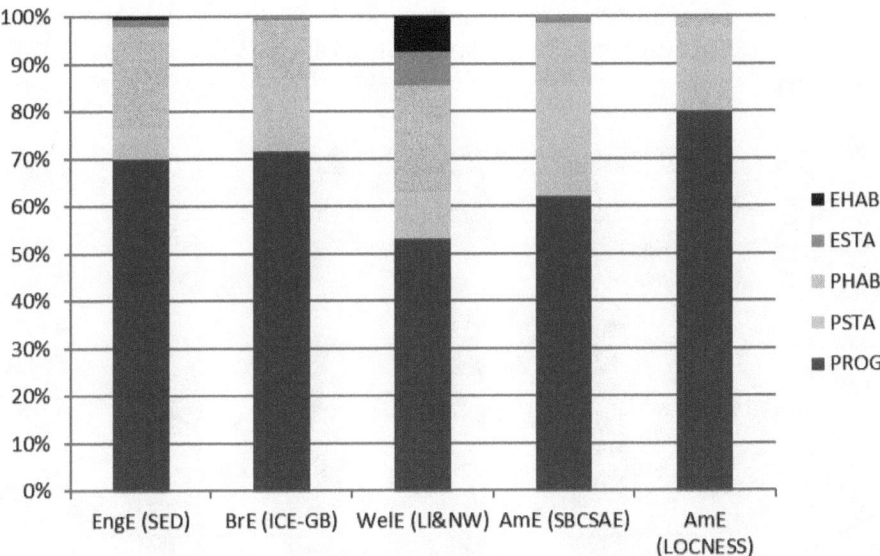

Figure 3: Proportional use of the imperfective categories in British and American corpora

Certain structural observations could also be made, although these are not central to the present study. The vernacular character of the SED corpus is revealed in the structural use of PF, as a remarkable 19% of all instances in the SED are ones without subject-verb concord in the auxiliary BE. In WelE, on the other hand, PF combines with modal verbs more often than in other varieties.

6.4 Outer Circle Englishes

The results from the Outer Circle in Figure 4 show that extended use is found in all corpora, but quite a bit more in some than in others. In SingE semantic extension is particularly infrequent. This might be partly due to the acrolectal nature of the corpus or the advancement of the variety to phase 4 in Schneider's Dynamic Model (Schneider 2007: 155–61). The norm-orientation of ICE-SIN in terms of PF use is observed also by Edwards (2014: 183, 186). The role of the substrate languages should be noted, as well: Although the private conversations section of ICE-SIN contains numerous other indigenized features, PF extension is not supported by the substrate languages Singapore Mandarin, Hokkien or Teochew, where imperfective marking is optional in non-progressive contexts (Sharma 2009: 186–188).

The varieties with the highest percentages of extended use are IndE (19 instances) and HKE (10), and the inclusion of ICLE-CH (HK) in Figure 4 shows that the results are similar in the learner corpus, with even more frequent use of ESTA (18 out of the 21 extended instances). KenE displays no instances of EHAB. The differences between the corpora are small, yet statistically significant ($p < 0.05$).

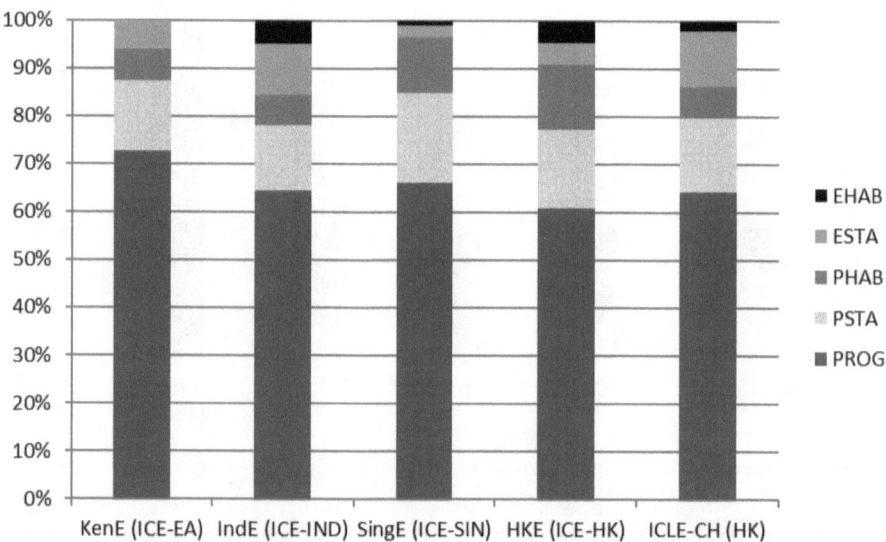

Figure 4: Proportional use of PF in imperfective categories in the Outer Circle corpora

In addition to cross-varietal differences, we can see that stative extension is the primary feature in all corpora while habitual extension is secondary. This aligns with the eWAVE finding (Kortmann and Lunkenheimer 2013) that stative extension is more widespread in World Englishes than habitual. This order of preference for the extended uses goes hand-in-hand with standard delimited/progressive stative and habitual functions, PSTA being more common than PHAB in every corpus.[12]

---

[12] This applies also to the raw frequencies (see Table 3 in the appendix).

As a further observation, extended uses correlate differently in the corpora with the general frequency of PF. There is a weak positive correlation in SingE, where there is less PF use than in BrE and AmE and fairly little semantic extension (M-coeff. 14.54), and a strong positive correlation in KenE (45.20) and especially IndE (83.70), where frequent PF use combines with extended uses (see Figure 1). In HKE, however, the correlation is negative: infrequent PF use combines with a relatively high percentage of extended use (22.38). These patterns are again indicative of substrate influence: the Chinese languages are analytic, with progressive aspect marking and only restricted imperfective aspect marking. Hindi and the Bantu languages, on the other hand, are more synthetic and aspect-marking; Hindi, for example, has obligatory imperfective marking, which clearly supports extended uses of PF (for Hindi and Chinese, see Sharma 2009: 184–188; for Swahili, see Deen 2005: 42).

In all corpora where ESTA is relatively frequent it occurs with a wide variety of verbs. IndE favours *having* to an extent (4/13 instances), as also observed by Balasubramanian (2009: 150) and Paulasto (2014: 263). In KenE, on the other hand, 5 of the 8 instances of ESTA are verbs of perception. There are, in other words, some variety-specific preferences in the extended uses.

6.5 The Expanding Circle

In the Expanding Circle learner corpora, extended uses are clearly more common among Chinese and Japanese learners than among Finnish and Swedish learners.[13] Figure 5 displays the results and includes the AmE LOCNESS for comparison. In ICLE-CH (HK) and ICLE-JP, extended use is statistically significantly more common than in other corpora ($p < 0.001$). This can be explained with L1 influence; unlike Finnish and Swedish, Chinese and Japanese are aspect-marking languages. The Chinese and Japanese progressive constructions are narrower in scope, though, than the English PF (see Sharma 2009: 184–188; Iwasaki 2013: 133–143). As discussed in Sharma (2009: 187), the L1–L2 mismatch may lead L2 speakers to search for the boundaries of the L2 category, resulting in non-standard use.

The differences between Chinese and Japanese vs. Finnish and Swedish learners may not be due to L1 influence alone, but also in part to the proficiency differences between the ICLE sub-corpora: as mentioned in section 5, samples from ICLE-FI (M-coeff. 1.98) and ICLE-SW (1.24) have been rated at a higher level

---

13 In the ICLE corpora, extended habitual and stative functions produce the following M-coefficients: ICLE-JP 26.78; ICLE-CH (HK) 21.00; ICLE-FI 1.98; ICLE-SW 1.24.

in CEFR than ICLE-CH and ICLE-JP. The latter two corpora also contain more structural nonstandard use of PF than the Finnish and Swedish ICLE data, which is telling of the proficiency differences between the learner groups. However, the Matriculation Examination data from intermediate level Finnish-speaking and Swedish-speaking students show that extended use is not solely due to lower proficiency. Rather, extended uses are rare for these learners, as there is no trigger in the L1, and there is little structural nonstandard use.[14]

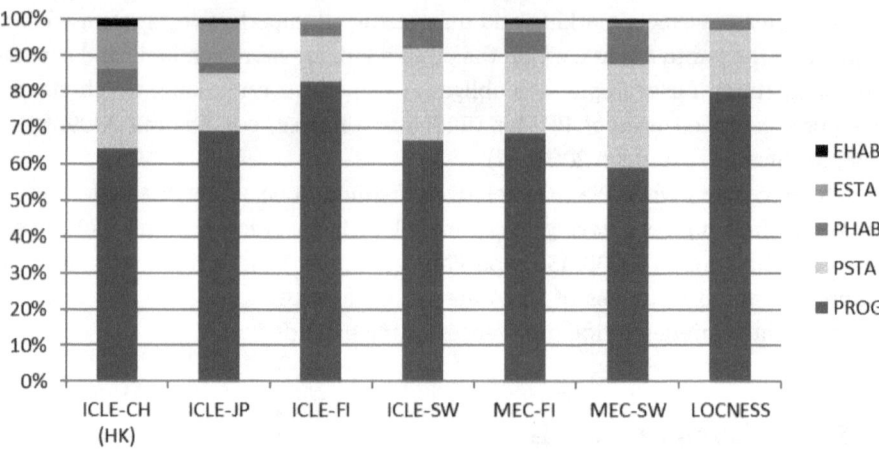

Figure 5: Proportional use of PF in the imperfective categories in the written learner corpora[15]

The results from ICLE-FI are functionally very similar to those of the native speaker comparison corpus LOCNESS, but as shown in Figure 1, the frequency of PF in LOCNESS is roughly twice that of ICLE-FI. In fact, all written learner corpora display lower total frequencies of use than the AmE comparison corpus. This is in line with Axelsson and Hahn (2001: 11), who show the frequencies of PF in learner English by L1 Finnish, Swedish and German learners to fall between AmE and BrE student writing, AmE displaying the highest frequencies.

The findings of this study contrast with earlier studies which have not found evidence for non-standard semantic use of PF in learner English (e.g. Axelsson and Hahn 2001; van Rooy 2006; Hundt and Vogel 2011). Hundt and Vogel (2011: 158), in fact, conclude that unlike ESL varieties, learner English does not tolerate combination of PF with stative verbs. It is noteworthy, however, that these earlier studies have only looked at advanced learners whose L1 does not mark

---

14 The M-coefficient for the extended functions in MEC-FI is 8.89 and in MEC-SW 3.55.
15 The raw frequencies are presented in Table 4 in the appendix.

the progressive aspect (L1 Finnish, Swedish and German learners from the ICLE). These findings have been interpreted as evidence for the exonormative nature of learner English is general. Our findings, however, show that extended use of PF may be found in written English by learners with lower English proficiency and whose L1 marks lexical aspect. L2 proficiency and L1 transfer thus emerge as important variables with regard to the occurrence of this feature.

6.6 Comparison of imperfective functions in all corpora

Figure 6 shows all corpora in the order of extended use in proportion to all imperfective categories. It comes as no surprise that the left-side end is held by academic student writing by native speakers, spoken standard BrE and AmE, and learners whose native languages do not offer support either to the progressive form or its semantically extended use. These varieties can be expected to follow StE norms most closely. The first vernacular data set, with traditional EngE dialects, is followed by SingE and intermediate-level student writing by L1 Finnish learners. The MEC-FI corpus is distanced somewhat from other L1 Finnish and Swedish learner corpora. This is probably indicative of the proficiency difference and the typological distance between Finnish and English, making the acquisition of PF, along with other grammatical categories, more challenging for L1 Finnish than Swedish learners.

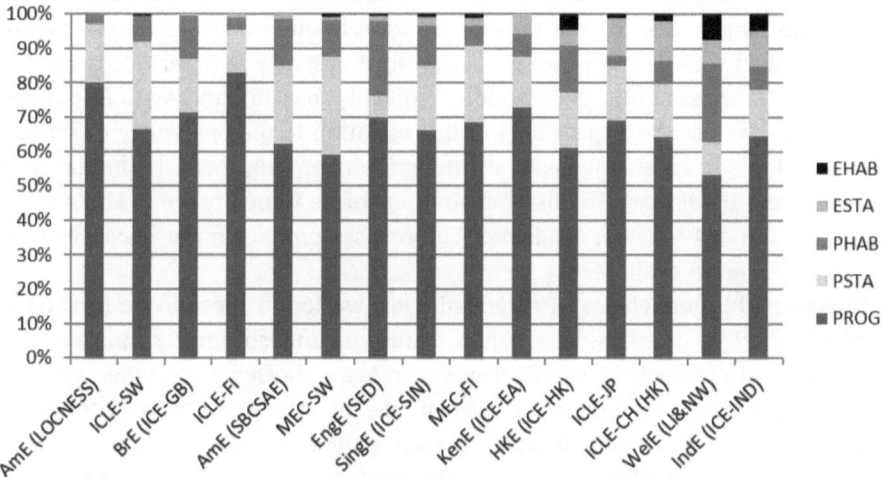

Figure 6: Proportional use of imperfective functions in all corpora

The six corpora on the right-hand side represent contact varieties or learner Englishes with a substrate or L1 which has overt aspectual marking. The imperfective constructions in Welsh and Hindi lead the English progressive form to be used in imperfective contexts as well. In both varieties these functions are also an established form of PF usage.

7 Discussion and conclusion

In the present study we set out to examine the frequencies of PF use and extended uses in particular in corpora spanning the Inner, Outer and Expanding Circles. The above results show that there is a great deal of variation in terms of the general frequencies of PF use, the primary variables being the type of data and the type of English. Our data consist of corpora which have been collected using different methods: casual conversation, interview data and written essays. As shown in previous studies (e.g. Leech et al. 2009: 125), PF use is highly register-dependent. The different types of Englishes along the dimensions of learner data and established varieties on the one hand and Inner and Outer Circles on the other are also bound to produce variation. The low frequencies in academic student writing and the high frequencies in established and indigenized spoken varieties are something that could be expected.

What is more interesting is the variation between mutually comparable data sets, particularly among the ICE corpora, where distinct varieties exhibit a considerable range: in KenE, the progressive form is three times as frequent as in HKE. Contact varieties, depending on the substrate, may in other words employ PF either 50% less or almost 50% more frequently than BrE and AmE. As pointed out above, we ascribe a great deal of this variation to the analyticity or syntheticity of the substrate languages. In the written corpora, then, the formality of the text and the learners' skills or desire to achieve formality are likely to influence the use of PF, as the academic ICLE corpora produce fewer instances than the matriculation exam texts.

As for the frequencies of extended uses, we found these to be in general quite low. PF is of course a common feature of English and its functions are varied, as also shown above. Our results indicate, however, that the extended uses play a relatively minor role also in the private conversation corpora of contact-induced Englishes, in spite of their proposed angloversality. This is of course partly the result of the upper mesolectal or acrolectal register sampled for the ICE corpora. Basilectal data would probably produce different results, as indicated, e.g. by Sharma (2009: 181): In her IndE corpus, extended (non-delimited) habitual use of PF is considerably more common than either progressive or stative uses. The ICE-corpora cannot therefore reveal the entire range of variation in PF use.

Based on the present data and our strict criteria, however, it seems clear that stative extension is more common in varieties of English worldwide than habitual extension. The former feature can to an extent be ascribed to the fluidity of the stative-dynamic continuum in English and the increasing use of PF in specific stative domains. There are, however, also variety-specific tendencies regarding stative extension, such as the emphasis on verbs of perception in KenE, which merit further examination. Extended habitual use, on the other hand, is typically found in varieties where the substrate or L1 supports an imperfective interpretation of the progressive form. The construction is not exactly salient as a habitual marker and it faces competition from other habitual constructions, which we believe is the reason why it is relatively unusual in this function.

The three main determining factors that emerge from the data are the type of English, the substrate language/L1 and the proficiency level of the learners. Semantic extension of PF is constrained in the traditional Inner Circle varieties (apart from the WelE corpus which is less standard in nature) and in advanced learner English (the L1 Finnish and Swedish subcorpora of the ICLE), which is in line with van Rooy (2006), Hundt and Vogel (2011) and Davydova (2012). In contrast, extended use is found in varieties and learner Englishes with a substrate or L1 which has verbal aspect marking. This applies particularly to Welsh, Hindi, Chinese, and Japanese contact influence. The contact language is thus in a key role for this feature. Finally, the learners' proficiency level affects their PF use, as can be seen from the comparison of ICLE subcorpora and the L1 Finnish and Swedish Matriculation Examination data: The higher frequency of extended use of PF in ICLE-CH and ICLE-JP may partially be explained by the learners' lower level of English proficiency in comparison to ICLE-FI and ICLE-SW. Yet, proficiency is outranked by the L1 effect, as shown by the more frequent use of semantic extension in ICLE-CH and JP than in the MEC corpora.

There are at least four explanations that have been proposed for the anglo-versal nature of extended progressive form usage: substrate influence (e.g. Gachelin 1997; Sharma 2009; Paulasto 2014), regularization or overgeneralization processes of SLA (e.g. Williams 1987), overgeneralization through a special emphasis in English language teaching (e.g. Platt, Weber and Ho 1984), and the broad semantic range and fluidity of the English PF (e.g. Sharma 2009; Mesthrie and Bhatt 2008: 67). We find that substrate or L1 influence is by far the most compelling of these, as extended uses seem to be infrequent in corpora where the contact explanation does not apply. Another explanatory factor that is readily acceptable is the general fluidity in the use of progressive forms, resulting from the aspectual ambiguity of the imperfective categories and the increasing acceptability of the construction in stative situations. These two explanations do not exclude one another; on the contrary, the fuzzy boundaries of the PF make it susceptible to language contact effects (see, e.g. Paulasto 2014).

The results do not, however, support general learner language or classroom explanations related to 'over-teaching' or, more significantly, regularization or overgeneralization strategies, as the learner corpora investigated here follow principles quite different from each other. We are, in fact, unaware of previous learner English studies which would give equally strong evidence of the influence of the L1 in progressive form use. On the basis of the present results, extended use of PF does not seem to be a universal feature of learner English. It is, therefore, questionable to resort to explanations relating to universal strategies of SLA in the context of World Englishes, either. Evidence from EFL corpora offers support for the contact-induced sources of this feature in World Englishes; since this feature is found in interlanguage by learners with an aspect-marking L1, it seems likely that extended use of the PF originates from transfer in the process of SLA, later becoming a stabilized feature in L2 varieties. The findings of this study thus call the angloversality of this feature into question.

In this paper, we hope to have demonstrated that combining the study of ENL, ESL and EFL is to be encouraged, especially when investigating proposed English language universals or angloversals. Our results show that it is possible to use data which are not fully consistent, as long as the methodological and register-related differences are taken into consideration and the analysis and classification of the features at hand is systematic across the data. The broad range of corpora representing many types and varieties of English, combined with the full-scale semantic analysis of PF, present a valuable addition to our prior knowledge about the behavior of PF in the English language complex. Our findings also show that the inclusion of learner English data may bring to light influential variables which cannot be reliably assessed in data on World Englishes alone. Further investigations to bridge this paradigm gap are certainly needed.

References

Aarts, Bas, Joanne Close, Geoffrey Leech & Sean Wallis (eds.). 2013. *The Verb Phrase in English. Investigating Recent Language Change with Corpora*. Cambridge: Cambridge University Press.

Axelsson, Margareta Westergren & Angela Hahn. 2001. The use of the progressive in Swedish and German advanced learner English – a corpus-based study. *ICAME Journal* 25. 5–30.

Balasubramanian, Chandrika. 2009. *Register Variation in Indian English*. Amsterdam, Philadelphia: John Benjamins.

Biber, Douglas, Stig Johansson, Geoffrey Leech, Susan Conrad & Edward Finegan. 1999. *Longman Grammar of Spoken and Written English*. London: Longman.

Brinton, Laurel J. 1987. The aspectual nature of states and habits. *Folia Linguistica* 21. 195–214.

Collins, Peter. 2008. The progressive aspect in World Englishes: A corpus-based study. *Australian Journal of Linguistics* 28(2). 225–249.

Comrie, Bernard. 1976. *Aspect: An Introduction to the Study of Verbal Aspect and Related Problems*. Cambridge: Cambridge University Press.

Couper-Kuhlen, Elizabeth. 1995. On the foregrounding progressive in American conversational narrative: A new development? In Wolfgang Riehle & Hugo Keiper (eds.), *Anglistentag 1994, Graz Proceedings*, 229–45. Tübingen: Niemeyer.

Davydova, Julia. 2012. Englishes in the Outer and Expanding Circles: A comparative study. *World Englishes* 31(3). 366–385.

Deen, Kamil Ud. 2005. *The Acquisition of Swahili*. Amsterdam: John Benjamins Publishing Co.

Edwards, Alison. 2014. The progressive aspect in the Netherlands and the ESL/EFL continuum. *World Englishes* 33(2). 173–194.

Fife, James. 1990. *The Semantics of the Welsh Verb: A Cognitive Approach*. Cardiff: University of Wales Press.

Filppula, Markku, Juhani Klemola & Heli Paulasto (eds.). 2009a. *Vernacular Universals and Language Contacts: Evidence from Varieties of English and Beyond*. London and New York: Routledge.

Filppula, Markku, Juhani Klemola & Heli Paulasto. 2009b. Digging for roots: universals and contacts in regional varieties of English. In Markku Filppula, Juhani Klemola & Heli Paulasto (eds.), *Vernacular Universals and Language Contacts: Evidence from Varieties of English and Beyond*, 231–261. London and New York: Routledge.

Gachelin, Jean-Marc. 1997. The progressive and habitual aspects in non-standard Englishes. In E.W. Schneider (ed.), *Englishes Around the World. Vol. 1, General Studies, British Isles, North America*, 33–46. Amsterdam & Philadelphia: John Benjamins.

Granger, Sylviane, Estelle Dagneaux, Fanny Meunier & Magali Paquot. 2009. *The International Corpus of Learner English. Version 2. Handbook and CD-Rom*. Louvain-la- Neuve: Presses Universitaires de Louvain.

Hilbert, Michaela & Manfred Krug. 2012. Progressives in Maltese English. A comparison of spoken and written text types of British and American English. In Marinne Hundt & Ulrike Gut (eds.), *Mapping Unity and Diversity World-Wide*, 103–136. Amsterdam/Philadelphia: John Benjamins.

Hope, Adery C. A. 1968. A simplified Monte Carlo significance test procedure. *Journal of the Royal Statistical Society* B 30. 582–598.

Huddleston, Rodney & Geoffrey Pullum. 2002. *The Cambridge Grammar of the English Language*. Cambridge: Cambridge University Press.

Hudson-Ettle, Diana & Josef Schmied. 1999. *Manual to Accompany the East African Component of the International Corpus of English (ICE-EA). Background information, coding conventions and lists of source texts*. Chemnitz. URL: www.tu-chemnitz.de/phil/english/real/eafrica/

Hundt, Marianne & Katrine Vogel. 2011. Overuse of the progressive in ESL and learner Englishes: fact or fiction? In Joybrato Mukherjee & Marianne Hundt (eds.), *Exploring Second-Language Varieties of English and Learner Englishes: Bridging the Paradigm Gap*, 145–165. Amsterdam/Philadelphia: John Benjamins.

Iwasaki, Shoichi. 2013. *Japanese*. Amsterdam/Philadelphia: John Benjamins.

Jarvis, Scott & Aneta Pavlenko. 2008. *Crosslinguistic Influence in Language and Cognition*. New York: Routledge.

Kachru, Braj B. 1985. Standards, codification and sociolinguistic realism: The English language in the outer circle. In Randolph Quirk & Henry Widdowson (eds.), *English in the World: Teaching and Learning the Language and Literatures*, 11–30. Cambridge: Cambridge University Press.

Klemola, Juhani & Mark J. Jones. 1999. The Leeds Corpus of English Dialects –project. In Clive Upton & Katie Wales (eds.), *Dialectal Variation in English: Proceedings of the Harold Orton Centenary Conference 1998*. (Leeds Studies in English, N.S. XXX, 1999), 17–30. Leeds: University of Leeds.

Kortmann, Bernd & Benedikt Szmrecsanyi. 2004. Global synopsis: morphological and syntactic variation in English. In Bernd Kortmann, Edgar W. Schneider, Kate Burridge, Rajend Mesthrie & Clive Upton (eds.), *A Handbook of Varieties of English: Volume 2*, 1142–1202. Berlin and New York: Mouton de Gruyter.

Kortmann, Bernd & Kerstin Lunkenheimer (eds.). 2013. *The Electronic World Atlas of Varieties of English*. Leipzig: Max Planck Institute for Evolutionary Anthropology. Available at: http://ewave-atlas.org. Accessed 22 January 2014.

Kranich, Svenja. 2010. *Progressive in Modern English: A Corpus-Based Study of Grammaticalization and Related Changes*. Amsterdam, New York: Rodopi.

Leech, Geoffrey, Marianne Hundt, Christian Mair & Nicholas Smith. 2009. *Change in Contemporary English: A Grammatical Study*. Cambridge: Cambridge University Press.

Levin, Magnus. 2013. The progressive verb in Modern American English. In Bas Aarts, Joanne Close, Geoffrey Leech & Sean Wallis (eds.), *The Verb Phrase in English. Investigating Recent Language Change with Corpora*, 187–216. Cambridge: Cambridge University Press.

Mair, Christian. 2003. Kreolismen und verbales Identitätsmanagement im geschriebenen jamaikanischen Englisch. In Elisabeth Vogel, Antonia Napp & Wolfram Lutterer (eds.), *Zwischen Ausgrenzung und Hybridisierung*, 79–96. Würzburg: Ergon.

Meriläinen, Lea. 2010. *Language Transfer in the Written English of Finnish Students*. Publications of the University of Eastern Finland. Dissertations in Education, Humanities, and Theology, no 9, Joensuu: University of Eastern Finland. Available at: http://epublications.uef.fi/pub/urn_isbn_978-952-61-0230-6/

Meriläinen, Lea & Heli Paulasto. 2017. Embedded inversion as an angloversal: Evidence from Inner, Outer and Expanding Circle Englishes. In Markku Filppula, Juhani Klemola & Devyani Sharma (eds.), *The Oxford Handbook of World Englishes*, 676–696. Oxford: Oxford University Press. Available at: http://www.oxfordhandbooks.com/view/10.1093/oxfordhb/9780199777716.001.0001/oxfordhb-9780199777716-e-26

Mesthrie, Rajend & Rakesh Bhatt. 2008. *World Englishes: The Study of New Linguistic Varieties*. Cambridge: Cambridge University Press.

Mukherjee, Joybrato & Marianne Hundt (eds.). 2011. *Exploring Second-Language Varieties of English and Learner Englishes: Bridging the Paradigm Gap*. Amsterdam/Philadelphia: John Benjamins.

Paulasto, Heli. 2006. *Welsh English Syntax: Contact and Variation*. Joensuu: University of Joensuu. Available at: http://epublications.uef.fi/pub/urn_isbn_952-458-804-8/

Paulasto, Heli. 2014. Extended uses of the progressive form in L1 and L2 Englishes. *English World-Wide* 35(3). 247–276.

Platt, John, Heidi Weber & Ho Mian Lian. 1984. *The New Englishes*. London: Routledge and Kegan Paul.

Quirk, Randolph, Sidney Greenbaum, Geoffrey Leech & Jan Svartvik. 1985. *A Comprehensive Grammar of the English Language*. London: Longman.
Ranta, Elina. 2013. *Universals in a Universal Language? Exploring Verb-Syntactic Features in English as a Lingua Franca*. Acta Electronica Universitatis Tamperensis 1366. Available at: https://tampub.uta.fi/handle/10024/94555.
Rautionaho, Paula. 2014. *Variation in the Progressive: A Corpus-based Study into World Englishes*. Acta Universitatis Tamperensis: 1997. Tampere: Tampere University Press. Available at: http://urn.fi/URN:ISBN:978-951-44-9636-3.
Römer, Ute. 2005. *Progressives, Patterns, Pedagogy: A Corpus-Driven Approach to English Progressive Forms, Functions, Contexts and Didactics*. Amsterdam: John Benjamins.
Schneider, Edgar W. 2003. The dynamics of New Englishes: From identity construction to dialect birth. *Language* 79(2). 233–281.
Schneider, Edgar W. 2007. *Postcolonial English: Varieties Around the World*. Cambridge: Cambridge University Press.
Sharma, Devyani. 2009. Typological diversity in New Englishes. *English World-Wide* 30. 170–195.
Smith, Nicholas & Geoffrey Leech. 2013. Verb structures in twentieth-century British English. In Bas Aarts, Joanne Close, Geoffrey Leech & Sean Wallis (eds.), *The Verb Phrase in English. Investigating Recent Language Change with Corpora*, 68–98. Cambridge: Cambridge University Press.
Smitterberg, Erik. 2005. *The Progressive in 19th-century English: A Process of Integration*. Amsterdam, New York: Rodopi.
Szmrecsanyi, Benedikt & Bernd Kortmann. 2011. Typological profiling: Learner Englishes versus indigenized L2 varieties of English. In Joybrato Mukherjee & Marianne Hundt (eds.), *Exploring Second-Language Varieties of English and Learner Englishes: Bridging the Paradigm Gap*, 167–187. Amsterdam/Philadelphia: John Benjamins.
van Rooy, Bertus. 2006. The extension of the progressive aspect in Black South African English. *World Englishes* 25(1). 37–64.
van Rooy, Bertus. 2014. Progressive aspect and stative verbs in Outer Circle varieties. *World Englishes* 33(2). 157–172.
Virtanen, Tuija. 1997. The progressive in non-native speaker and native speaker composition: Evidence from the International Corpus of Learner English. In Magnus Ljung (ed.), *Corpus-based studies in English: Papers from the Seventeenth International Conference on English Language Research on Computerized Corpora (ICAME 17). Stockholm, May 15–19, 1996*, 299–309. Amsterdam and Atlanta: Rodopi.
Williams, Jessica. 1987. Non-native varieties of English: A special case of language acquisition. *English World-Wide* 8. 161–199.

Appendix

Table 2: Raw frequencies of the semantic distribution of PF in the British and American corpora

Function	EngE (SED)	BrE (ICE-GB)	WelE (LI&NW)	AmE (SBCSAE)	AmE (LOCNESS)	Total
PROG	107	105	77	87	144	520
PSTA	10	23	14	32	31	110
PHAB	33	18	33	19	5	108
ESTA	2	1	10	2	0	15
EHAB	1	0	11	0	0	12
FUT	13	21	22	7	0	63
SUB	15	16	18	45	16	110
WR	8	9	12	5	3	37
OTH	2	0	0	0	1	3
IND	9	7	3	3	0	22
Total	200	200	200	200	200	1000

Table 3: Raw frequencies of the semantic distribution of PF in the Outer Circle corpora

Function	KenE (ICE-EA)	IndE (ICE-IND)	SingE (ICE-SIN)	HKE (ICE-HK)	ICLE-CH (HK)	Total
PROG	99	80	80	67	99	425
PSTA	20	17	23	18	24	102
PHAB	9	8	14	15	10	56
ESTA	8	13	3	5	18	47
EHAB	0	6	1	5	3	15
FUT	18	30	39	16	3	106
SUB	32	9	22	26	4	93
WR	4	31	8	43	4	90
OTH	0	1	1	1	4	7
IND	10	5	9	4	13	41
Total	200	200	200	200	182	982

Table 4: Raw frequencies of the semantic distribution of PF in the Expanding Circle corpora

Function	ICLE-CH (HK)	ICLE-JP	ICLE-FI	ICLE-SW	MEC-FI	MEC-SW	LOCNESS	Total
PROG	99	121	146	124	118	72	144	604
PSTA	24	28	22	47	38	35	31	173
PHAB	10	5	6	14	10	13	5	48
ESTA	18	19	2	0	4	1	0	7
EHAB	3	2	0	1	2	1	0	4
FUT	3	1	1	1	9	1	0	12
SUB	4	8	15	11	9	3	16	54
WR	4	13	6	1	5	0	3	15
OTH	4	0	0	1	2	1	1	5
IND	13	3	0	0	3	1	0	4
Total	182	200	198	200	200	128	200	926

III **Expanding the horizons: lingua franca, cognitive, and contact-linguistic perspectives**

Editors' Introduction to Part III

This final section of the book opens up new directions and new questions in understanding contemporary change in English, and language change more generally. All four chapters address questions concerning adequate models of language when the aim is to capture change, all use dialogic data, and all but one (Mortensen and Hazel) make use of corpora. The first three chapters, each from their different perspectives, take English as a Lingua Franca (ELF) in focus. In each, the attention is on observing ongoing change, and capturing the processes that help us gain insights into what change looks like in the making. For both Mauranen and Mortensen and Hazel, this is also the central object of theorising, whereas Vetchinnikova mainly draws her data from ELF, although she also contributes to its conceptualisation. ELF is not considered a variety of English in any of these approaches. The final chapter, by contrast, focuses on an established variety of English: Bao takes a given structure in Singapore English under close scrutiny, weighing alternative models of explanation for its existence in this variety.

The chapters that deal with ELF data are all very much aware of the instability of English in the hands of its second-language users, and of the communities using it. Mortensen and Hazel talk about transient multilingual communities, while Mauranen identifies three relevant levels: the macro-social, the micro-social, and the cognitive. The cognitive, or individual level, is the limiting case, but even the individual is a participant in social action. Vetchinnikova contrasts two levels of use, the communal and the cognitive – the latter, as in Mauranen, equalling the individual. In the last chapter, Bao views language from the collective viewpoint of corpus data.

Whether and to what extent native and non-native speakers might differ in terms of language behaviour from the cognitive and communal viewpoints (Vetchinnikova) and in terms of social position with greater linguistic authority (Mortensen and Hazel) is found not to follow the clear dichotomy often taken to be self-evident: in cognitive terms the differences look negligible, and in terms of epistemic authority the primacy of the L1 speaker is open to challenge when other social factors conferring epistemic authority step in. It may be time to shed some of the traditionally held demarcation lines as we search for fresh approaches to language change. The chapters below show that when traditional divisions into substrate, lexifier, and contact languages are intact, as in Bao's study, we can still fruitfully search and find explanatory models (like transfer in this case) that show a better fit to observed phenomena than more established ones (like replica grammaticalization), but the more radically new questions thrown up in the ELF studies here also result in more radical observations.

Grammaticalization features in Vetchinnikova and Bao's chapters. In both, reliance on usage-based models is an important point of departure. Vetchinnikova's take on grammaticalization is part of her view of language as a complex system, and thus emergent, while Bao juxtaposes grammaticalization with transfer.

As to the individual papers, first Anna Mauranen (*A glimpse of ELF*) distinguishes three social perspectives for approaching ELF as a site of language change: the macro-social, the micro-social or interactional, and the individual or the cognitive. For each, she makes predictions concerning ELF based on earlier research, after which she goes on to see how the predictions are borne out in a corpus of spoken English as a Lingua Franca. At the macro-social level, she describes ELF in terms of a higher-order contact, or second-order contact between *similects*, that is, those lects resulting from first-level contact between a particular L1 and English. In essence these are parallel individual idiolects which show recognisable similarities. At the interactional level these similects meet other similects and negotiate both form and meaning via various discourse strategies that help shape the grammar emerging from the hybrid encounters. Cognitive processing, in turn, operates on weakly entrenched means of expression, resulting not only in well-predicted structural simplification, but also less obvious phenomena like lexical simplification, and overall complexification through alternating processes of *approximation* and *fixing*. All three social levels interact at their boundaries, which helps explain the observable linguistic developments.

Janus Mortensen and Spencer Hazel (*Lending bureaucracy voice: negotiating English in institutional encounters*) set out to employ a conversation analytical methodology to tackle a wider social phenomenon, which enables them to scrutinise closely the processes of potential points of language change in the making as well as relate social and linguistic change to each other. They analyse service encounters in a multilingual university setting in Denmark where English is used as a lingua franca. By this specific focus on the transient multilingual communities that such encounters represent, they are well positioned to discover social and linguistic patterns in a type of unstable community that has been becoming more and more common in many parts of the world: internationalising higher education with its transnationally mobile students. They argue that these hybrid contexts, with their hyper-local registers that get formed under such circumstances provide insights into emergent English through joint meaning-making and negotiation by participants in interaction. Their analysis of illustrative encounters shows English as it is drawn on to verbalise concepts in a setting where direct equivalents may not exist in English, and the ensuing patterns of assigning and orienting to epistemic authority. While in many cases participants with English as their first language are positioned as linguistic norm providers, this is not necessarily the case, but people with knowledge of the institutional or bureaucratic system have considerable authority in defining the terms that are used, despite their non-native status relative to English. They position themselves and are positioned as linguistic norm-providers.

Svetlana Vetchinnikova (*On the relationship between the cognitive and the communal: a complex systems perspective*) sets out to explore the relationships between two separate levels of language representation: the individual or cognitive, and the communal. Her general approach builds on the theory of language as a complex system, and she argues that the communal plane of representation is *emergent* in relation to interactions between idiolects. She makes her case in the light of corpus evidence, contrasting an individual's or *cognitive* corpus with a collective corpus, which is of the kind we usually know as corpora. The particular case she uses is that of chunking, and how it differs on the two planes in terms of processes despite having also much in common in terms of the outcomes. The main difference is that individual usage is not only more fixed (at the cognitive level, resulting in variation at the communal level), but also less abstract than a communal corpus would suggest. The interrelationship is one of emergence, and as Vetchinnikova argues, fractal, in that the patterns at both planes are self-similar in a scale-free manner, in this case seen in their Zipfian distributions.

Finally, Zhiming Bao (*Transfer is transfer; grammaticalization is grammaticalization*) delves into the *one* construction in Singapore English that has been seen as a case of grammaticalization resulting from substrate influence of the Chinese *de* construction. He depicts the transfer process as a tripartite relationship between the substratum language, the contact language, and the lexifier. He argues that the analysis recognizing multiple grammatical meanings of the Chinese *de* construction is an artifact of the analysis of *one* in English morphosyntax, and that the usage pattern of the *one* construction does not support the prediction of a replica grammaticalization process, as seen in the light of an analysis of a 20-year time span, where the evidence points to the morphosyntactic frames of the *one* construction having arisen simultaneously. In a grammaticalization analysis, the prediction is that they occur sequentially. Bao uses two corpora of spoken Singapore English, compiled 20 years apart. In effect he shows that the substratum Chinese *de* is transferred to the contact language Singapore English and exponenced by *one* from the lexifier English.

Anna Mauranen
A glimpse of ELF

Abstract: English participates in an unusually multilingual and complex language contact: it is in contact with virtually any other language in the world, and from these contact varieties with traces of the other language, "similects", arises English as a lingua franca (ELF), a higher-order contact between contact varieties. This chapter presents a conceptualisation of ELF from three perspectives: the macro-social, the micro-social and the cognitive. The author derives a series of hypotheses from theoretical assumptions about ELF and from previous research in related fields. The hypotheses are then examined in the light of data from the corpus of English as a Lingua Franca in Academic Settings (ELFA). The results highlight tendencies towards both simplification and complexification in ELF. The principal processes involving all three perspectives of analysis (the macro, the micro and the cognitive) are approximation and fixing, which also drive change across each of these levels.

Keywords: approximation, complexification, entrenchment, fixing, fuzzy processing, lexical simplification, morpho-syntactic simplification, second-order language contact, second language use, shared cultural resources, similects, subjective simplicity

1 Introduction

The turbulent period of intense societal changes on a global scale that we are living in has consequences that make this a fascinating time to linguists: we are able to observe and record ongoing multiplex language contact on an unprecedented scale, with complex multilingual practices and language-mixing. These fast-changing scenes of language contact may result in rapid changes in the languages concerned, certainly blur their boundaries, and shake our notions of language, still surprisingly deeply rooted in thought patterns and terms of nation-states and clear-cut boundaries. Equipped with advanced and manageable technology, we are well situated for collecting endless data on the use and emergence of lingua francas, among which English is clearly only one. Why should, then, English be of particular significance in this turbulent multilingual world?

Anna Mauranen, University of Helsinki

DOI 10.1515/9783110429657-013

It would seem to me that English is important to understanding language, perhaps more than ever, not only on account of its ubiquity, but because it embodies current global flows more than any other language, and is in contact with more languages than any other.

English is used alongside other languages, gets mixed with them in a general process of "languaging" (Becker 1995) and "translanguaging" (Li Wei and Garcia 2014), and is involved in a plethora of circumstances where people from entirely different backgrounds come together. Varieties of English can overthrow traditional notions of social prestige (see, Pennycook 2008; Blommaert 2013), as Mair (this volume) argues in the cases of Jamaican creole and Nigerian pidgin. In other circumstances, language ideologies of a conservative kind can seriously affect individuals' lives and futures, as for instance in asylum seeker interviews (Guido 2008) or in testing language proficiency for university admission. In places of more conventional social prestige – from negotiating top-level world politics through business and trade to international research collaboration – English serves as the principal lingua franca. Even these high-stakes situations are fundamentally multilingual, and participants' command of Standard English varies considerably, yet with apparently few problems in communicative success. Social and political determinants thus govern our perceptions and constructions of linguistic difference as either manageable through communicative adaptation, or as a major obstacle.

Situations where speakers use a lingua franca are necessarily multilingual in that at least some participants must have other first languages and probably further additional languages in their repertoires. These other languages commonly surface in ELF situations (Klimpfinger 2009; Pietikäinen 2014; Mauranen 2013b), and it would appear that language-crossing or mixing is indeed a natural part of using a lingua franca. The resulting multiple language influences work in several directions, as cross-language research suggests (e.g. Jarvis and Pavlenko 2007). From the viewpoint of English with its globe-strapping usage this means that it leaves its traces in virtually all languages of the world, while they in turn inevitably affect English.

Why English in use as a Lingua Franca is of scholarly interest, then, derives above all from its potential contribution to understanding language, in addition to observing changes in English itself, and to working out how practitioners should go about teaching or translating it. We could frame this by adapting Habermas' (1976) typology of knowledge interests: a theoretical, descriptive and an applied interest. Possibly the principal and most enduring contribution of ELF research will turn out to be not the study of English, but a more general one: how we see language and its role in human communication. Research on ELF has opened the eyes of linguists working in English and also in other languages to look at languages as interconnected, drawing from a common pool of communicative resources. We are learning to appreciate the change that follows from the presence of second-language speakers and ubiquitous language contact. The questions that arise in an unusually complex, globally interrelated language contact are fundamental to understanding what languages are and what they do. In addition to this theoretical interest, it is clear that there is a great descriptive interest in ELF, particularly as one of the major developments in Englishes all over the world, in either colonial and postcolonial circumstances (roughly corresponding to Kachru's "Outer Circle"), or in the more established settings of the "Inner Circle" countries where it is a first language for a considerable proportion of citizens and has an official status. Finally, there is a definite applied interest that ELF holds for language professionals: what does this rapid change and new complexity mean for teaching, translating, and interpreting foreign languages?

This paper addresses mainly the first two knowledge interests, leaving the applications aside. The aim is to set the scene with a conceptualisation of ELF from three perspectives: the macro-social, the micro-social and the cognitive, and then go on to provide a brief overview of the processes and products that we have been able to observe thus far in analysing ELF data. Clearly, both can be regarded as interim stages in a development towards a more thorough understanding of the issues, or as developing hypotheses based on what we know now, with few answers as yet. The databases in existence are fairly modest so far, but clearly, in the 15 years or so that have passed since the seminal book on theorising and describing ELF (Jenkins 2000), we have witnessed much empirical and theoretical work that has taken the field forward, and we are in a far better position now than in the early days to see ELF in the big picture of languages and perceptions of language in change.

2 Conceptualising ELF

The term lingua franca is normally used to mean a contact language, that is, a vehicular language between speakers who do not share a first language. While some lingua francas are pidgins or jargons that arise without prior learning of a shared language, others are existing natural languages used for vehicular purposes. In the latter cases, at least one speaker or speaker group uses it as a second or additional language. Pidgins typically arise for restricted purposes, but any broad-purpose natural language can be employed as a lingua franca without restrictions on the uses or functions it can be put to. Although the term lingua franca is today most commonly used in connection with internationally widespread natural languages, especially (sometimes exclusively) English, smaller languages operate as local lingua francas. They need not even be "living" languages: "dead" languages also serve as vehicular languages, albeit for a limited range of purposes like religion or learning, like classical Arabic or mediaeval Latin.

The significance of ELF goes beyond the contact of any individual or group or community with English. ELF is unique on account of its non-local character as the means of communicating between people from anywhere in the world, not just where English is salient in the community. Neither is its global weight restricted to elite usages in politics, international business, or academia, but ELF enables communication to refugees, asylum seekers and ordinary tourists.

It is not difficult to recognise affinities between ELF and dialect contact; both incorporate contact between speakers of mutually intelligible varieties (or better, lects). We can therefore assume that phenomena discovered in dialect contact research, such as those that lead to dialect levelling, will also be in evidence in ELF. I try to avoid the term "variety" in connection with ELF because for many it entails a certain stability of use and user communities, which is essentially either inapplicable or irrelevant to ELF, and use a more neutral term, 'lect'. Lect reflects the affinity of ELF with dialect, and coheres with sociolect, idiolect, and similar terms. A number of English lects reflecting local language contact are jokingly, whether disparagingly or fondly, known by nicknames like Swinglish, Finglish, Czenglish, or Dunglish. Such nicknames have arisen from the common observation that when speakers who share a first language learn a given foreign or second language, their idiolects have recognisable similarities in pronunciation, accent, syntactic features, lexis, and so on. These lects, which arise from contacts of a particular L1 with English, I would like to call 'similects'.

Dialects arise in speech communities where people communicate with each other, and their specific features result from frequent interactions within that community. By contrast, similects are not lects of any community.

Similects arise in parallel, as speakers learn the same L2, but since they already share an L1, they normally use that rather than the L2 in communicating with each other. Similects are parallel also in that they develop similarities even though they are learned in different classrooms, schools, and locations, at different ages, and at different times. Similects, therefore, always remain first-generation hybrids. They do not go through developmental stages in the way community languages do, they do not diversify, change, develop sociolects, dialects, or other products of social interaction in a living community. They nevertheless embody language contact.

We might argue that language contact at the level of individuals is something that takes place in language learners, and therefore similects for individuals are manifestations of learner language. However, why similects cannot be placed under a general rubric of learner language, despite possible resemblance to L1-specific learner features (quite carefully recorded in learner language studies, notably in the Louvain projects: e.g. Granger, Hung and Petch-Tyson 2002; Gilquin, Granger and Paquot 2007) lies in their different social determinants. Similects thrive in actual second language use (SLU), in a plethora of contexts and speakers from professionals to tourists or refugees. Conversely, the sociolinguistic context of a language learning classroom is highly specific, with important repercussions to speaker identity and relationship to the language: a learner identity is reductive, one of a deficient communicator (Firth and Wagner 1997). Incorporating out-of-classroom experience into learning (e.g. Pickard 1996; Hyland 2004), or recently Blended Learning (e.g. Johnson and Marsh 2014), provides no remedy: if all SLU is perceived as practice towards the ultimate goal of learning, the language user orients to noticing, observing, and even deliberate memorising of language elements, whereas, clearly, SLU for co-construction of meaning towards immediate social goals orients speakers entirely differently – to achieving the goals at hand. A further distinction between SLA and SLU is that while learners are not in a position to change the language they are learning, any *user* of a language can initiate and diffuse changes. Therefore, the surface similarities of learner features and non-standard forms appearing in ELF hide much deeper incompatibilities (see further Mauranen 2012).

ELF, then, embodies contact between speakers from different similects. Put in another way, speakers who use ELF as their means of communication speak English which is a product of language contact between their L1 and the English they have encountered in their learning process. ELF, then, is a contact between these hybrid, contact-based lects – that is, ELF is a higher-order, or second-order language contact. Therein lies its particular complexity.

At this point it may be good to add some clarifications that often seem to create confusion around the notion of ELF. One is the question whether native speakers of English are included or excluded from the concept. In the definition of ELF adopted here, there is no basis for excluding those who have acquired English as their first language; the presence of English as a native language (ENL) is not unusual where ELF is spoken. Not only do they participate in speaking ELF, but they also contribute to its variability. Since there are so many varieties of ENL, it is easy to appreciate how this adds to overall variation in the total mix of Englishes from a global point of view, ELF included. A second matter that needs addressing is the inherent multilingualism in ELF. Since at least one group or individual necessarily uses any given lingua franca as an additional language, a minimum of two languages are involved in an instance of lingua franca use. A notable proportion of those who speak English know other languages besides their L1, and can have more than one L1. Since we know that a speaker's languages are all present and more or less active at any moment, relatively frequent language-crossing is also of theoretical importance as an underpinning of the ELF concept. The notion of English as "a multilingua franca" where the fundamental multilingualism of ELF (or presumably any lingua franca) occupies centre stage has recently been developed in Jenkins (2015).

Conceptualising ELF as a second-order contact language between similects is basically a sociolinguistic view on ELF. We could call this a macro-social perspective, which can be contrasted to or compared with two other perspectives for a rounded view of the whole, namely the micro-social, or interactive, and the individual, or cognitive. The interactive perspective focuses on speakers in interaction, which constitutes an interface between the individual and the collective, macro-social level. The individual's cognitive perspective attends to evidence on processing as well as idiosyncratic uses. Taking these three perspectives on board builds on earlier conceptualisations of language contact. Weinreich (1953/1963), in his classic study on language contact, talked about two levels where transfer would occur: the individual, or the level of speech, and society, or the level of language. A similar division is adopted by Jarvis and Pavlenko (2007), who also distinguish the levels of the individual (who shows cross-linguistic influence), and society (where transfer can be observed). In variationist sociolinguistics (e.g. Milroy 2002; Trudgill 1986; 2011), it is also customary to locate two key levels, the societal and the individual; yet their "individual" focus is in effect on individuals in interaction, so that it is interaction that becomes the other pivotal level. The micro-social level, interaction, is in its turn crucial to the social network theory (Granovetter 1983; Urry 2007) as developed for language change (Milroy and Milroy 1985; Raumolin 1998). We can thus see the present three-perspective approach as combining the main elements from previous approaches.

To return to the macro-social perspective briefly, it needs pointing out that ELF communities are non-local, that is, not based on physical proximity and the multiplex contacts within such communities. This is a key characteristic that distinguishes ELF from traditional dialect communities as well as many other communities typically described in sociolinguistic research, such as the speech community. In this respect ELF communities resemble academic discourse communities of the kind Swales (1990) talks about, which tend to be predominantly international. In many cases they also bear some likeness to Wenger's communities of practice (Lave and Wenger 1991), as noted by House (2003) Jenkins (2007) and Seidlhofer (2011). ELF communities also vary notably in their duration and stability, from ephemeral like those formed for just one occasion such as a conference, to task forces, international organisations, and finally to married couples with ELF as their family language (see, Pietikäinen 2014).

All these notions of "community" fit some ELF communities, but not all. Is there any unifying concept that could capture the whole? Clearly, a community of ELF speakers resembles a "diffuse language community" along the lines of LePage and Tabouret-Keller (1985), that is, one that consists of many kinds of speakers with varying language identities. The global ELF-using "community" is thus an umbrella community, which, apart from being diffuse, shares the feature with Anderson's (1991) imagined communities that the members may never meet each other in person, but nevertheless possess a general awareness of belonging to the "community", perceived as a category of speakers. An ELF identity may not be as binding or strong as the national communities Anderson talks about, and it can be self-contradictory in comprising both positive and negative elements, as many studies of language ideologies show (Jenkins 2007; Pilkinton-Pihko 2013; Kitazawa 2013). In such diffuse communities, some parts will be more likely to become "focused" than others, with the dimension of time potentially a central factor: both the duration of the community and its frequency of internal communication are likely to support the emergence of communal focus – as in the case of discourse communities or communities of practice (see also network theory in Milroy and Milroy 1985). Clearly, ELF as a whole is not a focused variety, but as Laitinen (2016) points out, in this respect ELF is not unlike the English language for the best part of its history, in which focused varieties only arose as standardised varieties in the modern period. This did not prevent change or evolution of its lexicogrammatical structures before that period.

3 What can we expect from ELF

Assuming the above, that is, taking ELF to be a complex, higher-order form of language contact between similects, what is it that we can reasonably expect to find when we delve into an ELF database? At this stage of ELF research, with roughly fifteen years of empirical research behind us, we already have a fair amount of evidence on different aspects of ELF. Most of the research has been carried out with small samples of data, but not quite everything, and when different studies come up with similar findings, even small-scale research shows its usefulness. However, in this section I am not drawing on that, but rather on the predictions we might derive from the current concept of ELF, what previous research has suggested, and the three perspectives that are relevant to the issues.

3.1 The macro-social perspective

To begin from the big picture, the first thing likely to affect the observable outcome of ELF speech is the vagueness of the aggregate or umbrella "community" discussed above of all thinkable speakers using ELF, and the complexity of the intersecting or independent smaller components that it consists of. The consequence is a plethora of contact situations with different constellations of similects. With vast numbers of similects coming into contact with each other, we can expect a considerable degree of variability. When speakers use a lingua franca, the combination of similects is multiplex and often ad hoc, rather than one of regular interactions between two similect groups, analogous to dialect contact. We can also assume variation along similectal lines from numerous SLA studies (including corpus studies like those from the ICLE project (https://www.uclouvain.be/en-cecl-icle.html.) which have systematically investigated individuals performing their idiolects in L2 English in a learner role, and found similarities based on their L1s. It is not necessary or interesting to try to replicate those studies with ELF data, because in ELF the similects meet in interaction and exert mutual influence: people do not perform their proficiency in terms of their individual repertoires but seek to co-construct meaning with their interlocutors. Speakers adjust their comprehension to deal with a range of unfamiliar forms that differ from their own idiolect features as well as their previous experiences of English, including Standard Englishes through formal education. This adjustment amounts to receptive expansion of classroom experience (much like assimilation in the Piagetian sense, but on occasion also leading to accommodation). It is matched by a productive expansion of adopting and trying out new forms for communicative needs. The combined effect pushes at the boundaries of English. We may thus expect to see unconventional features that do not cause turbulence or disruption in the ongoing communication.

In addition to variation, it is reasonable to expect repetitions of similar forms and similar expressions across speech events and language backgrounds. Such features can be expected on the basis of "Angloversals" (Mair 2003) as something in English itself that invites certain phenomena from L2 speech (in which case ELF characteristics should be similar to all other L2 varieties). Alternatively, there might be features that merely or primarily only occur in ELF (which would mean ELF is specific and different from other L2 uses). It is also possible that ELF patterns show similarities with either learner language or with other L2 Englishes, but not both (which could be used for testing whether or how SLU is different from SLA, as we would expect on the basis of the different social situational parameters). Finally, they may be innovations which have already been spreading in ELF.

Sociolinguistic research from the macro perspective typically suggests that the consequence of extensive language contact is simplification. So for instance Trudgill in his (2011) model lists language contact and adult SLA among factors conducive to overall simplification. Both are obviously fundamental components of ELF. Trudgill suggests that these social determinants lead to increasing morphological transparency, loss of redundancy, and loss of what he calls "historical baggage". Kusters (2003) looked at several language groups in a variety of sociolinguistic circumstances and found that languages used as lingua francas are more amenable to simplification than those spoken in closed speech communities, which is in agreement with Milroy and Milroy's (1985) earlier suggestion.

Even though structure seems to be a commonly assumed contact-induced site of simplification (also e.g. Croft 2000; Thomason 2001), it is important to note that simplification can be of many kinds – morphological, syntactic, semantic, pragmatic, for instance, and it seems trade-offs between these are hard to detect (Nichols 2009). Thus, an overall prediction of simplification may be insufficient for capturing nuances of what massive and multiplex language contact brings about, but it certainly looks likely that ELF is affected by simplification processes, in view of what is known about language contact in other circumstances.

The main macro-social consequences of ELF use would definitely be those that emanate from real-world contact, including the now ubiquitous digital contact, and less importantly reflections of the formal settings of learning. As part of this, we might reasonably expect to find regional trends, such as those based on shared cultural history, in addition to language typological similarities and previous language contact histories.

3.2 The cognitive perspective

From the individual's point of view, or the cognitive standpoint, we could expect ELF as based on the speaker's second language to be more weakly entrenched than the first. It would seem well grounded to expect a second language to display more fuzziness in processing compared to a first language. Even given the simplifications involved in talking about first and second languages (many people are bi- or multilingual from the start, their later languages may have become stronger, etc.), later acquired languages tend to provide less exposure, and their acquisition begins at a later stage of brain maturation, which can result in weaker entrenchment. In large numbers, then, the processing of a less strongly entrenched language should be fuzzier and manifest more approximate target items.

Thomason (2001) notes that in language contact situations imperfect learning tends to cause structural or phonological rather than lexical changes in the target language and more often than not lead to simplification rather than complication of the target language structure. While 'imperfect learning' is not a useful concept for ELF (e.g. Brutt-Griffler 2002; Mauranen 2012), post-childhood language learning has been implicated in structural simplification, as already noted. As this is the typical case for ELF, the prediction would follow that ELF displays structural simplification but probably not lexical changes. Moreover, on the whole syntheticity is found to be harder for learners, who prefer analyticity, and therefore analyticity can be presumed to be simpler. However, since English is a comparatively analytic language, the cognitive challenge may not be as substantial for learners as that posed by more synthetic languages.

Unlike structural simplification, lexical simplification has been rarely if at all predicted for language contact. This might appear motivated from a macro perspective since lexis travels fast and could just add to the lexical stores of both languages. But a cognitive viewpoint could suggest a different picture. Lexical simplification has been observed in learner language (e.g. Altenberg and Granger 2002; Granger et al. 2002) as well as in translations (e.g. Laviosa-Braithwaite 1996; Nevalainen 2005; Tirkkonen-Condit 2004). The established explanations for the prevalence of very frequent lexis in learner language relate to gaps in learning and to interference from the learner's first language. By contrast, since the overwhelming majority of translations are made into the translator's first language, interference from the target language is the accepted explanation, and learning difficulties are never implicated. I would argue, as I have done before (e.g. Mauranen 2010, 2013a), that there is a common, more general basis in each situation, and this is language contact. Language contact is activated whether an individual is translating from one language to another or speaking a less well entrenched language. In both instances two systems are activated and in competition for space in working memory. If two competing systems are active in a speaker's repertoire, the best entrenched parts of each are likely to become more salient in relative terms. As a corollary, unique features of the languages are likely to get suppressed (as found in translations by Tirkkonen-Condit 2004).

On account of the tendency of speakers to economise on their effort in expression and the limitations of working memory, we should also detect individuals settling on certain preferred expressions for given meanings, following the one-meaning-one-form principle or isomorphism that has been recognised in language learning. A phenomenon of this kind, fixing, has been observed in written SLU by Vetchinnikova (2014, this volume).

Moving on from production to reception, weak entrenchment applies to the hearer as well as to the speaker: an approximate form may not be harder to understand than a precise form for an ELF- speaking hearer, because a typical hearer is not precisely attuned to Standard English (or any particular variety of English) and is more likely to rely on fairly fuzzy processing in seeking to make sense of the interlocutor's speech. These matching cognitive processes in turn have interactional consequences: acceptance of approximate forms in interaction.

One mediating mechanism between language use and language change is frequency. It has been well established that frequent items behave differently from infrequent ones (see, e.g. Bybee and Hopper 2001), and survive longest in language even over very long periods of time (Pagel 2012). The cognitive correlate to this is stronger entrenchment of the most frequent items, which in ELF would mean that these are on the whole well represented; the interactional consequence of this would show in accommodation, especially in speakers' likelihood of finding common ground for fluent communication.

3.3 The micro-social perspective

At the interface of the two previous perspectives lies the micro-social, that of social interaction, with close relations to and partial intersection with the individual and the wider social entities. Innovations do not diffuse without interacting individuals, and at the same time, individual cognition is crucially shaped in interaction with its social environment, in other words with other people. The most obvious consequence of this is that children start by acquiring the language of their immediate circle of family and carers, and then go on to diversify their repertoires especially towards their peer groups. Secondary socialisation, such as formal education, is also imparted and absorbed through interaction.

As we saw above, accounts of language change in the macro-social perspective tend to assume that accommodation provides a key mechanism that explains the adoption of features from one language group to another, for instance in dialect contact (Trudgill 1986). Among other things, accommodation has been seen as a response to speakers from outside one's own community (Croft 2000). Accommodation in this interpretation would be used to compensate for the lack of common ground by adjusting one's speech, for instance by elaborating content or simplifying grammar as Giles and Smith (1979) suggest. These hypotheses derive from native speaker research, but accommodation would appear to be at least equally central in explaining what happens in successful ELF communication, as shown in Jenkins (2000) for phonology.

Features like enhanced explicitness and rephrasing would be closest to Giles and Smith's "elaborating the content". This need not exhaust their potential. Communicative strategies like these are also likely to result in discourse adaptations that can turn into drivers of grammar. In line with usage-based models of grammar (Du Bois 2003; Ford et al 2003; Barlow and Kemmer 2000) or second-language acquisition (Larsen-Freeman 2002; McWhinney 2005), which argue that linguistic structures are shaped by the demands of communication rather than communication reflecting available linguistic structures, we could expect discourse to be a key driver of ELF grammar. In the long term, then, there is good reason to expect structural changes to follow from continued large-scale ELF interaction. The clearest effect may perhaps be seen in altered preferences so that certain kinds of structures become more common while others get rarer.

Enhanced explicitness is also found in translation, and has become known in Translation Studies as explicitation (Blum-Kulka 1986). Explicitation is prioritised in the face of perceived or anticipated differences in writers' and readers' backgrounds, and has been one of the most strongly supported translation universals (e.g. Mauranen 2006a).

Some kind of "communicative fitness" in an element is further likely to help it spread into common use and become preferred. As Dabrowska puts it: "[o]ther things being equal, speakers naturally prefer structures which are easier to produce; and through failure to communicate, they learn to avoid structures which are difficult to understand" (Dabrowska 2004: 67).

The fuzziness in cognitive processing that is enhanced in SLU would presumably lead to the strengthening of approximate forms in production; their acceptance on the hearer's part may follow from a comparatively weak entrenchment of many items. If a hearer does not have a strong and well-defined notion of the correct form, an approximation is not likely to be disturbing; thus communicative success may follow forms that bear enough resemblance to a target for recognition to enable meaning construction. This in turn is likely to strengthen the speaker's perception of its acceptability further. The feedback loop on usage that arises in spontaneous interaction is a crucial link in the strengthening and spreading of expressions that might otherwise pass as random idiosyncracies. Or, if compared to environments of formal learning such as classrooms, they would be noted as errors, thus lack of success. Frequency also comes in here: the most frequent items are on the whole most strongly entrenched, since these are the items likely to be heard and used most often. Therefore, when speakers look for the common ground that would be particularly conducive to communicating with others with some knowledge of the chosen lingua franca, high-frequency items in the shared language are good candidates: they have the best chances of being known to both. We may therefore anticipate that very frequent items are well represented in ELF discourse.

Fuzzy cognitive processes concern interactants whether they adopt a speaker or hearer role at any moment. This should also lead to collaborative efforts in facilitating communicative fluency. Conversation is a joint achievement, and for instance collaborative completions (co-constructions) add to discourse fluency by taking the discussion forward. They also play a discourse facilitating role by indicating comprehension. The tendency of speakers to pick up each other's expressions in the course of interaction also smoothes the path of conversation, and like collaborative completions reflects communicative adaptation and accommodation.

As noted above, from a macro perspective the expectation regarding linguistic structure is that language contact results in simplification. From an interactional viewpoint this can be understood in terms of speakers from different backgrounds looking for the least common denominator that would support interactional fluency. The best guesses should be elements that are the most widely shared. These may also be especially salient or particularly learnable features of a given language, and in this way reflect a kind of "subjective simplicity" in analogy to what Miestamo (2009) calls user-oriented or "subjective complexity".

It would seem likely that interaction between speakers of different similects favours features that are vital to successful communication over those that are not (or are "ornamental" cf. Szmresanyi and Kortmann 2009). Whether this would mean that ELF tends towards creoles, which according to McWhorter (2001) display relatively little overall grammatical complexity on account of their pidgin origins and therefore have little that is unnecessary to communication, is an empirical question. Clearly, ELF is not of pidgin origin, or functionally reduced language use. It is used for everything languages are used for, and thus probably resists being stripped of ornamental uses.

3.4 In sum

We might summarise the above by noting that there are three relatively strong predictions to be made, and a few others that are also likely. Of the main predictions of ELF properties, simplification comes out strongly in any account of previous research and from all three perspectives considered here. There are two caveats, though: one is that overall simplification is unclear and difficult (maybe even pointless) to measure, as simplicity can be of different kinds. The second caveat is that English is a comparatively analytic language in structural terms, and therefore perhaps less likely to be in need of major structural simplification.

It is nevertheless structural simplification that is generally predicted for language contact or lingua franca use.

The second important prediction emanates from both cognitive and interactional considerations, and that is the manifestation of forms that approximate the target and may become strengthened, thus increasing variability. Variability in turn is also predicted on the basis of similect contact from the macro-social perspective. The third hypothesis follows from both cognitive and interactional positions: item frequency plays an important role, in other words highly frequent items should be strengthened in ELF.

The other predictions are hitherto somewhat less strongly supported on the basis of earlier research in related fields, but can still be reasonably postulated as probable in ELF: fixing, explicitation, and shared multi-word items across similects. Fixing is the counterpart of approximation, meaning that a speaker or a group settles on a given preferred expression, often either non-standard or rare in general English (otherwise it would hardly be noticed). This is predicted on both cognitive and interactional processes. Co-construction of utterances between interlocutors can strengthen certain patterns of expression, which may further support changes in discourse-driven grammar. Explicitation, as a discourse strategy, is likely to arise from speaker accommodation and recipient design, and it may result in preferences for explicit syntactic structures. Finally, we may find similar forms and similar multi-word expressions across speech events and language backgrounds. In principle these are particularly interesting, as they should represent the specifcally ELF-like features that arise from the particular combination of English and a complex similect contact.

4 The data

The descriptive analyses in this paper draw on a database of spoken academic English, the ELFA corpus (www.helsinki.fi/elfa), a just over million-word database at the University of Helsinki. This is a corpus of recorded interaction in authentic academic speech events in four Finnish universities (Helsinki, Tampere, Aalto, and Tampere Technological University) in their English-medium programmes and international conferences held in them. The data consist of both monologues such as lectures, graduate student presentations and conference presentations as well as dialogues such as seminar discussions, doctoral defence debates and conference discussion sections. The deliberate bias is on dialogic – or in this case, overwhelmingly polylogic – speech, which gives insights on linguistic processes in action. Slightly over two thirds of the material is of dialogic nature. The speakers were going about their academic activities, and being recorded was essentially trivial from their point of view. More vital concerns were at stake – how colleagues and fellow students received their presentations and took their points, or whether their doctoral theses were accepted. None of the recordings were made in same-L1-only situations, and none were made in situations where English was the object of study, to ensure that this would be a corpus of second language use (SLU), not a corpus of second language acquisition (SLA). ELFA is thus a corpus of speakers, not learners. In total, speakers reported 51 different first languages.

A one-million–word corpus may seem small, especially in comparison to the enormous web-based databases we now have. However, ELFA is spoken and specialized – both corpus types tend to be small compared to general, written or mixed-mode corpora (as large reference corpora usually are – and they are already looking small). Moreover, ELFA is not significantly smaller than, say, MICASE (Simpson et al. 2002), which is also spoken and specialised. The corpus was the first completed on ELF, and was intended as a basis for generating hypotheses about ELF rather than for finding conclusive proof on its characteristics. By now we already have points of comparison in other ELF corpora, albeit none of them compiled by absolutely identical principles: VOICE (2009), ACE (2014), EuroCoAT (MacArthur et al. 2015) and recently WrELFA (2015), the first corpus of written ELF. They are all small, but nevertheless offer a good basis for testing the robustness of some of the hypotheses based on ELFA, specifically in terms of the spread of the phenomena (see, e.g. Carey 2013).

The diversity of the population in ELFA might be perceived as a problem if the idea is to take up many background variables for corpus-internal comparisons, that is if the research rests on the assumption that as many population variables as possible need to be treated as potentially relevant to observable variation. If this had been our point of departure, we should have aimed at a different corpus structure altogether, for example by taking similar-sized samples of L1s, or ages, or gender. The population of ELF users is highly diverse in terms of linguistic backgrounds, not to speak of cultural backgrounds or trajectories of individual personal experience. The usual situation in actual ELF encounters is that such factors vary in interactions, and this is what ELF speech is made of: speech communities can be of varying duration, the fluency of English among the participants may be uneven and their expectations of interlocutors' skills and knowledge can vary. The aim in compiling the corpus was to maximise diversity in terms of language backgrounds, speech event types, disciplines, and academic status, which is a relevant social role in this context. The corpus reflects this diversity well, thus the multiplicity of factors need not present a problem as long as we pose questions that look for commonalities in linguistic features and do not want to compare, say, L1 influence on performance. It is an advantage that the corpus is focused in terms of genre, register, and speech event type, to balance out some of the diversity of the language. For a more detailed elaboration of the corpus rationale see Mauranen (2012).

5 What is ELF like?

Having gone through a few assumptions that could be reasonably made of ELF it is time to look at what empirical evidence from ELFA we have to bear on the issues. In this section, the hypotheses posed above in section 3.4 are reviewed in the light of the data presented in section 4.

5.1 Simplifying

ELFA reveals a number of cases where regularization of irregular forms takes place. This concerns many irregular verbs (*losed*; *digged*; *teached*) and uncountable nouns regularised into countable nouns (*advices*; *independencies*; *informations*; *staffs*). Losing the third person singular ending from present tense verbs can also be seen as regularization (*the co-participant **need** to share the knowledge; he can make everything he **want***). Yet, although these phenomena are well in evidence and suggest a common tendency, regularisation, this does not mean that they are more typical or frequent in ELF speech than conventional irregular verb forms, conventional mass nouns, or the standard third person –s. Some of these forms seem nevertheless to be gaining ground, for instance some mass nouns (*informations*, *furnitures*) that appear to be spreading based on anecdotal evidence from the media and field notes, even though in the present corpus *advices* was the only notable competitor to *advice* (6 and 20 occurrences, respectively, distributed over independent files). Initial analyses from the WrELFA corpus of written academic ELF (www.eng.helsinki.fi/elfa/wrelfa) in turn suggest that *evidences* appears quite commonly as a noun.

It is reasonable to take regularisation to be a form of simplification. In addition to morphological regularisation, simplification can to some extent be detected in other linguistic domains like syntax and lexis. Speech data is not ideally suited for studying syntactic processes, but Ranta (2013; see also Mauranen, Carey and Ranta 2015) carried out an extensive study of frequently occurring non-standard syntactic features in ELFA, and also compared their use to comparable ENL data from MICASE. Ranta's work included the extended use of the progressive, *would* in hypothetical *if*-clauses, embedded inversions, and singular agreement in existential *there*-constructions with plural notional subjects. All of these were common in both sets of data. Arguably, expanding the applicability of certain forms beyond their former domain means diluting existing structural distinctions and thereby simplifying a system.

Progressives were used[1] among both ELF and ENL speakers with stative verbs (1a), punctual events (1b), and general truths/habits (1c) – all thus deviating from the prescribed standard. Only 'habits' use did not appear much in ENL data.

(1a) okay my name is er it's difficult to pronounce **i'm coming from croatia** i'm teaching in the faculty of law university of Zagreb

(1b) even when **i was referring** er the nordic countries were divided eastern and western orientation @@ i had in mind finland to east- eastern orientation

(1c) i mean er er properties and relation **are belonging to** the same erm ontological general er area

The use of progressives has been on the increase in English generally (Leech, Hundt, Mair and Smith 2009; Leech and Smith 2009), which is interesting in respect of the findings in ELFA: either ELF follows general trends or, as actual majority usage, plays a role in leading the change. It certainly supports the trend. Hypothetical *if*-clauses (2) and embedded inversions (3) did not much differentiate between the speaker groups any more than *ing* forms, but in the case of *there* constructions with plural notional subjects, singular agreement (4) was actually more common in native English speech.

(2) these relations **if they would be called** the intensional containment they are those ones that come er about

(3) the yukos affair of course one can go in great le- length **discussing why was it** er er what actually happened

(4) and **there is** many success stories

Even if the embedded inversions did not much differentiate between the corpora, simple inversions (5) also appear in ELFA, and although infrequent, they add another simplifying facet.

(5) **what you think** is the reason for that

---

[1] The examples illuminate Ranta's findings and are from the ELFA corpus but not from her study.

Apart from morpho-syntactic simplification, a far less discussed kind is lexical simplification. It is nevertheless worth exploring since it is found in other contact situations besides ELF. Lexical simplicity or complexity can be measured for example by means of estimated vocabulary sizes of individuals, type/token ratios in texts, and the relative proportion of the most frequent items in large text masses. The last-mentioned measure lends itself to corpus comparisons. As already noted by Zipf (1935), frequent words largely follow a power law pattern, thus the most frequent ones cover a very substantial proportion of language in use. This has been confirmed in corpus data time and again. If we take the classic Brown corpus as a standard, equalling ELFA in size, 135 top-ranking words account for half of the data. In other words, the 135 most common types constitute 50% of the tokens. By contrast, in ELFA, 44 words (types) suffice to account for 50% of the data (tokens) (Mauranen 2012). This is a dramatic difference: only a third of the types reported for Brown is required to cover half of the tokens in ELFA. Issues of mode and genre spring to mind: Brown is far more varied in genre, and it is written. Since written corpora tend to show less concentration of high-frequency lexis than spoken (e.g. Biber and Conrad 2009), it is worth exploring the effect of comparing ELFA to MICASE, which, like ELFA, is both spoken and academic.

Table 1 shows that there is a clear effect of mode and genre and that MICASE and ELFA are closer to each other than either is to Brown.

Table 1: Shares of the most frequent words in ELFA and MICASE (from Mauranen 2012: 91)

Words	ELFA %	MICASE %
Top 44	50.05	
Top 58		50.0
Top 200	68.7	68.0

As we can see, MICASE requires 58 most common words to account for half of the corpus, which is well under a half (43%) of the number in Brown. What is also clear from the table is that this effect is at its strongest at the very top frequencies, whereas the difference levels out at the rank order of 200, which is still quite high. A third of the lexis used thus falls under this frequency level in both. While we therefore have no grounds for dismissing ELF as wholly or predominantly limited to the most frequent lexis, the tendency to proportionally higher representation of top-frequency items still holds. The evidence supports lexical simplification, although this is not the case solely in ELF (see section 3.2 above); rather, it would seem to be an effect of language contact more generally.

Moreover, the present findings lend support to the hypothesized significance of item frequency in language change. The most frequent words in ELFA and MICASE are very similar at the very top, but start bifurcating gradually as we move down the rank order, and the same is true of trigrams (Mauranen 2012). These findings compare interestingly to Gilner's recent (2016) results from three spoken corpora: the spoken part of ICE-CORE (Gilner and Morales 2011) and two ELF corpora, VOICE (2009) and ELFA. Gilner's figures differ slightly from the above, as she had removed all fillers and non-words, but the differences are small. The identical comparison in her study and mine was the coverage of the top 200 words, where the respective coverage was 69.61% of (VOICE), 64.63% (ELFA) and 62.68% (ICE spoken) (Gilner 2016: 33). ELFA is in the middle, suggesting that academic vocabulary may be comparatively varied after all, but the main finding confirms the above: at 200 words, about two thirds of spoken lexis is covered, and the distinction between first and second language use is negligible. On the whole, Gilner suggests a greater reliance of what she calls "dominant vocabulary" (DOVO) in ELF compared to English at large, where local considerations have more prominence. This is compatible with the idea of relative lexical simplification in ELF, and especially the notion that the key factor in this is language contact.

5.2 Complexifying

If structural simplification in the light of currently available evidence largely manifests itself in regularisation, other ELF features such as approximation and cross-linguistic similect influence do not follow suit. As a kind of counterpart to the tendency to regularise, ELF speech manifests tendencies that are quite irregular compared to conventional English usage. One is unusual productivity in morphology, such as a fairly free use of negative prefixes (*undirectly*; *insuitable*; *unuseful*), and either adding affixes (*the promoting and **securing** of human rights*; *it is recognised that, and **theoretisised**, to make it a theory about it*) or dropping them (*it's er difficult to change from one day to the other because it's so **routined***; *initiatives are **couraged** or discouraged in these two countries*; *ASEAN has developed signi- **significally** towards a security community*).

The mechanisms generating approximate forms can sometimes be guessed or gleaned from the context. They would appear to include various kinds of analogy – which may also lead into regularising – and not differ materially from those generally found in language change. A case in point is backformation, for which contextual support could often be found, as illustrated in (6 a–b).

(6a) one researcher of us was doing really the opposite studying the er effect of **standardisation** that if he could **standardise** more, er in that company

(6b) is it er **bio-degradation** er there are, are, so it's it's fairly fairly known that polycaprolactone **bio-degradates** so yeah

In both instances the likely source of backformation is in the immediately preceding context, and in both the verb is modelled on a noun. Similar phenomena were observed with a number of verbs.

Articles and prepositions are among the most conspicuous forms showing variable or unstable use in ELF. They are common enough to enable fairly reliable identification of L2 speakers even from very short snippets of data. Articles may get dropped (*and **bigger company** the better*), added (*they are deprived of **the** liberty they are transported into different countries*), or used in unconventional ways (*kind of **a** same process*). Prepositions show similar processes: dropping a preposition (*so I was **listening the experiences** of er turkish women*), adding one (*maybe we can **discuss about** it*), or choosing an unconventional one (*this kind of **obsession in** progress that the modern west at least I think has*). These tendencies can be regarded as a typical ELF feature at the collective level, i.e. social usage. At the individual, cognitive level another facet is revealed: the same individuals can display fluctuating use, as in (7).

(7) four criteria i believe **first** is the sh- social participation of women **second one** is the accessibility and presence at all levels of power **the third one** is the legal infrans- infrastructural framework on women in society and **the last one** is non-governmental institutions for women

Such fluctuation within one utterance would seem to suggest weak entrenchment of the conventional usage. Consequently, we can speak of weak entrenchment at the level of the individual, which then manifests itself as loosening up of norms at the collective level represented in a corpus. A social norm, which linguistic conventions essentially are, starts losing its bind when people come across more and more breaches of it, especially if noncompliance works effectively. Acceptability is tested in interaction. In effect, relaxing norms leads to increased fuzziness. For reception at individual level this means further demands towards processing and making sense of variable forms.

Widening morphological productivity has consequences beyond individual words: it affects phraseological units. For example, using the frame *–ly speaking* in the MICASE and ELFA corpora reveals a clear difference. In MICASE *–ly speaking* is strongly biased towards *generally speaking*, with other adverbs (*objectively*, *roughly* etc.) as one-off occurrences (apart from *strictly*, which appears twice). By contrast, ELFA shows much more variation, a larger number of instances, and a less clear preference for any one alternative: three hits for both *historically* and *generally* and two each for five others, including *basically*, *formally*, and *frankly* (Mauranen 2012). This wide dispersion involves no breach of structural standards, only challenging conventionalised preferences. Approximation of this kind is less obvious than the kinds altering structures, but despite its subtlety it may be quite influential; unlikely to get corrected, it frees up productivity and plays down conventions.

Repeated patterns in the corpus data allow us to see that approximation is not merely a matter of individual processes (such as dropping a particular morpheme or article by a given speaker) that can fall into a type (say, unusual prepositions), but a more interesting tendency of speakers settling for similar preferences across speech events and language backgrounds. I suggest such collectively manifest repeated preferences can usefully be called fixing, although Vetchinnikova (2014, this volume) coined the term originally to describe individuals' usage. Such fixing, when it concerns several speakers, not only adds to aggregate variability, but more importantly shows incipient signs of new usages that diffuse over particular instances and similects.

Fixing can best be seen in multi-word units, starting from simple combinations like *discuss about* to phraseological units like *in my point of view* (in the sense of 'in my view'), *let me say some words about* (for 'let me say a few words about') (Mauranen 2012), *on the other side* (for 'on the other hand'), *so to say* (for 'so to speak') (Carey 2013).

Phraseological, multi-word units of meaning are at the very heart of change potential. As they combine lexis and structure, they are more powerful than either on their own. Lexical elements and the schematic whole ensure that meanings get across; structures come along under their protection as it were. When these expressions get accepted they serve as analogical formations and models for others. They also explain how a language tolerates fuzziness in very frequent items: approximative items are communicatively successful if they (i) give a sufficient hint of what the target item might be, such as analogy (*discuss about* – *talk about*), (ii) are embedded in recognisable schemata like multi-word units (*how to put the end on x* – *how to put an end to x*), or (iii) if the preceding context supplies enough backup to enable recognition.

In an important sense these are also quintessentially ELF features in that all the examples above appear in different speech events in ELFA, spoken by different speakers from different language backgrounds – in brief, they come from different similects. Example 8 is another illustration a of set of instances that come from four similects in different speech events.

(8)

i'll try to be quick	**in term of**	methodology and move directly to
so that's very very limited	**in term of**	aphasia and conves- conversation
clones can be described	**in term of**	the notion of preservation presented by
i try to skip all that	**in term of**	aphasia people have start working on
which can be presented	**in term of**	rela- relation and automorphism
if we think rather	**term of**	knowledges mostly used you find
mass library it is er t- er	**term of**	totalitarian society is

Fixing is an intriguing phenomenon. We observe individuals adopting particular expressions for particular meanings, along the lines of isomorphism, which undoubtedly lightens the cognitive burden in production. For receptive processing, however, it offers no advantage but can be a disadvantage, unless some form rises to dominance. From a cognitive productive perspective we can take fixing to represent simplification. For the larger whole, the macro level of language, it rather adds to variability: if several individuals or groups settle for a given unconventional expression in a particular meaning, it introduces an additional option to the wider system or the whole language.

Above (5.1) we made the assumption that regularisation is a form of simplification. By the same logic, it would seem motivated to postulate that increased variability makes a system more complicated. We can also see variability as making the system more complex in the sense that the new elements entering it through the process of approximation have the potential of throwing the system (or any subsystem in it) off balance. When unsettling features enter it, the system will be in need of reshuffling itself. This may not seem dramatic in individual cases, but a large number of approximations produces this effect in the aggregate. And approximations are ubiquitous. If we take languages to be complex, self-organising systems, approximations and subsequent fixings work towards the self-renewal of language.

5.3 Discourse driven

At discourse level, we find speakers engaging in "strategic" processes. They draw on shared resources, be these linguistic or cultural, in this way making the discourse more accessible to recipients ("recipient design"), say, by means of explicitation. If we accept that usage drives language and is the basis on which regularities can be adopted, observed, and described, then we must assign an important role to discourse processes in ELF. Thanks to a fairly large body of research into ELF interactions, quite a few points can be identified on which a number of studies converge. The strongest generally observed tendencies are enhanced cooperativeness (Seidlhofer 2011), creativity (Hülmbauer 2009; Pitzl 2011), accommodation (Jenkins 2000; Cogo 2009; Mauranen 2012), and enhanced explicitness (Mauranen 2007, 2012; Seidlhofer 2011). Presumably they all play a role in shaping English.

A general propensity to cooperate is fundamental in linguistic activity. Language – languaging – can be seen as a cooperative achievement for a good reason, so ELF is hardly exceptional, but researchers have nevertheless observed particularly pronounced cooperativeness in ELF. Among other things, speakers resort to various tactics for getting a message constructed with or without engaging help from their interlocutors. They may for example draw on shared cultural resources, as in (9 a–b).

(9a) ... it is a way of controlling us sort of eh i don't know *divide and govern* sort of a thing

(9b) ... i don't know *what's the hen and what's the egg*

Both cases make use of expressions that have spread about the European cultural area long before English has, with variants shared among people from the region. That the variants do not comply with the dominant way of using them in contemporary English is unlikely to present an obstacle to their intelligibility, and it is reasonable to assume that such alternative variants disperse within the L2 English speaking community. Resorting to anecdotal evidence, *hen or egg* is a frequently heard form. Similarly, linguistic resources that are widely borrowed constitute shared knowledge (10a–b).

(10a) ... the lesson learned within this tradition of *ostpolitik* is that this really

(10b) ... you could do the same for *the dooming cathedral* in Turku

While (a) above illustrates a term from international politics that has lost its topicality outside political history, similar terms (like *Grexit* or *Brexit*) float around as a shared cultural underpinning, and likely to come and go as regional or global items that are equally well-known in different languages. The latter example is less direct, since it builds its transparency not only on Swedish (*domkyrka*) and related Scandinavian terms, but also variants of *duomo*, familiar from Romance languages. Variants of *cathedral* also exist in European languages. Altogether, it is not surprising that this somewhat odd coinage passed without notice in its context. Cases like these show that we should not blithely assume that ELF speech rests on no shared cultural or linguistic knowledge apart from variably learned English.

Enhanced explicitness, or explicitation, is another frequently used strategic discourse feature, takes many forms and has the potential for altering preferences for syntactic patterns. Rephrasing (12a–b), discourse reflexivity or metadiscourse (13a–b), and negotiating topic (14a–b) are common manifestations of explicitation.

(12a) because *we are the candidate we got the status of the candidate country* for the membership

(12b) this is *the first civil is the first political institution* within the parliament

(13a) *so you're saying* that probabilistic system is fair

(13b) okay, basically *what i'm trying to get to* is that, is it possible to have

(14a) *the communities they* are kind of isolated

(14b) *this* is our greatest problem the *the regional tensions*

What we see in (14a) is what I like to call "negotiating topics" based on its discourse function, but which from a syntactic viewpoint can be seen as a "header" or even "left dislocation". What such fronting does is add explicitness to the discourse by starting with a topic noun, which is then followed by a clause with a co-referential pronoun in subject position. Traditional descriptive terminology ("left dislocation") of this phenomenon is writing-based, although topic announcement followed by a resumptive co-referential pronoun is definitely a property of spoken language. The sequential mirror image ("right dislocation") involves adding a noun after an utterance (14b) as if to ensure the retrievability of the pronominal referent. Discourse tactics like these are conducive to communicative success by keeping interlocutors aware of the topic. Their common use in ELF may be driving grammar towards more explicit and transparent structures. This, in turn, may manifest itself in alterations in preference patterns rather than new grammatical patterns relative to Standard English syntax.

6 Conclusion

This paper has presented ELF as a complex, higher-order form of language contact between similects. As shown above, ELF manifests tendencies of simplification as well as complexification. Moreover, we can arguably view ELF as a complex dynamic system in that its shifts towards simplicity or variability will lead to occasional unsettling and imbalance in the system or its parts, causing the system to self-organise anew. Interactions between speakers generate and diffuse linguistic innovations, which then manifest themselves as changes in the language system. Since languages can be seen in terms of modular systems in the sense that they comprise lects (idiolects, sociolects, dialects, similects...) of various kinds in addition to grammatical and lexical systems – we could talk about "polysystems" – they are heterogeneous and variable, and ELF is no exception.

Many researchers have recently questioned the appropriateness of talking about languages as if they were distinct homogeneous entities with clearly demarcated boundaries (e.g. Canagarajah 2013; Pennycook and Makoni 2006; Blommaert 2010). As long as we accept that natural languages are in many ways convenient fictions supported by standardising infrastructures, we can continue talking about them, or ELF, without taking their unified nature too literally.

I have argued here that we can distinguish three important interacting levels in language contact processes: that of the individual, or cognitive processing, that of social interaction, or micro-social processes which crucially mediates between the individual and the third, societal level of language change.

The processes of cognition, approximation, and fixing are elements of speech production. At the receptive end they are recognizable on the basis of function, form, or meaning, and their consequences entail tolerance of variability in the recipient role, encouraging fuzzy processing. In social interaction, the hearer's readiness to tolerate approximate forms leads to their reinforcement, through the positive feedback of achieving communication. Interactional success may also help further strengthen the position of the most frequent items in the language, given that they are likely to be shared across a large number of speakers. Plausibly, the deep entrenchment of the most frequent lexis may also underlie its strong representation in translations: when the processing load gets heavier, as in demanding bilingual processing, the best entrenched items gain proportionally more prominence.

Social interaction is also prone to explicitation when crossing language boundaries is involved – another similarity between ELF and translation. This is a facet of recipient design, which helps support the notable collaborative tendency in ELF interaction. The crucial bridge built in interaction is the strengthening and diffusion of approximations and innovations, enabling them to make their way from individual processing to alterations in linguistic systems. The macro-social consequences of ELF interactions result in similect mixing and levelling in second-order language contact. The central processes result in simplification as well as complexification. The main macro-social consequences of

ELF use emanate from face-to-face (including digital) contact, which are also shaped by regional trends, such as those based on shared cultural or linguistic history, in addition to language typological similarities.

Apart from the social categories of individual, interaction, and society we also looked at ELF from the viewpoint of levels of language. The "strategic" resources of discourse, largely explicitation, no doubt drive change in their own way, in addition to lexicogrammatical simplification and complexification. Discourse features such as using discourse markers or metadiscourse are in well in evidence in ELF, like expressions of vagueness and evaluation, which would support hypotheses of the universality of such phenomena. The linguistic level that straddles lexis and grammar nevertheless seems to be at the heart of change in ELF communication: multi-word units of meaning give rise to analogical formations and models for other expressions.

In addition to what we now know about ELF, much more needs to be discovered and understood. For instance, unconventional lexical expressions are sometimes detected in ELF that are functionally equivalent to conventionalised, "pragmaticised" discourse in evaluation or metadiscourse. This would call for large-scale systematic studies. Neither is there much, if anything, on discourse intonation. A plethora of accents is an obvious fact of ELF, and the centrality of pronunciation in achieving mutual intelligibility, but the role of intonation is unclear: is there something in "universal" intonation that marks a question as a question, for instance? ELF data can also help unravel the roles, amount and sources of shared non-linguistic understanding in communication. The common assumption has been that ELF speakers share little if anything in terms of "cultural" background. But surely there must be much that has not been discovered. ELF is well positioned to shed light on the relationships of language with various contextual and multimodal phenomena.

References

Altenberg, Bengt & Sylviane Granger. 2002. The grammatical and lexical patterning of make in native and non-native student writing. *Applied Linguistics* 22(2). 173–189.

Barlow, Michael & Suzanne Kemmer (eds.). 2000. *Usage Based Models of Language*. Chicago: CSLI Publications.

Becker, Alton. 1995. *Beyond Translation: Essays toward a Modern Philosophy*. Ann Arbor: The University of Michigan Press.

Biber, Douglas & Susan Conrad. 2009. *Register Genre and Style*. Cambridge: Cambridge University Press.

Blum-Kulka, Shoshana. 1986. Shifts of cohesion and coherence in translation. In J. House & S. Blum-Kulka (eds.). *Interlingual and Intercultural Communication: Discourse and Cognition in Translation and Second Language Acquisition Studies*, 17–35. Tübingen: Gunter Narr.

Blommaert, Jan. 2010. *The Sociolinguistics of globalization*. Cambridge: Cambridge University Press.
Brutt-Griffler, Janine. 2002. *World English. A Study of its Development*. Clevedon: Multilingual Matters.
Bybee, Jean L. & Paul Hopper. 2001. *Frequency and the Emergence of Linguistic Structure*. Amsterdam: John Benjamins.
Canagarajah, Suresh. 2013. *Translingual Practice: Global English and Cosmopolitan Relations*. London: Routledge.
Carey, Ray. 2013. On the other side: formulaic organizing chunks in spoken and written academic EFL. *The Journal of English as a Lingua Franca (JELF)* 2(2). 207–228.
Christiansen, Morten H. & Nick Chater. 2015. The Now-or-Never Bottleneck: A Fundamental Constraint on Language. *Behavioral and Brain Sciences*, Available on CJO2015 doi:10.1017/S0140525X1500031X
Cogo, Alessia. 2009. Accommodating Difference in ELF Conversations: A Study of Pragmatic Strategies. In Mauranen, A. & Ranta, E. (eds.), *English as a Lingua Franca: Studies and findings*, 254–273. Newcastle: Cambridge Scholars Publishing.
Croft, William. 2000. *Explaining language change: an evolutionary approach*. London: Longman.
Dabrowska, Ewa. 2004. *Language, Mind and Brain. Some Psychological and Neurological Constraints on Theories of Grammar*. Edinburgh: Edinburgh University Press.
Du Bois, John W. 2003. Discourse and Grammar. In Michael Tomasello (ed.), *The New Psychology of Language. Vol. 2*, 47–87. Mahwah, NJ: Lawrence Erlbaum.
Firth, Alan & Johannes Wagner. 1997. On discourse, communication, and (some) fundamental concepts in SLA research. *Modern Language Journal* 81. 285–300.
Ford, Cecilia E., Barbara A. Fox & Sandra A Thompson. 2003. Social Interaction and Grammar. In Tomasello, Michael (ed.), *The New Psychology of Language. Vol. 2*, 119–143. Mahwah, NJ: Lawrence Erlbaum.
Giles, Howard. 1973. Accent mobility: A model and some data. *Anthropological Linguistics* 33. 27–42.
Giles, Howard & Philip Smith. 1979. Accommodation Theory: Optimal Levels of Convergence. In Giles, Howard & Robert N. St. Clair (eds.), *Language and Social Psychology*, 45–56. Oxford: Blackwell.
Gilner, Leah. 2016. Dominant vocabulary in ELF interactions. *The Journal of English as a Lingua Franca (JELF)* 5(1). 27–51.
Gilner, Leah & Franc Morales. 2011. The ICE-CORE word list: The lexical foundation of 7 varieties of English. *Asian Englishes* 14(1). 4–21.
Gilquin Gaetanelle, Sylviane Granger & Magali Paquot. 2007. Learner corpora: The missing link in EAP pedagogy. *Journal of English for Academic Purposes* 6(4). 319–335.
Granger, Sylviane, Joseph Hung & Stephanie Petch-Tyson (eds.). 2002. *Computer Learner Corpora, Second Language Acquisition and Foreign Language Teaching*. Amsterdam: John Benjamins.
Granovetter, Mark. 1983. The Strength of Weak Ties: A Network Theory Revisited. *Sociological Theory* 1. 201–233.
Guido, Maria Grazia. 2008. *English as a Lingua Franca in Cross-Cultural Immigration Domains*. Frankfurt: Peter Lang.
Habermas, Jürgen. 1976. Tieto ja intressi. [Knowledge and interest.] In R. Tuomela and I. Patoluoto (eds.), *Yhteiskuntatieteiden filosofiset perusteet I*, 118–141. Helsinki: Gaudeamus.
House, Juliane. 2003. English as a lingua franca: a threat to multilingualism? *Journal of Sociolinguistics* 7(4). 556–578.

Hülmbauer, Cornelia. 2009. "We don't take the right way. We just take the way we think you will understand" – the shifting relationship between correctness and effectiveness in ELF. In Mauranen, Anna & Elina Ranta (eds.), 2009. *English as a Lingua Franca: Studies and findings*, 323–347. Newcastle: Cambridge Scholars Publishing.

Hyland, Fiona. 2004. Learning Autonomously: Contextualising Out-of-Class English Language Learning. *Language Awareness* 13(3). 180–202.

Jarvis, Scott & Aneta Pavlenko. 2007. *Crosslinguistic Influence in Language and Cognition*. London: Routledge.

Jenkins, Jennifer. 2000. *The Phonology of English as an International Language*. Oxford: Oxford University Press.

Jenkins, Jennifer. 2007. *English as a Lingua Franca: Attitude and Identity*. Oxford: Oxford University Press.

Jenkins, Jennifer. 2015. Repositioning English and multilingualism in English as a Lingua Franca *Englishes in Practice* 2(3). 49–85. DOI 10.1515/eip-2015-0003.

Johnson, C. P. & David Marsh. 2014. Blended language learning: An effective solution its challenges. *Higher Learning Research Communications*, 4(3), 23–41. http://dx.doi.org/10.18870/hlrc. vb4i3 213.

Kitazawa, Mariko. 2013. *Approaching Conceptualisations of English in East Asian Contexts: Ideas, Ideology, and Identification*. University of Southampton Doctoral dissertation.

Klimpfinger, Theresa. 2009. "She's mixing the two languages together" – Forms and Functions of Code-Switching in English as a Lingua Franca. In Mauranen, A. and E. Ranta (eds.), *English as a Lingua Franca. Studies and Findings*, 348–370. Manchester: Cambridge Scholars Publishing.

Kortmann, Berndt & Benedict Szmrecsanyi. 2012. *Linguistic Complexity: Second Language Acquisition, Indigenization, Contact*. Berlin: de Gruyter.

Kusters, Wouter. 2003. *Linguistic Complexity. The influence of social change on verbal inflection*. Utrecht: LOT.

Laitinen, Mikko. 2016. Ongoing changes in English modals: On the developments in ELF. In Olga Timofeeva, Sarah Chevalier, Anne-Christine Gardner & Alpo Honkapohja (eds.), *New Approaches in English Linguistics: Building Bridges*, 175–196. Amsterdam: John Benjamins.

Larsen-Freeman, Diane. 2002. Language acquisition and language use from a chaoe/complexity theory perspective. In C. Kramsch (ed.), *Language Acquisition and Language Socialization: Ecological Perspectives*, 33–46. Clevedon: Multilingual Matters.

Lave, Jean & Etienne Wenger. 1991. *Situated Learning. Legitimate peripheral participation*. Cambridge: Cambridge University Press.

Laviosa-Braithwaite, Sara. 1996. *The English Comparable Corpus (ECC): A Resource and a Methodology for the Empirical Study of Translation*. UMIST: Doctoral dissertation.

Leech, Geoffrey & Nicholas Smith. 2009. Change and Constancy in Linguistic Change: How Grammatical Usage in Written English Evolved in the Period 1931–1991. In Antoinette Renouf and Andrew Kehoe (eds.), *Corpus Linguistics: Refinements and Reassessments*, 173–200. Amsterdam: Rodopi.

Leech, Geoffrey, Marianne Hundt, Christian Mair & Nicholas Smith. 2009. *Change in Contemporary English. A Grammatical Study*. Cambridge: Cambridge University Press.

LePage, Robert B. & Andrée Tabouret-Keller. 1985. *Acts of Identity: Creole-Based Approaches to Language and Ethnicity*. Cambridge: Cambridge University Press.

Li Wei & Ofelia Garcia. 2014. *Translanguaging. Language, Bilingualism and Education*. London: Palgrave.

MacWhinnney, Brian. 2005. The emergence of linguistic form in time. *Connection Science* 17. 191–211.

Mair, Christian. 2003. Kreolismen und verbales Identitätsmanagement im geschriebenen jamaikanischen Englisch. In Elisabeth Vogel, Antonia Napp, and Wolfram Lutterer (eds.), *Zwischen Ausgrenzung und Hybridisierung*, 79–96. Würzburg: Ergon.

Makoni, Sinfree & Alastair Pennycook (eds.). 2006. *Disinventing and Reconstituting Languages*. Clevedon: Multilingual Matters.

Mauranen, Anna. 2006. Translation Theory, Translation Universals. In Brown, K. (ed.) *Encyclopaedia of Language and Linguistics, 2nd Ed*. Oxford: Elsevier.

Mauranen, Anna. 2007. Hybrid Voices: English as the Lingua Franca of Academics. In Fløttum, Kjersti, Dahl, Trine and Kinn, Torodd (eds.), *Language and Discipline Perspectives on Academic Discourse*, 244–259. Newcastle: Cambridge Scholars Press.

Mauranen, Anna. 2010. Translation corpora and the quest for Translation Universals. Presentation at the UCCT conference, Edge Hill University, 29 July 2010.

Mauranen, Anna. 2012. *Exploring ELF*. Cambridge: Cambridge University Press.

Mauranen, Anna. 2013a. Translational corpora – better in search for the general of the specific? Presentation at the joint ICLC7 and UCCT 3 conferences, University of Ghent, 10 July 2013.

Mauranen, Anna. 2013b. Lingua franca discourse in academic contexts: shaped by complexity. In Flowerdew, J. (ed.), *Discourse in Context*, 225–246. London: Bloomsbury Academic.

Mauranen, Anna, Ray Carey & Elina Ranta. 2015. New answers to familiar questions: English as a lingua franca. In Biber, D and R. Reppen (eds.), *The Cambridge Handbook of English Corpus Linguistics*, 401–417. Cambridge: Cambridge University Press.

McWhorter, John. 2001. The world's simplest grammars are creole grammars. *Linguistic Typology* 6. 125–166.

Metsä-Ketelä Maria. 2012. Frequencies of vague expressions in English as an academic lingua franca. *The Journal of English as a Lingua Franca (JELF)* 1(2). 263–285.

Miestamo, Matti. 2009. Implicational hierarchies and grammatical complexity. In G. Sampson, D. Gil, and P. Trudgill (eds.), *Language Complexity as an Evolving Variable*, 80–97. Oxford: Oxford University Press.

Milroy, James & Lesley Milroy. 1985. Linguistic change, social network and speaker innovation. *Journal of Linguistics* 21. 339–384.

Milroy, Lesley. 2002. Social Networks. In Chambers, J.K., Trudgill, P. & Schilling-Estes, N. (eds.) *The Handbook of Language Variation and Change*. Oxford: Blackwell, 549–572.

Nevalainen, Sampo 2005. Köyhtyykö kieli käännettäessä? – Mitä taajuuslistat kertovat suomennosten sanastosta. [Does language get poorer when translated? – What does the frequency of occurrence tell about Finnish translated vocabulary.] In Mauranen, A. & J. Jantunen (eds.), *Käännössuomeksi. Tutkimuksia käännössuomen kielestä*, 139–160. Tampere: Tampere University Press.

Nichols, Johanna. 2009. Linguistic complexity: a comprehensive definition and survey. In G. Sampson, D. Gil, and P. Trudgill (eds.), *Language Complexity as an Evolving Variable*, 64–79. Oxford: Oxford University Press.

Pagel, Michael. 2012. *Wired for Culture. Origins of the human social mind*. New York: Norton.

Pickard Nigel. 1996. Out-of-class language learning strategies. *ELT Journal (English Language Teaching Journal)* 50(2). 150–159.

Pietikäinen, Kaisa. 2014. ELF Couples and automatic code-switching. *The Journal of English as a Lingua Franca (JELF)* 3(1). 1–26.

Pilkinton-Pihko Diane. 2013. *English-medium instruction: Seeking assessment criteria for spoken professional English*. University of Helsinki Doctoral dissertation.

Pitzl, Marie-Luise. 2011. *Creativity in English as a lingua franca: Idiom and metaphor*. University of Vienna: Doctoral dissertation.

Ranta, Elina. 2013. *Universals in a universal language? Exploring verb-syntactic features in English as a Lingua Franc*a. University of Tampere Doctoral dissertation.

Raumolin-Brunberg, Helena. 1998. Social factors and pronominal change in the seventeenth century: the Civil War effect? In Jacek Fisiak & Marcin Krygier (eds.*)*, *Advances in English Historical Linguistics*, 361–388. Berlin: Mouton de Gruyter.

Seidlhofer, Barbara. 2011. *Understanding English as a Lingua Franca*. Oxford: Oxford University Press.

Swales, John M. 1990. *Genre Analysis*. Cambridge: Cambridge University Press.

Szmrecsanyi, Benedict & Berndt Kortmann. 2009. Between simplification and complexification: non-standard varieties of English around the world. In G. Sampson, D. Gil, and P. Trudgill (eds.), *Language Complexity as an Evolving Variable*, 64–79. Oxford: Oxford University Press.

Szmrecsanyi, Benedict & Berndt Kortmann. 2012. Introduction: Linguistic Complexity, Second Language Acquisition, indigenization, contact. In B. Szmrecsanyi and B. Kortmann (eds.), *Linguistic Complexity: Second Language Acquisition, Indigenization, Contact, Lingua & Litterae*, 6–34. Berlin/Boston: Walter de Gruyter.

Thomason, Sarah G. 2001. *Language Contact*. Edinburgh University Press.

Tirkkonen-Condit, Sonja. 2004. Unique items – over-or underrepresented in translated language? In Mauranen, A. & Kujamäki, P. (eds.) *Translation Universals. Do they exist?*, 177–184. Amsterdam/Philadelphia: John Benjamins.

Trudgill, Peter. 2001. Contact and simplification: historical baggage and directionality in linguistic change. *Linguistic Typology* 5(2/3). 371–374.

Trudgill, Peter. 1986. *Dialects in contact*. Oxford: Blackwell.

Trudgill, Peter. 2011. *Sociolinguistic typology: social determinants of linguistic complexity*. Oxford, New York: Oxford University Press.

Urry, John. 2007. *Mobilities*. Cambridge: Polity.

Vetchinnikova, Svetlana. 2014. *Second language lexis and the idiom principle*. Unigrafia: Helsinki.

Vetchinnikova, Svetlana. (this volume) On the relationship between the cognitive and the communal: A complex systems perspective.

Weinreich, Uriel. 1953/1963. *Languages in Contact: Findings and Problems*. New York: Linguistic Circle 1953. Reprinted: The Hague: Mouton 1963.

Zipf, George K. 1935. *The Psychobiology of Language*. Boston: Houghton-Mifflin.

Corpora

ACE. 2014. *The Asian Corpus of English*. Director: Andy Kirkpatrick; Researchers: Wang Lixun, John Patkin, Sophiann Subhan. http://corpus.ied.edu.hk/ace

A Standard Corpus of Present-Day Edited American English, for use with Digital Computers (Brown). 1964, 1971, 1979. Compiled by W. N. Francis and H. Kučera. Brown University. Providence, Rhode Island.

ELFA. 2008. *The Corpus of English as a Lingua Franca in Academic Settings*. Director: Anna Mauranen. http://www.helsinki.fi/elfa/elfacorpus.

MacArthur, F.; Alejo, R.; Piquer-Piriz, A.; Amador-Moreno, C.; Littlemore, J.; Ädel, A.; Krennmayr, T.; Vaughn, E. 2014. EuroCoAT. *The European Corpus of Academic Talk*. http://www.eurocoat.es.

Simpson, R. C., Briggs, S. L., Ovens, J., & Swales, J. M. 2002. *The Michigan corpus of academic spoken English*. Ann Arbor, MI: The Regents of the University of Michigan. http://quod.lib.umich.edu/m/micase/

VOICE. 2009. *The Vienna-Oxford International Corpus of English. (version 1.0 online)*. Director: Barbara Seidlhofer; Researchers: Angelika Breiteneder, Theresa Klimpfinger, Stefan Majewski, Marie-Luise Pitzl. http://voice.univie.ac.at.

WrELFA. 2015. *The Corpus of Written English as a Lingua Franca in Academic Settings*. Director: Anna Mauranen. Compilation manager: Ray Carey. http://www.helsinki.fi/elfa/wrelfa.html.

Janus Mortensen and Spencer Hazel
Lending bureaucracy voice: negotiating English in institutional encounters

Abstract: This study explores how English, used in the context of university internationalisation, is habitually called upon to verbalize concepts and practices which are intimately tied to local settings but which do not necessarily have direct equivalents in English. Focusing on institutional encounters at a Danish university, the study illustrates how speakers negotiate expressions for local bureaucratic terms and procedures as well as their meaning, and argues that such instances of joint meaning making carry the potential to contribute to the hyper-local emergent register of English found in the setting. A key finding of the analysis is that speakers in the data are afforded different epistemic rights and obligations with relation to the lingua franca being used, depending on their institutional role, (inter)national status and general familiarity with the linguistic resources mobilised. English first language speakers are shown to be positioned as linguistic norm providers in several cases, but participants who use English as a foreign language also introduce new terms and re-define old ones, particularly when they use English to lend bureaucracy voice in interactional roles associated with institutional power. Methodologically, the chapter makes a case for the detailed study of social interaction in transient multilingual communities as a window on linguistic and social change, which may, as one avenue of future research, stimulate cross-fertilization between sociolinguistics and the emerging body of research on the use of English in lingua franca scenarios.

Keywords: boundary object, conversation analysis, emergent register, epistemic authority, epistemic rights, exonormativity, face-to-face interaction, hyper-local register, lingua franca scenario, transient multilingual communities

1 Introduction

For the past 10–20 years, internationalization of Higher Education in Europe has been fuelled by a steady increase in transnational student mobility, facilitated by a widespread adoption of English as a lingua franca at universities across Europe (Fabricius, Mortensen and Haberland 2017; Jenkins 2013; Mauranen 2012; Preisler, Klitgård and Fabricius 2011). The increased traffic of transnationally

---

Janus Mortensen, University of Copenhagen
Spencer Hazel, Newcastle University

DOI 10.1515/9783110429657-014

mobile students and staff entails that many university programmes today constitute examples of what can be called "transient multilingual communities" (Mortensen 2013), understood as social configurations of people from diverse sociocultural and linguistic backgrounds coming together (physically or otherwise) for a limited period of time around a shared activity, in this case university education.

For English to serve as a tool for communication in such contexts, it must provide the necessary means for carrying out academic as well as administrative activities associated with the local university, and English has responded readily to this challenge. Although there is a widespread and problematic tendency to ignore the use and relevance of languages other than English in the process of university internationalization in Europe (Haberland and Mortensen 2012), it remains a truism that English, for better and for worse, has become the language that is most frequently used to lend 'the international university' voice.

In its role as the dominant lingua franca at internationalizing European universities, English is habitually called upon to verbalize concepts and practices which are intimately tied to local settings, but which do not necessarily have direct equivalents in English. In the present chapter we introduce a small set of micro-analytic studies of interaction in institutional encounters at a Danish university to illustrate how this process can be studied and conceptualised as a window on linguistic and social change. We demonstrate how speakers negotiate expressions for local bureaucratic terms and procedures as well as their meaning, and argue that these instances of joint meaning making carry the potential to contribute to the hyper-local emergent register of English found in the setting.

A key finding of our analysis is that speakers are afforded different epistemic rights and obligations with relation to the lingua franca being used. Previous research has shown how participants display sensitivity to their own and others' relative rights to know about the topic of the talk or focus of activity in social interaction (Heritage and Raymond 2005; Raymond and Heritage 2006). Co-participants orient to a person's epistemic authority, the "relative epistemic rights to describe and evaluate objects within different knowledge domains" (Heritage and Raymond 2005), depending on their relative epistemic status in relation to the matter at hand. Sacks (1984), for example, notes how members differentiate between the status of knowledge gained from direct experience and from that gained through hearsay, with members accorded primary epistemic rights to know about and narrate their own experiences. Elsewhere, Raymond and Heritage (2006) show how grandparents are oriented to as having privileged rights to evaluate their grandchildren, while Hayano (2011) describes how particular formatting components in turn-design, specifically the use of the Japanese particle *yo* in assessment sequences, display claims by speakers to greater access to knowledge about a referent. In our data, we note how (inter)national status, institutional status, and general familiarity with the language(s) and registers typically used in the setting are all aspects that may be relevant to the epistemic status of a member with regard to the situated use of English as a lingua franca. English first language speakers are shown to be positioned as linguistic norm providers in several cases, but they are not the only relevant providers in the setting. On the contrary, our analysis suggests that people in institutional power who habitually call on English to lend bureaucracy voice have a considerable say in introducing new terms and re-defining old ones, thereby contributing to the local development and change of English, and quite clearly asserting their role as proficient language users rather than language learners (Firth and Wagner 1997; Firth and Wagner 2007).

2 Data and method

The data for the current chapter forms part of the CALPIU storehouse located at Roskilde University. At the CALPIU research centre, researchers have taken a special interest in how the cultural and linguistic practices at international universities are being shaped on a day-to-day basis through interactions in a variety of settings. Previous studies carried out under the auspices of CALPIU include investigations into the use of English in Danish second/foreign language classrooms (Hazel and Wagner 2015; Kirkebæk 2013); epistemic stance-marking in student project group work (Mortensen 2010); language choice and alternation in group oral examinations, in informal settings, and student project groups (Hazel and Mortensen 2012; Mortensen 2014; Nevile and Wagner 2008); displays of understanding in group tutorials (Day and Kjærbeck 2012); and multimodal resources for developing interaction in encounters between students and administrative staff (Hazel 2012), for which the data for the current study was initially collected.

In this chapter, we focus on face-to-face service encounters between students and university administrative staff where English is used as a lingua franca. The two settings featured in the data are sites where university students interact with designated members of staff on administrative and procedural issues, or concerns relating to their own well-being.

One part of the data set comes from the International Office of a Danish university where access was granted to carry out an exploratory study of the interactional practices of staff and students at the office's help desk. The help desk serves both international – or "inbound" – students who may have inquiries or administrative tasks to perform concerning their stay at the host university, and local "outbound" students who may for example be interested in participating in an international study exchange programme. In these encounters, staff members are either called on to personally assist with a student's request, or alternatively to provide the student with information on where they are able to obtain the desired information or support.

The other part of the data set is comprised of study guidance meetings where students have turned to the university study guidance counsellors (*studievejledere*) in order to discuss in private one or more of a range of concerns relating to their studies, including the organisation of their studies and study trajectories, personal issues, study group dynamics and the like. The data of the counselling meetings were recorded in three sites, situated in different departments at the university. In all cases the counsellors are themselves students at the university.

The complete video-recorded data set consists of some 120 helpdesk and study-counselling encounters, which vary in length between 20 seconds and 85 minutes. The data involve 6 help desk staff members and 5 study guidance counsellors. The data were recorded from multiple angles with fixed cameras. Both first language and second/ additional language conversations are present in the larger data set, with a number of languages represented. In the present chapter, we pay detailed attention to interactional exchanges drawn from 2 study guidance session and 2 help desk encounters, all of which were primarily conducted in English.

Our analysis focuses particularly on the specific and sometimes novel ways in which English is mobilized in these settings as a resource to "name" the world. Unlike traditional stable sociolinguistic communities where members can be expected to have substantially overlapping linguistic repertoires and shared cultural experiences, members in transient multilingual communities cannot *a priori* be expected to have the same linguistic and cultural frames of reference. We do not mean to suggest that participants in transient multilingual communities do not share frames of reference at all, nor do we imply that members in stable communities have completely overlapping frames. Still, there are significant differences of degree, and it is the importance of these differences that we explore in this chapter. Similarly, transient communities do not, unlike communities of practice (Lave and Wenger 1991), typically count "masters" among their members who can initiate novices into the practices, linguistic or otherwise, of the group. Indeed, what we see in the data is that the meaning of particular linguistic items is often negotiated in situ, in interaction between participants.

The analysis below concerns four such negotiation sequences, where participants work together to converge on adequate terminology and mutual understanding of the administrative work being undertaken. The selected sequences were transcribed in CLAN (MacWhinney and Wagner 2010) and analysed drawing on methods and theoretical insights originating in the Conversation Analytic tradition (see Sacks, Schegloff, and Jefferson, 1974).

3 Analysis

3.1 L1 English speakers, linguistic hybridity and epistemic authority

Participants in our data often need to refer to certain procedures or particular forms of documentation as they discuss questions relating to administrative matters. In such cases, what might look like everyday terms are often imbued with very specific meanings tied to the institutional context. For example, in the context of study exchange programmes the term *learning agreement* is not a general, everyday term but a specific administrative term that refers to a particular bureaucratic artefact that requires a signature from a person who holds a particular institutional position in order to be valid.

Since they are firmly embedded in the local institutional culture, the terms used to describe such administrative documents and processes have typically been coined in Danish, and students and members of staff may therefore occasionally struggle to locate adequate equivalents in English. An example of this is represented in Example 1 below. On this occasion, an East-Asian student, Sally (SAL), who speaks English as a second language and a study guidance counsellor from an English speaking country, Tod (TOD), are discussing 'SU', which is an acronym used to refer to the monthly allowance (*Statens Uddannelsessstøtte*, literally State Education Support) awarded to Danish national students by the state.

(1)   *Locating an equivalent in English for Danish administrative term*

```
61   TOD:   I think then you'll have to wr- write to the
62          excha- erm excha- xx
63          (0.8)
64   TOD:   yeah exchange
65          (0.3)
66   SAL:   by the way=
67   TOD:   = office=
68   SAL:   = erm now erm I can't get SU
69          ⌈p- er⌉ now erm I er (0.2)
70          what is er opholdstillad- (0.3)
71          op⌈holdstillad-⌉
72   TOD:   ⌊ejr er resident (0.2) permit=
73   SAL:   resident perm- residence permit (0.4)
74          so it means that I have the same
75          (0.2)
76   SAL:   rights as a danish er student (.) right
```

In line 66, Sally initiates a new topic, eventually introducing the term 'SU' in line 68. The term is not given any further gloss here, and does not appear to cause the counsellor any trouble, and Sally proceeds to start formulating a question relating to access of non-Danish students to financial support. However, she immediately projects upcoming trouble in line 69, where she produces a number of intra-turn hesitation markers and a pause, before suspending the progression of the turn to produce an insertion sequence, where she can attend to trouble in locating a particular term. The term in question appears to be the Danish word *opholdstilladelse*, which is the full form of what is here produced in truncated shape as *opholdstillad-*. Tod treats Sally's contribution as a request for the translation of the Danish term into English (line 72), and this is ratified by Sally in next position (line 73): he offers a candidate term "resident permit", and she accepts the action performed by Tod, that of suggesting a candidate translation of the term in English. This is a qualified acceptance, however, as she suspends the repetition of the term 'resident permit' to produce the more "formally correct" version 'residence permit'.

In this case, the participants are successful in identifying a relevant pre-existing term in English, 'residence permit', to name the Danish bureaucratic term in question. What is notable is that both student and counsellor, neither of whom is Danish, deploy Danish terms to serve as tools to advance their conversation. This indexes the talk's embeddedness in the local, Danish context, and constructs and reflects the status of the English used in this setting as a hybrid localised register that draws on features associated with multiple "languages", not simply "English".

Furthermore, the sequence demonstrates the presence of a number of shared understandings between the participants. First, there is an understanding that the staff representative should be able to understand Danish, at least with regard to terminology relevant to the topics that these meetings may encompass: Sally orients to Tod as a person able to understand the Danish administrative terms she slots into her talk. This indicates that the use of English in this setting to some extent presupposes a multilingual backdrop which is particular to that setting. We might say that the participants implicitly acknowledge the hybrid nature of the "language scenario" (Mortensen 2013: 36) that their interaction unfolds within. Second, and perhaps paradoxically considering the multilingual nature of the interaction, there is an orientation to a requirement for the procedures to be named in English, even where the participants already display their understandings of the matters as referred to in Danish. Sally and Tod both treat the term *opholdstilladelse* as a term that needs to be translated into English and

Tod takes on the role of L1 English language expert in providing a candidate term, even when they each appear to display knowledge of what the term means in Danish. This suggests that they do not consider the use of a bilingual medium (Gafaranga and Torras 2001) appropriate for the encounter, despite its multilingual base. Finally, the participants display a concern for using terms that may be considered "formally correct" even when what would appear to be an adequate variation has been used and oriented to as understood: it is not sufficient to use the term 'resident permit' when the more formally accepted 'residence permit' can be employed. This suggests that the participants here, contrary to what is often suggested to be the case in scenarios where English is used as a lingua franca (Cogo 2008; Firth 1996), orient to "form" and not merely "function" or communicative success. In other words, despite the fact that the language used here is remarkably local, the participants nevertheless to some extent seem to adopt an exonormative approach in their use of English, with the L2 speaker of English being the one who displays this orientation most clearly in producing an embedded repair (Jefferson 1987) of 'resident permit' to 'residence permit'.

In our second example, it is a student counsellor who displays difficulties in locating a relevant term in English for a particular administrative procedure, and turns to the student, who in this case is an L1 speaker of English, to confirm a candidate term. Although the sequence resembles the one described above, it is not as straightforward, and the outcome is very different. The sequence is taken from a study guidance meeting between a North-American student, Zara (ZAR), and a German student guidance counsellor, Adam (ADA). They are discussing the possibility for Zara to take a year out from her studies.

Early in the encounter, Zara positions herself as a competent speaker of Danish. This happens during a section where she argues that she would be sufficiently proficient to attend a Danish language Bachelor's programme in her subject, which she hopes to do in the future. This assessment of her Danish skills appears to make relevant an account for why the current meeting is being held in English, rather than in the local language. She provides this by a) saying that she would in principle be able to handle the encounter in Danish (lines 19 and 22 in Example 2a), and then b) going on to explain why she would nevertheless prefer English. In accounting for her preference for English, she explains that using English is important for her to achieve full understanding of the issues addressed in the meeting (lines 35–36 and 38 in Example 2a).

(2a)   *Accounting for language preference and claiming language competence*

Zara – student; Adam – counsellor

```
19  ZAR:  I mean I'm I'm obviously I'm good enough to handle ⌈taking⌉
20  ADA:                                                    ⌊okay  ⌋
21        so ⌈you you you ⌉
22  ZAR:     ⌊in in Danish⌋
23  ADA:  you studied the international humanistic basic studies
24  ZAR:  yes=
25  ADA:  =okay=
26  ZAR:  =and then while I was studying that I was learning Danish
27        (0.5)
28  ADA:  yeah
29  ZAR:  and then this is my first time to ⌈do  ⌉ university in Danish
30  ADA:                                    ⌊yeah⌋
31        (0.2)
32  ADA:  o⌈kay ⌉
33  ZAR:   ⌊this⌋ semester
34        (1.4)
35  ZAR:  I just want to make sure that I understand (0.4)
36        a hundred percent of ⌈this⌉ conversation and not
37  ADA:                       ⌊yeah⌋
38  ZAR:  ninety ⌈nine percent⌉
39  ADA:         ⌊ sure sure  ⌋ ha ha
```

Interestingly, in raising this point Zara implicitly claims epistemic authority as an English user, stating that when the conversation is conducted in English she can understand a "hundred percent of th[e] conversation and not ninety nine percent". At a certain point in the meeting this claimed epistemic authority is made relevant in the interaction. This happens when a particular administrative term is sought by the counsellor, who then orients to Zara and positions her as the language expert, inviting her to ratify a candidate term.

(2b)   *L1 English speaker ratifying a local English term*

```
83  ADA:  I mean what what happens is (.)
84        ⌈you will⌉ you will officially be (0.2) um
85  ZAR:  ⌊perso-?⌋
86        (1.3)
87  ADA:  do you say ex-matriculated
88        (1.4)
89  ZAR:  ↑yeah↘
90  ADA:  yeah e⌈heheh⌉ ·hhh
91  ZAR:        ⌊heheh⌋
92  ADA:  you know so um
```

The term in question is 'ex-matriculated', which we take to be an anglicization of the German – or Danish – noun *eksmatrikulation* or its related verbal and adjectival forms. In line 84, we note how the way this item is introduced flags up that the word may constitute a source of uncertainty on Adam's part. Following his use of the adverb "officially", and the projection of an upcoming progressive or passive verb form through the use of the auxiliary *be* (or a complement if *be* is functioning as a main verb), he breaks off, punctuating the progression with a pause and a hesitation marker. This is followed by a lengthy 1.3 second pause, upon which Adam then produces the candidate term, 'ex-matriculated'. Interestingly, this candidate is embedded in a question "do you say ex-matriculated" (line 87). Although the "you" here could possibly constitute either a 2nd person or generic pronoun, it is treated here by Zara as orienting to her as the person with superior epistemic rights to be able to confirm or reject the candidate: responding to the "do you say", Zara in line 89 displays an understanding that Adam has singled *her* out as the arbiter of correct English.

Zara's response to Adam's question is interesting. She does not respond immediately, indeed, her confirmation is very delayed.

(2c)   *L1 English speaker ratifying a local English term – refined transcript*

```
87  ADA:    do you say ex-matriculated
88   ->     #(1.0)-------------   #(0.4)----
            #Zara eyes to Adam    #Zara looks over at the camera
89  ZAR:    #↑yeah↘
            #looks back to Adam; smiles
90  ADA:    yeah e⌈heheh⌉ ·hhh
91  ZAR:          ⌊heheh⌋
```

Following a 1 second pause, Zara fixes her gaze on the video camera, which is situated on an adjacent shelf. Turning her gaze back to Adam, she then produces a somewhat hesitant confirmation "yeah", which ends up in a smile. Adam acknowledges the response with his own "yeah", which he also follows up with a smile. Both then produce collaborative laughter.

Research has shown that participants often glance at recording equipment at moments when there is an orientation to some form of transgression of normative appropriate conduct pertaining to the ongoing interaction (Speer and Hutchby 2003; Hazel 2016). This is often accompanied by the mitigating resource of laughter. If this is also the case in this example, we could consider what kind of transgression this sequence constitutes, and it is very possible that it relates particularly to the confirmation ultimately offered by Zara. This would not be altogether surprising, since the term 'ex-matriculated' has not, to the best of our knowledge, been "officially" ratified as an L1 English term, for instance through inclusion in major dictionaries. 'Matriculation' and 'matriculated' are included in many such dictionaries and the construction used here clearly conforms to common morphological principles of English. Nevertheless, 'ex-matriculation' has a distinct "local" flavour and we suggest that this is partly what Zara displays awareness of in this sequence. She is being positioned as "the English expert" and asked to ratify a word which she may in fact not know, or simply not perceive to be "correct". So, on camera, she produces a little white lie in response to the question "do you say ex-matriculated" and this may be said to amount to a transgression of normative appropriate conduct, however innocent it may be.

It could be suggested that the word 'ex-matriculated' is a nonce item which has limited relevance beyond this encounter. However, we would argue that both parties to the encounter have now agreed that this is a legitimate lexical term, and as such, we could hypothesize that they may use it elsewhere to denote the process of de-registering from a university programme. In this way, the joint ratification of the term that takes place in this face-to-face encounter – uneventful as it may seem – could be perceived as a potentially important step in the gradual emergence of this lexical item as an accepted and commonly employed bureaucratic term which may eventually find its way into more public domains. In fact, we believe that is possible that a process like this is – or has been – taking place elsewhere in similar settings. An online search for the term 'ex-matriculation' may not provide links to established English dictionaries, but it does nevertheless throw up a number of results, all of which point to German university websites, where the anglicised equivalent of *exmatrikulation* appears to be quite common on web pages written in English. Interestingly, there are no hits from Danish university web pages at the time of writing (2015), so Adam may be seen as a first-mover here, making an aspect of his personal linguistic repertoire available for the general benefit of the transient linguistic community that he is part of.

In both of the examples we have looked at so far, we have seen that an L1 English user is ascribed superior epistemic rights to name or confirm candidate terms in English. In Example 1 we saw Tod, the student counsellor with English as his L1, provide a candidate term in English for a term initially introduced in Danish; and in the case of Example 2 we found ratification of the anglicised version of what appears to be a non-standard term ('ex-matriculated'). In the first example, it was the counsellor who was L1 English speaker, and the epistemic primacy afforded him also matched that of his institutional role; in the latter example, it was the client who was the L1 English speaker afforded epistemic primacy, at odds with the institutional role arrangement of the particular phase of the encounter, where the counsellor is at work explaining procedural aspects relating to the client's issues.

Examples 1 and 2 thus illustrate that L1 English speakers are occasionally considered – and treated – as relevant linguistic norm providers, contrary to what have been found in other studies (e.g. Hynninen 2013). However, L1 English speakers are by no means seen as the *only* relevant norm providers in this setting. This was to some extent foreshadowed in the embedded repair that the student in Example 1 offered in relation to an uncommon noun phrase composed of entirely common individual parts (*resident permit* > *residence permit*). In this case, the epistemic authority of the L1 speaker is arguably challenged by an L2 English speaker as his candidate term is not deemed to be sufficiently in accordance with the perceived appropriate linguistic norm. However, moving beyond cases of this kind, what our data suggest is that people in institutional power who habitually call on English to lend bureaucracy voice (irrespective of their own first language) have a considerably say in introducing new terms and redefining existing ones, thereby contributing to the local development and change of English. In the following, we turn to a number of examples where there are no L1 speakers of English present, and explore who is afforded epistemic rights to name or confirm a term that is causing one or more of the participants trouble.

3.2 L2 English speakers, linguistic hybridity and epistemic authority

In our data, we often observe students asking for clarification of the meaning of particular terms and procedures at the interface between administrative or institutional domains and the life of the student. In such instances, the onus is on the student counsellor or help desk staff member to provide an explanation. In the following sequence, for example, we see how a particular standard administrative expression is flagged up as problematic for two students from East Asia, Suzy (SUZ) and Andy (AND). Karen (KAR), a Danish member of staff, offers assistance.

(3)   *L2 English speaker explaining the meaning of a 'standard' term*
         Suzy & Andy – students; Karen – help desk staff

```
60    KAR:   so: (0.3) you have to ask the person you are staying with↗
61           if you can use that address as a cee oh (0.2) ⌈ a⌉ddress↗=
62    SUZ:                                                ⌊ah⌋
63    AND:   = uh huh
64    SUZ:   cee oh what ⌈is cee oh means⌉
65    KAR:               ⌊ ∇cee   oh∇    ⌋
66           (0.5)
67    KAR:   this means that you are (0.2) ∇care of∇
68           (0.5) ↓that person
69    SUZ:   oh
70    KAR:   okay↗
71    SUZ:   okay=
72    KAR:   +≈ yeah
73           (0.3)
74    KAR:   so you put your name cee oh:
75           and the name of the person
76           you are staying ⌈with⌉ and his address=
77    SUZ:                   ⌊yeah⌋
```

In line 61, Karen introduces the term *c/o*, which Suzy immediately flags up as problematic. Karen subsequently unpacks the abbreviation, and explains that it means *care of*, an expression denoting that the address where one lives has a named primary occupant, in whose residence you are staying or living. We note that Karen does not really *explain* the term 'c/o' initially: *care of* is in fact quite insufficient as an explanation to clarify what this expression denotes. However, she subsequently expands on her initial reply with an explanation as to how the term is employed in formulating your address and living circumstances.

In this case, we see that the member of staff is expected to have – and willingly claims – epistemic authority to define/explain what *c/o* means. It is interesting though, that in this case, the authority is premised on a particular interactional/institutional role, not on English L1-speaker status. This suggests that the normative centres of linguistic development in this setting are not necessarily English L1 speakers. This becomes even clearer in the next example.

In part 1 of the analysis we looked at the use of the term 'ex-matriculation' and argued that this could be seen as a lexical item that has emerged in response to the need for English to be able to "name" the practices and concepts that exist in the local setting. In Example 4, we turn to a similar case, but now with different participants. Like the example we have just seen, Example 4 is also connected to residence permits, in this case the application form that EU citizens need to fill out when they come to Denmark to work, study or live. We will start out by looking at the application form itself, and then later return to the interaction that develops around it in a particular case in our data.

Figure 1 shows a screenshot of a section of the 7 page legal document through which non-Danish EU-citizens must apply for permission if they wish to stay longer than three months in Denmark. As the screenshot illustrates, the form is bilingual, in Danish and English. Exchange students and other transnational students tend to stay in Denmark for more than three months, so this is a form that most of them do in fact encounter. The process of filling out legal documents in order to be granted temporary permission to reside in a country may be a commonplace and perhaps even trivial matter seen from the point of view of the system, but for the individual student this nevertheless amounts to a high-stakes activity. It is essential that the information is filled out correctly by the student, who in turn is required to sign the document stating that it has been, thereby assuming legal responsibility for the veracity of the information.

Section 2 of the document is called *Oplysninger om anledningen til ansøgningen*, translated as 'Information about the reason for application'. In this section, there is a box where the applicant may indicate that the purpose of the stay is *Studier/Education*. In the same box, the document stipulates that the applicant must include two forms of documentation with the application if this box is ticked: 1. 'a letter of enrolment' (*optagelsesbrev* in Danish), and 2. 'a declaration of sufficient means', which is offered as an English equivalent to the Danish term *forsørgelseserklæring*.

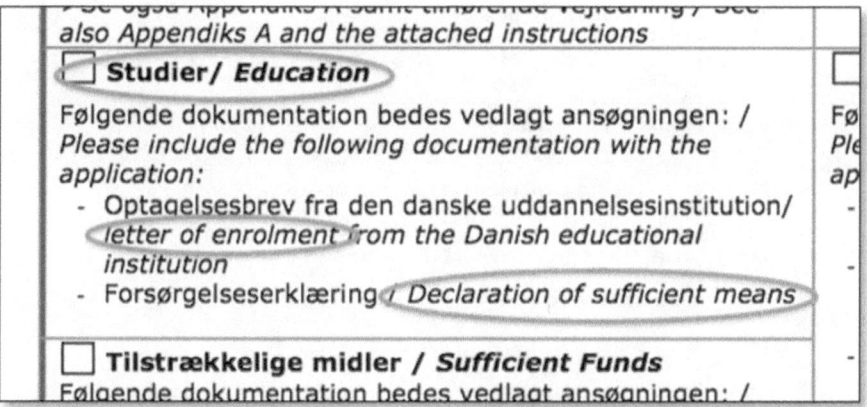

Figure 1: A screenshot of a bilingual section of the 7 page legal document for non-Danish EU-citizens

'Declaration of sufficient means' does not read like an English stock phrase, and it is most definitely not a term one would encounter in L2 English education materials. Indeed, an online search at the time of writing (2015) indicates that as a standalone phrase the expression is almost exclusively used in Denmark. It also appears in similar documents in The Netherlands, Germany and Slovenia, though in these contexts the term is typically embedded in a larger structure, for example 'declaration of sufficient financial means', or 'declaration of sufficient means of existence'. The truncated form that we find in the Danish application form is not very self-explanatory. In fact, the applicant is not given any help in ascertaining exactly what form of documentation he or she is required to provide to satisfy the requirement of enclosing a 'declaration of sufficient means' with the application. It is unclear what is to be understood by 'declaration' in this context, and it is also unclear what the term 'means' refers to, let alone 'sufficient means'. In sum, what an applicant needs to provide here, as part of their application for a residence permit, is somewhat opaque.

So, not surprisingly, in the following extract, taken from the help desk data set, an Italian student on the Erasmus exchange programme, Paulina (PAU), has arrived at the desk to ask for advice from Tanja (TAN) on the filling out of the application. This sequence occurs approximately 50 seconds into the meeting.

(4)   *L2 English speaker explaining the meaning of a 'non-standard' term*

Tanja-staff; Paulina-client

```
69  PAU:   and declaration of sufficient (0.2) means↗
70         (0.5)
71  PAU:   what it does it means↗=
72  TAN:   =that you have money enough
73         to support yourself
74         while you are here
75         (0.3)
76  PAU:   ah okay (.) ⌈erm::→⌉
77  TAN:          ⌊a bank⌋ statement or something like that
78  PAU:   yeah↗
79  TAN:   or a sti- a statement from the bank↗
80         (0.6)
81  PAU:   o⌈kay↗ ⌉
82  TAN:    ⌊or:↗⌋ if you have (0.3) a grant↗
83         (0.8)
84  PAU:   what is a grant↗
85         (0.3)
86  TAN:   ↑stipend↗
87         (1.6)
88  PAU:   n::::
89         (1.4)
90  PAU:   i don:::'t know what ↑is it↘
91         (2.3)
92  TAN:   oh dear
93         (0.3)
94  TAN:   ·hhh it's money that you receive as a student→
95  PAU:   ah: okay ⌈perfect ⌉
96  TAN:           ⌊to: supp⌋ort you→
97         (0.7)
98  PAU:   okay→
99         (0.5)
100 PAU:   maybe::→
101        (0.2)
102 TAN:   do you ha⌈ve any funding ⌉ of that kind↗
103 PAU:            ⌊i have something⌋
104        (0.6)
105 PAU:   yes maybe yes↘
106        (0.6)
107 PAU:   o⌈kay⌉
108 TAN:    ⌊okay⌋
109 PAU:   i ⌈think i have a pa⌉per:
110 TAN:     ⌊that's what they want⌋
```

We see that the expression in question, 'declaration of sufficient means', is problematic for Paulina[1], and she turns to a help desk officer for an explanation. In such a service provision activity, the staff member is required to take responsibility to ensure the student has an adequate level of understanding of the legal jargon that is featured in the application form, which in turn will allow the student to complete the form in the required manner. This task is complicated by the fact that the student will often have limited knowledge of the "logic" of the administrative system, but also by the fact that the terms available in English to describe procedures and concepts that are closely tied to the local

---

[1] Although the phrase she is reading aloud is 'sufficient', she adds an additional 'n' making it sound like *suffincient*.

Danish context may not be available. Finally, differences in linguistic proficiency may complicate things even further.

In the case at hand, the help desk officer's initial formulation appears to be geared towards unpacking the meaning of 'sufficient means', or rather of 'having sufficient means':

```
(5)  69  PAU:  and declaration of sufficient (0.2) means↗
     70        (0.5)
     71  PAU:  what it does it means↗≈
     72  TAN:  ≈that you have money enough
     73        to support yourself
     74        while you are here
     75        (0.3)
     76  PAU:  ah okay (.) ⌈erm::→⌉
     77  TAN:            ⌊a bank⌋ statement or something like that
     78  PAU:  yeah↗
```

So, the initial formulation relates to what the declaration needs to address, rather than what format it should take and what sort of "evidence" would be appropriate. However, following the delayed, minimal uptake from the student in line 76, the member of staff extends her explanation with a number of suggestions as to what could satisfy the requirement. Again however, none of these suggestions (*stipend, grant, bank statement, statement from the bank*, being *an Erasmus student*) conforms to the format of a *declaration*. They are examples of types of documentation which may prove that a student has sufficient financial resources to undertake the exchange, but they are not in themselves 'declarations'.

Although the member of staff is neither providing an explanation of what the 'declaration of sufficient means' entails, nor offering a particularly uniform set of alternative descriptors, the manner in which she responds to the student's request appears to embody some level of epistemic authority. This of course may point to the institutional nature of the encounter, where she is present as an institutionally designated person-in-the-know. The help desk encounters in our data carry an overall interactional fingerprint of asymmetrical epistemic rights and obligations, with participants working from asymmetry of knowledge to symmetrical positions (Heritage 2012). Where clients in these encounters tend to have epistemic primacy with regard to their personal affairs (whether they are an Erasmus student for example), the members of staff are deemed to possess superior knowledge of procedural matters pertaining to the institution (what goes where in filling out a document) and – very importantly for our analysis here – the language that goes with these matters. In the current sequence we observe this very pattern.

The participants start out with asymmetrical levels of understanding of the phrase in question and its relevance to the situation of this particular student, and collaboratively move towards a convergent understanding. The initial part of the sequence (lines 69–73) displays clear knowledge asymmetry, but then we observe how the participants in the subsequent steps (from line 94 onwards) gradually seem to be building mutual understanding. This process eventually leads to the participants agreeing that the requested declaration could simply be a "paper" stating that the student is an Erasmus student (lines 108–109). This appears to amount to a pragmatically relevant understanding of what 'declaration of sufficient means' means, although as outside observers, we may still think that it is all but clear what format this paper should actually have in order to fulfil the requirement of providing 'a declaration of sufficient means'.

Nevertheless, the example shows how a phrase that is introduced as an English equivalent to a Danish administrative term denoting a particular legal requirement, may develop a certain meaning through repeated use in a particular context. The member of staff responds pragmatically to the question about what the phrase means, with an explanation of *what would satisfy the requirement*, rather than an *explanation* of the term. As the understanding of the technical term is negotiated between the participants, a particular meaning for the term may emerge, driven by the attempts by the staff member to assist the student in completing the requirements.

So, in parallel to our discussion of 'ex-matriculated' above, we would argue that the term 'declaration of sufficient means' has in this encounter been ratified as a legitimate lexical item by the participants and a shared understanding of its meaning has been negotiated. In this way, the interaction that takes place in this face-to-face encounter – uneventful as it may seem – could be perceived as a potentially important step in the gradual emergence of this phrase as a generally accepted and commonly employed bureaucratic term in the linguistic repertoire of the international university in Denmark.

4 Discussion

In this chapter, we have presented a number of illustrative examples from service encounters at a Danish university that demonstrate how speakers negotiate "local" bureaucratic terms and their meaning, and thereby contribute to the hyper-local emergent register of English. Obviously, we do not wish to make sweeping claims about linguistic change on the basis of the analyses we have carried out. However, we would like to suggest that what we have presented amounts to a study of the kind of social processes that necessarily underlie – and which are therefore likely to facilitate the ongoing process of – linguistic change. Social interaction in face-to-face encounters may be considered the primordial site of language variation and change, and by studying such sites in detail, we may be able to catch a glimpse of – and hopefully describe in some detail – some of the multiple factors that relate to what Weinreich, Labov and Herzog (1968) call "the actuation riddle", i.e. the problem of explaining why and how linguistic change actually comes about. By focusing on lexical items, we have arguably been studying one of the less obscure elements of the riddle, since changes at other linguistic levels are less likely to become the object of metalinguistic discourse of the kind we have studied here. Yet, if we assume that the processes driving linguistic change are to some extent parallel or at least similar irrespective of the (analytically determined) level of language we investigate, the study of processes related to lexical innovation and change may have a bearing on our understanding of changes at other levels.

In our view, the use of language in transient multilingual communities constitutes a particularly interesting site of investigation for research that takes an interest in the link between social and linguistic change, since many of the changes that we only have access to "after the fact" in traditional stable communities are often unfolding in real time in transient communities. By studying social interaction in transient multilingual communities, we may not be able to describe or predict the formation of particular linguistic varieties (because the use of language may never result in sedimented patterns that we might want to describe as varieties), but we are ideally positioned to study the processes that may be said to underlie linguistic change, in stable as well as transient communities.

Today, English is used as a lingua franca "locally everywhere" as Latour (2005) might have put it. Under these conditions, English can either be conceptualized as an "immutable mobile" Latour (1987), an object that can be transported across social borders and between intersecting social worlds while remaining stable, or as a "boundary object". In Star and Griesemer's description (1989) boundary objects are:

> (...) objects which are both plastic enough to adapt to local needs and constraints of the several parties employing them, yet robust enough to maintain a common identity across sites. They are weakly structured in common use, and become strongly structured in individual-site use. They may be abstract or concrete. They have different meanings in different social worlds but their structure is common enough to more than one world to make them recognizable, a means of translation. The creation and management of boundary objects is key in developing and maintaining coherence across intersecting social worlds. (Star and Griesemer 1989: 393)

Where we see an orientation to correcting slight "imperfections" in language use (Example 1) and L1 speakers of English being oriented to as having greater epistemic authority in producing candidate terms as well as confirming or disconfirming linguistic forms (Examples 1 and 2), it appears that the language is being conceptualised by participants as a fully formed set of linguistic resources that can be transported to and applied across local settings internationally. It is treated as a language that can stand in for local terms in other languages, regardless of the way the local terms are bound up with e.g. local practices, institutions and concepts. However, with those present not always being representative of groups traditionally afforded primary epistemic rights for adjudicating on language matters – i.e. L1 speakers or language teachers – others may assume this position, acting as language experts within particular areas of knowledge. This is what we see in Example 3 and, very clearly, in Example 4. In these cases, the language is treated as being more closely bound up with local practices, and in this way it could be said to possess a level of plasticity that affords users opportunities for structuring the linguistic resources more strongly in their individual-site use (cf. the terminology of Star and Griesemer).

The metaphor pursued here may also be applied at the level of individual words. In instances where we see candidate terms emerging from the demands of the local setting in this way, we might describe these as "intermediary objects" (Brassac et al. 2008; Jeantet 1998; Vinck 1999). Brassac et. al. (2008: 217) describe intermediary objects as 'virtual objects' that are 'yet to be manufactured' and go on to say that,

> [b]y way of these representations, actors assume they will be able to communicate their idea of the problems they have to solve, the possible solutions, and the constraints to be taken into account. Intermediary objects mediate the way each specialist expresses himself or herself and the setting up of a compromise. When the object is robust enough to support interactions between various social worlds, they can be called boundary objects (Star and Griesemer, 1989). (Brassac et al. 2008: 217).

Terms such as those observed in our data, 'ex-matriculated' and 'declaration of sufficient means', could be representative of the different stages of this process, from intermediary objects to boundary objects, i.e. terms that gradually assume a level of usability in their own right and can be deployed across different contexts within the local settings. No matter whether the terms eventually come to be adopted and ratified as English terms "proper", for instance through inclusion in dictionaries, or not, the cases illustrate how English is constantly changing in response to its use in increasingly more diversified local settings.

5 Concluding remarks

In writing this chapter, we hope to have illustrated one way in which it might be possible to pursue what we consider a desirable cross-fertilization between the general research area of sociolinguistics, particularly the study of language variation and change, and the emerging body of research on the use of language in lingua franca scenarios, particularly scenarios where English is used as the lingua franca. Considering traditional demarcations between disciplines, it might seem peculiar to enlist a CA-inspired micro-analytical approach as the methodological go-between in this process since conversation analysts and sociolinguists are not the most obvious bedfellows, but we believe that the study of transient, multilingual communities calls for new and perhaps unconventional approaches to problems that may appear familiar from the study of stable communities, but which are nevertheless not quite the same in transient communities, and it is in that spirit that we have offered this chapter.

References

Brassac, Christian, Pierre Fixmer, Lorenza Mondada & Dominique Vinck. 2008. Interweaving objects, gestures, and talk in context. *Mind, Culture, and Activity* 15(3). 208–233.
Cogo, Alessia. 2008. English as a lingua franca: Form follows function. *English Today* 24(3). doi:10.1017/S0266078408000308.
Day, Dennis & Susanne Kjærbeck. 2012. Treating student contributions as displays of understanding in group supervision. In Gitte Rasmussen & Catherine E. Brouwer (eds.), *Evaluating Cognitive Competences in Interaction*, 67–88. Amsterdam: John Benjamins Publishing Company.
Fabricius, Anne, Janus Mortensen, Hartmut Haberland. 2017. The lure of internationalization: Paradoxical discourses of transnational student mobility, linguistic diversity and cross-cultural exchange. *Higher Education* 73(4). 577–595. doi:10.1007/s10734-015-9978-3.
Firth, Alan. 1996. The discursive accomplishment of normality: On conversation analysis and "lingua franca" English. *Journal of Pragmatics* 26. 237–259.
Firth, Alan & Johannes Wagner. 1997. On discourse, communication, and (some) fundamental concepts in SLA research. *The Modern Language Journal* 81(3). 285–300. doi:10.1111/j.1540-4781.1997.tb05480.x.
Firth, Alan & Johannes Wagner. 2007. Second/foreign language learning as a social accomplishment: Elaborations on a reconceptualized SLA. *The Modern Language Journal* 91. 800–819. doi:10.1111/j.1540-4781.2007.00670.x.
Gafaranga, Joseph, and Maria.-Carme. Torras. 2001. Language versus medium in the study of bilingual conversation. *International Journal of Bilingualism* 5(2). 195–219. doi:10.1177/13670069010050020401.
Haberland, Hartmut & Janus Mortensen. 2012. Language variety, language hierarchy and language choice in the international university. *International Journal of the Sociology of Language* (216). 1–6. doi:10.1515/ijsl-2012-0036.
Hayano, Kaoru. 2011. Claiming epistemic primacy: *Yo*-marked assessments in Japanese. In Tanya Stivers, Lorenza Mondada & Jakob Steensig (eds.), *The Morality of Knowledge in Conversation*, 58–81. Cambridge: Cambridge University Press. doi:10.1017/CBO9780511921674.004.
Hazel, Spencer. 2012. *Interactional competence in the institutional setting of the international university: Talk and embodied action as multimodal aggregates in institutional interaction*. Roskilde: Roskilde University PhD Thesis.
Hazel, Spencer. 2016. The Paradox from Within – Research Participants Doing-Being-Observed. *Qualitative Research* 16(4). 446–467. doi:10.1177/1468794115596216

Hazel, Spencer & Janus Mortensen. 2012. Kitchen talk: Exploring linguistic practices in liminal institutional interactions in a multilingual university setting. In Hartmut Haberland, Dorte Lønsmann & Bent Preisler (eds.), *Language Alternation, Language Choice and Language Encounter in International Education*, 3–30. Dordrecht: Springer.

Hazel, Spencer & Johannes Wagner. 2015. L2 and L3 integrated learning: Lingua franca use in learning an additional language in the classroom. In Christopher Joseph Jenks & Paul Seedhouse (eds.), *International Perspectives on ELT Classroom Interaction*. Basingstoke: Palgrave Macmillan. 149–167.

Heritage, John. 2012. The epistemic engine: Sequence Organization and territories of knowledge. *Research on Language & Social Interaction* 45(1). 30–52. doi:10.1080/08351813.2012.646685.

Heritage, John & Geoffrey Raymond. 2005. The terms of agreement: Indexing epistemic authority and subordination in talk-in-interaction. *Social Psychology Quarterly* 68(1). 15–38. doi:10.1177/019027250506800103.

Hynninen, Niina. 2013. *Language Regulation in English as a Lingua Franca: Exploring Language-regulatory practices in academic spoken discourse*. Helsinki: University of Helsinki PhD Thesis. https://helda.helsinki.fi/handle/10138/38290.

Jeantet, Alain. 1998. Les objets intermédiaires dans les processus de conception des produits. *Sociologie du travail* 3(98). 291–316.

Jefferson, Gail. 1987. On exposed and embedded correction in conversation. In Graham Button & John R.E. Lee (eds.), *Talk and Social Organisation*, 86–100. Cleveland, Philadelphia: Multilingual Matters.

Jenkins, Jennifer. 2013. *English as a Lingua Franca in the International University: The Politics of academic English language policy*. London: Routledge.

Kirkebæk, Mads Jakob. 2013. "Teacher! Why Do You Speak English?" A discussion of teacher use of English in a Danish language class. In Hartmut Haberland, Dorte Lønsmann & Bent Preisler (eds.), *Language Alternation, Language Choice and Language Encounter in International Tertiary Education*, 143–159. Dordrecht: Springer.

Latour, Bruno. 1987. *Science in Action: How to Follow Scientists and Engineers Through Society*. Cambridge (MA): Harvard University Press.

Latour, Bruno. 2005. *Reassembling the Social: An Introduction to Actor-Network-Theory*. Oxford: Oxford University Press.

Lave, Jean, and Etienne Wenger. 1991. *Situated Learning: Legitimate Peripheral Participation*. Cambridge: Cambridge University Press.

MacWhinney, Brian & Johannes Wagner. 2010. Transcribing, searching and data sharing: The CLAN software and the TalkBank data repository. *Gesprächsforschung – Online-Zeitschrift zur verbalen Interaktion* 11. 154–173.

Mauranen, Anna. 2012. *Exploring ELF: Academic English Shaped by Non-Native Speakers*. Cambridge: Cambridge University Press.

Mortensen, Janus. 2010. *Epistemic Stance Marking in the Use of English as a Lingua Franca: A Comparative Study of the Pragmatic Functions of Epistemic Stance Marking in Problem-Solving Sequences at Student Project Group Meetings, with Special Emphasis on Meetings Where English is Used as a Lingua Franca*. Roskilde: Roskilde University PhD Thesis.

Mortensen, Janus. 2013. Notes on English used as a lingua franca as an object of study. *Journal of English as a Lingua Franca* 2(1). 25–46. doi:10.1515/jelf-2013-0002.

Mortensen, Janus. 2014. Language policy from below: Language choice in student project groups in a multilingual university setting. *Journal of Multilingual and Multicultural Development* 35(4). 425–442. doi:10.1080/01434632.2013.874438.

Nevile, Maurice & Johannes Wagner. 2008. Managing languages and participation in a multilingual group examination. In Hartmut Haberland, Janus Mortensen, Anne Fabricius, Bent Preisler, Karen Risager & Susanne Kjærbeck (eds.), *Higher Education in the Global Village*, 149–175. Roskilde: Roskilde Universitetscenter.
Preisler, Bent, Ida Klitgård & Anne H Fabricius. 2011. *Language and Learning in the International University: From English Uniformity to Diversity and Hybridity*. Bristol: Multilingual Matters.
Raymond, Geoffrey & John Heritage. 2006. The epistemics of social relations: Owning grandchildren. *Language in Society* 35(05). 677–705. doi:10.1017/S0047404506060325.
Sacks, Harvey. 1984. On doing "being ordinary". In J. Maxwell Atkinson (ed.), *Structures of Social Action*, 413–429. Cambridge: Cambridge University Press. doi:10.1017/CBO9780511665868.024.
Sacks, Harvey, Emanuel A. Schegloff & Gail Jefferson. 1974. A simplest systematics for the organization of turn-taking for conversation. *Language* 50. 696–735.
Speer, Susan A. & Ian Hutchby. 2003. From ethics to analytics: Aspects of participants' orientations to the presence and relevance of recording devices. *Sociology* 37(2). 315–337. doi:10.1177/0038038503037002006.
Star, Susan Leigh & James R. Griesemer. 1989. Institutional ecology, "translations" and boundary objects: Amateurs and professionals in Berkeley's Museum of Vertebrate Zoology, 1907–39. *Social Studies of Science* 19(3). 387–420. doi:10.1177/030631289019003001.
Vinck, Dominique. 1999. Les objets intermédiaires dans les réseaux de coopération scientifique. Contribution à la prise en compte des objets dans les dynamiques sociales. *Revue française de sociologie* 40(2). 385–414. doi:10.2307/3322770.
Weinreich, Uriel, William Labov & Marvin I. Herzog. 1968. Empirical foundations for a theory of language change. In Winfred P. Lehmann & Yakov Malkiel (eds.), *Directions for Historical Linguistics: A Symposium*, 97–105. Austin, TX: University of Texas Press.

Transcription conventions

Identifier	TEA:
Pause	(0.2)
Overlap markers top	⌈ ⌉
Overlap markers bottom	⌊ ⌋
Intonation: rising	↗
continuing	→
falling	↘
Pitch shift	↑
Latched turns	≈
Smiley voice	☺
Unsure	ʔUnsureʔ
Within word laughter	ʜ
Inbreath	·hhhh
Stress	no<u>w</u>
Accelerated speech	Δand youΔ
Translation	*In italics*

Svetlana Vetchinnikova
On the relationship between the cognitive and the communal: a complex systems perspective

Abstract: This paper presents a specific take on the relationship between the global and the local in language. In particular, it draws a distinction between the cognitive and the communal plane of language representation and attempts to model the relationship between the two using complexity theory. To operationalise this relationship and examine it with corpus linguistic methods, it proposes a concept of a cognitive corpus, setting it against the more usual idea of a corpus as representing the language of a certain community of speakers. As a case study, the paper compares the properties of chunking at the cognitive and communal planes. The study shows that (1) chunks at the cognitive plane seem to be more fixed than at the communal, (2) their patterning at the communal plane can be seen as emergent from the patterning observable in individual languages, but that (3) there is also similarity in the shape of the patterning across the two planes. These findings suggest that although the processes leading to multi-word unit patterning are different at each of the planes, the similarity in the shape the patterning takes might be regarded as an indication of the fractal structure of language which is a common property of complex adaptive systems. For example, Zipf's law, which is able to model the patterning at each of the planes, can be seen as one of the symptoms of such structure. Since the cognitive and the communal planes of language are in constant interaction with each other, such conceptualisation suggests intriguing implications for ongoing change in English and the role second language users might play in it.

Keywords: cognitive corpus, individual language, lexical bundles, chunking, complex adaptive system, fractal, Zipf's law, emergence, fixing, unit of meaning, approximation, *it is* ADJ *that*, second language use, ELF

> [A fractal is] a rough or fragmented geometric shape that can be split into parts, each of which is (at least approximately) a reduced-size copy of the whole.
> Mandelbrot 1982: 34

Svetlana Vetchinnikova, University of Helsinki

1 Introduction

There is a number of ways *language* can be split into parts. If language behaves as a complex adaptive system (CAS), then in each case (1) a part will be a reduced-size copy of the whole, a fractal and (2) the relationship between the parts and the whole will be characterised by emergence. This should also apply to the distinction between the global and the local, focused on in this volume. I will now introduce this hypothesis in more detail.

The CAS approach to language modelling (see notably Larsen-Freeman 1997; Ellis and Larsen-Freeman 2006; Ellis 2011; Larsen-Freeman and Cameron 2008; de Bot et al. 2007) has developed from a usage-based, emergentist theoretical orientation (Hopper 1987; Bybee and Hopper 2001; Tomasello 2003). In this paradigm, the understanding of how language works is in stark contrast to the traditional view where grammar rules are seen to work top-down rather than merely be a description of what happens bottom-up. Conversely, language structure is seen to emerge dynamically in usage and to be shaped by "interrelated patterns of experience, social interaction, and cognitive processes" (Beckner et al. 2009: 2). This view entails an intricate relationship between every individual and every language event and language change at the global level. On the one hand, as Larsen-Freeman (1997) points out:

> [There is] no distinction between current use and change/growth, they are isomorphic processes. Every time language is used, it changes. As I write this sentence, and as you read it, we are changing English. [...] as the user's grammar is changed, this sets in motion a process, which may lead to change at the global level. (Larsen-Freeman 1997: 148)

At the same time, every instance of language use, necessarily performed by an individual, is itself a product of interaction of different forces, such as the user's cognitive processes, previous experience of language and social motivations. As a result, we have a multiply embedded system with a complex interrelationship between the communal and the individual. As Beckner et al. (2009: 15) observe "an idiolect is emergent from an individual's language use through social interactions with other individuals in the communal language, whereas a communal language is emergent as the result of the interaction of the idiolects".

Here, the concept of *emergence* takes on a new meaning. Hopper (2011) distinguishes between *emerging* and *emergent* grammar, pointing out that what is commonly foregrounded by the former is inquiry into the historical origins of present-day grammar and, as a consequence, its conceptualisation as a stable system which *has emerged*, while the latter sees grammar as always temporary, ephemeral and provisional. While forming a fundamental background, neither of the two interpretations captures the specifics of emergence conceptualised as a property of a CAS (see e.g. Ellis and Larsen-Freeman 2006). A CAS is a product of interaction of different types of elements where each element is itself a product of interaction of even smaller elements. In other words, we see multiply embedded complex systems at different levels of abstraction. It is the relationship between the levels that can be characterised by emergence. At every level, a CAS *emerges* from the interaction of the elements at a lower level, that is, it does not equal the sum of the elements but arises from their interaction, and thus can have properties which are not present at the lower level. In this way, a traffic jam is not the property of an automobile but emerges in the interaction of many automobiles, or, to be more precise, their trajectories (de Bot and Larsen-Freeman 2013: 17).

At the same time, another common property of complex adaptive systems, namely, fractal structure, also called scale-free self similarity, predicts that an element or component part participating in the interaction at the lower level will have the same shape as the system as a whole. In other words, multiply embedded complex systems located at different levels or scales of a certain dimension will be self-similar. For example, Mandelbrot (1963) examined variation in cotton prices over short and long time periods and found that the pattern of change was similar regardless of the scale. Language appears to be an entity which is particularly suitable for fractal analysis since we routinely talk about langauges at different levels of abstraction, such as English language, British language, academic language, newspaper language, Early Modern English language, child language, Hip Hop nation language, individual language.

In principle, there seems to be three major dimensions along which one can split language into parts: (1) across different groups of speakers, from individuals and discourse communities to nations and global networks, (2) across different levels of language organisation, such as phonological, morphological, lexico-grammatical, discoursal and (3) across different time-scales . We can tentatively refer to them as 'social', 'structural' and 'temporal' dimensions (cf. e.g. Ellis 2006; de Bot et al. 2013). The first two can also be thought of as breadth and depth, to borrow the terms from vocabulary studies (Anderson and Freebody 1981; Read 2004). If the hypothesis about the fractal structure of language is correct, we should be able to see inherent similarity in shape whether we zoom in or zoom out along each of the dimensions. Thus, if we take the temporal dimension, for example, short-term and long-term changes in language can exhibit similarity in their patterning. At the same time, the temporal dimension can be kept separate as there is no need to impose it on either the social or the structural dimension: the behaviour of complex systems on these two dimensions, including the property of emergence which might not be so intuitively obvious, can be studied from a synchronic point of view.

The contrast of the global and the local of this volume is then situated on the social dimension, that of breadth or spread. Thus, we can think of English as comprised of different varieties, dialects and registers (e.g. see Mair this volume for a suggestion of a currently relevant taxonomy for English). In this paper, I am drawing a distinction between the individual and the communal plane of language representation which is another way of breaking up language on the social dimension. In principle, the properties of the relationship between these two planes should be applicable to other divisions into planes on the social dimension. Here, I equate the individual with the cognitive for reasons I discuss in Section 3. I will refer to the levels of the social dimension as planes to set them apart from the time-scales of the temporal dimension and the levels of the structural dimension.

In what follows, I first further explain in which way the communal plane of language representation can be seen as emergent from the interaction of idiolects by giving two examples of observed language patterning. It must be mentioned that while complex system properties must apply to language representation across different levels of its organisation, this paper contextualises the model by focusing on the type of patterning which is often referred to as 'phraseological' (see Section 4 for an outline of this approach). Thus, the examples examined in Section 2 directly relate to the case study described in Sections 4, 5 and 6. But before that, in Section 3, I argue for the feasibility of making a connection between the individual and the cognitive and suggest a concept of a cognitive corpus. Then, in Section 4, I move on to exploring the relationship between the individual and the communal by looking at the properties of chunking at each of them and describe the data I am going to use for this purpose. In Section 5, I focus on the variation in the construction *it is* ADJ *that* at each of the planes to see whether the relationship between the two can be described as emergent and fractal, in line with CAS predictions. In Section 6, I take a more quantitative approach to inspect whether there is further support for the chunking differences observed in Section 5. In the final section, I summarise the findings and relate them to research on grammaticalization and ongoing change in English as possible avenues for further research.

2 Emergence of the communal from the cognitive

In this section, I will show in which way language representation at the communal plane can be seen as emergent from the cognitive and what implications this might have for understanding the mechanisms underlying phraseological patterning observable at each of the planes. To do this, I will take two linguistic units, a more lexical and a more grammatical one, as my examples and see how they can be represented at each of the planes.

I will start with Sinclair's unit of meaning (Sinclair 1996, 2004), a form-meaning pairing which, in contrast to many other conceptualisations of meaningful units, allows for fixed as well as variable components. Its fixed components are obligatory: the core, the most invariable formal element, and the semantic prosody, which is defined here as the communicative purpose of a unit (Vetchinnikova 2014; see also Hunston 2007 who defines semantic prosody as a discourse function of a unit of meaning). The variable components are optional: they are collocation, colligation and semantic preference. Collocation is a verbatim association between two or more words. In contrast, colligation and semantic preference are abstracted associations: association with a grammatical feature and association with a semantic set respectively. A well-known example of a unit of meaning is the case of *naked eye* (Sinclair 1996). *Naked eye* itself is a collocation because it is a verbatim co-occurrence of two words. It also has a semantic preference for words from the semantic set of 'visibility', like *seen, discernible, visible*, rather than collocates with just one of them, and colligates with the class of prepositions, including *by, with* or *via*, again rather than collocates with just one of them. The whole patterning associates with the communicative purpose of saying that something is difficult to see, which is the semantic prosody of this unit.

The patterning of a unit of meaning was first revealed through corpus observations of language (Sinclair 1996), i.e. at the communal plane. But there is evidence for its psycholinguistic reality too (Vetchinnikova 2014). Yet, the fact that the unit of meaning seems to be represented at both planes, cognitive and communal, does not yet mean that the processes leading to its emergence at each of the planes are the same.

At the cognitive plane, the existence of colligation and semantic preference can be explained by effects of frequency on entrenchment and the properties of human memory, which is stronger for meaning than for linguistic form (Bock and Brewer 1974; Gurevich et al. 2010). As such, if a sequence or a certain component of it has not been frequent enough (or the type/token ratio is tipped towards the higher type frequency) in the language experience of a user, its representation in memory is abstracted in grammatical or semantic terms rather than is verbatim. Thus, a language user might associate the verb *undergo* with a semantic set of words meaning some kind of 'change' (*surgery, transformation, change, treatment, operation*) rather than with a specific word from this set. This abstracted representation would be explained by the cognitive reality of semantic preference. At the same time it is possible for a language user to associate *undergo* with e.g. *change* in particular due to his/her specific experience of language, i.e. have the unit represented as a collocation in memory. Over time, due to continuous change in the experience of language, these associations can also change: become more fixed, from abstracted to verbatim or collocational, and loosen, abstract from a collocation to a semantic preference or a colligation. These reverse processes have been called *fixing* (Vetchinnikova 2014) and *approximation* (Mauranen 2012).

At the communal plane, the picture is a bit different. When we examine the patterning of the verb *undergo* and find that it co-occurs with words belonging to the same semantic set, such as *surgery, change, transformation, operation, endoscopy* (BNC) and therefore can postulate the category of semantic preference for it, it does not yet mean that this semantic preference is valid for all language speakers, or for all native speakers or for all speakers of British English. It is just as well possible that the category of semantic preference we observe in a corpus is a result of averaging[1] across speakers: that is, each of the speakers represented in the BNC might have his/her own collocational preference which together look like a semantic preference. Therefore we can say that semantic preference exists at both planes but is driven by different mechanisms.

Let us imagine for a moment that due to certain socio-economic developments *undergo change* becomes a fixed expression at the communal plane, say, to refer to restructuring of an organisation due to severe cuts in budget.[2] Then the processes of fixing at the individual plane and conventionalisation at the communal plane can also be seen as similar, even though again the mechanisms underlying them are different. It seems that this similarity across different planes can be regarded as an example of scale-free self-similarity or fractal scaling (Mandelbrot 1982; Gleick 1987), mentioned at the outset of this paper. Fractal scaling is also another common property of complex systems. I will come back to this idea in the analysis of data in Section 5.

But let me give another example of how emergence might be conceptualised. Mollin (2009a) studies the distribution of maximiser adverbs, such as *absolutely, completely, entirely* and *totally* in a three-million corpus of Tony Blair's public speeches and finds a clear preference for specific combinations, for example,

---

[1] See Larsen-Freeman 2013 for the discussion of the problem of averaging and thus abstracting away from variability in research on language development, including second language research.
[2] It is important to mention at this point that in Sinclair's conceptualisation of lexis and meaning, when a combination of words starts to be treated as a unit, i.e. on the idiom principle, it always means a change in meaning, a meaning shift, however small (e.g. Sinclair 2004; Cheng et al. 2009). This view is not dissimilar to views expressed in the study of grammaticalization in relation to the mechanisms underlying language change which suggests a possibility for cross-fertilisation between these theoretical frameworks, but which would not be further discussed here for reasons of space.

completely unacceptable, entirely understand or *absolutely blunt*. Such preferences sometimes align with the BNC collocational patterns, sometimes do not and sometimes are clearly "Blairisms". To me, this might mean that the grammatical category of maximiser adverbs as an abstraction of regularities in language patterning emerges only at the communal plane, when we aggregate different speakers and different discourses and average across them. To put it in other words, many aspects of linguistic structure might be an emergent property of language at the communal plane and might not be present at the individual level.

If this hypothesis is correct, it might help to explain often conflicting findings of the studies examining the psycholinguistic reality of co-occurrence patterns observed in corpora, an issue which has recently drawn attention of many scholars (e.g. Hoey 2005; Mollin 2009b; Ellis and Frey 2009; Ellis et al. 2009; Durrant and Doherty 2010). The solution it suggests is that corpus-linguistically attested patterns do not necessarily have to be psycholinguistically real in order to be valid observations of language at the communal level. It is possible, and plausible, that the patterning at the two levels is different, in a qualitative way.

3 A *cognitive* corpus

In many ways, the distinction between the individual and communal levels of language is not new. For example, in the study of language contact we find the distinction between transfer at the level of the society and at the level of individual already in Weinreich (1953). Mauranen (2012 and this volume) adds another, microsocial level, and builds a framework based on three interrelated levels: the societal or macrosocial, the individual or cognitive and the level of social interaction between speakers or the microsocial. Both Weinreich (1953) and Mauranen (2012) make an explicit connection between the individual and the cognitive, after all cognition is the property of an individual. But can we make the same connection in corpus linguistic research and treat a corpus of an individual's language use as his/her cognitive corpus, that is, a corpus enabling observation of individual's cognitive processes and representations? Let us have a look at what research on idiolects can tell us.

The study of idiolects is not a particularly popular topic in almost any field of linguistics, mostly for reasons of limited generalisability as it seems, but not a non-existent one. Idiolectal preferences have been studied in forensic linguistics for the purposes of authorship identification (Coulthard 2004; Wright 2015) and in a few other corpus linguistic studies, such as Mollin (2009a) and Barlow (2013). All these studies come to the conclusion that idiolectal preferences are clearly identifiable and are able to distinguish an individual from other language speakers or from the "communal average".³ In a way these studies, and especially Barlow (2013), continue in the tradition of studies on language variation and suggest that there is no reason to stop at the already well acknowledged fact of register variation: idiolectal variation seems to be just as palpable.

The case of idiolects has also been brought to attention in historical sociolinguistic studies of grammaticalization, but in a bit different way (see Raumolin-Brunberg and Nurmi 2011 for a review). These studies are interested in the role of the individual in language change. Taking a historical perspective and using the benefit of hindsight, they examine in which way language changes attested at the communal plane reflect in language use of specific individuals across their life span. What they find is "a great deal of variation between individuals concerning their participation in ongoing linguistic changes" (Raumolin-Brunberg and Nurmi 2011: 262). In fact, Raumolin-Brunberg and Nurmi observe that "[t]he patterns that arise from studies of large groups of people do not necessarily surface in the language of individuals" (262). This conclusion makes one think whether what we see is mere variation or whether it is possible that the relationship between the individual and communal is not straightforward but rather can indeed be described by emergence.

One thing this brief glance at research on idiolects shows is that interestingly while collective corpora have been used in research on psycholinguistic reality of corpus-attested patterns, as mentioned in the previous section, individual corpora have not (though, see Vetchinnikova 2014). I will try to give several theoretical arguments in support of such uses, i.e. in support of cognitive corpora. First, in the tradition of usage-based linguistics, there is no propensity to make a distinction between competence and performance. Therefore, language produced by an individual is the language available to him/her. Second, as discussed in the previous section, the distinction is also not made between language use and language change. Language acquisition can thus be seen as a language change at the individual or cognitive plane. Therefore, again, language produced by an individual can be taken to represent his/her stage of language acquisition/ development/change at this particular moment in time. And lastly, language produced by an individual is a product of his/her cognition. Therefore, it reflects the properties of cognition just as individual's answers to physiological and psychological tests used in cognitive science do.

One reason why cognitive corpora have not been compiled might lie in the obvious practical problems of collecting all the language an individual produces

---

3 In relation to this, see also studies in psychology (Molenaar 2004; Molenaar 2008; Molenaar and Campbell 2009; van Geert 2011) showing that "we cannot argue from group to individuals" (Schumann 2015: xv), that is, individual trajectories cannot be inferred from aggregated data.

even for a short period of time (e.g. Mollin 2009a refers to this problem as a limitation of her study). Yet, given the evidence from studies on register variation (most notably Biber 1988 and Biber et al. 1999), it is reasonable to hypothesise that individual language use will exhibit the same kind of variation across different domains of language use. Therefore, it might not be absolutely necessary to compile a 24/7 cognitive corpus, but rather enough to focus on a specific domain, for example someone's academic writing, spoken communication at work or online interaction in social media as a representative sample of his/her language use in this context. At least it would be clear what such a corpus is representative of and what it can be compared to.

So, in this paper a *cognitive corpus* will be defined as a corpus of an individual's language use which is compiled in a way that enables observation of cognitive aspects of language production. As such, in contrast to most other corpora, which can be called communal, it does not aggregate data from different individuals, but rather focuses on a specific individual. And at the same time, it differs from a corpus of an idiolect compiled for the purposes of sociolinguistic research as it does not sample one's language use across genres, domains or the life span. In contrast, it deliberately tries to get rid of sociolinguistic variables as far as possible to pave the way for examining cognitively important factors of recency and frequency as they work within an individual. As Ellis (2006: 104) writes "[f]requency, recency, and context are [...] the three most fundamental influences on human cognition, linguistic and non-linguistic alike". In a cognitive corpus by keeping the context constant as it were, one should be in a good position to examine the effects of frequency and recency. For example, frequency in such a corpus gains a new significance: rather than serving as a predictor of how likely a pattern is to occur in general, it has a direct relationship to the strength of entrenchment of this pattern in the cognition of an individual. Compiling what I call a cognitive corpus is certainly not the only way to do "cognitive corpus linguistics" (Arppe et al. 2010). And indeed there is a growing number of corpus linguistic studies which aim at examining different aspects of human cognition and Cognitive Linguistics studies which use corpora (see Arppe et al. 2010; Grondelaers et al. 2007; Gilquin and Gries 2009; Gries and Stefanowitsch 2006).[4] Yet, to my knowledge there have not been any studies

---

4 As I see it, it is important to distinguish between Cognitive Linguistics and cognitive linguistics, such as cognitive corpus linguistics. Cognitive Linguistics is an established field of research with its own traditions and theoretical framework which grew out of the work of notably Lakoff, Langacker and Talmy. Cognitive linguistics, in contrast, is a type of research undertaken by cognitively oriented linguists, i.e. linguists of any theoretical background who take an interest in human cognition and believe that human cognitive processes can at least in part explain phenomena we see in language.

which use a corpus of an individual's language use for this purpose. In the next section, I will rely on the definition of a cognitive corpus and describe a case study based on the comparison between cognitive and communal corpora.

4 Cognitive vs. communal: focus on chunking

In this case study, I will compare chunking at the cognitive and communal planes. By chunking researchers usually mean a cognitive predisposition of language speakers towards holistic, rather than compositional processing (e.g. Wray 2002), also called sequential processing (e.g. Ellis 1996 or Bybee 2012), or the idiom principle (Sinclair 1987, 2004) which, being one of the domain-general cognitive processes underlying language use, leads to the emergence of complex patterning at all levels of language organisation. This is one of the central tenets of usage-based theory and emergentism (see e.g. Ellis 2003; Bybee 2012). At the same time, such complex patterning is usually explored at the communal rather than cognitive level of language use, for example in collective corpora. Corpus studies have yielded observations of numerous patterns in language use, from various methodologically defined n-grams, skipgrams, phrase-frames (Fletcher 2002), concgrams (Greaves 2009), PoS-grams (Stubbs 2007) to formulaic sequences (Wray 2002), units of meaning (Sinclair 1996), collocational frameworks (Renouf and Sinclair 1991), grammar patterns (Hunston and Francis 2000) and lexical bundles (Biber et al. 1999). Whether we can draw a direct line between the patterning observed in corpora and cognitive processes is an unresolved question. Here I would like to probe the hypothesis that cognitive processes lead to patterning at the individual level, which I call cognitive for precisely this reason. While such patterning certainly feeds into the patterning at the communal level, they are not in direct correspondence, as the property of emergence predicts. So chunking might be co-existent at two levels: language speakers chunk, but language can also have its "chunking processes". Such chunking at the communal plane is probably better described as a *phraseological tendency* of language (Sinclair 1996; Cheng et al. 2009), "syntagmatic organisation in language in use" (Stubbs 2009: 115) or simply a phraseological phenomenon, as corpus linguists usually do. Yet, for the ease of presentation I will also talk about "chunking at the communal level".

As my data, I will use a corpus of interaction within one blog over a period of seven years. In order not to mention the actual name of the blog, let us call it the Diachronic Blog Community Corpus (the DBCC). The corpus comprises comments posted to an exceptionally active blog by over 4,000 unique commenters over 7 years, amounting to 7.3 million words in more than 73,000 comments.

Note that the corpus contains comments to the blog entries only and excludes the blogs themselves. This includes 1.77 million words of comments written by a single person, the author of the blog. In addition to this exceptionally large individual contribution, there are five more commenters who produced from 160k to 250k words and ten more who produced from 50k to 100k words. Thus, the corpus allows sampling of language representation at three different levels: 1) the individual or the cognitive level – language use of the author of the blog and its most active commenters taken individually; 2) the communal level – all comments, excluding the heavily represented commenters (24 commenters who contributed over 400 comments to the blog); 3) and the inter-individual microsocial level (Mauranen 2012 and this volume) – the interaction between the most active commenters, including the author of the blog. In this way, the corpus operationalises a complex systems perspective on language. It is important to mention that there are native as well as non-native speakers of English among the active and regular commenters of the blog. The author of the blog is a non-native speaker. In this sense, the blog exhibits typical ELF interaction. Also, blog comments are relatively spontaneous and unedited in contrast to, for example, books or articles which can be more easily put together in an individual corpus of language production. Thus, blog comments are more likely to reflect the common usage patterns of an individual rather than adherence to established norms of standard language introduced through many stages of revision and editing common in more formal writing.

For the purpose of the present article, I will use the following subsets of data extracted from the DBCC:
1) Josef_1750k, which contains ca. 1,750,000 words written by the main author of the blog;
2) Non24_1750k, which contains ca. 1,750,000 words extracted from the DBCC excluding 24 of its most frequent commenters as well as Josef himself;
3) five additional cognitive sub-corpora (C1 to C5 where C1 stands for Commenter 1, C2 for Commenter 2 etc.), each equalling ca. 150,000 words produced by a single commenter.

It is thought feasible to compare these sub-corpora because all of them contain comments posted in response to blog entries or other comments. That is, the corpora are matched in terms of genre. The difference between them might reside in the types of comments made since their contributors in the Non24 corpus are by definition less active in blog discussions that the author of the blog and most active commenters. Figure 1 shows the mean length of comments calculated for five 150k samples extracted chronologically from Non24_1750k and Josef_1750k as well as five additional 150k sub-corpora (Commenters 1 to 5).

It shows that: 1) Josef's comments tend to be on average somewhat longer than comments of other contributors; 2) there is variation in the mean length of comments Josef contributes across time; 3) there is some variation in the mean length of comments different people contribute (C1 to C5 bars); 4) Non24 corpus, comprised of comments by over 4, 000 commenters, is relatively homogeneous with regard to the mean length of comments.

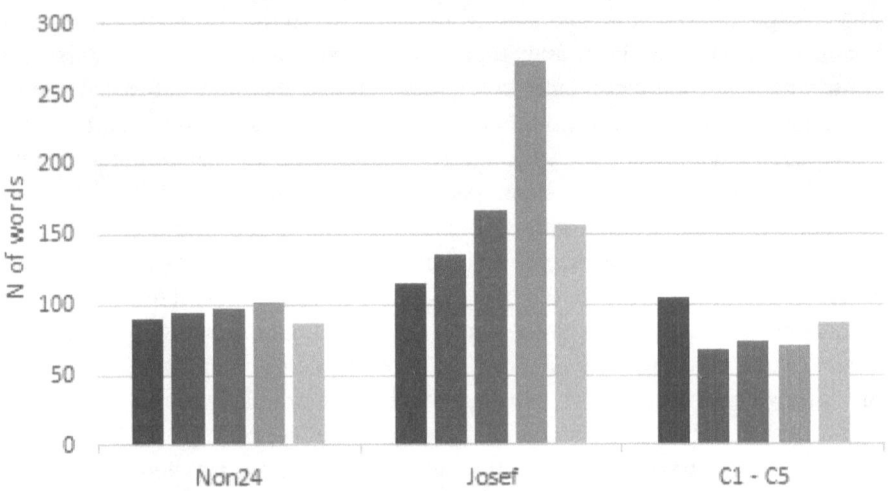

Figure 1: Mean length of comments across sub-corpora (150k samples)

These features of the sub-corpora should not have a large confounding effect in the retrieval of chunks or multi-word units. What might interfere are extremely short or extremely long comments: the former because they might not give possibility for a multi-word unit to occur, the latter because they might become substantially different in terms of text structure. As an extremely short comment, I will treat any comment which is less than five words[5], and as an extremely long, any comment longer than 500 words since 500–570 words is a very common maximum length of a comment across the corpora. Yet, the numbers of such comments are relatively small and equal across all corpora: the proportion of

---

[5] Since in part of the analysis I will use lexical bundles or immediate co-occurrences of 4 words, I have taken the impossibility for a lexical bundle to occur as a criterion for an extremely short comment. In principle a 4-word comment can be a lexical bundle. However, in practice, when comments of up to 4 words were searched for lexical bundles occurring at least twice, none were found. Comments of up to 5 words yielded one lexical bundle in Josef_1750k: *Thanks for the link*. This is thus used as a yardstick.

short comments per 150k corpus varies between 0 and 2.3 per cent, the proportion of long comments between 0 and 1.2 per cent, with the exception of Josef3_150k (5.3%) and Josef4_150k (16.3%): he clearly had a period when he wrote longer comments, this is visible in the mean length of comments presented in Figure 1 too. This dynamics of Josef's writing will be taken into account in the analysis to follow (see Appendix 1 for more details on the statistics of comments).

5 The case of *it is* ADJ *that*: is there evidence for emergence and fractality?

To probe the relationship between the cognitive and the communal and examine the predictions of complexity theory as applied to language, I will first focus on one construction – *it is* ADJ *that* – and see how it is represented at the two planes.

It is ADJ *that* is a well-known construction, very common for academic language in particular. It belongs to a wider grammar pattern *it* v-link ADJ *that* as documented in *Collins COBUILD Grammar Patterns* (Francis et al. 1998: 480) which itself, making a grammatical generalisation, can be subsumed under 'introductory' or 'anticipatory' *it* structures which "make forward reference to produce an end-focus" (Carter and McCarthy 2006: 891), so characteristic of English in general (see e.g. Quirk et al. 1985). It is also possible to classify it as an extraposed *that*-clause (Biber et al. 1999: 671–675). Further, it is often noted that this pattern carries an evaluative meaning (e.g. Francis 1993, Biber et al. 1999), while Hunston and Sinclair (2000) actually use the pattern[6] (or, "a collection of several patterns" as they say, [84]) to identify evaluative adjectives showing that in fact evaluation is the primary purpose of the pattern. Groom (2005) further points out that this evaluative function combined with the impersonality of *it* used as a grammatical subject makes the pattern very useful for writers of academic texts in particular. Charles (2004) has analysed the use of the pattern in academic discourse and noted further regularities of its more specific realisation, *it is clear/apparent/obvious/evident that*, i.e. the one where the adjectives filling the slot in the *it* v-link ADJ *that* grammar pattern fall into the 'obvious' group according to *Collins COBUILD Grammar Patterns* (Francis et al. 1998: 481). Hunston has later used Charles's findings to reinterpret the observed regularities as semantic sequences, i.e. "sequences of meaning elements rather than as formal sequences" (Hunston 2010 [2008]: 7) since they are much more abstract

---

[6] "*it* + link verb + adjective group + clause" (Hunston and Sinclair 2000: 84)

than simple co-occurrences of words as her representation of them clearly suggests:
- 'Logical basis + *it is clear that* + claim'
- 'Consensual information + *it is clear that* + claim'
- '*It is clear that* + claim + exception or caveat' (Hunston 2010 [2008]: 21)

What this substantial body of previous research on the pattern suggests is that from the point of view of language organisation *it is* ADJ *that* is an instance of a grammatical structure which, when it comes to actual language use, is at the same time lexically restricted, for example, to only a few semantic sets of adjectives, with a very clear communicative purpose of evaluation. Taking a step down from this rather high level of generality and looking at the use of the pattern with its adjectives from the specific 'obvious' group and focusing only on academic discourse, we detect further regularities in the way meaning elements are arranged. Still, even at this level of specificity, when we have restricted our observations to the use of a specific group of instances in a particular discourse, the pattern displays a lot of variability. What happens if we look at the patterning of the construction at the individual level?

In my analysis, I am deliberately simplifying the grammar pattern *it* v-link ADJ *that* to *it* BE ADJ *that* so that there is only one variable slot left since there are reasons to expect specific lexicalised preferences for the verb-slot across individual languages.[7] Thus, the most direct way to examine such predictions is to leave just one possible point of variability. It is also reasonable to assume that *it* BE ADJ *that* is probably the prototypical variant of constructions at progressively higher levels of abstractness.

As presented in Table 1, *it* BE ADJ *that* occurs 585 times in Josef_1750k with 69 different adjectives[8]. In comparison, it occurs twice less often in Non24_1750k but with almost the same number of different adjectives which results in a larger type-token ratio. Larger type-token ratio usually means more diversity in lexical choice. Yet, lexical diversity does not seem to be a plausible explanation here since the number of different adjectives used in the construction is almost exactly the same in the two corpora.

Table 1: Type-token distribution of adjectives in *it* BE ADJ *that* in Josef_1750k and Non24_1750k

Corpus	Adj.: Types	Adj.: Tokens	TTR
Josef_1750k	69	585	0.12
Non24_1750k	61	288	0.21

---

7 Variation in the tenses of the verb BE will probably be determined by the context only.
8 The DBCC was tagged with Stanford Log-linear Part-Of-Speech Tagger (Toutanova et al. 2003).

Interestingly, if we look at the type-token distribution of adjectives within the construction, it turns out to be Zipfian in both corpora as approximately linear log-log plots show (Figures 2 and 3), where the slope (y) is close to −1 and coefficient of determination (r^2) is close to +1.

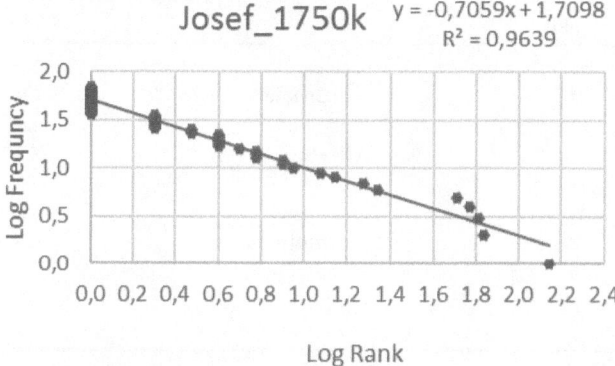

Figure 2: Type-token frequency distribution of adjectives in the *it* BE ADJ *that* in Josef_1750k

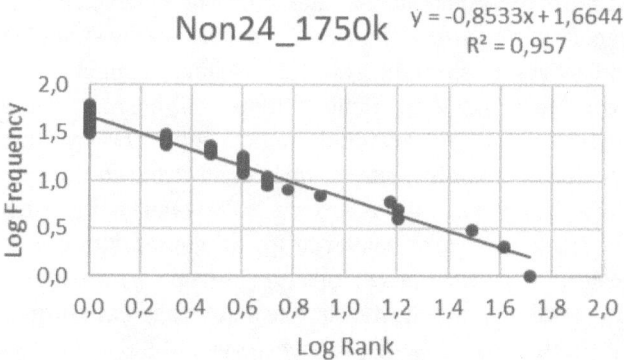

Figure 3: Type-token frequency distribution of adjectives in *it* BE ADJ *that* in Non24_1750k

Looking closer at frequency ranked lists of the 10 most frequent adjectives in each of the two corpora (see Table 2), there are three aspects that become apparent: (1) the order in which different adjectives are preferred in Non 24 and Josef is different; (2) most frequent adjectives on Josef's list are much more frequent than most frequent adjectives on Non24 list[9] and (3) not all adjectives are shared between the two lists (the non-overlapping adjectives are marked in bold)[10].

Table 2: 10 Most frequent adjectives used in *it* BE ADJ *that* in Non24_1750k and Josef_1750k

Non24		Josef	
Adj.	Freq.	Adj.	Freq.
true	52	clear	139
clear	41	**plausible**	69
obvious	31	obvious	65
interesting	16	likely	59
possible	16	true	51
likely	15	unlikely	22
unlikely	8	**conceivable**	19
important	6	important	14
odd	5	good	12
sad	5	possible	9

In fact, both the overlap and the difference between the lists are interesting. In principle, if we assume that the choice of an adjective to fill the open slot in the construction is determined by grammatical rules only, the convergence of four thousand commenters from all parts of the world with Josef in the exhibited preference for certain adjectives is stunning. Even if we take a much more realistic view and acknowledge semantic restrictions, there still remains a large number of adjectives to choose from: for example, Francis et al. 1998 mention 249 different adjectives which commonly occur in this construction in English. So there is clearly a lot of coherence even in a very variable language use such as ELF use. At the same time, there is no evidence for an equilibrium either, such as would be expected in a usage-based scenario driven to its extreme where one's language use would be so adjusted to one's language exposure as to be a mere replica of it. In this case, Josef's preferences would have to reflect the communal average much closer. Yet, he clearly exhibits some individual preferences.

---

9 It is possible to argue that the main reason for the frequency difference between the most common adjectives on Josef's and Non24 lists is that Josef overall used the construction more often than it was used in Non24 (585 vs 288 occurrences). Yet, it is also possible to reverse the cause-effect explanation: Josef might have used the construction more often because some of the realisations of the construction, such as *it is clear that* and *it is plausible that* have become fixed and therefore come to mind easily adding up to other uses of the construction.

10 Further down the lists the proportion of non-overlapping adjectives increases. In the next 10 most frequent adjectives, it changes from 20% to 80% (i.e. 8 out of 10 adjectives are nor shared). Yet, since the frequencies of occurrence also decrease, this might be due to chance.

To interpret the distribution of preferences for adjectives in Non24 and Josef, it seems helpful to appreciate that the reasons why some adjectives attain high frequencies on each of the lists are different. *True*, *clear* and *obvious* are frequent in Non24 because they are most popular choices across different speakers. These are the choices different speakers converge on. The fact that all of them are on Josef's list supports this conclusion. In contrast, adjectives on Josef's list are likely to be the result of the process of fixing mentioned in Sections 2 and 3. That is, in frequent use of the construction Josef has started to associate it with specific adjectives. So instead of selecting an adjective from a (semantically) restricted set of variants, he has several adjectives which he commonly uses in the construction and which therefore come to mind first. The choice has changed from being abstract, colligational or that of a semantic preference, to verbatim, i.e. collocational. Such lexicalised realisations of the construction can further develop into separate multi-word units instead of being merely variants of the construction.

In search of further evidence of fixing in Josef's use, I will look at an extended pattern of the construction and in particular at the patterning of the adv. + adj. combinations within it. Again, in principle, allowing for a combination with an adverb should result in an even higher type-token ratio since the chances for recurrence of specific combinations become lower. As Table 3 shows, this is indeed the case for the Non24 corpus: the TTR becomes much closer to 1, meaning that there are a few combinations which occur more than once but there are much fewer of them. Interestingly, in Josef's case the picture is different: his TTR indeed becomes a bit higher than for single adjectives, but it still remains very low implying a lot of reuse of identical combinations.

Table 3: Type-token distribution of adv.+adj. combinations in *it* BE ADV+ADJ *that* in Josef_1750k and Non24_1750k

Corpus	Adv.+adj.: Types	Adv.+adj.: Tokens	TTR
Josef_1750k	167	635	0.26
Non24_1750k	110	180	0.61

Table 4 showing frequency ranked lists of 10 most frequent adv.+adj. combinations used in Josef_1750k and Non24_1750k confirms the conclusions drawn based on calculations of TTRs. There is clearly more divergence between what is common at the communal level and what Josef prefers. But perhaps the biggest difference is the fact that in contrast to Josef's use, there are no exceptionally frequent adv.+ adj. combinations in the Non24 corpus. In other words, Non24 does not exhibit any specific uses which have become conventional or popular at the communal level, and, therefore, *it* BE (ADV+) ADJ *that* indeed can be said to function at an abstracted level as a grammar pattern. In Josef's corpus, while there are some adverbs which combine with adjectives in the construction relatively freely, as a long tail of one-off occurrences suggests (n = 115), others form pretty fixed combinations. For example, *it's still true that* occurs 104 times which is almost as often as the most frequently chosen single adjective *clear* (*it's clear that,* n = 139). It is interesting to mention that both *it's still true that* and *it's clear that* in an overwhelming number of cases (n = 92 and n = 105, respectively) occur with the contracted form *it's*. This preference for a contracted over a non-contracted form which becomes set can also be regarded as an effect of the process of fixing the unit is undergoing. Such settling of a preference for a contracted form within a multi-word unit seems to be very similar to observations of phonetic reduction due to frequency effects (see e.g. Bybee 2006), but at the individual level.

Table 4: 10 Most frequent adv.+adj. combinations used in *it* BE ADV+ADJ *that* in Josef_1750k and Non24_1750k

Non24_1750k		Josef_1750k	
Adv.+adj.	Freq.	Adv.+adj.	Freq.
not true	11	**still true**	104
very clear	9	not true	82
more likely	7	very clear	65
not surprising	5	**very likely**	21
pretty clear	5	**also true**	18
certainly true	4	pretty clear	15
extremely unlikely	4	more likely	14
not obvious	4	**not shocking**	14
almost certain	3	not surprising	12
also clear	3	**totally obvious**	10

There are other trends which become visible in Table 4. First, the frequency difference between the most common adv.+adj. combinations on Josef's and Non24 lists becomes even more pointed suggesting indeed a qualitative difference between a realisation which happens to be used by several people in the case of Non24 and a fixed realisation which has in fact become a separate multi-word unit in Josef's case. And second, while Josef's individual patterns not shared with the Non24 are spread out on the frequency list and can be both very frequent as *it's still true that* and relatively infrequent, distinct patterns on the Non24 list are all at the end of the list, just as it was the case with single adjectives. This again suggests that the main determinant of the frequency distribution in Non24 is the popularity of the pattern which means that with the decrease in frequency a certain pattern is less and less likely to be popular with a specific speaker, like Josef in this case. In contrast, the main determinant of the frequency distribution in Josef's list is the cognitive strength of association, which in extreme cases can lead to the development of a separate multi-word unit (with presumably a separate cognitive representation).

Obviously, so far we have dealt with just one speaker who is also a non-native speaker. How generalisable are the observations? For this purpose, I will take 150k samples from five other speakers, in this case NSs of English, as well as 150k samples from Non24 and Josef for comparison purposes. Since it has become apparent from the analysis of Josef's use that a combination of adv.+adj. filling the slot in the *it* BE (ADV+) ADJ *that* construction can be just as frequent as a single adjective and form a fixed holistic pattern, like one "big word" (Ellis 1996: 111; Wray 2002:7), I will collapse adjectives and adv.+adj. combinations in one frequency ordered list for each corpus. Table 5 presents the results.

Table 5: 5 most frequent adj./adv.+adj. combinations across cognitive and communal corpora

C1/Freq.		C2/Freq.		C3/Freq.		C4/Freq.		C5/Freq.	
true	16	obvious	5	interesting	7	true	7	quite conceivable	12
likely	5	quite possible	5	unfortunate	5	amazing	3	true	8
clear	4	true	4	apparent	3	unfortunate	3	best	4
obvious	3	possible	3	clear	2	too bad	3	conceivable	4
possible	3	ironic	2	likely	2	clear	2	not true	4
TTR: 43/74 = 0.58		24/41 = 0.59		24/42 = 0.57		37/50 = 0.74		39/67 = 0.58	
Non24_150k		Non24_1750k		Josef150_1		Josef150_5		Josef_1750k	
obvious	5	true	52	likely	13	clear	20	clear	139
true	5	clear	41	clear	6	still true	15	still true	104
clear	3	obvious	31	plausible	6	plausible	10	not true	82
possible	3	interesting	16	true	6	not true	7	plausible	69
unlikely	3	possible	16	conceivable	4	obvious	6	obvious	65
28/45 = 0.62		171/468 = 0.37		43/85 = 0.51		40/117 = 0.34		236/1220 = 0.19	

Analysis of the data presented in Table 5 provides the following observations. First, just like Josef, most other commenters (4 out of 5) have individual preferences, which are not popular at the communal plane or with any other commenter in the table (non-overlapping slot fillers are marked in bold), which, together with the different ordering of preferences overall, makes their profiles distinct from the communal average. Also, very often in individual language use combinations of adv.+adj. are among the five most frequent slot fillers which supports the assumption that such combinations can become quite fixed and treated holistically as "one word". This does not happen at the communal level which means that such combinations usually stay as individual preferences. In fact it appears possible that when a new/separate multi-word unit is developing in an individual's language use, it attracts new components,[11] in this case a modifying adverb. Frequency lists of slot fillers taken from chronologically different samples of Josef's use, the first and the fifth 150k words, as well as the total 1750k words point to the possibility of such diachronic development. Josef's preferences in the fifth sample of 150k words are in general closer to his overall preferences counted for 1750k words. If we look at the development of preferences for the adjective *true* in particular, we will see that in the first 150k words it appears among the first five most frequent slot fillers for the construction. In the fifth sample, it already appears in combinations *still true* and *not true* which together make the occurrence of *true* almost four times as frequent as in the first sample. This gives tentative evidence that with increase in frequency of use, the pattern becomes more fixed and attracts new associations.

What does this lead us to? The interim conclusions we can draw so far is that individual languages seem to exhibit distinct preferences in their lexical patterning. This lexical patterning at the individual/cognitive plane also seems to be more fixed than the patterning at the communal plane. At the extreme, certain patterns at the cognitive plane appear to be lexicalised while corresponding patterns at the communal plane are schematic or grammatical. Therefore, the more abstracted patterning at the communal plane can be seen as emergent from the more specific patterns of the individual languages. That is, the patterning at the communal plane is not the sum of individual patterns, but is qualitatively different from them. This in fact is not surprising since the processes leading to lexical patterning at the two planes are different: convergence of individual speakers on certain popular patterns in the first case, and cognitive propensity to chunking and forming progressively stronger associations between chunk components with increase in frequency of use, in the second.

At the same time, there is indisputable similarity in the overall shape of the patterning between the two planes. This similarity can be viewed as evidence of the fractal structure of language, another property of complex systems, as it was put forward in Section 1. In other words, we can distinguish between the communal and the cognitive/individual planes of language representation but the relationship between them is fractal, i.e. individual language is a "reduced-size

---

[11] Acquisition of new components/associations, such as new collocations, colligations or semantic preferences, in a unit of meaning was discussed as part of the process of fixing in Vetchinnikova 2014.

copy" of language as represented at the communal plane. The processes at work at the communal and the cognitive planes are different but they result in similar patterning. Conformity of this patterning at both planes to Zipfian frequency distribution can be regarded as a symptom of such fractality.

In fact, as we know from previous research, Zipfian distributions seem to be pervasive in language. Zipf's law holds for frequency distribution of words in any single text in general (Zipf 1935; Manning and Schütze 1999 on Mark Twain's *Tom Sawyer*) and in any corpora (see Manning and Schütze 1999 on the Brown corpus), for type-token frequency distribution of verbs in verb argument constructions (Ellis and Ferreira-Junior 2009; Ellis and O'Donnell 2012; Ellis et al. 2014; see also Goldberg 2006) and for other types of frequency distributions at different levels of language representation (see e.g. Kretzschmar 2009). Researchers of language as a complex adaptive system have already referred to Zipf's law as an indication of the fractality of language when it is split into different levels or time scales. For example, Larsen-Freeman 1997 writes that: "[a]n example of the fractality of language can be seen in Zipf's power law connecting word rank and word frequency for many natural languages" (150). Ellis (2006) mentions Mandelbrot's fractal geometry when discussing language as emergent at all its levels, starting from neurological and physical. De Bot et al. (2013) argue for the "fractal approach to time and change" (207). In a similar vein, it seems reasonable to suggest then that the relationship between the communal and the cognitive can also be described by fractality.

In this study, Zipfian power law relationship was found to apply to the type-token frequency distribution of adjectives in the *it* BE ADJ *that* construction for Josef_1750k (cognitive plane) and Non24_1750k (communal plane). The distribution of adj./adj.+adv combinations in the construction in the rest of the cognitive corpora (C1 to C5) do not really fit Zipfian profile (see Appendix 2 for the log-log plots), but the reasons for this may be different. It is possible that there is simply not enough data in these individual cognitive corpora to produce clearly Zipfian distributions for specific constructions (yet, see the log-log plot for Josef's fifth 150k sample which yields a well-fitting Zipfian distribution). It is also possible that commenters C1 to C5 do not use the construction often enough for it to develop very fixed and frequently occurring preferences. It is clear though that the smaller the TTR, i.e. the less diversity the profile shows, the more the frequency distribution fits Zipfian power law relationship. Out of all the profiles, those of Non24_1750k, Josef1750k and Josef150k_5 provide best fits to Zipfian linear distributions (Josef150_5: $y = -1.05$; $r^2 = 0.96$; Josef1750k: $y = -0.88$; $r^2 = 0.94$; Non24_1750k: $y = -1.16$, $r^2 = 0.93$). It remains to be clarified in future studies which factors warrant a neat Zipfian distribution.

6 Chunking at communal vs. cognitive planes: evidence of fixing?

The analysis of the *it is* ADJ *that* construction has revealed two clear trends: the lack of a one-to-one relationship between the cognitive and the communal levels and a tendency for fixing in individual preferences. In this section, I would like to further test the hypothesis that lexical patterning at the cognitive plane is overall more fixed than at the communal plane. This hypothesis entails that individual language use should contain more chunks or lexical patterns, which also exhibit less variability, than observed at the communal plane. Therefore, to gauge the level of fixedness of a corpus, it is convenient to focus on lexical bundles (Biber et al. 1999) or immediate co-occurrences of four words.[12] In the following, I compare a cognitive corpus, Josef_1750k, to a communal corpus, Non24_1750k, in terms of the number of types and tokens of lexical bundles which occur at least 17 times, which approximates a commonly used threshold of 10 instances per million (Biber et al 1999; Conrad and Biber 2004; Biber 2009). To retrieve lexical bundles from the corpora, I use AntConc's Clusters/N-grams Tool (Anthony 2014). Table 6 presents the results of this comparison.

Table 6: Number of types and tokens of lexical bundles (freq. threshold = 17) in Josef_1750k and Non24_1750k

Corpus	Types (N)	Tokens (N)
Josef_1750k	1351	50,292
Non24_1750k	550	17,747

As Table 6 shows, there are 2.5 times more different types of bundles in Josef_1750k compared to Non24_1750k. Such frequent bundles also occur 2.8 time more often in Josef's use than at the communal plane. These results seem to support the hypothesis: there are more fixed lexical patterns at the cognitive plane, as Josef's use suggests, than at the communal plane. Yet, it is certainly possible that this is an idiosyncratic feature of Josef's use. To test this possibility, I take five more individual samples of comments data each equalling 150k words (C1 to C5) and retrieve lists of lexical bundles occurring at least five times from them. For these much smaller corpora, a frequency threshold of 10 per million would

---

[12] Please note that in this paper I am not interested in the properties of lexical bundles as such but the phenomenon of verbatim co-occurrence. Thus, I will use the term only in the methodological sense, as a convenient tool.

mean that a lexical bundle needs to occur only once. Thus, a frequency threshold of 5 was chosen since it is in the mid-range between resulting in too many bundles as frequency thresholds of 2 and 3 do, and too few, as frequency thresholds of 9 and higher do. I also include Josef and Non24 in the comparison. To do this, I take five 150k samples from Non24_1750k and one sample from Josef_1750k, Josef_1, with the mean length of comments closest to the C1–C5 corpora (n = 114) (see Section 4 for details). Josef_1 also dates back to the very beginning of the blog which means that these are the first 150k words he wrote for this blog in comments making the selected sample closer to the samples of comment data from other contributors. Figure 4 shows the number of types of lexical bundles occurring at least five times across five communal (Non24_1 to Non24_5) and six cognitive corpora (Josef and Commenters 1 to 5).

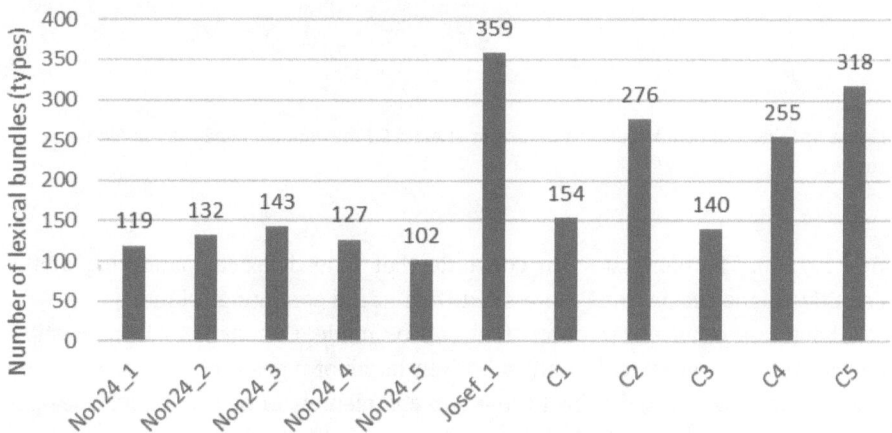

Figure 4: Types of lexical bundles occurring at least 5 times in communal and individual corpora

Figure 5, in turn, shows the number of tokens of lexical bundles occurring at least five times across five communal (Non24_1 to Non24_5) and six cognitive corpora (Josef and Commenters 1 to 5).

The two figures show that 1) cognitive corpora exhibit a greater variety of types and a larger number of tokens of lexical bundles than the communal corpora and 2) variation in the cognitive corpora is wider than in the communal (for types: SD_{com} = 15.34; SD_{cog} = 87.77; for tokens: SD_{com} = 101.72; SD_{cog} = 835.05). Yet, if the unequal variance t test (the Welch t test) is applied, the difference between the means of the two sets of data, communal and cognitive, is statistically significant (for types: two-tailed p = 0.0183; for tokens: two-tailed

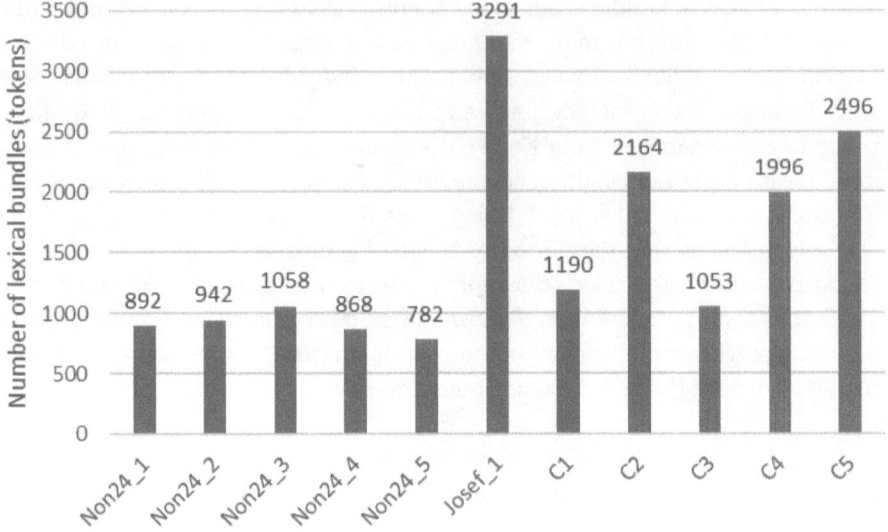

Figure 5: Tokens of lexical bundles occurring at least 5 times in communal and individual corpora

p = 0.0223). Therefore, we can conclude that indeed lexical patterning at the cognitive plane seems to be more fixed than at the communal plane.

There are other observations that can be made. Commenters 1 and 3 show substantially fewer lexical bundles both in terms of types and tokens. Based on SLA literature, we would expect these two commenters to be non-native speakers of English for many SLA studies on second language phraseology have been persistently demonstrating that "learners' phraseological skills are severely limited" (Granger 1998: 158) and that "the non-native speaker, however accurate in grammar and knowledgeable at the level of words, would always be a potential victim of that lesser store of formulaic sequences" (Wray 2002: 210). Yet, among the six individuals examined in this study, Josef is the only non-native speaker, and he is also the one showing the greatest variety and number of lexical bundles in his writing. Should we then make a conclusion that actually the situation with the use of multi-word units is the other way round: that it is the NNSs "who have a greater store of formulaic sequences"? Probably not, since in fact there is another variable involved which is rarely taken into account: the amount of practice in a certain genre. I have taken the first set of 150k words from Josef's comments, so what must make a difference is not the amount of writing he has done for the blog in total but the period of time in which he wrote his 150k words, the density of practice. For Josef this period of time is 15 months, for Commenters 1 and 3, who had smallest numbers of bundles, 40 and 72 months respectively, for Commenters C4 and C5, who had more bundles than C1 and C3 but less that Josef, 27 and 31 months respectively. Commenter C2 wrote his 150k words in the period of only 7 months. Pearson test shows that indeed there is a negative correlation between the time span of writing and the number of lexical bundles (for types, $r = -0.7752$; for tokens, $r = -0.7439$). Thus, a more plausible explanation of the numbers seems to be that lexical patterns get fixed with regular practice and do not so much depend on the native/non-native speaker status.

Section 6 has demonstrated further evidence to suggest that lexical patterning at the cognitive plane, i.e. in individual languages, is more fixed that at the communal. It is proposed that this happens due to the process of fixing in which associations between components of multi-word units strengthen in frequent use, up to becoming verbatim, and attract further associations which can also become entrenched with time.

7 Conclusions

In this paper, I have attempted to separate the communal and the cognitive/individual representation of language and examine the relationship between them. Modelling the two planes using complexity theory suggests that the relationship between them can be characterised by the properties of perpetual dynamics (continuous interaction), emergence and fractality or scale-free self-similarity. In other words, according to this view, the two planes are in constant interaction with each other, the communal plane emerges from the interaction of individual languages and is therefore qualitatively different from them, and the processes underlying language representation at each of the planes are different but lead to similar overall patterning.

Examination of the properties of chunking at the two planes seems to corroborate these predictions. It was observed that multi-word unit patterning at the communal plane is likely to result from averaging, while at the cognitive plane it is determined by the cognitive propensity to chunking and strengthening of internal associations with frequent use. In this way, multi-word unit patterning at the communal plane can be seen as emergent from individual preferences. At the same time, the frequency distribution of preferences is similar at both planes and seems to conform to Zipf's power law: it holds for both planes that while there are only a few very frequent preferences, the number of one-off occurrences is very large. This similarity of frequency distributions can be described as fractal.

The argument that language patterning at each of the two planes is qualitatively different is further supported by the evidence that lexical patterning at the cognitive plane seems to be more fixed than at the communal: all individuals examined in this paper use a greater variety and a higher number of lexical bundles, which are in essence immediate verbatim co-occurrences of four words, than identified at the communal plane. The reason why we see more four-word bundles at the cognitive plane might be that it contains quite many patterns which are very fixed. Since, presumably, each speaker has his/her own preferences for a particular variant of a pattern, cumulatively these preferences result in variation observable at the communal plane which also leads to fewer lexical bundles: thus, we can say, an *average* form of a pattern is less often fixed than a *cognitive* form.

As a possible avenue for further research, it seems pertinent to mention that the process of fixing in an individual's language use seems to be remarkably similar to the evolutionary processes leading to emergence of phraseological patterns, conventionalisation and grammaticalization observed in language change at the communal plane. Certainly, an item in an individual's use cannot go all the way toward becoming grammatical since this stage of grammaticalization requires diffusion and acceptance of a language community. However, if the process of grammaticalization is viewed as a continuum, then an item in an individual's use seems to be able to move along this continuum at least to the point of becoming non-compositional. The case of *it's still true that* is a good example of this. So the proposition that it is frequency which drives grammaticalization (Bybee and Hopper 2001; Bybee 2003) seems to have a lot of explanatory power. Growing frequency leads to chunking or, in other words, a switch to processing on the idiom rather than the open-choice principle, which in its turn leads to structural reanalysis (see e.g. Beckner and Bybee 2009) or in Sinclair's terms, delexicalisation and meaning-shift (see Cheng et al. 2009), which may or may not in the end lead to grammaticalization. This way, the processes observed in an individual's language use can be seen as micro-processes of language change which feed into macro-processes of language change observed at the communal plane. The fact that such micro-processes look remarkably similar to the macro-processes can be again described as scale-free self-similarity or fractal structure.

With respect to changing English, the importance of the processes underlying individual language use means that recent dramatic increase in second language use of English and especially ELF must inevitably have a visible impact at the communal plane. For example, if second language users are prone to approximation (Mauranen 2005, 2012), or communicatively unproblematic but slightly non-standard use of multi-word units, it is possible that these approximative uses can also get fixed in their repertoires (see also Mauranen this volume). As a hypothesis, this might lead to more distinct individual preferences resulting in more divergence between idiolects or wider inter-individual variation and eventually in more variability at the communal plane. Such variability will be an emergent property since it clearly does not characterise language use at the individual plane: both native and non-native individual languages were more fixed in their lexical patterning than the communal representation in this study and the extent of their fixedness depended on the density of practice rather than native or non-native speaker status. This fits well with previous research on ELF which describes it as highly variable language use.

For the discussion of the global and the local in changing English, this study therefore suggests two tentative hypotheses. First, if indeed current language use can be characterised by wider inter-individual variation, then idiolects gain more weight in language variation and change and thus present an interesting object of further research. Second, it seems promising to continue modelling language as a CAS on the social dimension, or that of spread. In this study, I have chosen the relatively safe option of exploring the relationship between individual languages and the communal representation of discourse in which these individual languages participate. Modelling Global English as the communal plane and identifying the component parts from whose interaction it emerges certainly present more challenges as well as intriguing possibilities for further research. I hope this study can serve as a step in this direction.[13]

References

Anderson, Richard C. & Peter Freebody. 1981. Vocabulary knowledge. In John T. Guthrie (ed.), *Comprehension and teaching: Research reviews*, 77–117. Newark, DE: International Reading Association.

Anthony, Laurence. 2014. AntConc (Version 3.4.3w) [Computer Software]. Tokyo, Japan: Waseda University. Available from http://www.antlab.sci.waseda.ac.jp/

Arppe, Antti, Gaëtanelle Gilquin, Dylan Glynn, Martin Hilpert & Arne Zeschel. 2010. Cognitive Corpus Linguistics: five points of debate on current theory and methodology. *Corpora* 5(1). 1–27.

Barlow, Michael. 2013. Individual differences and usage-based grammar. *International Journal of Corpus Linguistics* 18(4). 443–478.

---

[13] I would like to thank the author of the blog used in this study for generously providing his blog data for research purposes. I am also grateful to Ray Carey† and Nina Mikusova for their help in preparing the data for corpus linguistic analysis. Special thanks to all the readers for their valuable comments on different versions of this paper.

Beckner, Clay & Joan Bybee. 2009. A usage-based account of constituency and reanalysis. *Language Learning* 59(1). 27–46.
Beckner, Clay, Richard Blythe, Joan Bybee, Morten H. Christiansen, William Croft, Nick C. Ellis, John Holland, Jinyun Ke, Diane Larsen-Freeman & Tom Schoenemann. 2009. Language is a complex adaptive system: Position paper. *Language learning* 59(s1). 1–26.
Biber, Douglas. 1988. *Variation across speech and writing*. Cambridge: Cambridge University Press.
Biber, Douglas. 2009. A corpus-driven approach to formulaic language in English: Multi-word patterns in speech and writing. *International Journal of Corpus Linguistics* 14(3). 275–311.
Biber, Douglas et al. 1999. *Longman grammar of spoken and written English*. London: Longman.
Bock, Kathryn J. & William F. Brewer. 1974. Reconstructive recall in sentences with alternative surface structures. *Journal of Experimental Psychology* 103(5). 837–843.
Bybee, Joan & Paul Hopper. 2001. *Frequency and the emergence of linguistic structure*. Amsterdam, Philadelphia: John Benjamins.
Bybee, Joan. 2002. Sequentiality as the basis of constituent structure. In Talmy Givón & Bertram Malle (eds.), *The evolution of language from pre-language*, 109–32. Amsterdam: John Benjamins.
Bybee, Joan. 2003. Mechanisms of change in grammaticalization: The role of frequency. In Brian D. Joseph & Richard D. Janda (eds.), *The handbook of historical linguistics*, 602–623. Malden (MA): Blackwell.
Bybee, Joan. 2006. From usage to grammar: The mind's response to repetition. *Language* 82(4). 711–733.
Bybee, Joan. 2010. *Language, usage and cognition*. Cambridge: Cambridge University Press.
Bybee, Joan. 2012. Domain-general processes as the basis for grammar. In Maggie Tallerman & Kathleen R. Gibson (eds.), *The Oxford Handbook of Language Evolution*, 528–536. Oxford: Oxford University Press.
Carey, Ray. 2013. On the other side: Formulaic organizing chunks in spoken and written academic ELF. *Journal of English as a Lingua Franca* 2(2). 207–228
Carter, Ronald & Michael McCarthy. 2006. *Cambridge grammar of English: A comprehensive guide*. Cambridge: Cambridge University Press.
Charles, Maggie. 2004. *The construction of stance: A corpus-based investigation of two contrasting disciplines*. University of Birmingham. Unpublished PhD thesis,
Cheng, Winnie, Chris Greaves, John McH. Sinclair & Martin Warren. 2009. Uncovering the extent of the phraseological tendency: Towards a systematic analysis of concgrams. *Applied Linguistics* 30(2). 236–252.
Conrad, Susan & Douglas Biber. 2004. The frequency and use of lexical bundles in conversation and academic prose. *Lexicographica* 20. 56–71.
Coulthard, Malcolm. 2004. Author Identification, Idiolect, and Linguistic Uniqueness. *Applied Linguistics* 25(4). 431–447.
de Bot, Kees, Wander Lowie & Marjolijn Verspoor. 2007. A dynamic systems theory approach to second language acquisition. *Bilingualism: Language and Cognition* 10(1). 7–21.
de Bot, Kees & Diane Larsen-Freeman. 2013. Researching second language development from a dynamic systems theory perspective. In Marjolijn Verspoor, Kees de Bot & Wander Lowie (eds.), *A dynamic approach to second language development: Methods and techniques*, 5–23. Amsterdam; Philadelphia: John Benjamins.
de Bot, Kees, Wander Lowie, Steven L. Thorne & Marjolijn Verspoor. 2013. Dynamic systems theory as a theory of second language development. In María del Pilar García Mayo, María

Junkal Gutiérrez Mangado & María Martínez Adrián (eds.), *Contemporary approaches to second language acquisition*, 199–220. Amsterdam: John Benjamins.

Durrant, Philip & Alice Doherty. 2010. Are high-frequency collocations psychologically real? Investigating the thesis of collocational priming. *Corpus Linguistics and Linguistic Theory* 6(2).

Ellis, Nick C. 1996. Sequencing in SLA: Phonological memory, chunking and points of order. *Studies in Second Language Acquisition* 18. 91–126.

Ellis, Nick C. 2003. Constructions, chunking, and connectionism: The emergence of second language structure. In Catherine J. Doughty & Michael H. Long (eds.), *The handbook of second language acquisition*, 63–103. Oxford: Blackwell.

Ellis, Nick C. 2006. Cognitive perspectives on SLA: The associative-cognitive CREED. *AILA Review* 19(1). 100–121.

Ellis, Nick C. 2011. The emergence of language as a complex adaptive system. In James Simpson (ed.), *The Routledge handbook of applied linguistics*, 666–679. London: Routledge.

Ellis, Nick C. & Diane Larsen-Freeman. 2006. Language emergence: Implications for Applied Linguistics–Introduction to the special issue. *Applied Linguistics* 27(4). 558–589.

Ellis, Nick C. & Eric Frey. 2009. The psycholinguistic reality of collocation and semantic prosody (2): Affective priming. In Roberta Corrigan, Edith Moravcsik, Hamid Ouali & Kathleen Wheatley (eds.), *Formulaic language (vol. 2): Acquisition, loss, psychological reality, and functional explanations* [Typological Studies in Language, 83], 473–497. Amsterdam: John Benjamins.

Ellis, Nick C., Eric Frey, & Isaac Jalkanen. 2009. The psycholinguistic reality of collocation and semantic prosody (1): Lexical access. In Ute Römer & Rainer Schulze (eds.), *Exploring the lexis-grammar interface* [Studies in Corpus Linguistics, 35], 89–114. Amsterdam: John Benjamins.

Ellis, Nick C. & Fernando Ferreira–Junior. 2009. Construction learning as a function of frequency, frequency distribution, and function. *The Modern Language Journal* 93(3). 370–385.

Ellis, Nick C. & Matthew Brook O'Donnell. 2012. Robust language acquisition: An emergent consequence of language as a complex adaptive system. In Patrick Rebuschat & John M. Williams (eds.), *Statistical learning and language acquisition, vol. 1* [Studies in Second and Foreign Language Education], 265–304. Berlin; Boston: De Gruyter Mouton.

Ellis, Nick C., Matthew Brook O'Donnell & Ute Römer. 2014. The processing of verb-argument constructions is sensitive to form, function, frequency, contingency and prototypicality. *Cognitive Linguistics* 25(1).

Fletcher, William H. 2002. *Phrases in English.* http://phrasesinenglish.org/ (last accessed 23 April 2015).

Francis, Gill, Susan Hunston & Elizabeth Manning. 1998. *Collins COBUILD Grammar Patterns: Nouns and adjectives*. London: HarperCollins.

Francis, Gill. 1993. A corpus-drive approach to grammar: Principles, methods and examples. In Mona Baker, Gill Francis & Elena Tognini-Bonelli (eds.), *Text and technology: In honour of John Sinclair*, 137–156. Amsterdam: John Benjamins.

Gilquin, Gaëtanelle & Stefan Th. Gries. 2009. Corpora and experimental methods: A state-of-the-art review. *Corpus Linguistics & Linguistic Theory* 5(1). 1–26.

Gleick, James. 1987. *Chaos: Making a new science*. New York: Viking.

Goldberg, Adele. 2006. *Constructions at work*. Oxford: Oxford University Press.

Granger, Sylviane. 1998. Prefabricated patterns in advanced EFL writing: Collocations and formulae. In Anthony P. Cowie (ed.), *Phraseology: Theory, analysis, and applications*, 145–160. Oxford: Clarendon.

Greaves, Chris. 2009. *ConcGram 1.0: A phraseological search engine* [Software]. Amsterdam: John Benjamins.
Gries, Stefan Th. 2013. 50-something years of work on collocations: What is or should be next.... *International Journal of Corpus Linguistics* 18(1). 137–166.
Gries, Stefan Th. & Anatol Stefanowitsch (eds). 2006. *Corpora in Cognitive Linguistics: Corpus-based approaches to syntax and lexis.* Berlin: Mouton de Gruyter.
Grondelaers, Stefan, Dirk Geeraerts and Dirk Speelman. 2007. A case for a cognitive corpus linguistics. In Monica Gonzalez-Marquez, Irene Mittelberg, Seana Coulson & Michael J. Spivey (eds.), *Methods in Cognitive Linguistics*, 149–169. Amsterdam: John Benjamins.
Groom, Nicholas. 2005. Pattern and meaning across genres and disciplines: An exploratory study. *Journal of English for Academic Purposes* 4(3). 257–277.
Gurevich, Olga, Matthew A. Johnson & Adele E. Goldberg. 2010. Incidental verbatim memory for language. *Language and Cognition* 2(1). 45–78.
Hoey, Michael. 2005. *Lexical priming: A new theory of words and language.* London: Routledge.
Hopper, Paul J. 1987. Emergent grammar. *Berkeley Linguistics Society* 13. 139–57.
Hopper, Paul J. 2011. Emergent grammar and temporality in interactional linguistics. In Peter Auer & Stefan Pfänder (eds.), *Constructions: Emerging and emergent*, 22–44. Berlin: De Gruyter Mouton.
Hunston, Susan. 2007. Semantic prosody revisited. *International Journal of Corpus Linguistics* 12(2). 249–268.
Hunston, Susan. 2008. Starting with the small words: Patterns, lexis and semantic sequences. *International Journal of Corpus Linguistics* 13(3). 271–295.
Hunston, Susan. 2010. Starting with the small words. In Ute Römer & Rainer Schulze (eds.), *Patterns, meaningful units and specialized discourses*, 7–30. Amsterdam; Philadelphia: John Benjamins.
Hunston, Susan & Gill Francis. 2000. *Pattern grammar.* Amsterdam: John Benjamins.
Hunston, Susan & John McH. Sinclair. 2000. A local grammar of evaluation. In Susan Hunston & Geoff Thompson (eds.), *Evaluation in text: Authorial stance and the construction of discourse*, 74–101. Oxford: Oxford University Press.
Kretzschmar, William A. 2009. *Linguistics of speech.* Cambridge: Cambridge University Press.
Larsen-Freeman, Diane. 1997. Chaos/complexity science and second language acquisition. *Applied Linguistics* 18(2). 141–165.
Larsen-Freeman, Diane. 2013. Complexity Theory/Dynamic systems theory. In Peter Robinson (ed.), *The Routledge encyclopaedia of Second Language Acquisition*, 103–106. New York: Routledge.
Larsen-Freeman, Diane & Lynne Cameron. 2008. *Complex systems and Applied Linguistics.* Oxford: Oxford University Press.
Mandelbrot, Benoit B. 1963. The variation of certain speculative prices. *The Journal of Business* 36(4). 394–419.
Mandelbrot, Benoit B. 1982. *The fractal geometry of nature. 1 edition.* San Francisco: W. H. Freeman and Company.
Manning, Christopher D. & Hinrich Schütze. 1999. *Foundations of statistical natural language processing.* Cambridge, Massachusetts: MIT Press.
Mauranen, Anna. 2005. English as a Lingua Franca – an unknown language? In Giuseppina Cortese & Anna Duszak (eds.), *Identity, community, discourse: English in intercultural settings*, 269–293. Frankfurt: Peter Lang.
Mauranen, Anna. 2009. Chunking in ELF: Expressions for managing interaction. *Journal of Intercultural Pragmatics* 6(2). 217–233.

Mauranen, Anna. 2012. *Exploring ELF: Academic English shaped by non-native speakers*. Cambridge: Cambridge University Press.
Mauranen, Anna. 2013. Hybridism, edutainment, and doubt: Science blogging finding its feet. *Nordic Journal of English Studies* 12(1). 7–36. (23 September, 2014).
Mauranen, Anna. Forthcoming. *Reflexively speaking: Uses of metadiscourse in ELF*. Berlin: De Gruyter Mouton.
Molenaar, Peter C. M. 2004. A manifesto on psychology as idiographic science: Bringing the person back into scientific psychology, this time forever. *Measurement: Interdisciplinary Research and Perspectives* 2(4). 201–218.
Molenaar, Peter C. M. 2008. On the implications of the classical ergodic theorems: Analysis of developmental processes has to focus on intra-individual variation. *Developmental Psychobiology* 50(1). 60–69.
Molenaar, Peter C. M. & Cynthia G. Campbell. 2009. The new person-specific paradigm in psychology. *Current Directions in Psychological Science* 18(2). 112–117.
Mollin, Sandra. 2009a. Combining corpus linguistic and psychological data on word co-occurrences: Corpus collocates versus word associations. *Corpus Linguistics and Linguistic Theory* 5(2).
Mollin, Sandra. 2009b. "I entirely understand" is a Blairism: The methodology of identifying idiolectal collocations. *International Journal of Corpus Linguistics* 14(3). 367–392.
Pawley, Andrew & Frances H. Syder. 1983. Two puzzles for linguistic theory: Nativelike selection and nativelike fluency. In Jack C. Richards & Richard W. Schmidt (eds.), *Language and communication*, 191–227. London: Longman.
Quirk, Randolph, Sidney Greenbaum, Geoffrey Leech, & Jan Svartvik. 1985. *A comprehensive grammar of the English language*. Harlow: Longman.
Raumolin-Brunberg, Helena & Arja Nurmi. 2011. Grammaticalization and language change in the individual. In Heiko Narrog & Bernd Heine (eds.), *The Oxford Handbook of Grammaticalization*, 251–262. Oxford: Oxford University Press.
Read, John. 2004. Plumbing the depths: How should the construct of vocabulary be defined? In Paul Bogaards & Batia Laufer (eds.), *Vocabulary in a second language: Selection, acquisition, and testing*, 209–226. Philadelphia, PA, USA: John Benjamins.
Renouf, Antoinette & John McH. Sinclair. 1991. Collocational frameworks in English. In Karin Aijmer & Bengt Altenberg (eds.), *English corpus linguistics: Studies in honour of Jan Svartvik*, 128–143. London: Longman.
Schumann, John H. 2014. Foreword. In Dörnyei, Zoltán, Alastair Henry & Peter D. MacIntyre (eds.), *Motivational dynamics in language learning*, xv- xix. Bristol: Multilingual Matters.
Sinclair, John McH. 1987. Collocation: A progress report. In Ross Steele & Terry Treadgold (eds.), *Language topics: Essays in honour of Michael Halliday*, 319–331. Amsterdam: John Benjamins.
Sinclair, John McH. 1996. The search for units of meaning. *Textus* 9(1). 75–106.
Sinclair, John McH. 2004. *Trust the text*. London: Routledge.
Stubbs, Michael. 2007. An example of frequent English phraseology: Distributions, structures and functions. In Roberta Facchinetti (ed.), *Corpus Linguistics 25 years on*, 89–106. Amsterdam and New York: Rodopi.
Tomasello, Michael. 2003. *Constructing a language: A usage-based theory of language acquisition*. Cambridge (MA): Harvard University Press.
Toutanova, Kristina, Dan Klein, Christopher D. Manning & Yoram Singer. 2003. *Feature-rich Part-of-speech Tagging with a Cyclic Dependency Network. Proceedings of the 2003 Conference of the North American Chapter of the Association for Computational Linguistics on*

Human Language Technology – Volume 1, 173–180. (NAACL '03). Stroudsburg, PA, USA: Association for Computational Linguistics.
van Geert, Paul. 2011. The contribution of complex dynamic systems to development. *Child Development Perspectives* 5(4). 273–278.
Vetchinnikova, Svetlana. 2014. *Second language lexis and the idiom principle*. Unigrafia: Helsinki.
Weinreich, Uriel. 1953. *Language in contact: Findings and problems*. New York: Linguistic Circle.
Wray, Alison. 2002. *Formulaic language and the lexicon*. Cambridge: Cambridge University Press.
Wright, David. 2015. Testing the theory of idiolect. Paper presented at the BAAL Annual Meeting "Breaking theory: New directions in Applied Linguistics", Birmingham, September 3–5.
Zipf, George K. 1935. *The psycho-biology of language: An introduction to dynamic philology*. Cambridge, MA: MIT Press.

Databases

BNC: The British National Corpus. http://bncweb.lancs.ac.uk/

Appendix 1

Subsets of the Diachronic Blog Community Corpus (the DBCC) used in the study

Corpus	Corpus size	N of comments	Mean length[14]	MAX length	N of short comments (< 5 words)		N of long comments (> 500 words)	
					N	%	N	%
Non24_1	150401	1673	90	525	36	2,2	10	0,6
Non24_2	150164	1598	94	554	37	2,3	16	1,0
Non24_3	150234	1556	97	1869	33	2,1	18	1,2
Non24_4	150488	1472	102	539	25	1,7	11	0,7
Non24_5	150212	1726	87	571	16	0,9	10	0,6
Josef_1	150287	1313	114	538	8	0,6	11	0,8
Josef_2	150299	1111	135	529	4	0,4	11	1,0
Josef_3	150962	906	167	1554	0	0,0	48	5,3
Josef_4	150786	551	274	1695	1	0,2	90	16,3
Josef_5	150486	959	157	520	4	0,4	4	0,4
C1	150156	1442	104	507	9	0,6	1	0,1
C2	150445	2215	68	504	46	2,1	1	0,0
C3	150162	2051	73	724	26	1,3	4	0,2
C4	150435	2126	71	817	43	2,0	5	0,2
C5	150157	1716	88	1171	2	0,1	4	0,2

---

14 Pearson test shows only a weak correlation between the mean length of a comment and the number of lexical bundles retrieved from a corpus (for types r = −0.0021; for tokens r = 0.0781).

Appendix 2

Logarithmic plots of type-token frequency distributions of adj./adv.+adj. combinations in the *it* BE ADJ (+ADV) *that* construction across cognitive and communal corpora

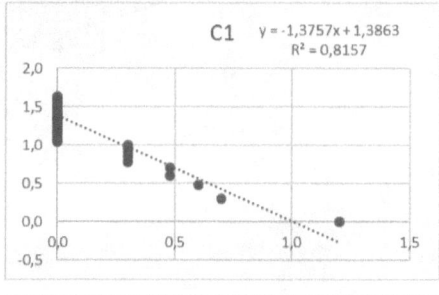

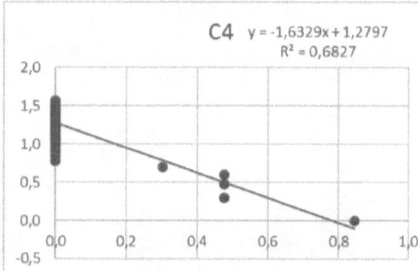

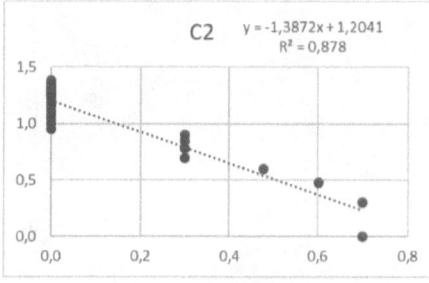

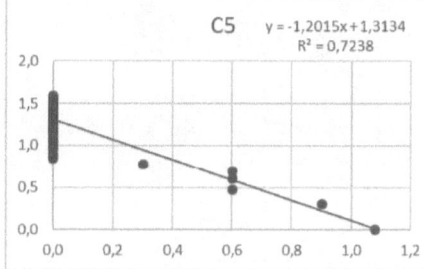

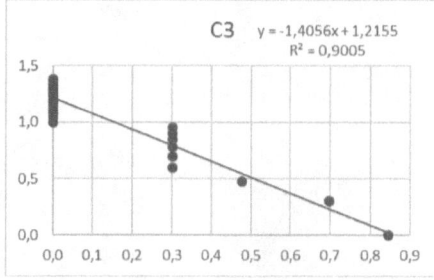

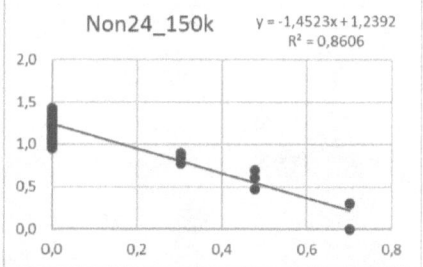

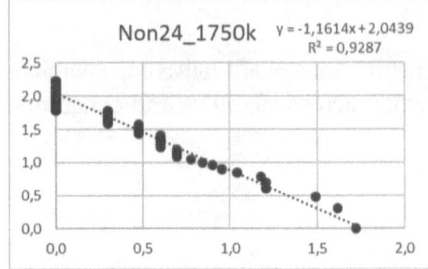
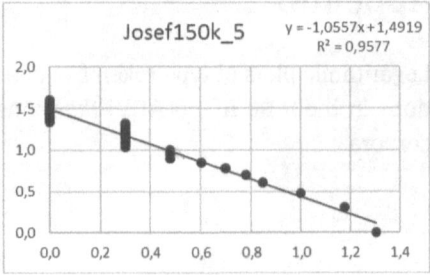
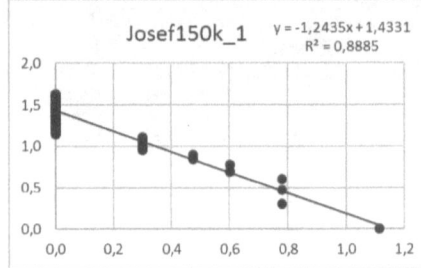
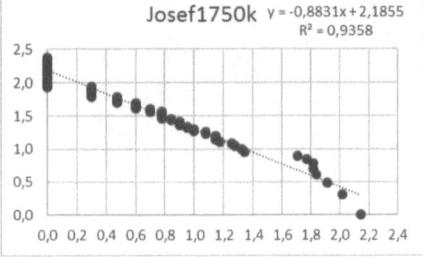

Zhiming Bao
Transfer is Transfer; Grammaticalization is Grammaticalization

Abstract: It is well-known that languages borrow not only words but also grammatical constructions. The latter is known as substratum transfer. One central question in contact-induced grammatical change is whether substratum transfer can be reduced to grammaticalization. Heine and Kuteva (2003, 2005) argue that it can, citing examples such as the Irish English *after*-perfect, among others. In this paper, I examine the grammar of *one* in Singapore English, which has acquired novel grammatical meanings from Chinese *de*. On the basis of speaker intuition, *one* parallels *de*, which can be accounted for in terms of parallel grammaticalization. Usage tells a different story. The usage data obtained through ICE-SIN (ca. 1990) and SCoRE (ca. 2005) reveal a marked decline in token counts of the Chinese-derived functions over the 15 year period that separates the two spoken Singapore English corpora. I argue that the data are consistent with post-transfer stabilization, a process in which English, the lexifier, plays an important role.

Keywords: Singapore English, substrate-driven grammatical change, transfer, appropriation, Chinese *de* construction, Singapore English *one* construction, replica grammaticalization, parallel grammaticalization, contact ecology

1 The issue

Substrate-driven grammatical change is a phenomenon well-known among students of language contact. How to characterize and explain the phenomenon is a matter of intense and fractious debate in the contact linguistics literature. Many theories have been proposed to account for the presence in the contact language of grammatical features which are demonstrably derived from the languages which are part of its contact ecology and thus contribute to its emergence and development. Inevitably the contact-theoretic models are informed by various formal linguistic theories and built on different assumptions about the nature of the contact ecology and the relative weight assigned to the factors

---

Zhiming Bao, National University of Singapore

DOI 10.1515/9783110429657-016

that contribute to the success or failure of grammatical features derived from the linguistic substratum in the contact language.

There is no doubt that contact languages of all sorts, be they pidgins, creoles or New Englishes, contain grammatical features obtained from the languages in their respective contact ecologies. One central question is how such grammatical features enter the contact language. The common descriptive terms include TRANSFER, when the said feature transfers from the source to the contact language, or APPROPRIATE, when the contact language appropriates the said feature into its own grammar. While substratist theories tend to see substrate influence in terms of transfer,[1] superstratist theories see it in terms of appropriation. The difference is not just a simple matter of perspective – the former from the perspective of the substrate language and the latter that of the lexifier. It reflects how the contact language itself is viewed. Substratists tend to see it through the prism of broken transmission (Thomason and Kaufman 1988) or typological convergence (Keesing 1988; Lefebvre 1998; Siegel 1999, 2008), whereas superstratists tend to see it as a dialect of the lexifier (Mufwene 1996, 2001; Chaudenson 2001), rejecting the claim of broken transmission. In terms of formal mechanisms of substratum transfer, there have been many proposals, including phonological relabeling (Muysken 1981; Lefebvre 1998), surface congruence (Siegel 1999, 2008), pivot-and-match (Matras and Sakal 2007), and transfer and filter (Bao 2005, 2009, 2010). Although they differ in theoretical orientation and formal approach, these accounts all consider substratum transfer as an independent mechanism by which substrate grammatical features enter the contact language. In this respect, they differ from Heine and Kuteva (2003, 2005), who approach substratum transfer from the perspective of grammaticalization. Grammatical borrowings are no different from the normal process of grammaticalization, whether a lexifier morphosyntactic construction acquires a single grammatical meaning, or multiple grammatical meanings, from the linguistic substratum.

In what follows, I discuss the grammar and usage of the pronominal *one* in Singapore English, which is based on Chinese *de*, and show that transfer is not reducible to grammaticalization. By transfer or substratum transfer, I mean the

---

1 In this paper, I use the term *transfer* to refer broadly to the phenomenon that lexical and grammatical features from one language are found in another, genetically unrelated, language. We will not distinguish between the transfer of lexical items, or lexical borrowing, and the transfer of grammatical features, or interference (Weinreich 1964; Thomason and Kaufman 1988). There have been attempts to link contact language to interlanguage in the literature on second language acquisition (Mufwene 1990; Siegel 2008). Here we will not be concerned with the approach to transfer in second language acquisition. Suffice it to say that substrate-derived grammatical features in general, and the *one* construction in particular, are not attributable to the structural properties in the interlanguage or interlanguages of second language learners.

process in the mind of the erstwhile creator-developer of the contact language by which the morphosyntactic resources of one language (the lexifier) are used to exponence the grammatical constructions of another (the substratum). So, it is essentially a tripartite relationship among the contact language, the lexifier, and the substrate language. I have argued elsewhere (Bao 2005, 2012) that substratum transfer targets the grammatical system. It involves the following steps, stated in the style of Heine and Kuteva (2003, 2005):

(1) a. Speakers of the substrate language identify a grammatical system in the substrate language;

b. They use the morphosyntactic resources of the lexifier language to exponence the targeted grammatical subsystem;

c. The component features of the targeted system that can be exponenced will emerge in the contact language;

d. The component features of the targeted system that cannot be exponenced will be filtered out of the contact language;

e. Post-transfer stabilization is subject to the interaction between the contributing languages, and linguistic universals.

In this paper, I argue two main points. First, there is no known grammaticalization process that is responsible for the multiple grammatical meanings of the Chinese *de* construction, the substrate source for the novel meanings of the Singapore English *one* construction. In fact, the purported multi-functionality of *de* is an artifact of our analysis of the English morphosyntax of *one*, as we shall see. Second, I show that the usage pattern of *one* in two separate corpora constructed over a 20-year span suggests that the various morphosyntactic frames of the *one* construction emerge together at once, which are then subjected to post-transfer stabilization, as described in (1). In other words, the usage pattern is contrary to the prediction of replica grammaticalization.

2 Replica grammaticalization

Heine and Kuteva (2003, 2005) recognize two types of contact-induced grammaticalization, which they call ordinary grammaticalization and replica grammaticalization. The former deals with a single substrate-derived grammatical meaning, whereas the latter deals with multiple grammatical meanings that result from some grammaticalization chain presumed to have taken place in the substrate source. In this paper, we will focus on replica grammaticalization. In their account, instead of individual grammatical categories or meanings associated with a given construction, the proverbial creator-developer of the contact language targets the grammaticalization process that produces the meanings. The targeting takes the following form (Heine and Kuteva 2003: 539) (R, recipient; M, model):

(2) Replica grammaticalization
    a. Speakers of language R notice that in language M there is a grammatical category Mx.
    b. They develop an equivalent category Rx, using material available in their own language (R).
    c. To this end, they replicate a grammaticalization process they assume to have taken place in language M, using an analogical formula of the kind [My > Mx] = [Ry > Rx].
    d. They grammaticalize category Ry to Rx.

Central to the operation is (2c), which extends the grammatical polysemy of a feature in the model language (the substrate language) to an equivalent feature in the recipient language (the contact language). Substratum transfer is reduced to replica grammaticalization. Bruyn (1996, 2009) proposed a similar model, calling it parallel grammaticalization.

Heine and Kuteva (2003, 2005) cite a rich array of cases that can be given an analysis along the lines outlined in (2). We will discuss two cases familiar in the literature, the so-called hot-news perfect in Irish English and the perfect and focus marker *nao* in Solomons Pijin. The Irish hot-news perfect has been studied extensively (Harris 1991; Filppula 1999). The data below are cited from Heine and Kuteva (2003: 540):

(3) a. Irish
    tá   sí   tréis   an   bád   a dhíol.
    be:NON-PAST   she   after   the   boat   selling
    'She has just sold the boat.'

    b. Irish English
    She's after selling the boat.
    'She has just sold the boat.'

In Irish, the locative preposition *tréis* 'after' is used to express the meaning of hot-news perfect. The bilingual speakers of Irish and English replicate the

Irish *tréis*-grammaticalization, thereby attributing the same aspectual meaning to *after* in Irish English.

In Solomons Pijin, *nao* (< now) marks both the perfect aspect and the topic, as shown in (4) (Keesing 1991: 320–321):

(4) a. Perfect
 Kwaio: e 'akwa no'o
 he run away PRF
 'He has run away.'

 Solomons Pijin: hem-i runawe nao
 'He has run away.'

 b. Topic
 Kwaio: gila no'o la age-a
 them TOP they do-it
 'They are the ones who did it.'

 Solomons Pijin: hem nao i save
 he TOP he know
 'He's the one who knows.'

According to Keesing (1988, 1991), *no'o* has undergone the grammaticalization process from perfect marker to topic marker in Kwaio, and indeed in other indigenous languages of Melanesia. The dual grammatical meanings of *no'o* are calqued in Solomons Pijin as *nao*, which is derived from English *now* on account of phonological similarity.[2] However, for lack of historical evidence this remains a conjecture. In Heine and Kuteva's (2003) account, Solomons Pijin replicates the perfect-to-topic grammaticalization through analogical reasoning (2c), which can be represented as follows:

(5) no'o (perfect) > no'o (topic) = nao (perfect) > nao (topic)

See Matras and Sakal (2007), Gast and Auwera (2012), and Ziegeler (2013) for critiques and elaborations of the grammaticalization account of contact-induced grammatical borrowing.

---

[2] It is possible to see *nao* as a direct borrowing of *no'o*, rather than as a result of English *now* being drafted to express the grammatical meanings of *no'o*. If so, the point-by-point identity between *nao* and *no'o* needs no explanation. This sort of grammatical borrowing is not uncommon in contact languages that emerge in areas with extensive bilingualism. For example, Daohua, a product of Tibetan-Chinese contact, borrows the Tibetan case marking system in its entirety; see Acuo (2001).

There is no doubt that some of the substrate influences discussed in the literature can be given a grammaticalization analysis modeled on an established or assumed grammaticalization process in the substrate source. The case for Irish English hot-news perfect is strong, given the fact that modern scholarship has clearly shown the trajectory of the hot-news perfect in Irish and subsequently in Irish English (Filppula 1999). The analysis of Solomons Pijin *no'o* requires a leap of faith in that we have to accept Keesing's (1988) conjecture that Kwaio has completed the perfect-to-focus grammaticalization in *no'o*. The process, for which Keesing (1988) offers no historical evidence, relies on phonological similarity in the modern language rather than on known cognitive motivations or actual historical trajectories involving the perfect; see, for example, Bybee, Perkins and Pagliuca (1994).

We now proceed to examine the *one* construction in Singapore English and the *de* construction in Chinese.

3 The functional range of Singapore English *one*

In Singapore English, it has been shown that the pronominal *one* has acquired novel grammatical meanings from Chinese (Gupta 1992; Alsagoff and Ho 1998; Brown 1999; Lim 2004; Bao 2009). In addition to the pronominal uses which are inherited from English, *one* has two additional grammatical functions, as a pronominal with an expanded range and as a marker of emphasis. These are exemplified below, adapted from Bao (2009: 342).

(6)   frame   example
     a.   A-one   large *one*
     b.   N-one   silk *one*
     c.   P-one   my *one*
     d.   XP-one   i.   PP-*one*
                                      from Thailand *one*
                                      'one from Thailand'
                            ii.   VP-*one*
                                      showing in Cathay *one*
                                      'one which is showing in Cathay'
                            iii.   S-*one*
                                      those wear black *one*
                                      'the ones who wear black'

e. XP-*ONE* i. I always use microwave *one*
               'I ALWAYS use microwave!'
            ii. Wah like that *one*.
                'Wow, LIKE that!'
            iii. Very rough *one*, you know.
                 'Very ROUGH, you know.'

The term FRAME refers to the syntactic type of the phrase in which *one* occurs. So *large one* is a token of frame A-*one*, *silk one* a token of frame N-*one*, and so on. In addition, English also has frame *one*-XP (*the one I like*). Frames (6a–d) exemplify one as pronominal, with (6d) being ungrammatical in standard English. In frame (6e) *one* is not pronominal; instead, it is used as a sentence-final particle of emphasis. We use the label 'XP-*ONE*' to distinguish it from XP-*one* (6d). Structurally, all the *one* frames are NPs headed by *one*, with the exception of (6e), where *one* functions as a clause-final marker of emphasis. This is the crucial difference between the pronominal frame XP-*one* (6d) and the emphatic frame XP-*ONE* (6e).

Chinese does not have a pronominal that corresponds to English *one*. The translation-equivalent of pronominal *one* is the particle *de*, as has been noted in the literature. The Chinese equivalents of (6) are listed in (7), adapted from Bao (2009: 342).

(7)   frame   example
  a. A-*de*   dà   de
             big   *de*
             'large one'

  b. N-*de*   sī   de
             silk *de*
             'silk one'

  c. P-*de*   wǒ   de
             I   *de*
             'mine/my one'

  d. XP-*de* i. PP-de
             zài   wū-lǐ   de
             in   house-inside   *de*
             'that which is in the bowl'

ii. VP-de
   zài guótài fang de
   in Cathay show *de*
   'that which is showing in Cathay'

iii. S-de
   nàxiē chuān hēi de
   those wear black *de*
   'those who wear black'

e. XP-*DE*[3]

i. *wǒ (shì) yòng wēibōlú de*
   I be use microwave *de*
   'I ALWAYS use a microwave oven.'

ii. *(shì) xiàng nà yà de*
   be like that type *de*
   'LIKE that!'

iii. *(shì) hěn chūzhào de*
   be very rough *de*
   'Very ROUGH.'

As in Singapore English, all frames are noun phrases except the emphatic frame (7e). Descriptions of the *de* construction are readily available in English-medium linguistics literature; see, among many others, Chao (1968) and Li and Thompson (1986).[4]

The apparent *de-one* convergence, however, hides important differences between the two systems in structure and frequency. We will discuss the frequency

---

3 The emphatic frame XP-*DE* optionally contains the copula verb *shì* 'be' with no change in emphatic force. Contrastive stress may fall on any syllable, although usually not on *de*. So (7e-iii) may be read as follows:

i. SHÌ hěn chūzhào de
ii. shì HĚN chūzhào de
iii. shì hěn CHŪZHÀO de

4 Chinese data are cited in Mandarin out of convenience. The heritage dialects of Chinese are mainly Southern Min (Hokkien, Teochew and Hainanese) and Cantonese. They share the *de* construction, with *de* being replaced by *e* in Southern Min and *goh* in Cantonese. In all relevant respects the *e/goh* construction is identical with the *de* construction.

issue in section 3. Structurally, *de* is a particle that marks pre-modification, except in the emphatic frame (7e). This is illustrated in (8):[5]

(8) a. *dà   de   shū*
    big de book
    'large book'

   b. *sī   de   shū*
    silk de book
    'silk book'

   c. *wǒ   de   shū*
    I   de book
    'my book'

   d. *zài   wū-lǐ   de   shū*
    in   house-inside de book
    'book in the house'

   e. **hěn   chūzhào   de   shū*[6]
    very rough   de book
    '*very ROUGH book'

The morphosyntax of *one* can be represented as follows:

(9) a. Modification: Modifier *de* (N)

   b. Emphasis: XP *DE*

The Modifier in (9a) can be of any phrasal type. When the nominal head is not expressed, the form is functionally equivalent to the English pronominal *one*.

---

[5] We will exclude the use of *de* which stresses the completion of an event, as exemplified in (i) (Lü 1999: 162):

i. *Wǒ zuótiān   jìn   de chéng*
   I   yesterday enter DE city
   'I entered the city yesterday.'

Here, [wǒ zuótiān jìn] is not a pre-modifier. Of course, we can also interpret it as a pre-modifier, in which case (i) means the city which I entered yesterday.

[6] (8e) is acceptable if it is non-emphatic, with *de* introducing the pre-modifier *hěn chūzhào* 'very rough'. In this sense, it is a token of frame XP-*de*.

Singapore English *one* frames cannot pre-modify nominal heads:

(10) a. *large *one* durian

b. *silk *one* blouse

c. *my *one* auntie

d. *from Thailand *one* durian

Native-speaker intuition is strong on the ill-formedness of these forms. We formalize this intuition as follows:

(11) * ... *one* N

This constraint is not surprising, given the categorial status of *one* as pronominal. The grammars of *de* and *one* are summarized in Table 1.

Table 1: Chinese *de*, English and Singapore English *one* compared. X, lexical category; XP, phrasal category

	Chinese	Sing Eng	English
Pronominal			
a. X-*one*	yes	yes	yes
b. XP-*one*	yes	yes	no
c. *one*-XP	no	yes	yes
Emphasis	yes	yes	no
Pre-modification	yes	no	no

For ease of exposition, I use the label X-*one* and so on to refer to frames associated with both the *one* construction and the *de* construction.

From the above discussion we can safely conclude that the Singapore English *one* construction inherits the frames from English *one*, and acquires the new frames from Chinese *de*. Bao (2009) argues for a set-theoretic account, according to which the set of *one* frames in the contact language (Singapore English) is the union of the set of frames of *de* in the substrate language (Chinese) and that of its exponent from the lexifier (English), subject to well-formedness constraints such as (11), which rules out [... *one* N], the putative exponent of well-formed [... *de* N]. The facts summarized in Table 1 supports the union analysis.

Prima facie, we may be tempted to assume that the pronominal function of *one* is basic, and the construction acquires the other grammatical functions through replica grammaticalization. Two forms are shown in (12).

(12) a. [*de*: pronominal] > [*de*: emphatic] = [*one*: pronominal] > [*one*: emphatic]

b. [*de*: pronominal] > [*de*: relative pronoun] = [*one*: pronominal] > [*one*: relative pronoun]

(12a) derives the emphatic frame XP *ONE*, which is exemplified in (6e) for English *one* and in (7e) for Chinese *de*. As shown in (7) and in footnote 3, this frame has the form *shi ... de*, with *shi* being optional in modern Chinese. Historically, the emphatic force is derived from *shi*, not *de* (Ota 2003: 325). The premise in (12a) has no historical support.

In the literature on Singapore English, *one* in frame XP-*one* has been analyzed as a relative pronoun, and the whole frame as a relative clause. The example below is due to Alsagoff and Ho (1998: 131) (*kachang* is a Malay word which means 'bean'):

(13) The man [sell ice-*kachang one*] go home already.
'The man who sells ice-beans has gone home.'

Since the nominal head cannot follow *one* in Singapore English, courtesy of (11), the relative clause follows the head, as it does in English. In Alsagoff and Ho's (1998) analysis, the relativized noun phrase in Singapore English shows the influence of both Chinese and English:[7] the position of the relative pronoun *one* is derived from Chinese, and the position of the relative clause XP-*one* from English. This is shown below:

(14) a. Relativized NP in Chinese: [XP *de*] N

b. Relativized NP in English: N [*that* XP]

c. Relativized NP in Singapore English: N [XP *one*]

In the structures, XP is the relative clause. Position aside, the relative pronoun function of *one* in Singapore English is derived from the pronominal *one*, through the analogy shown in (12b).

Close scrutiny of the relevant data reveals serious problems with the grammaticalization analysis of the *de-one* convergence. As we have remarked earlier, *one* is pronominal, whereas *de* is a grammatical morpheme that links premodification with the nominal head. The pre-modifier in the *de* construction

---

[7] Alsagoff and Ho (1998) also consider Malay, another major language spoken in Singapore. Malay relativized NP has the same structure as its English counterpart.

can be any lexical or phrasal category. When it is a lexical category, X-*de* and English X-*one* are functionally equivalent, cf. (6a–c) and (7a–c). When the pre-modifier is a phrasal category, as in (7d), XP-*de* is the equivalent of English *one*-XP, with XP being often analyzed as a relative clause. I set out the functional equivalents between the *de* and *one* constructions as follows:

(15)   The Chinese *de* construction:
    a. α is lexical and N is null, cf. (7a–c):
        De is functionally equivalent to pronominal *one* in English, cf. (6a–c)

    b. α is lexical and N is nonnull, cf. (8a–c):
        De has no functional equivalent in English, cf. (11)

    c. α is phrasal and N is null, cf. (7d):
        [α *de*] is functionally equivalent to relative clause in English, cf. (6d)

    d. α is phrasal and N is nonnull: cf. (8d)
        De has no functional equivalent in English, cf. (11)

    e. α is phrasal and N is null, with optional *shì*, cf. (7e):
        De has no functional equivalent in English

XP in XP-*de*, the putative relative clause, is just one type of pre-modification introduced by *de*; it is not derived through grammaticalization from any of the other types of pre-modification. The analogical formula (12b) has no empirical basis.

4 The use of *one*

We have shown that the functional range of Singapore English *one* cannot be derived from Chinese *de* through replica grammaticalization, for the simple reason that the functions of *de* are not due to grammaticalization, so there is no model or path for *one* to follow to acquire the new grammatical meanings. In Bao's (2009) analysis, Singapore English *one* is due to direct transfer: the *de* construction is exponenced with the English pronominal *one*. Given the different analytical slant, the transfer and grammaticalization analyses see the usage pattern of the *one* frames differently. In the transfer analysis, usage reflects post-transfer stabilization, which is subject to many factors, including the impact of the continued presence of the lexifier in the contact ecology. As long as the ecological conditions are maintained, there will be no substantial change over time in the structural range of the frames associated with the novel *one* construction, including those which violate English morphosyntax. Usage of the *one* frames is circumscribed by the morphosyntax of the contributing languages, English and Chinese, in addition to the usual nonlinguistic or paralinguistic, communicative factors. The grammaticalization analysis sees usage as a reflection of the developmental stages along the path that the model construction, here Chinese *de*, is presumed to have undergone in the source language. As grammaticalization proceeds in the language over time, novel *one* frames emerge or stabilize through usage. The usage pattern of *one* in Singapore English over some 20 years supports the transfer analysis.

We have at our disposal the Singaporean component of the International Corpus of English (ICE-SIN), compiled in the early 1990s and the Singapore Corpus of Research in Pedagogy (SCoRE), compiled in the mid-2000s. The ICE corpus is made up of a series of register-based subcorpora, including the 100,000-word spoken register. SCoRE is a corpus of some 4 million words of classroom discourse in Singaporean schools (Hong 2009). Although classroom discourse is guided by teachers to achieve lesson objectives, it is conversational in nature. Table 2 displays the overall uses of *one* in ICE-SIN, ICE-GB, and the English-lesson portion of SCoRE:[8]

Table 2: The uses of *one* in ICE-GB, ICE-SIN, and SCoRE. The percentage figures do not add up to 100 due to rounding

	ICE-GB		ICE-SIN		SCoRE	
	Count	Percent	Count	Percent	Count	Percent
Pronominal	456	49.8	662	46.9	2,901	41.0
Numeral	476	50.2	751	53.1	4,182	58.9
Total	932		1,413		7,083	

The *pronominal* category includes the emphatic tokens of *one*. For convenience I include in the *numeral* category repetitions and instances of *one of* (*one of them*, *one of two marks*). Normalized at 1,000 words, the pronominal *one* is 4.56 in ICE-GB, 6.62 in ICE-SIN, and 2.42 in SCoRE. There is no statistically significant difference in usage between ICE-GB and ICE-SIN. In Singapore English, the incidence of use has declined from 6.62 to 2.42 between ICE-SIN and SCoRE.

We now turn to the detailed usage patterns of the pronominal *one* in British English and Singapore English. The pronominal uses of *one*, and the emphatic

---

[8] The data are culled from the 100,000-word spoken subcorpora of ICE-SIN and ICE-GB, and from the English-lesson portion of the SCoRE corpus, which amounts to some 1.2-million words. The SCoRE is a much larger corpus than what is discussed in Hong (2009).

frame XP-*ONE*, are exemplified in (16). The data are cited from ICE-SIN, and the English-lesson portion of SCoRE.

(16) a. A-*one*
Later you write the proper *one*. (ICE-SIN:sla-017)
You think of an adjective, a positive *one*. (SCoRE)

b. N-*one*
The bottle *one* not the cheap cheap can type. (ICE-SIN:sla-054)
'The one in the bottle, not the cheap can type.'
T-shirt. Small boy *one*. (SCoRE)
'T-shirt, the one for small boys.'

c. Pr-*one*
No I never put down my *one*. (ICE-SIN:sla-079)
'No I did not put down my one.'
I use my one. (SCoRE)

d. *One*-XP
Can you see that *one* on the cabinet? (ICE-SIN:sla-030)
Yah, we are going to do the *one* on page twenty three. (SCoRE)

e. XP-*one*
From Thailand *one* ... Is it from Thailand? (ICE-SIN:sla-080)
'The one from Thailand ... Is it from Thailand?'
Yesterday we give you *one*. (SCoRE)
'The one we gave you yesterday.'

f. XP-*ONE*
Uh but turned out she very fun-loving *one*. (ICE-SIN:sla-013)
'Uh but turned out she (is) VERY fun-loving.'
Usually you can talk very loudly *one*. How come suddenly so shy ah? (SCoRE)
'Usually you can talk VERY loudly. How come suddenly so shy ah?'

On native-speaker judgment, the data in (16) are all acceptable, although the acceptability judgment varies in robustness. For many, the frames exemplified in (16e,f) are marginal features of the basilectal variety of the language (Tay 1982; Gupta 1992, 1994). This is largely reflected in usage. Table 3 displays the frequencies of English-derived *one* frames in ICE-GB and ICE-SIN:

Table 3: The frequencies of English-derived *one* frames in ICE-GB and ICE-SIN. The percentage figures do not add up to 100 due to rounding. $\chi^2 = 2.09$, $p = 0.555$

	ICE-GB		ICE-SIN	
Frame	token	percent	token	percent
A-*one*	99	21.7	114	19.6
N-*one*	23	5.0	40	6.9
one-XP	90	19.7	120	20.6
Others	244	53.5	308	52.9
Total	456		582	

There are 5 tokens of Pr-*one* in ICE-GB and 4 in ICE-SIN. For this reason I combine the frame with N-*one*. The *others* category includes tokens of *every one*, *this one*, and the bare *one*. There is no difference between the two varieties of English in the use of *one* frames.

Differences emerge when we compare the usage patterns of *one* in ICE-SIN and SCoRE. The relevant data are displayed in Table 4.

Table 4: The frequencies of the *one* frames in ICE-SIN and SCoRE, excluding the others category of Table 3. $\chi^2 = 112.56$, $p < 0.00001$

	ICE-SIN		SCoRE	
Frame	token	percent	token	percent
A-*one*	114	32.2	714	57.9
N-*one*	40	11.3	126	10.2
one-XP	120	33.9	313	25.4
XP-*one*	6	1.7	8	0.6
XP-*ONE*	74	20.9	73	5.9
Total	355		1234	

There are two notable differences in the usage patterns. First, the frame A-*one* has a higher incidence of use in SCoRE than in ICE-SIN. Second, the Chinese-derived frames of XP-*one* and XP-*ONE* have declined in productivity over the nearly two decades between ICE-SIN and SCoRE. We can explain the difference by appealing to the nature of the discourse represented in the two corpora, especially SCoRE. In fact, more than half of the SCoRE's A-*one* tokens, or 489 out of 714, are of the form *first one, next one, and last one*. ICE-SIN contains only 9 such tokens. Three specimens from SCoRE follow:

(17) a. If you can't think of an example for the *first one*, move on to the *second one*.

b. Okay the *next one*. Am I going to fast?

c. Okay, let's look at the *last one*. Why did the man pick up the rubbish eventually?

Clearly, such tokens are motivated by the instructional needs of the English lessons, increasing the token count of A-*one* that exaggerates the importance of the frame. If we discard such tokens, we can recast Table 4 as Table 5:

Table 5: The frequencies of the *one* frames in ICE-SIN and SCoRE, excluding A-*one* tokens exemplified in (17). The percentage figures do not add up to 100 due to rounding. $\chi^2 = 32.03$, $p < 0.00001$

Frame	ICE-SIN		SCoRE	
	token	percent	token	percent
A-*one*	105	30.4	225	30.2
N-*one*	40	11.6	126	16.9
one-XP	120	34.8	313	42.0
XP-*one*	6	1.7	8	1.1
XP-*ONE*	74	21.4	73	9.8
Total	345		745	

The difference between ICE-SIN and SCoRE is narrower if we exclude A-*one* tokens exemplified in (17). In fact, there is no statistically significant difference in the frequencies of the English-derived frames A-*one*, N-*one* and XP-*one* ($\chi^2 = 3.49$, $p = 0.174$). The crucial difference lies in the use of the Chinese-derived frames, the pronominal XP-*one* and the emphatic XP-*ONE*. Interestingly, the productivity of these two frames has declined over the nearly 20 years that separate the two corpora. The decline is more dramatic if we take into account the sizes of the corpora: the English-lesson portion of SCoRE is 12 times the size of the spoken subcorpus of ICE-SIN; see footnote 8.

The corpora ICE-SIN and SCoRE provide two snapshots of the grammar and use of the *one* construction in Singapore English. The decline in usage of the Chinese-derived frames posts a challenge to the grammaticalization analysis, while lending support for the transfer analysis. One crucial difference between the two analyses is the timing of the various frames of *one*. In the transfer analysis, the frames occur at the same time; in the grammaticalization analysis, the frames follow a sequential path. The difference is schematized below:

(18) a. Transfer analysis:
{A, B} → {A′, B′}

b. Grammaticalization analysis:
{A > B} → {A′ > B′}

Here the arrow represents the stabilization of the construction with frames A and B (or functions A and B) and the double arrow represents grammaticalization. In the transfer analysis, frames A′ and B′ are presumed to have appeared in the contact language at the same time, and their productivity may diverge as post-transfer stabilization proceeds. In the grammaticalization analysis, frame B′ is derived from frame A′ through the same grammaticalization process that links frames A and B in the source, i.e. substrate, language. Over time the productivity of frame B′ increases as the substrate grammaticalization deepens in the contact language.[9] In the case of the *one* construction, one would expect XP-*one* and XP-*ONE* to have undergone further grammaticalization over the time period between the two corpora, leading to an increase, at least not a decrease, in the productivity of the two frames. The usage pattern reported in Table 5 is consistent with the transfer analysis. According to this analysis, outlined in (1), the *de* construction transfers to Singapore English, to be exponenced by the English pronominal *one*, which is subject to the circumscriptive effect of English. Given the fact that XP-*one* and XP-*ONE* violate the *one*-related morphosyntax of English, the stigma associated with them stunts their stabilization post transfer.

5 Concluding Remarks

In the preceding pages we examined the emergence of the *one* construction in Singapore English against the adequacy of the explanatory models of replica grammaticalization and of transfer and filter. The grammar and usage of *one* in Singapore English support a usage-based analysis that recognizes substratum transfer as an independent mechanism of contact-induced grammatical change.

---

9 One anonymous reviewer points out that under Heine and Kuteva's (2005) analysis the result of grammaticalization in the model language may be replicated in the recipient language, not necessarily the grammaticalization process itself. However, what distinguishes the transfer analysis from the grammaticalization analysis, outlined respectively in (1) and (2), is the latter model's focus on the grammaticalization process, not the result of that process. The transfer analysis makes no commitment as to the source of the multifunctionality of the construction in question, here, the *one/de* construction. I thank the anonymous reviewer for the critique.

Transfer targets the grammatical system, and operates on abstract linguistic representation. Upon transfer, the system is exponenced with suitable morphosyntactic materials from the lexifier, which acts like a filter that limits the productivity of the individual features that make up the system. In the case of *one*, the English-derived frames stabilize without a hitch. But the post-transfer stabilization of the Chinese-derived frames is impacted by English morphosyntax. The decline in productivity between ICE-SIN and SCoRE can be interpreted as the effect of English morphosyntax slowing the development of the Chinese-derived frames.

References

Acuo. 2001. Zhàng-Hàn hùn hé yǔ "dǎohuà" shùluè [A description of Tibetan-Chinese mixed language "Daohua"]. *Yǔyán Yánjiū* 2001(3). 109–126.

Alsagoff, Lubna and Ho Chee Lick. 1998. The relative clause in colloquial Singapore English. *World Englishes* 17(2). 127–138.

Bao, Zhiming. 2005. The aspectual system of Singapore English and the systemic substratist explanation. *Journal of Linguistics* 41(2). 237–267.

Bao, Zhiming. 2009. One in Singapore English. *Studies in Language* 33(2). 338–365.

Bao, Zhiming. 2010. A usage-based approach to substratum transfer: The case of four unproductive features in Singapore English. *Language* 86(4). 792–820.

Brown, Adam. 1999. *Singapore English in a nutshell: An alphabetic description of its features*. Singapore: Federal Publications.

Bruyn, Adrienne. 1996. On identifying instances of grammaticalization in Creole languages. In Philip Baker and Anand Syea (eds.), *Changing meanings, changing functions: Papers relating to grammaticalization in contact languages*, 29–46. London: Westminster University Press.

Bruyn, Adrienne. 2009. Grammaticalization in creoles: ordinary and not-so-ordinary cases. *Studies in Language* 33(2). 312–337.

Bybee, Joan, Revere Perkins and William Pagliuca. 1994. *The evolution of grammar: tense, aspect, and modality in the languages of the world*. Chicago: The University of Chicago Press.

Chao, Yuen Ren. 1968. *A grammar of spoken Chinese*. Berkeley: University of California Press.

Chaudenson, Robert. 2001. *Creolization of language and culture*. Tr. from the French by Sheri Pargman. London: Routledge.

Filppula, Markku. 1999. *The grammar of Irish English: language in Hibernian style*. London: Routledge.

Gast, Volker and Johan van der Auwera. 2012. What is 'contact-induced grammaticalization'? Evidence from Mayan and Mixe-Zoquean languages. In Björn Wiemer, Bernhard Wälchli and Björn Hansen (eds.), *Grammatical replication and borrowability in language contact*, 381–426. Berlin: Mouton de Gruyter.

Gupta, Anthea F. 1992. Contact features of Singapore Colloquial English. In Kingsley Bolton and Helen Kwok (eds.), *Sociolinguistics today: International perspectives*, 323–345. London: Routledge.

Gupta, Anthea F. 1994. *The step-tongue: children's English in Singapore*. Clevedon: Multilingual Matters.
Harris, John. 1991. Conservatism versus substratal transfer in Irish English. In Peter Trudgill and J.K. Chambers (eds.), *Dialects of English: Studies in grammatical variation*, 191–212. London: Longman.
Heine, Bernd and Tania Kuteva. 2003. On contact-induced grammaticalization. *Studies in Language* 27(3). 529–572.
Heine, Bernd and Tania Kuteva. 2005. *Language contact and grammatical change*. Cambridge: Cambridge University Press.
Hong, Huaqing. 2009. *A corpus-based study of educational discourse: the SCoRE approach*. Singapore: National University of Singapore PhD dissertation.
Keesing, Roger M. 1988. *Melanesian pidgin and the Oceanic substrate*. Stanford: Stanford University Press.
Keesing, Roger M. 1991. Substrates, calquing and grammaticalization in Melanesian Pidgin. In Elizabeth C. Traugott and Bernd Heine (eds.), *Approaches to grammaticalization*, 315–342. Amsterdam: John Benjamins.
Lefebvre, Claire. 1998. *Creole genesis and the acquisition of grammar: the case of Haitian creole*. Cambridge: Cambridge University Press.
Li, Charles N. and Sandra A. Thompson. 1981. *Mandarin Chinese: A functional reference grammar*. Berkeley: University of California Press.
Lim, Lisa (ed.). 2004. *Singapore English: A grammatical description*. Amsterdam: John Benjamins.
Lü, Shuxiang. (ed.). 1999. *Xiandai Hanyu babai ci (zeng ding ben)* [Eight hundred words of Modern Chinese (expanded edition)]. Beijing: Commercial Press.
Matras, Yaron and Jeanette Sakel. 2007. Investigating the mechanisms of pattern replication in language convergence. *Studies in Language* 31(4). 829–865.
Mufwene, Salikoko S. 1996. The founder principle in creole genesis. *Diachronica* 13(1). 83–134.
Mufwene, Salikoko S. 1990. Transfer and the substrate hypothesis in creolistics. *Studies in Second Language Acquisition* 12(1). 1–23.
Mufwene, Salikoko S. 2001. *The ecology of language evolution*. Cambridge: Cambridge University Press.
Muysken, Pieter. 1981. Halfway between Quechua and Spanish. In Arnold Highfield and Albert Valdman (eds.), *Historicity and variation in creole studies*, 52–78. Ann Arbor, MI: Karoma.
Ota, Tatsuo. 2003. *Zhongguo yu li shi wen fa* [A historical grammar of modern Chinese]. Tr. from the Japanese by Jiang Shaoyu and Xu Changhua. Beijing: Beijing University Press.
Siegel, Jeff. 1999. Transfer constraints and substrate influence in Melanesian Pidgin. *Journal of Pidgin and Creole Languages* 14(1). 1–44.
Siegel, Jeff. 2008. *The emergence of pidgin and creole languages*. Oxford: Oxford University Press.
Tay, Mary W. J. 1982. The uses, users and features of English in Singapore. In John B. Pride (ed.), *New Englishes*, 51–70. Rowley, Mass: Newbury House.
Thomason, Sarah G. and Terrence Kaufman. 1988. *Language contact, creolization, and genetic linguistics*. Berkeley: University of California Press.
Weinreich, Uriel. 1964. *Languages in contact: findings and problems*. The Hague: Mouton.
Ziegeler, Debra. 2014. Replica grammaticalisation as recapitulation: the other side of contact. *Diachronica* 31(1). 106–141.

Subject index

accent 248
accommodation 33, 230, 233, 236, 245
ACE (Australian Corpus of English) 171, 237
acquisition, language 41–6 *see also* second language acquisition (SLA)
acquisitional universals 147
acrolects 93, 146, 149n23, 205–6, 210
actuation of change 27, 32–8, 41, 42, 47, 48–51, 264, 271, 278, 284
adjectives 289–97
adnomial relative clauses 89–108
adverbs 69, 77–82, 243, 282–3, 293–5
affixes 241
afterthoughts 77, 78
aggregative analysis methods 69–71, 75–6, 81n12, 83
analogical inferencing 36–7, 243, 248
angloversals 164–5, 166, 192, 195, 196, 210, 211–12, 230
animacy 92, 95–7, 165
Animacy Hierarchy 165
AntConc 93, 179, 298
apparent-time method 148
appropriation 312
approximation 233, 236, 241, 243, 244, 282, 302–3
archaic usages 17, 181
areal convergence 148
argument structure mapping 50
article usage 155–68, 242
aspect 36, 65, 193, 314–15 *see also* imperfective aspect; perfect aspect
assimilation 230
association 295
auxiliaries 115–16, 199

backformations 241–2
basilects 210, 324
BE + *V-ing* 193, 199
BE-perfects 64n2
bilingualism *see also* multilingualism
– and actuation of contact-induced change 27, 32

– Cape Flats English 114, 116, 120, 121
– English as a Lingua Franca (ELF) 261
– functional transfer 49–50
– grammaticalization 37, 314–15
Blended Learning 227
blogs, as corpora 286–9, 298–301
BNC (British National Corpus) 172, 175, 178–9, 180, 185–6, 282–3
borrowing 10, 116, 312, 315
boundary objects 271–2
BRICS (Brazil, Russia, India, China, South Africa) 8
British Imperialism 9
broken transmission 312
Brown corpus 240
Brown/LOB quartet 171, 176

CALPIU 257–9
calques 116, 117
CCJ (Corpus of Cyber-Jamaican) 20n
CCN (Corpus of Cyber-Nigerian) 13–16
central languages (World System) 8
chunking 286–9, 296, 298–301, 302
CLAN 258
CLAWS part-of-speech tagger 68, 175
CLMET3.0 (Corpus of Late Modern English Texts) 179, 183–5, 187
cluster analysis 69–71, 73–4, 113
CNZNE (Corpus of New Zealand Newspaper English) 171–9, 182–7
COCA (Corpus of Contemporary American English) 67, 175, 178–9, 185–6
co-construction of meaning 230, 235, 236
code switching 20, 112, 113, 114, 116
cognitive corpora 280, 283–6, 299–300
Cognitive Linguistics 285n4
cognitive/ psycholinguistic processes
– analogical inferencing 36–7
– chunking 286–9
– contact-induced language change 27, 46–51
– imposition 37

– individual versus communal planes of language 280–303
– lingua francas 228, 231–3, 242, 244, 247
– processing constraints 42–4, 48
– and study of New Englishes 26
– units of meaning 281
colligation 281–2, 293
Collins COBUILD Grammar Patterns 289
Collins Corpus 67
collocation 281–2, 283, 286, 293
colonial innovation 181
colonial lag 170, 181–2, 183, 184, 188
colonial settings, variety of 30–2
Coloured communities (South Africa) 111–12
Common European Framework of Reference (CEFR) 198
communal plane of language representation 280–3
communities of practice 228, 229, 258
community, lingua franca notions of 228–9
complementisation 175–81
completive perfect 35–6
complex adaptive systems 277–310
complexification 232, 241–4, 247–8
Complexity Principle 177
conservativeness 181–2, 224
contact ecologies 311–12, 322
contracted forms 294
convergence
– areal convergence 148
– complex adaptive systems 293
– creoles 50n
– South Africa 114–15, 116
conversation analysis (CA) 259–70, 273
co-occurrence 283, 289–90, 298n12
cooperativeness 245, 247
co-referentiality 143, 246
corpus projects *see also specific corpora by name*
– article usage 157–8
– authentic data 66
– cognitive corpus 283–6
– diasporic communities 13–21
– English as a Lingua Franca (ELF) 236–48
– and globalisation 13
– idiolects 283
– and nation state ordering 6–7

– New Zealand newspaper English verb complementation 169–90
– problems with 171
– progressive form (PF) 193, 197–212
– psycholinguistics 281, 283
correlative structures 102–3, 106
count nouns 16, 238
creoles
– creole formation 25–55
– creole/non-creole colonial Englishes 31–2, 40
– in Ecology of Language model 31
– and lingua francas 235
– prestige 12
– similarity to indigenized varieties 40
– syntax 43–4
creolization 40
cultural frames of reference 244–6, 248, 258, 259

dative constructions 116–17
DBCC (Diachronic Blog Community Corpus) 286–9
definite article 155–88
delexicalization 302
dendrograms 70, 73–4
diachronic studies
– article usage 158
– individual's role in language change 284
– New Zealand newspaper English verb complementation 170, 172, 183, 184
– progressive form (PF) 193, 204
dialect contact 32, 38–41, 164, 226, 230, 233
dialect leveling 40
diasporic communities 12, 13–21
diffuse language communities 229
diffusion of language change 147–8, 264–5, 302
direct objects 129–53
discourse markers 116, 248
ditransitivity 131, 137
divergence 33
do 115–16, 117
do be 117
dominant vocabulary (DOVO) 241
double relativizers 101–2, 106
Dynamic Model 6, 71, 82, 89, 197, 206

Ecology of Language (EL) framework 28–48
ELFA (English as a Lingua Franca in Academic Settings) 7
ELFA corpus 236–48
embedded inversions 239
embedded repairs 261
emergence 278–9, 282–3, 284, 286, 289–97, 303
emergent register 270
emphatic frames 317, 323
en third person singular pronoun 34
endangered languages 9
endonormativity 7–8, 21, 82, 90
English as a Foreign Language (EFL) 6, 22, 192, 195–6, 198–9, 207–9, 212 *see also* Expanding Circle Englishes
English as a Lingua Franca (ELF) 7, 10, 22, 195, 223–53, 255–75, 287
English as a Native Language (ENL) 6, 192, 195–6, 212, 227 *see also* Inner Circle Englishes
English as a Second Language (ESL) 6, 192, 195–6, 212 *see also* Outer Circle Englishes
English Language Complex 10
enhanced explicitness 234, 245, 246
entrenchment 231–2, 233, 234, 242, 247, 281
epistemic authority 256, 259–70, 271–2
ethnolects 121
ethnoscapes 12
EuroCoAT 237
evaluative functions 289, 290
evolution, language 26, 27, 32–41, 139n10
evolutionary framework of language change 27
eWAVE (Electronic World Atlas of Varieties of English)
– direct object omission 130, 149
– Present Perfect (PrPf) 76, 78
– progressive form (PF) 194–5, 206
– relative clauses 89, 94, 95, 97, 98, 100, 101–2, 104
exogenous prestige-driven mimicry 147–8
exonormative standards 72, 82, 90, 91, 209, 261

Expanding Circle Englishes 6, 22, 113, 196, 197–201, 207–9 *see also* English as a Foreign Language (EFL)
explicitation 234, 236, 246
exploitation colonies 30
extraterritorial English (ETE) 181, 184, 188

Fairfax archives 169, 171, 172–5
feature pool approaches 43, 48, 121, 138
fixing 232, 236, 243–4, 282, 296n11, 298–301, 302
fluency 18–19
forensic linguistics 283
formulaic sequences 286, 300
founder effects 47, 138, 147, 182
Founder Principle 138
fractals 278, 279, 282, 289–97, 301–2
Freiburg 13
from-less complementation 185–7
Full Access/Full Transfer model 50
functional transfer 37, 49, 79
futurates 199, 200, 203–4
fuzzy processing 231, 233, 234–5, 242, 243, 247

generic nouns 95–6
genre 69, 82, 175, 240
geolinguistic signals 71
global power 8–9, 11–12
globalization 12–21, 82, 255–6
global-local distinction 277–310
GloWbE (Corpus of Global Web-based English)
– nation states as ordering principle 6
– Present Perfect (PrPf) 67n4
– prestige 16n, 17n
– relative clauses 96, 100, 102, 106
Goals 50
grammaticalization 311–29
– cognitive/psycholinguistic processes 282 n2, 284, 302
– contact-induced grammaticalization 36–7
– progressive form (PF) 193
– replica grammaticalization 313–16
– Simple Past 76, 83

habitual functions of the progressive form 192, 194–5, 196, 199–201, 204–10, 211, 239
Harry Potter 10n
HAVE + past participle 63–86
hesitations 77–8, 260, 263
historical linguistics 34 *see also* diachronic studies
holistic processing 286
human/non-human referents 95–7, 165
hybridity, linguistic 259–70
hybridization 47, 50–1
hyper-central language 8
hyper-local register 270

ICE (International Corpus of English)
– article usage 158
– lack of metadata on L1s 197
– nation states as ordering principle 6
– overview of 67–8, 171
– Present Perfect study 63–86
– progressive form (PF) 197, 201–3, 210, 211
– relative clauses study 93–105
– Singapore English *one* study 323–6
– transitivity study 132
– word frequencies 241
ICLE (International Corpus of Learner English) 197–203, 206, 207–9, 210, 211, 230
identity, and choice of variety 20–1
idiolects
– cognitive/psycholinguistic processes 48–51, 280, 283–4, 303
– corpora 283–6
– emergentist theoretical perspectives 278
– English as a Lingua Franca (ELF) 226, 230, 247
– and language change 32, 33, 35, 37, 41, 43, 47, 48–51
idiom principle 286, 302
idioms 116
if-clauses 239
imagined communities 22, 229
imperfect learning 232
imperfective aspect 193, 204–10
implementation/propagation of change 27, 32, 33, 37

imposition 37, 49–51
indigenized varieties of English 21, 30, 31, 40, 47, 90
inflection 43
Inner Circle Englishes *see also* English as a Native Language (ENL)
– article usage 166
– direct object omission 129
– Ecology of Language (EL) framework 30
– and ELF speakers 225
– and nation state ordering 6
– progressive form (PF) 195, 196, 197–201, 204–5, 211
– typology 113
innovation
– colonial innovation 181
– Ecology of Language (EL) framework 33, 46, 47
– first-movers 264
– fixing 243–4
– grammaticalization 37
– Indian English as linguistic epicentre 148
– and lingua francas 230
– Present Perfect (PrPf) 79
– relative clauses in indigenized L2 Asian English varieties 83–108
– social interactions 233, 263–4
insertions 77, 260
institutional encounters 255–75
interlanguage 43–4, 212, 312n1
intermediary objects 272
internally/externally motivated change 34–8 *see also* cognitive/psycholinguistic processes
internationalization 255–6
intonation 97, 112, 248
inversions 239–40
involved vs. informational text type 75–6
isomorphism 232, 244
it BE (ADV+) ADJ *that* 294–5
it is ADJ *that* 289–97, 298, 302
iterative statements 77

jargons 225

killer languages 9

Subject index

L1 transfer *see* substrate influences
L1 varieties
- in corpora 67
- and innovative features 90
- NeighborNets 118–20
- Present Perfect (PrPf) 72, 73
- Simple Past 77
- transplanted L1s 72, 82
L2 varieties *see also* English as a Second Language (ESL)
- article usage 165–6
- in corpora 67
- institutional encounters 259
- NeighborNets 118–20
- Present Perfect (PrPf) 71–2, 73, 79
- progressive form (PF) 195
- relative clauses in indigenized L2 Asian English varieties 89–108
- Simple Past 77
- South Africa 113
- substrate influences 110
language boundaries 247
language contact *see also* dialect contact
- article usage 164
- Ecology of Language (EL) framework 25–55
- English as a Lingua Franca (ELF) 223–53
- grammaticalization 311–29
- "high" and "low" 164
- progressive form (PF) 195
- second-order language contact 227, 228, 247
- translations 232
language crossing/mixing 224, 228, 247
language death 9
language ideologies 11, 229
language modelling 277–310
language planning 8
language proficiency 269
languaging 224, 245
laughter 263
layering 76
learner English
- corpora 197–8
- and lingua francas 226–7, 230
- Present Perfect (PrPf) 79, 83
- progressive form (PF) 195, 201–10, 211, 212

- similects 226–7
- simplification 232
left-dislocation 102–3, 246
leveling
- and ELF 226, 247
- Present Perfect and Simple Past 76–82
- relative clauses 98
lexical bundles 288n5, 298–301, 302
lexical equivalents 259–60
lexical negotiation 255–75
lexical patterning, individual 296, 298
lexical simplification 231, 232, 240–1, 248
leyenda negra 9
lingua francas
- English as a Lingua Franca (ELF) 7, 10, 22, 195, 223–53, 255–75, 287
- Kenya 139
- Singapore 139
linguistic hybridity 259–70
LOCNESS (Louvain Corpus of Native English Essays) 197, 198, 201, 202, 203, 204, 207–8, 209, 227
-ly speaking 242–3

marked/unmarked structures 44, 48
mass nouns 16, 238
maximiser adverbs 282–3
MEC (Matriculation Examination Compositions) corpus 198, 201–3, 204, 208, 209, 211
media industry 11, 12
mediascapes 12
memory 232, 281
metadiscourse 246, 248
MICASE 237, 238, 240–1, 242–3
migration 12–21, 111–12
mobility, global 12–21
modals 15–16
monotransitivity 131, 137
morphology/morphosyntax
- in interlanguage 43
- in lingua francas 241–2
- morpho-syntactic simplification 231, 233–4, 238–40
- Present Perfect (PrPf) 65
- relative clauses in indigenized L2 Asian English varieties 89–108

– typology 109–28
multilingualism
– BRICS (Brazil, Russia, India, China, South Africa) 8
– cognitive/ psycholinguistic processes 231
– English as a Foreign Language (EFL) 227–8
– English as a Lingua Franca (ELF) 224, 260–1
– transient multilingual communities 255–75
multi-word units 243–4, 248, 288–9, 293, 295, 300, 302–3
MWAVE (Mouton World Atlas of Variation in English) 110, 113, 114–17, 120–1

nation states 6–8, 9, 11
national standards 6–8
nativized varieties of English 21n, 30, 82, 90
natural second language acquisition (SLA) 37, 42, 47
N-CAT (Net Corpora Administration Tool) 13
negation 44, 49, 117, 241
NeighborNets 70n9, 71, 76, 81, 110, 113, 118–20
network graphs 70
network theory 228, 229
newspaper corpora 171–5
nonce items 264
non-reduction relativization strategy 103
non-restrictive relative clauses (NRRCs) 97–8
NORM (non-mobile older rural male) informants 197, 205
Northern Subject Rule 34

object omission 129–53
one 92, 312, 316–27
Outer Circle Englishes *see also* English as a Second Language (ESL)
– article usage 166
– and ELF speakers 225
– endonormativity 21
– progressive form (PF) 196, 197–201, 205–7
– relative clauses 90
– typology 113
– in World Englishes model 6

overgeneralization 195, 196, 211, 212
overlapping turns 134

passive constructions 40, 177–8, 179, 200, 201
pauses 133, 260, 263
perfect aspect 36, 199, 200, 314–15
– Present Perfect (PrPf) 63–86, 116
performance errors 78, 90, 94
peripheral languages (World System) 8, 9
peripheral varieties (English Language Complex) 10
peripheral varieties (World System) 11
phenograms *see* phylogenetic networks
phraseological patterning 280–3, 286, 300, 302
phylogenetic networks 69, 71
pidgins
– based on non-standard varieties 30
– and colonies 30
– as lexifier languages of creoles 42, 49
– and lingua francas 225, 235
– prestige 12
– in trade versus settlement colonies 30
planning errors 94, 97, 102
plantation colonies 30–1, 44
politeness 20
polysystems 247
population structures 30–2
poss -ing 176n8, 179
power law patterns 240, 291, 297, 301
pragmatics
– article usage 155, 160, 165
– and lingua francas 248
– Present Perfect (PrPf) 77–8, 83
– relative clauses 97
– South African English 117
prepositions
– English as a Lingua Franca (ELF) 242
– Ghanaian English 92
– *from*-less complementation 176–8, 180, 183, 184–5
– preposition chopping 104–5, 106
– prepositional objects 131
– in verb complementation 175–8, 180, 183, 184–5
Present Perfect (PrPf) 63–86, 116

Subject index

prestige 11–21, 147–8, 224
prevention, verbs of 175–83
pro-drop languages 141, 145
progressive form (PF) 191–216, 239
pronouns
– co-referentiality 143, 246
– *one* 317–20, 323–4
– pronominalization 103
– second person pronouns 117, 263
– *yous* 117
propagation of change 27, 32, 33, 37
prosody 112, 248, 281
prototypical states 194, 199
psycholinguistics *see* cognitive/psycholinguistic processes
publishing industry 10

quantifying expressions 156

reanalysis 37
reflexives 117
register
– article usage 166
– hybrid localised register 260
– hyper-local register 270
– and language change diffusion 79
– Present Perfect (PrPf) 66, 69, 75, 77, 82
– progressive form (PF) 193
regularization 43, 49, 211, 212, 238, 241–2, 244
relative clauses 89–108, 321
relativization 39, 89–108, 321
relexification 37, 46–7, 50
Relexification Hypothesis 46–7, 50
replica grammaticalization 313–16, 322
restrictive vs non-restrictive relative clauses 97
restructuring 32, 34–5, 38–9, 40, 41–6, 47, 51
rhythm 112
rich agreement 140–1, 146
right dislocation 246

salience marking 103
SBCSAE (Santa Barbara Corpus of Spoken American English) 132, 158, 163n7, 164, 197, 198, 200, 201, 203

scale-free self similarity 279, 282, 302
SCoRE (Singapore Corpus of Research in Pedagogy) 323–6
second language acquisition (SLA)
– and actuation of contact-induced change 38–9
– cognitive/psycholinguistic processes 284
– and contact-induced language change 42–6
– direct object omission 147, 149
– Full Access/Full Transfer model 50
– and lingua francas 227, 230
– natural second language acquisition (SLA) 37, 42, 47
– phraseological patterning 300
– progressive form (PF) 192, 195, 211, 212
– restructuring 42
– and transfer 312n1
– typology 120
– universals 192, 197
second language use (SLU) 227, 230, 234
second person pronouns 117, 263
second-order language contact 227, 228, 247
SED (Survey of English Dialects) 157, 197, 198, 201, 202, 203, 204–5, 209
self-forms 34
semantics
– article usage 155, 165
– Cape Flats English 116
– and contact-induced language change 50–1
– meaning shift 302
– Present Perfect (PrPf) 65, 69, 77, 83
– progressive form (PF) 192, 199, 200, 201, 203–4, 205–6, 208, 211
– relative clauses 97
– semantic preference 281–2, 293
– semantic prosody 281
– semantic sequences 289
– transitivity 132, 137
– units of meaning 281, 286
– verbs of prevention 177
sequential processing 286
serial verb constructions 45, 49
settlement colonies 30, 31

shared cultural resources 236, 244–6, 248, 258
similects 226–7, 228, 230, 235, 244, 247
Simple Past 66, 76–82, 116
simplification
– left-dislocation 103
– lexical simplification 231, 232, 240–1, 248
– lingua francas 231, 232, 235, 235–6, 238–41, 247–8
– morpho-syntactic simplification 231, 233–4, 238–40
– restructuring 43, 49
slaves 31, 47, 112
social institutions, names of 155–88
social interactions 29, 226, 233–5, 247, 270–2, 283
social networks 33, 228, 229
social norms 242
socio-ecological approaches 26
sociolinguistics
– African American Vernacular English (AAVE) 12
– cognitive corpus 285
– Ecology of Language (EL) framework 29–32
– of globalisation 12
– lingua francas 227, 228, 230–1, 258
– MWAVE (Mouton World Atlas of Variation in English) 120–1
– Standard American English 11, 12
– and study of New Englishes 26
speaker attitude 193, 194, 199
spelling 7, 10
spoken language versus written 73–4, 93, 201, 204, 240–1
Stammbaum model 35
stance 194, 205, 257
Stanford Log-linear Part-of-Speech Tagger 290n8
stative functions of the progressive form 192, 194–5, 196, 199–201, 204–10, 211
stop 182–3
stylistics 90, 158, 193, 199, 204
subcultural movements 11, 12
subjective function 193n3, 199, 201, 203, 204

subjective simplicity 235
substrate influences
– article usage 162, 164, 165–6
– Cape Flats English 112, 116–17
– direct object omission 138–47, 148
– Ecology of Language (EL) framework 37, 39–40, 41, 43, 46, 47, 50
– grammaticalization 311
– New Zealand English 170
– Present Perfect (PrPf) 79, 83
– progressive form (PF) 195, 197, 202, 206, 207, 210, 211, 212
– as reinforcement of retention of features 117
– relative clauses 106
– relativizers 99, 103, 104
– South African English 110
– transfer versus appropriation 312
– World System of Englishes model 11
super-central languages 8, 9
super-central varieties 10, 11
superstrates, restricted access to 38–9
symbolic usages 18

tags 116
temporal adverbials 69, 77–82
tense 63–86, 114–15 *see also* aspect
text type 66, 69, 73, 76, 82
that 92, 97–8, 99, 101, 105, 289
Themes 50
third person singular endings 238
Three Circles model 6, 22, 113, 192, 225
topic marking 315
topic salience 103
topic-comment 142
topic-prominence 103, 141–7, 148–9, 246
transfer
– of features into L2 superstrates 38–9
– and grammaticalization 311–29
– individual versus societal level 283
– from L1 44, 47, 49
– lingua francas 228
– natural second language acquisition (SLA) 47
– progressive form (PF) 197
– and universals 165
transient multilingual communities 255–75

transitivity 129–53
translanguaging 224
translations 232, 234, 247, 259–60
transparency 43
typology 38–41, 109–28

units of meaning 281, 286
universals
– acquisitional universals 147
– angloversals 164–5, 166, 192, 195, 196, 210, 211–12, 230
– Animacy Hierarchy 165
– and definite articles 164–5, 166
– as explanation of features 147
– language universals 149
– pragmatic universals 165
– progressive form (PF) 197
– second language acquisition 192, 212
– semantics 196–7
– of topic 142
– translations 234
– vernacular universals 44
universities, encounters in 255–75

verb complementation 169–90
video-recorded data 258, 263
VOICE (Vienna-Oxford International Corpus of English) 7, 237, 241

wahala 18
WAVE (World Atlas of Varieties of English) 156 *see also* eWAVE (Electronic World Atlas of Varieties of English)
Wcopyfind 174n6
wetin be 18
what 99–101, 105
where 92, 98–9, 106
which/ who relativizers 95, 102, 105
whose 92
wh-questions 44
wh-relativizers 92, 93, 95–7, 98–101, 104
will 15–16, 199
women 20
word order 43, 49
WordSmith Tools 68, 133
World Language System 8–12
World System of Englishes model 8–12
WrELFA 237, 238
WWC (Wellington Corpus) 171, 176

yous 117

Zipf's law 240, 291, 297, 301
Zulu 110

Languages and Varieties index

African American Vernacular English
  (AAVE) 11, 12, 31, 98, 100, 101
Afrikaans 110, 111, 113, 114–15, 116, 117, 120
Afrikaner South African English (ASAE) 111, 116
American English
– Americanization 187
– article usage 160, 164
– and colonial lag 182, 183
– direct object omission 129, 135–8, 147–8, 149
– as endonormative standard 82
– as hub/ hyper-central variety 10
– language-ideological myth of 11
– and nation state ordering 7
– *prevent* verb complementation 176–7
– progressive form (PF) 193–4, 197, 200, 201, 202–5, 208, 209
– Simple Past 81
– verb complementation 178–81, 182–7
American Southern English 31
Appalachian English 100
Australian English 72, 73, 78, 104

Bahamas English 8, 117
Bangladesh English 101
Bantu languages 47, 139, 141, 145, 202, 207
Bazaar Malay 139, 143–4
Black South African English (BSAE) 111, 113, 120, 121, 195
British English
– article usage 155, 157, 158, 160, 162–3, 164
– and colonial lag 182, 183
– conservativeness 81
– direct object omission 129, 135–8, 147–8, 149
– and nation state ordering 7
– not the hub/ hyper-central variety 10
– *one* 323
– *prevent* verb complementation 176–8
– progressive form (PF) 193–4, 197, 202–5, 208, 209

– regional varieties of 99
– relativizers 99
– and transplanted L1 varieties 72
– verb complementation 179–81, 182–7
Butler English 104, 130

Cameroon English 104
Canadian English 7, 72, 162–3
Cantonese 139, 143–4, 146, 202, 318n4
  see also Chinese
Cape Flats English 109–28
Celtic languages 34, 162
Chicano English 117
Chinese *see also* Cantonese; Hokkein; Mandarin; Teochew
– article usage 164
– *de* 312, 313, 317–22, 323, 325–6
– direct object omission 139
– progressive form (PF) 198, 202, 207, 211
– relative clauses 99, 104, 105, 106
– and Singapore English 40, 316–22
– topic-prominence 142, 143–4
Colloquial Singapore English (CSE) 39–40, 130, 149n22
Cornish 9

Daohua 315n5
Dravidian languages 103, 106
Dutch 112
Dutch English 196

East African English 81, 159, 162–3, 164
  see also Kenyan English
East Anglian English 100
English English 7, 157, 160–2, 202–4, 209

Fiji Hindi 139, 140n14, 145
Fijian 139, 141
Fijian English 113, 120, 130, 132, 135–8, 140–7, 149
Filipino 139
Finnish 9
French 9, 47

Gbe languages 36, 45, 47, 48, 50
German 9, 44
Ghanaian English 92
Gujarati 39
Gullah 31
Guyanese Creole 43, 44

Hindi
– article usage 164
– direct object omission 139, 140, 141, 144–5, 146, 148n21
– progressive form (PF) 203, 207, 210, 211
– relative clauses 103, 106
Hip Hop nation language 11
Hokkein 139, 206, 318n4
Hong Kong English
– article usage 162–3
– direct object omission 129, 130, 135–8, 146, 148, 149–50
– nativized varieties of English 90
– Present Perfect (PrPf) 72, 77, 79
– progressive form (PF) 197, 198, 200, 202–4, 206, 207, 209, 210
– relative clauses 92, 93–105
– substrate influences 139

Indian English
– article usage 160, 162–3, 165
– direct object omission 129, 130, 135–8, 140–7, 148, 149
– as linguistic epicentre 148
– nativized varieties of English 90
– Present Perfect (PrPf) 72, 77, 79
– progressive form (PF) 195, 196, 197, 200, 201, 202–4, 206, 207, 209, 210–11
– relative clauses 92, 93–105
– substrate influences 139
Indian South African English (ISAE) 39, 104, 111, 113, 120, 121
Irish 162, 314, 316
Irish English
– article usage 156, 157–8, 161–3, 164
– and Cape Flats English 117
– dative constructions 117
– hot-news perfect 314, 316
– negation 117

– perfect aspect 64n2, 314, 316
– preposition chopping 104
– Present Perfect (PrPf) 72
– relativizers 98
– *yous* 117

Jamaican Creole
– article usage 164
– direct object omission 140, 145, 149
– preposition chopping 104
– prestige 12, 19–21, 224
– social ecology of 31
– "space of flows" of cultural globalisation 12
Jamaican Standard English
– article usage 162–3, 164
– diasporic corpus projects 19–21
– direct object omission 130, 132, 135–8, 147, 149, 150
– Present Perfect (PrPf) 72
– prestige 12
– relative clauses 92
– Simple Past 81
– social ecology of 31
– substrate influences 140
– World System of Englishes 11, 12
Japanese 207, 211

Kaaps 112
Kenyan English
– direct object omission 130, 135–8, 140–7, 149–50
– progressive form (PF) 197, 200, 201, 202–4, 206, 207, 209, 210, 211
– substrate influences 139–40
Kikuyu 139, 140, 141, 145
Kwaio 315, 316

Luo 139, 140, 141

Malay 40, 139, 143–4, 202, 321
Malaysian English 103, 104, 129, 130
Maltese English 113, 120, 130
Mandarin 139, 142, 143, 202, 206, 318n4
Manx 9
Māori 170
Multicultural London English 92

Namibian English 7
New England English 31
New Zealand English 11, 72, 78, 169–90
Niger-Congo languages 145
Nigerian English 12, 13–17, 71–2, 73, 81, 92
Nigerian Pidgin 12, 13, 17–19, 224
Nilo-Saharan languages 139

Paamaka 45, 49
Palenquero 47
Philippine English
– article usage 159, 162–3
– direct object omission 130, 135–8, 147, 149–50
– Present Perfect (PrPf) 71–2, 77, 79
– relative clauses 92
– Simple Past 81
– substrate influences 139–40

Received Pronunciation (R.P.) 7
Rope River Creole 130

Sami 9
Sanskrit 148n21
Scottish English 7
Singapore English
– article usage 160, 162–3, 164
– Colloquial Singapore English (CSE) 39–40, 130, 149n22
– direct object omission 130, 135–8, 146, 148, 149
– endonormative stabilization 90
– grammaticalization 312, 316–22
– postcolonial language planning 8
– Present Perfect (PrPf) 72, 79, 81
– progressive form (PF) 196, 197, 201, 202–4, 205–6, 207, 209

– relative clauses 92, 93–105
– Simple Past 81
– substrate influences 139
Singlish *see* Colloquial Singapore English (CSE)
Solomons Pijin 314, 315, 316
Sotho 110
South African English 7, 109–28
South African Indian English (SAIE) 39 *see also* Indian South African English (ISAE)
Sranan 44
Sranan Tongo 35–6
Sri Lankan English 130
St Kitts and Nevis English 8
Surinamese creoles 35–6, 45, 48
Swahili 139, 140, 141, 145, 207

Tagalog 139, 145
Tamil 39, 139, 202
Teochew 139, 206, 318n4
Tibetan 315n5
Tok Pisin 121, 130

Vietnamese 45

Wacigbe 45, 49
Welsh 162, 210, 211
Welsh English
– article usage 158, 159, 160–2
– progressive form (PF) 195, 197, 200, 201, 202–5, 209, 211
White South African English (WSAE) 111, 113, 116, 117, 120, 121

Xhosa 110, 111, 112

Zambian English 7

Author Index

Aboh, Enoch O. 43n, 48
Adhikari, Mohamed 111
Agnihotri, Rama Kant 121
Alo, Moses A. 16
Alsagoff, Lubna 92, 99, 316, 321
Altenberg, Bengt 232
Anderson, Benedict R. 22, 229
Anderson, Richard C. 279
Ansaldo, Umberto 43n, 48, 139n10
Anthony, Laurence 298
Appadurai, Arjun 12
Aranovich, Raúl 140, 141
Arppe, Antti 285
Arts, Bas 69
Awonusi, Victor O. 72
Axelsson, Margareta Westergren 208

Bache, Carl 97
Backus, Ad 27
Balasubramanian, Chandrika 207
Bao, Zhiming 40, 139n13, 312, 313, 316, 317, 320, 322
Barlow, Michael 234, 283
Bauer, Gero 64, 65
Bauer, Laurie 170, 171, 172, 181
Becker, Alton 224
Beckner, Clay 278, 302
Bernaisch, Tobias 148
Bhatt, Rakesh M. 10, 156, 191, 195, 211
Biber, Douglas 64, 65, 67, 69, 73, 75, 98, 157, 199, 201, 240, 285, 289, 298
Blommaert, Jan 12, 224, 247
Blum-Kulka, Shoshana 234
Bock, Kathryn 281
Bowerman, Sean 110
Bowie, Jill 69
Brassac, Christian 272
Brewer, William F. 281
Brinton, Laurel J. 200
Brown, Adam 316
Brutt-Griffler, Janine 232
Bruyn, Adrienne 314
Bryant, David 69, 110, 118

Buthlezi, Qedusizi 110
Bybee, Joan 36, 76, 233, 278, 286, 294, 302, 316

Calude, Andreea 172
Cameron, Lynne 278
Canagarajah, Suresh 247
Carey, Ray 237, 243
Carter, Ronald 131, 289
Castells, Manuel 12
Chambers, J.K. 44
Chamoreau, Claudine 30
Charles, Maggie 289
Chaudenson, Robert 312
Cheng, Winnie 286, 302
Cheshire, Jenny 92, 139n10
Christian, Donna 100
Coetzee-Van Rooy, Susan 111, 112, 113
Cogo, Alessia 245, 261
Collins, Peter 68n5, 80n11, 81, 192, 198
Comrie, Bernard 193n2
Conrad, Susan 69, 73, 240, 298
Coronel, Lilian 92, 95, 97
Coulthard, Malcolm 283
Couper-Kuhlen, Elizabeth 199n5
Croft, William 231, 233
Cysouw, Michael 118

Dabrowska, Ewa 234
Dahl, Östen 76
Davies, Mark 67n4, 96, 100, 102, 106, 178n12
Davydova, Julia 69, 79, 83, 195, 196, 211
Day, Dennis 257
De Bot, Kees 278, 279, 297
De Klerk, Vivian 111
de Swaan, Abram 8–12
Deen, Kamil Ud. 207
Dixon, R.M.W. 131
Dollinger, Stefan 181
Dryer, Matthew 166
Du Bois, John W. 234
Dunne, Timothy T. 39

Eckert, Penelope 30, 33
Edwards, Alison 195, 196, 206
Ellis, Nick C. 278, 279, 283, 285, 286, 295, 297
Elsness, Johan 66, 79
Erasmus, Zimitri 111

Fabricius, Anne 255
Ferreira-Junior, Fernando 297
Fife, James 205
Filppula, Markku 156, 157, 162, 164, 192, 195, 314, 316
Finn, Peter 113
Firth, Alan 227, 257, 261
Fischer, Olga 36, 37
Ford, Cecilia E. 234
Francis, Gill 289
Freebody, Peter 279
Fuchs, Robert 67n4, 96, 100, 102, 106, 148

Gachelin, Jean-Marc 192, 195, 211
Gafaranga, Joseph 261
Garcia, Ofelia 224
Garside, R. 175
Gast, Volker 315
Giles, Howard 33, 233–4
Gilner, Leah 241
Gilquin, Gaëtanelle 285
Gisborne, Nikolas 92, 104
Givón, Talmy 103
Gleick, James 282
Goldberg, Adele 297
Görlach, Manfred 181
Graddol, David 139
Granger, Sylviane 197, 198, 227, 232, 300
Granovetter, Mark 228
Greenbaum, Sidney 67
Gries, Stefan Thomas 66, 132n6, 138, 148, 285
Griesemer, James R. 271, 272
Grondelaers, Stefan 285
Groom, Nicholas 289
Guido, Maria Grazia 224
Gupta, Anthea F. 31, 139, 316, 324
Gurevich, Olga 281
Gut, Ulrike 72, 92, 95, 97

Habermas, Jürgen 224
Hahn, Angela 208
Hannah, Jean 7
Harris, John 156, 314
Hay, Jennifer 170, 172
Hayano, Kaoru 256
Hazel, Spencer 257, 263
Heine, Bernd 36, 312, 313, 314, 315, 327n9
Helms-Park, R. 44, 45
Heritage, John 256, 269
Hermann, Tanja 95, 100
Herzog, Marvin I. 271
Heyvaert, Lisbet 176n8
Hickey, Raymond 156
Himmelmann, Nicolaus P. 145
Ho Chee Lick 92, 99, 316, 321
Hong, Huaqing 323
Hopper, Paul 132, 233, 278
House, Juliane 228
Huber, Magnus 90, 92
Huddleston, Rodney 64, 98, 131, 176n8, 177, 180, 199n5
Hudson-Ettle, Diana 199n4
Hülmbauer, Cornelia 245
Hulstijn, J. 42
Hundt, Marianne 34, 66, 67n4, 68, 75, 76, 82, 90, 92, 148, 170, 171, 181–2, 187, 188, 192, 195, 196, 208, 211, 239
Hung, Tony T.N. 90, 92
Hunston, Susan 281, 289
Huson, Daniel H. 69
Hutchby, Ian 263
Hyland, Fiona 227
Hynninen, Niina 259–70

Jacobsson, Bengt 97
Jakobsen, Leif 97
James, Paul 172
Jantjies, Wesley 116
Jarvis, Scott 198, 224, 228
Jaszczolt, Kasia M. 65
Jefferson, Gail 261
Jenkins, Jennifer 225, 228, 229, 233, 245, 255
Johnson, C.P. 227
Jones, Mark J. 197
Junghare, Indira Y. 142, 144, 146, 148–9

Kachru, Braj 6, 22, 192, 225
Kallen, Jeffrey L. 164
Kaufman, Terrence 35, 312
Keesing, Roger M. 312, 315, 316
Kemmer, Suzanne 234
Khin Khin Aye 143–4
Kirk, John M. 164
Kirkebaek, Mads Jakob 257
Kitazawa, Mariko 229
Kittilä, Seppo 130, 131, 132, 137, 141, 146
Kjaerbeck, Susanne 257
Klein, Wolfgang 64, 65, 77
Klemola, Juhani 34, 197
Klimpfinger, Theresa 224
Kortmann, Bernd 65, 89, 93, 94, 95, 97, 98, 100, 101, 103, 104, 109, 110, 113, 118, 120, 121, 130, 145, 149, 156, 192, 194, 196, 206, 235
Koul, Omkar N. 140, 141
Kouwenberg, Silvia 49
Kranich, Svenja 192, 193, 194, 199, 204
Kretzschmar, William A. 11, 297
Kroeger, Paul 145
Krug, Manfred 81n12, 83
Kusters, Wouter 231
Kuteva, Tania 36, 312, 313, 314, 315, 327n9

Labov, William 30, 33, 64, 271
Laitinen, Mikko 229
Lakoff, George 285
Lange, Claudia 103
Lanham, Leonard W. 110
Larsen-Freeman, Diane 234, 278, 279, 282n1, 297
Latour, Bruno 271
Lave, Jean 228, 258
Laviosa-Braithwaite, Sara 232
Leech, Geoffrey 192, 193, 194, 198, 199, 201, 204, 210, 239
Lefebvre, Claire 37, 46, 47, 312
Léglise, Isabelle 30
Leimgruber, Jakob 8
LePage, Robert 229
Levin, Magnus 199
Li, Charles N. 142–3, 145
Li Wei 224
Lim, Lisa 139, 316
Lippi-Green, Rosina 11
Loftman Bailey, Beryl 145–6
Lumsden, John 47, 50
Lunkenheimer, Kerstin 76, 77, 89, 94, 95, 97, 98, 100, 101, 103, 104, 109, 110, 113, 118, 120, 121, 130, 145, 149, 156, 192, 194, 196, 206

Macalister, John 174
MacArthur, F. 237
Macdonald, Carol Ann 110
MacWhinney, Brian 234, 258
Mair, Christian 10, 13n6, 67, 148, 171, 175n7, 177, 178, 180, 184, 187, 192, 224, 230, 239, 280
Makoni, Sinfree 247
Malan, Karen 111, 113
Mandelbrot, Benoit B. 277, 279, 282
Manning, Christopher D. 69, 71, 297
Marckwardt, Albert 181
Marsh, David 227
Matras, Yaron 312, 315
Matthews, Stephen 40, 143–4
Mauranen, Anna 224, 232, 234, 238, 240, 241, 243, 245, 255, 282, 283, 287, 302, 303
Maurer, Philippe 47
Maxwell, Dan 103
McArthur, Tom 10
McCarthy, Michael 131, 289
McCawley, James D. 65, 103
McCormick, Kay 112, 113, 114, 115, 116
McWhorter, John 235
Meierkord, Christiane 112
Meriläinen, Lea 192, 195, 198, 199n4
Mesthrie, Rajend 10, 16, 39, 104, 110, 111, 112, 114, 116, 117, 156, 191, 195, 211
Miestamo, Matti 235
Migge, Bettina 36, 45
Milroy, James 30, 33, 228, 229, 231
Milroy, Lesley 30, 33, 228, 229, 231
Mintz, Sidney W. 31
Molenaar, Peter C. 284n3
Mollin, Sandra 282, 283, 285
Mortensen, Janus 256, 257, 260
Moulton, Vincent 110, 118

Mufwene, Salikoko 27, 28, 29, 30, 31, 32, 33, 34, 35, 37–8, 40–1, 41–2, 46, 47, 48, 50, 51, 138, 312
Mugane, John M. 140, 141n15
Mukherjee, Joybrato 68, 92, 132n6, 138, 192, 195, 196
Muysken, Pieter 312
Myachina, E.N. 140
Myers-Scotton, Carol 50n

Neeleman, A. 145
Nelson, Gerald 67
Nemser, W. 44, 47
Nevalainen, Sampo 232
Nevile, Maurice 257
Newbrook, Mark 92, 97, 104
Nichols, Johanna 231
Nurmi, Arja 284

O'Donnell, Matthew Brook 297
Ota, Tatsuo 321

Pagel, Michael 233
Parviainen, Hanna 148
Paul, Herman 32, 33, 41
Paulasto, Heli 158, 192, 195, 197, 199, 205, 207, 211, 212
Pavlenko, Aneta 198, 224, 228
Pennycook, Alastair 11, 224, 247
Pettman, Charles 116
Piaget, Jean 230
Pickard, Nigel 227
Pienemann, M. 44, 49
Pietikäinen, Kaisa 224, 229
Pilkinton-Pihko, Diane 229
Pitzl, Marie-Luise 245
Plag, Ingo 43, 44, 48, 49
Platt, John T. 129, 130, 164, 191, 195, 211
Ponelis, F.A. 114
Portner, Paul 65
Poussa, Patricia 99
Pratt, Mary Louise 6
Priesler, Bent 255
Prince, Ellen F. 103
Pullum, Geoffrey K. 64, 98, 131, 176n8, 177, 180, 199n5

Quirk, Randolph 64, 65, 76, 98, 131, 155, 157, 160, 176n8, 193, 194, 199, 289

Ranta, Elina 195, 238
Rastall, Paul 77
Raumolin-Brunberg, Helena 228, 284
Rautionaho, Paula 138, 163n7, 192, 195, 203
Raymond, Geoffrey 256
Read, John 279
Rissanen, Matti 95
Ritz, Marie-Eve A. 76
Roberge, Paul T. 112
Rohdenburg, Günter 177
Römer, Ute 199
Romesburg, H. Charles 69
Rudanko, Juhani 176n8

Sacks, Harvey 256
Sahgal, Anju 121
Sakal, Jeanette 312, 315
Salkie, Raphael 65
Sanchez, Liliana 47
Sand, Andrea 82, 156, 160, 164, 165
Sato, Yosuke 141, 142, 144
Schilk, Marco 68
Schlüter, Norbert 66, 68n7, 69
Schmied, Josef 164, 199n4
Schneider, Edgar 6, 7, 21, 22, 31, 71, 73, 79, 82, 89, 90, 97, 100, 101, 113, 197, 206
Schneider, Gerold 82
Schreier, Daniel 34
Schumann, John H. 284n3
Schütze, Hinrich 69, 71, 297
Scott, Mike 68
Seidlhofer, Barbara 228, 245
Seoane, Elena 66, 79
Sharma, Devyani 147, 148, 149, 165, 192, 195, 196–7, 199, 203, 206, 207, 210, 211
Siegel, Jeff 37, 44, 47, 49, 140n14, 145, 312
Siemund, Peter 156, 165–6
Simpson, R.C. 237
Sinclair, John McH 281, 282n2, 286, 289, 302
Smith, N. 175
Smith, Nicholas 66, 76, 199, 239
Smith, Philip 233–4

Smitterberg, Erik 134, 192, 193, 194, 199, 199n5, 204
Speer, Susan A. 263
Sprouse, Rex A. 50
Sridhar, Shikaripur 103
Srivastav, Venneta 103
Stafford, Roy Lawrence 141
Star, Susan Leigh 271, 272
Stefanowitsch, Anatol 285
Stubbs, Michael 286
Suárez-Gómez, Cristina 66, 79, 90, 92, 94, 99, 100
Swales, John M. 228
Szendrői, K. 145
Szmrecsanyi, Benedikt 71, 156, 192, 196, 235

Tabouret-Keller, Andrée 229
Tagliamonte, Sali 100
Tay, Mary W.J. 324
Thomas, Deborah A. 21
Thomason, Sarah Grey 34, 35, 231, 232, 312
Thompson, Sandra A. 132, 142–3, 145
Thorne, David A. 162
Tirkkonen-Condit, Sonja 232
Toefy, Tracey 111, 113, 114
Torras, Maria-Carme 261
Tottie, Gunnel 160
Toutanova, Kristina 290n8
Traugott, Elizabeth Closs 36
Trudgill, Peter 7, 164, 181, 182, 228, 231, 233
Turner, G.W. 172

Urry, John 228

van Buren, Paul 41–2
van Coetsem, Frans 37, 49

van der Auwera, Johan 315
van Dulm, Ondene 116
van Rooy, Bertus 110, 111, 112, 113, 121, 192, 195, 208, 211
Veloudis, Ioannis 64
Vetchinnikova, Svetlana 232, 243, 281, 282, 284, 296n11
Vigouroux, Cécile B. 29, 30, 33, 46
Vinck, Dominique 272
Vogel, Katrin 68, 75, 195, 196, 208, 211

Wagner, Johannes 227, 257, 258
Wahid, Ridwan 166
Walker, Jim 66, 76
Watermeyer, Susan 110
Wee, Lionel 40, 164
Weinreich, Uriel 27, 28, 32, 46, 51, 228, 271, 283, 312n1
Wenger, Etienne 228, 258
Werner, Valentin 64, 65, 66, 69, 70, 73, 75, 76, 77, 78, 79, 80, 81, 83
Whaley, Lindsay J. 165
Williams, Jessica 211
Wilmot, Kirsten 111
Winford, Donald 35, 36, 37, 40, 45, 49, 69
Wolfram, Walt 100
Wood, Tahir M. 113
Wray, Alison 286, 295, 300
Wright, David 283
Wright, Laura 35
Wynne, Terence 68n7

Yao, Xinyue 68n5, 80n11, 81
Yip, Virginia 40, 143–4

Ziegeler, Debra 315
Zipf, George K. 240, 291, 297, 301

www.ingramcontent.com/pod-product-compliance
Lightning Source LLC
Chambersburg PA
CBHW030431300426
44112CB00009B/953